DATE DUE

NY 26 04			

DEMCO 38-296

DEVELOPMENT ECONOMICS

DEVELOPMENT ECONOMICS

FROM THE POVERTY TO THE WEALTH OF NATIONS

YUJIRO HAYAMI

CLARENDON PRESS · OXFORD

1997

Riverside Community College

OCT '99 Library

4800 Magnolia Avenue

Riverside, CA 92506

HD82 .H344 1997
Hayami, Yujiro, 1932–
Development economics : fro
the poverty to the wealth of
nations

Clarendon Street, Oxford OX2 6DP
New York
ngkok Bogota Bombay
Cape Town Dar es Salaam
Delhi Florence Hong Kong Istanbul Karachi
Kuala Lumpur Madras Madrid Melbourne
Mexico City Nairobi Paris Singapore
Taipei Tokyo Toronto
and associated companies in
Berlin Ibadan

Oxford is a trade mark of Oxford University Press

Published in the United States by
Oxford University Press Inc., New York

Copyright © Yujiro Hayami, 1997

All rights reserved. No part of this publication may be reproduced,
stored in a retrieval system, or transmitted, in any form or by any means,
without the prior permission in writing of Oxford University Press.
Within the UK, exceptions are allowed in respect of any fair dealing for the
purpose of research or private study, or criticism or review, as permitted
under the Copyright, Designs and Patents Act, 1988, or in the case of
reprographic reproduction in accordance with the terms of the licences
issued by the Copyright Licensing Agency. Enquiries concerning
reproduction outside these terms and in other countries should be
sent to the Rights Department, Oxford University Press,
at the address above

British Library Cataloguing in Publication Data
Data available

Library of Congress Cataloging in Publication Data
Hayami, Yūjirō, 1932–
Development economics: from the poverty to
the wealth of nations / Yujiro Hayami.
Includes bibliographical references (p.   )
1. Economic development.   I. Title.
HD82.H344   1997   338.9—dc20   96–30616
ISBN 0–19–829207–4

Typeset by Pure Tech India Ltd., Pondicherry
Printed in Great Britain
on acid-free paper by
Bookcraft Ltd, Midsomer Norton, Somerset

To Dr Lee Teng-hui

Preface

This book is intended to be a comprehensive, cohesive treatise on development economics, organized to serve the possible interests of professionals and, at the same time, to be usable as a text for graduate and advanced undergraduate curricula.

This volume addresses one major question: Why has a small set of countries in the world achieved a high level of affluence to which a limited number of developing economies have been converging, while the majority still remain poor and stagnant? An obvious factor underlying this global divergence is difference in the ability to develop and adopt advanced technology. Why, then, has the number of developing economies set on the track of closing their productivity gap with advanced economies been so limited? An answer appears to be the difficulty for low-income economies to prepare appropriate institutions for borrowing advanced technology under their social and cultural constraints. The major task of this volume is to explore the nature of these binding constraints with the aim of identifying the ways and means to remove them through comparison with cases in which constraints have been successfully lifted.

By nature, the scope is interdisciplinary, covering non-economic aspects such as political process and social value systems. The analysis, however, is based on the logic of standard economics. It is hoped that non-economist readers, including political scientists and sociologists (as well as non-technical economists), will be able to grasp the major thrust of development economics by reading through this book while skipping over the sections marked with an asterisk in the table of contents.

Quantitative characteristics of Third World development in terms of population growth, natural resource depletion, capital accumulation, and technological change are outlined. However, the major approach used in this volume is comparative institutional analysis, i.e. comparing the patterns of institutional evolution in response to changes in resource endowments and technology under different social and cultural traditions across space and time. Serving as a benchmark for this comparison is my experience and knowledge on economic development in East Asia, especially Japan. Admittedly my perspective is biased, as were those both of Adam Smith based on observations in eighteenth-century Britain and Friedrich List in nineteenth-century Germany. Presumptuously, I intended to prepare a block for building a new *Wealth of Nations* from the East Asian perspective, although the present achievement is as yet only one step toward a goal lying several hundred miles away.

My perspective evolved through grass-roots investigations into rural villages in tropical Asia while I served as an economist at the International Rice Research Institute (IRRI) in the Philippines during 1974–6. IRRI was then a relatively small research institute strongly orientated to its mission of bridging the agricultural technology gap between temperate and tropical zones. Through dialogue with scientist colleagues and observations on their agronomic and biological research, I was firmly convinced of both the decisive role of technology transfer for the development of developing economies, as well as the critical need for preparing institutional infrastructure in support of such transfer.

I learned even more from rural people in the Philippines than from my IRRI colleagues. I observed how small farmers were rational and capable of maximizing incomes within their limited means by optimally utilizing the modern technology made available to them. Yet, their advancement was limited by underdeveloped input and product markets as well as poor public support on transportation, communication, and other infrastructure. In fact, government policies and regulations often blocked rather than promoted their progress. I also found that village communities were less strongly organized than in Japan for the supply of local public goods such as communal irrigation systems. These observations raised a question in my mind as to what would be a right combination of market, state, and community for economic development. This idea evolved as I extended my field study over other parts of tropical Asia, including communist Vietnam, culminating in the central theme of this volume.

Another basic experience underlying my perspective was the surprising development of the Japanese economy. As I experienced childhood during World War II and its aftermath, poverty and hunger were not something unusual to me. It was when I went to Iowa State University for graduate study in 1957 under a Rockefeller Foundation scholarship at the age of 24 that I first realized how backward my nation was, and how poor our life had been. (Indeed, my salary from the Japanese Ministry of Agriculture was then only about $30, as compared with as much as $500 for my US counterparts.) Completely overwhelmed by the affluence of the USA, I couldn't conceive that Japan could reach even half that level within my life time. Therefore, the subsequent development of the Japanese economy was more than a surprise. The same surprise was repeated as I observed later developments in Korea and Taiwan. From this experience I have become convinced that the mechanism of development is latent in apparent backwardness, and that catch-up development is possible if this mechanism is exploited. It is my sincere desire that this perspective, based on my life experience and elaborated in this volume, will increase understanding about the mechanism of economic development among scholars in low-income economies.

The Japanese version of this book under the title *Kaihatsu Keizaigaku* was published in 1995 by Sobunsha Publishing Company in Tokyo. Preparation of this English edition was done during my visiting professorship to the Lee Teng-hui Chair of World Affairs at Cornell University from August 1995 to March 1996. A secluded environment in the beautiful Cornell campus over-looking Cayuga Lake was ideal for concentrating on the preparation of the manuscript. A series of lectures for my graduate seminar were instrumental for testing and improving the manuscript. I thank Andy Novakovic and William Tomek of the Department of Agricultural, Resource, and Managerial Economics, Tapan Mitra and Kaushik Basu of the Department of Economics, and Theodore Bester of the East Asia Program, for arranging my stay in Ithaca to be both comfortable and productive.

Keijiro Otsuka, Gustav Ranis, Vernon Ruttan, and Erik Thorbecke kindly read earlier manuscripts and gave me valuable comments. Useful advice and suggestions were given at various stages of research by Masahiko Aoki, Randolph Barker, Robert Evenson, Gary Fields, Yoshihisa Godo, Masayoshi Honma, Shigeru Ishikawa, Motoshige Itoh, Masao Kikuchi, Fukunari Kimura, Hirohisa Kohama, Ryutaro Komiya, Laurence Lau, Justin Lin, Tim Mount, Takashi Negishi, Hiroshi Ohta, Masahiro Okuno-Fujiwara, Gustav Ranis, T. N. Srinivasan., and Henry Wan, Jr. Support in referencing, data processing, and manuscript typing from two capable assistants at Cornell, Rhonda Blaine and Eveline Ferretti, was just invaluable. For all these benefits, I express my deepest gratitude.

This book is dedicated to Dr Lee Teng-hui not as a political leader in Taiwan today but as a leading agricultural economist in Asia. His classic study on intersectoral resource transfer in Taiwan broke a path for the agricultural economics profession in East Asia to catch up with the international academic frontier—the path I have followed in my professional life.

Yujiro Hayami

Cornell University, Ithaca, NY
March 1996

Contents

Detailed Contents

* General readers not interested in technical detail may wish to skip sections marked with an asterik (*)

List of Figures

List of Tables

Introduction

The world today is characterized by extremely large income inequality among countries. According to World Bank's *World Development Report 1992*, average per-capita income per year in 1990 ranged from the level of around $US 20,000 in high-income countries belonging to the Organization for Economic Cooperation and Development (OECD), to the meagre level of only about $100 in countries at the bottom of the low-income group, such as Mozambique, Tanzania, and Ethiopia in Sub-Saharan Africa.

In that year total world population amounted to 5.3 billion, of which the population in high-income countries with per capita income above $10,000 numbered only 800 million. Yet this 15 per cent share of the global population received more than 70 per cent of world income. In contrast, 3.1 billion people, or about 60 per cent of world population, in low-income countries with per capita income below $600 were entitled to only about 4 per cent of the world income.

These per capita income comparisons are made in terms of the UN estimates of gross national product (GNP) converted to US dollars using the official exchange rates. Such comparisons tend to underestimate the level of economic welfare being enjoyed by people in low-income relative to those of high-income economies because of differences between exchange rates and purchasing power parities, as well as incomplete enumeration of non-market goods and services in GNP statistics. Yet, even after this statistical bias is corrected, it is certain that an extremely wide gap in the levels of real income and living remains between low-income and high-income countries, though the gap might be reduced from an order of one to several hundreds to an order of one to several tens.

In addition, there are many indicators other than national income statistics to show poverty and destitution in low-income economies. For example, according to a joint study by the Food and Agriculture Organization and the World Health Organization (FAO/WHO, 1992), in 1990 chronically undernourished people amounted to 800 million or about one-quarter of population in low-income countries, and to as high as nearly 40 per cent in Africa. Another indication is the high infant mortality rate, with about 100 out of 1,000 newly born babies dying before the age of 5 in Sub-Saharan Africa and South Asia, in contrast with only about 10 in high-income countries.

The escape from such destitution and misery through economic development must be the common national goal of low-income countries. Indeed,

developing countries that achieved independence after World War II have
almost unanimously undertaken ambitious development programmes aimed
at catching up with high-income economies. Several success stories have
been recorded. Especially remarkable are the so-called 'Newly Industrializing Economies' (NIEs) in Asia, such as Korea, Taiwan, Hong Kong, and
Singapore. Starting the early post-World War II period with per capita
income levels not much different from those of low-income countries today,
these NIEs have by now advanced to the verge of joining the ranks of high-
income economies. Following the NIEs, economies in the Association of
South-East Asian Nations (ASEAN) such as Indonesia, Malaysia, and
Thailand have been growing at rates more than twice as fast as high-income
countries. However, the rates of growth in low-income economies, especially
in Sub-Saharan Africa, have been lower than in high-income economies,
with the result of widening worldwide differentials in per capita income.

It should not be difficult to imagine how such growing inequality in the
world economy has been exacerbating tension in international relations. For
many years after World War II, the confrontation between the North (high-
income developed economies) and the South (low-income developing economies) represented one of the two major axis for mapping international
relations, together with the confrontation between the West (capitalist market economies) and the East (socialist centrally planned economies). Since
the end of the cold war, the global confrontation between two superpowers
in the East and the West has been replaced by multidimensional ethnic and
local conflicts. These relatively minor but numerous and pervasive conflicts,
if amplified by growing international economic disparity, will be likely to
result in major instability in the world political system. Emancipation of
people in developing countries from poverty is, therefore, not only desirable on humanitarian grounds but also necessary for developed countries
whose peace and prosperity hinge critically on the stability of international
order.

Scope of development economics

The major task of development economics is to explore the possibility of
emancipation from poverty for developing economies. It should be strongly
focused on low-income developing countries where poverty is especially
acute. How can low-income economies in the world today be set on the
track of sustained economic development for the immediate goal of reducing
poverty and the long-run goal of catching up to the wealth of developed
economies? The ultimate goal of development economics is to obtain an
answer to this question.

In order to achieve this goal, it is of course necessary to understand the
structure and mechanism of low-income economies. However, the characteristics of low-income economies cannot be properly understood without

comparisons with those of high-income economies. A key to identifying the causes of poverty and stagnation in low-income economies may be found in the experiences of economies that escaped from the same trap. It was through the process of economic development over a 200-year period since the Industrial Revolution that the majority of people in developed countries in the West were emancipated from poverty. The process was shortened to less than 100 years in Japan, and further to less than forty years in Asian NIEs.

An effective theory of development economics should be based on under-standing the similarities and differences of these histories compared with current situations in low-income economies. For this understanding it is vital to learn the theories of economic development by great economists in the past, who aimed to identify effective policies to promote and sustain devel-opment in their ages. Indeed, 'an inquiry into the nature and the causes of the wealth of nations' (Adam Smith, 1776) is equivalent to the inquiry into the causes of poverty and underdevelopment.

While it is critically important to learn from the experience of successful development, it is equally useful to learn from cases of failure. A dramatic example in our days was the recent collapse of centrally planned economies, which until only a few decades ago were considered by many to represent an effective model for developing economies to catch up and even surpass advanced market economies. Identifying the factors underlying both the failure of centrally planned economies as well as the relative stagnation of some developing economies that tried to adopt the central planning model, would be a vital step towards understanding the sustainable development mechanism.

It is relatively common to distinguish the term 'economic development' from 'economic growth,' though they are used interchangeably in some cases. 'Economic growth' has a connotation of quantitative expansions in economic variables, especially aggregate and per capita national incomes as measured by such statistics as GNP and NNP (net national product). There-fore, the analysis of economic growth is concerned mainly with measuring of growth in economic variables and identifying their interrelationships such as between the national income growth rate and the speed of capital formation.

On the other hand, 'economic development' is usually conceived as a process involving not only quantitative expansions but also changes in non-quantitative factors such as institutions, organizations, and culture under which economies operate. If we follow this usage, economic growth is considered a quantitative aspect of economic development. If so, in addi-tion to the analysis of economic growth, the study of economic development must investigate the influences of institutional and cultural factors on eco-nomic growth as well as the impacts of economic growth on those factors.

Since this book is focused on the development of low-income economies towards catching up with high-income economies, the range of economic

growth concerned is so wide that major cultural and social changes are
necessarily involved. Thus, it is inevitable that this book intends to be a
treatise of economic development as its title connotes. To be effective,
however, development economics must incorporate the achievements of
economic growth analysis to the maximum extent.

Among the many issues and subjects pertaining to development economics, this book is strongly focused on the role of technology borrowing as a
major means for low-income economies to catch up with advanced ones. A
critical condition for the transfer of foreign technology is development of
appropriate institutions. For new institutions to function effectively, they
must be consistent with people's value system in the recipient economy.
Thus, a major agenda of this book is to investigate the potential of developing economies endowed with different social and cultural heritages to
achieve institutional innovations needed for effective technology borrowing.
The overall aim is to identify possible means to facilitate this process.

An equally strong focus is placed on the choice of economic system for
development. In this book, this issue is posed as a question of what would be
the optimum combination of market, state, and community. These three
organizations co-ordinate the division of labour among people—the market
by means of competition, the state by means of coercion, and the community
by means of co-operation. They have both merits and demerits in co-
ordinating people's economic activities toward a socially desirable direction.
How to combine market, state, and community in the economic system for
maximizing growth in social productivity, under the unique cultural and
institutional conditions in each economy will be the ultimate question
addressed by our investigation.

While the special focus is placed on low-income economies, the book
covers broadly 'developing economies' at various stages of development.
However, no consensus exists on the definition of 'developing economies'.
Until recently, a common practice was to classify as developing economies
all countries other than OECD members, high-income oil exporters, and
centrally planned economies in Eastern Europe and the Soviet Union, while
it was customary to include the centrally planned economies in East Asia
such as China and Vietnam in this category as well. Since the collapse of the
socialist bloc, ex-socialist economies in Eastern Europe and Soviet Union
are now also often classified as developing economies. This conventional
usage is generally followed in this volume, though the term is too broad to be
useful for many purposes. For more specific analyses, the World Bank
classification (*World Development Report 1992*) of 'low-income economies'
(with per capita GNP less than $600 in 1990), 'low-middle income econo-
mies' (between $600 and $2,500) and 'upper middle-income economies'
(between $2,500 and $10,000) is used.

'High-income economies' (more than $10,000) in the World Bank de-
finition include not only OECD members but high-income oil exporters

(United Arab Emirates and Kuwait) and a few others (Israel, Singapore, and Hong Kong) in 1990. Yet, in this book the term 'high-income economies' is used to represent OECD members alone. Also it is used interchangeably with 'developed economies,' 'industrial economies', and 'advanced economies.'

Organization of the book

This book is organized in the following manner. Chapter 1 aims to establish a theoretical framework for the whole volume. As a basic framework, development of the social system is considered a process of dialectic interactions between the economic subsystem and the cultural-institutional subsystem. The economic subsystem consists of activities combining economic resources (labour, capital, and natural resources) through technology to produce goods and services useful for human living. These activities expand through accumulation of resources and progress in technology to result in economic growth. People's economic activities are co-ordinated and controlled by institutions (which here means the rules of society) and culture (which represents people's value system). As relative endowments of economic resources change—for example when natural resources like land become scarcer relative to labour owing to population growth—new agricultural technology may be required to save land relative the labour. For this technology to be developed and adopted, a new set of institutions may become necessary. A model is developed to conceptualize how such technological and institutional changes are interrelated with each other, how they respond to changes in resource endowments, and how such responses are governed by cultural traditions.

Chapter 2 tries to develop a bird's-eye view on the current status and growth potential of developing economies by means of highly condensed international comparative statistics in order to postulate broad hypotheses for the analyses in the subsequent chapters. The development pattern thus drawn is far different from that of the growth stage theories *à la* Rostow (1966) in which countries are supposed to advance linearly to higher developmental stages according to the order and sequence of their economic 'take-offs'. A dramatic contrast to Rostow's model is that per capita income in Argentina, which used to be one of the wealthiest nations in the period immediately after World War II, is now about to be surpassed by that of Korea, which ranked among the poorest in the early post-war years. Similar examples are abundant if not quite so dramatic. It is evident that an apparent 'take-off' does not guarantee sustained growth. It is also clear that wide differences in economic growth rates among developing countries are due little to differences in natural resource endowments, but may instead be explained mainly by investment in both physical and human capital. Data seem to support a hypothesis that the magnitude of such broadly defined capital formation does not depend so much on the level of per capita income. If so, it should be reasonable to hypothesize that even poverty-stricken economies can be set on the track of rapid economic development depending on the policies adopted.

Chapters 3 and 4 analyse the effects of explosive population growth and resulting relative scarcity in natural resources in the low-income economies that are characterized by high dependency on the production and export of primary commodities. Chapter 3 tries to identify the causes of 'population explosion' in developing countries today in the light of demographic histories in both developed and developing economies in order to draw future predictions. Further, development theories by classical economists such as Malthus and Ricardo who incorporated population as an endogenous variable in the economic system relative to fixed natural resources are examined to draw implications for developing economies today. Chapter 4 identifies the shift from resource-based to science-based agriculture as the basic force that prevented dismal predictions by Malthus and Ricardo from being realized. This chapter investigates the process in which the mechanism of science-based agriculture has now been transferred to developing economies and how such process can be promoted and sustained. As concluded in the chapter, it is no longer possible today to sustain economic development through nineteenth-century-type natural resource exploitation, and any resource-rich economy is bound to stagnate in poverty without major efforts to improve natural resource conservation and utilization efficiencies.

Chapters 5 and 6 examine the roles of capital accumulation and technological progress in industrial development. Chapter 5 traces the major currents in development thought and ideology after World War II which have resulted in the adoption by many newly independent nations of a strategy geared towards maximizing capital accumulation in the industrial sector by means of government planning and command. This strategy tends to consider 'capital' synonymous with large-scale machinery and equipment embodying modern labour-saving technologies developed in advanced industrial countries. It thereby tends to overlook the importance of finding appropriate technologies for efficient use of scarce capital and abundant labour in developing economies. In more recent years, the basic defect of such strategy has increasingly been evident in the economic stagnation plaguing its faithful adherents. It has thus become recognized that accumulated capital can not be an effective basis of economic development unless it is combined with appropriate technology and manpower under an appropriate organization. Chapter 6 examines institutional conditions by which appropriate technology and human resources are developed for rapid industrialization. A conclusion is that government investment in scientific research and education as well as the organization of competitive markets to facilitate innovations by Schumpeterian entrepreneurs are necessary conditions for sustained industrial development.

Chapter 7 examines the problems of growing inequality and environmental degradation that developing economies will have to face in their development processes. In the early phase of development, strong population pressure on limited land resources tends to push up land rent and pull down labour wage rates in the rural sector. In the urban sector the importation of labour-saving technologies from advanced countries tends to increase returns to capital relative to labour. Altogether, income disparity between asset-owning and assetless classes widens. Concurrently, as farmlands become short to support growing rural population, people tend to open and cultivate fragile lands in hills and mountains which would better be conserved for forest and pasture, with the result of serious soil erosion. In major cities air and water pollution tends to worsen at an accelerating pace because early industrialization often proceeds with little investment in pollution control. There is a real danger that the growing inequality and deteriorating environment might create so much social tension as to result in major social disruptions. Yet, importation of social welfare institutions such as minimum-wage laws for the purpose of income transfer risks worsening the lot of the majority of poor people who stake out a living in informal sectors lying outside the realm of such programmes. A solution should be sought that is directed at counteracting the basic economic forces to creating problems instead of trying to cure only their apparent symptoms.

Chapters 8 and 9 discuss what kind of institutional set-up would be appropriate for promoting economic development. In Chapter 8, this problem is considered from the question of how to combine market and state for the design of an economic system. In Chapter 9, the discussion is expanded to include the question of how to incorporate community relations into the economic system. The market is an organization co-ordinating competition among people seeking profits by impersonal means of prices. The community organizes collective actions based on mutual trust within a small group characterized by intensive personal interactions. The state intervenes in matters of resource allocations through the use of coercive power. Theoretically, the market is efficient in the supply of private goods, and the community's comparative advantage lies in the supply of 'local' public goods, of which the beneficiaries are locally confined. The supply of 'global' public goods such as basic scientific research and judicial systems should be left to the state. However, in developing economies where markets are poorly organized and characterized by highly imperfect information, they tend to fail to achieve efficient resource allocations even for private goods. Also, in some rural communities that had hitherto enjoyed free use of abundant natural resources under sparse population, it would be difficult to develop the ability to manage common-property resources at an adequate pace to cope with rapidly growing resource scarcity under accelerated population growth. In these cases it may appear necessary for the government to become involved in activities supplying private goods and local public goods. However, it must be recognized that in the economies where the market is undeveloped and local communities' resource-management capacity is low, the government's administrative and information-collecting capacity is also weak. Therefore, the expansion of the scope of government activities for the correction of market and community failure could well be subject to the high probability of government failure, which may be much more costly to society.

What should be the right combination of community, market, and state for promoting economic growth is thus the problem of high research priority in development economics. There is no single optimum combination uniformly applicable to developing economies. Under different cultural and social traditions, the efficiency of the market may be relatively higher in one economy, whereas the organizational ability of community is relatively stronger in another. In the former it would be effective to increase the role of the market, whereas in the latter it would be better to expand the role of community. For example, in the course of modernization in Japan, a rather unique form of economic organization has been created under a different cultural and social tradition from that in the West. On the basis of this unique institutional set-up, Japan was able to catch up with the economic power of Western Europe and North America. Chapter 10 concludes with the argument that if developing economies today are to catch up with developed economies, they must develop effective economic systems each suitable to their unique cultural and social traditions.

1

A Theoretical Framework for Economic Development

In this book we will examine the economic development necessary to bridge the extremely wide gap in per capita income between the low-income developing economies and the high-income developed economies in the world today. Such extensive economic growth cannot be realized without examining the requisite major changes in social organizations and people's value systems. Understanding the process by which quantitative expansions in economic variables (such as capital and labour force) interact with culture and institutions to evolve a social system that supports major growth in per capita income should be the ultimate goal of development economics. As a step towards this goal, development of a theoretical framework for the analysis of complex relationships among economic, cultural, and institutional changes is presented in this chapter.

1.1 Development of the Social System

1.1.1 A model of dialectic social development

A broad conceptual framework for development of social systems is outlined in Figure 1.1. This figure illustrates a model of the evolution in social systems through dialectic interactions between economic and cultural-institutional variables. The lower section of this figure represents the economic sector as a subsystem of society. This subsystem consists of interactions between technology and 'resources'—broadly defined as 'factors of production', including natural resources, labour, and capital. Technology is the determinant on the value of product to be produced from a given combination of production factors, commonly called 'the production function' in economics.

If we measure economic growth by the increase in average per capita product (or income), it is realized through increases in per capita endowments of resources and/or 'progress in technology' defined as an increase in product for given inputs of resources. 'Product' is defined here as economic value newly added to society by the inputs of labour, capital, and natural resources within a period; this 'value added' is distributed to owners of the resources to become their incomes, which are aggregated into the income of the society.

Increases in economic resources and progress in technology are not independent. For example, as the technology of controlling water-flows is developed and necessary investments are made for use of the technology—such as construction of irrigation canals and diversion dams—hitherto useless barren lands could be converted into economically useful arable lands. If more food could be produced on the increased land resources, the food surplus might be stored, allowing a greater portion of labour input to be diverted from food production to capital formation activities in the next period.

Thus, while the progress of technology provides a basis of resource augmentation, it is promoted by purposive resource-using activities. For example, advances in irrigation technology are achieved through research on the identification of water-flow patterns as well as the development of irrigation facilities for adequate control of the water-flows through experiments of various designs, be it done by scientists and engineers in modern research laboratories or by primitive trial and error by peasants on their farms. Those activities use both human effort and capital for the addition of the stock of engineering knowledge. Since this increase in knowledge has the same output-increasing effect as investment in tangible capital—such as the construction of irrigation canals and dams—research and development activities can be called 'investment in intangible capital'.

Similar to the production of tangible capital, it is possible to formulate a process of producing technical knowledge from the inputs of labour and capital. A critical element in augmenting this knowledge production function is 'investment in human capital', defined as enlargement of human capacity by such means as education, training, and health care. Investment in human capital will increase the efficiency of knowledge production, which in turn will improve the efficiency of production of economic value added from given resources in the society. Thus, cumulative increases in average product per capita will result from investments in both tangible and intangible capital.[1]

The productivity of an economic subsystem, consisting of its resource endowments and technology, is conditioned by culture and institutions in society. Broadly defined, institutions as well as technology are a part of culture. However, culture is here narrowly defined to imply the value system of people in the society, while institutions are defined as 'rules sanctioned by the members of the society' including both formally stipulated laws and informal conventions. Cultures and institutions thus defined are inseparably related. The rules that contradict the morals of people would not be sanctioned socially and, if stipulated formally, would not function effectively. For example, the institution of slavery to stipulate a person's property rights on other human beings could hardly be expected to function as a social institution today as it is inconsistent with the culture of the modern world. Yet, it was a perfectly legitimate and effective institution under different cultures such as in ancient Greece and Rome.

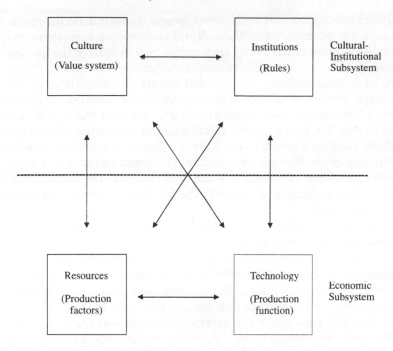

FIG. 1.1 *Interrelated developments in the social system*

Culture and institutions indicated in the upper section of Figure 1.1 as components of the social system exert significant influences on the economic subsystem located in the lower section. For instance, an important parameter to determine the rate of investment is the ratio of saving to income; this parameter is determined largely by people's future preference over present consumption, which is a part of their value system. It has been the tradition of modern neoclassical economics to analyse the workings of the economic subsystem under the assumption of fixed preferences. Such an approach would be effective for the analysis of a situation in which the upper subsystem was relatively constant. Yet, the approach would be grossly inadequate for dealing with the wide range of economic development within which major cultural and institutional changes inevitably occur. In this respect, the theory of Max Weber (1920) identifying the Protestant ethic as a source of modern capitalist development represents an important methodological suggestion, irrespective of its empirical validity.

1.1.2 A historical example

While accumulation of resources and progress in technology are conditioned by culture and institutions, changes in the latter are also induced by the former. Such a process of social development through dialectic interactions between the economic and the cultural-institutional subsystems may be understood more concretely by tracing the transition from the hunting and gathering economy to the agricultural (and pastoral) economy.

A basic force inducing this epochal change in human history was the increased scarcity of natural resources under the pressure of population growth.[2] As long as population was sparse and land was felt to infinitely exist like air, the killing of wild animals and the harvesting of wild crops in unlimited amounts would have shown no sign of exhaustion. However, as population grew (though very gradually), it was inevitable that the day would come when exploitation of the wild resources began to exceed their reproductive capacity and, thereby, the hunting-gathering economy could not be sustained.

To avoid the subsistence crisis that arose from this resource exhaustion, it became imperative for hunters to augment/increase the reproduction process by raising animals instead of killing and eating them immediately, and for gatherers to plant nuts and cereals for future harvests. An economic basis of the increased reproduction was the accumulation of capital. A limited list of capital items was required for hunting and gathering, such as stones, knives, clubs, and bows and arrows. A larger capital stock was required for shifting to the agriculture-based system, especially in the forms of reared animals, standing crops and trees, and opened and cultivable farmlands. Capital requirement increased further as the agricultural production system advanced to the stage at which it began to rely heavily on man-made land infrastructure, such as irrigation and drainage facilities.

To convert animals and plants to productive capital, it was necessary to accumulate knowledge to identify useful animals and plants for domestication as well as the appropriate methods to feed and grow them. Countless efforts of primitive producers to advance agricultural technology through trial and error were the major source of investment in intangible capital. These efforts to enlarge the reproduction process under the growing scarcity of natural resources are likely to have been induced by the producers' need for survival.

While such advancement in technical knowledge was necessary, it was not sufficient for the development of the agriculture-based economic system. This development required a major institutional change: establishment of property rights on productive resources. A basic rule in ideal primitive hunting and gathering economies was free access to natural resources, under which all the resources were the property of everyone but no one person's property in particular. Under this rule anyone could capture and consume any useful animals and plants as they found them. As long as this rule prevailed, a person who attempted to engage in agricultural production had to face the difficulty of preventing others from taking away the animals and crops he raised. In such circumstances there would have been little incentive for anyone to start agricultural production by investing in livestock and standing crops. Therefore, the requisite for the formation of an agricultural economy was the establishment of a new social order of clearly defined property rights by which the person who made efforts to invest in productive capital could exclude others from its use (Demsetz, 1967; Alchian and Demsetz, 1973). In the course of this development of agrarian civilization, property rights were first assigned to livestock and standing crops, and later extended to cover agricultural lands.

Those who were assigned property rights on land would have been equipped with strong incentives to invest in improving the quality of the land, from removing stones and tree roots, fencing and terracing, to irrigation and drainage. The form of property rights also evolved from communal ownership by tribe or village to private ownership by household or individual, with a stronger power of exclusion and, hence, a stronger incentive for private investment.

Common to all institutions, stipulation and enforcement of property rights entail costs. The most profitable situation for an individual is for him to break the rules (e.g. steal others' properties) while others are observing the rules (e.g. do not steal others' properties). Thus, the temptation is always high for anyone to become a 'free-rider' who tries to gain from breaking the rules. To the extent that people's propensity to become free riders is high, it is costly to enforce the property rights by such means as police and courts. It is the ethics as a part of culture that reduces the cost of enforcing the rules of society. Indeed, 'thou shall not steal' is a unanimous moral code in the commandments of the great religions that coincided with the development of agrarian civilizations. It seems reasonable to hypothesize that such a religious doctrine was both the cause and the consequence of establishment of the agriculturally based economic system.

Economic and social development through such interactions between economic forces and cultural-institutional elements have been repeated over history. For instance, the patent system that was established with the development of modern industrial society was aimed at assigning property rights on engineering knowledge and information, thereby promoting private investment in this critical component of intangible capital (Evenson and Westphal, 1995). Recent negotiations in the GATT (General Agreement on Tariffs and Trade) Uruguay Round on intellectual property rights represented an attempt to establish internationally uniform rules on the protection and the transactions of property rights over a wide range of knowledge and information including computer software. This attempt was a response to the growing need of the world today in which the role of knowledge and information, as a factor of economic production, has been rising faster than that of tangible capital. Likewise, the establishment of the International Law of the Sea creating exclusive economic zones over 200 nautical miles from each country's coast was an attempt to mobilize conservation efforts for marine resources at the national level in response to growing scarcity and high prices of fish and other marine products (Hannesson, 1991). These are among the efforts to achieve the institutional innovation of the same nature as developing property rights on livestock, crops, and lands in the prehistoric initiation of agriculture.

1.1.3   Marx and new institutionalism

The theoretical framework outlined above has a basic similarity with the perspective on evolution of the social system described by Karl Marx and Friedrich Engels.[3] The economic subsystem and the cultural-institutional subsystem in Figure 1.1 correspond broadly with what they term 'infrastructure' and 'superstructure', respectively. In their system, the core of the superstructure is the property-rights relations of production factors (so-called 'production relations'), while infrastructure is the technology needed to determine the capacity of material production from available resources. While the institution is believed to determine realization of the technology's production potential, technology is identified as the basic force in structuring the institution; at the origin the institution is so structured as to best exploit the potential of material production. This view on the formation of institutions in response to economic demand is analogous to the theory of induced institutional innovation.

Marx and Engels assumed a major time-lag between increases in material production capacity and changes in institutions; this made changes in the social system discontinuous and abrupt. In their perspective technical knowledge and tangible capital are accumulated gradually to bring about continuous growth in productive capacity. In contrast, institutions cannot adjust immediately—they must be stable over time so that the rules of society for structuring people's stable expectations in dealing with others could effectively function.

Moreover, the core institution in the Marx–Engels theory is the property-right assignment of a key production factor at each stage of economic development—such as slaves in the ancient classical world, land in medieval feudalism, and capital in modern industrial capitalism. Changes are bound to take time as it will be strongly resisted by the prestige class to whom property ownership is exclusively bestowed. As a result, even though the institution was originally designed to best exploit the productive potential of society, as it becomes inconsistent with the changed conditions of material production resulting from technological progress and capital accumulation, it tends to survive. In other words, the institution that was once a carrier of economic development over time turns out to be the 'fetter' against further development under a new technology regime. Marx and Engels theorized that this gap between the institution and the production potential would be ultimately closed through a violent political revolution. This perspective was forcibly marshalled in a classic statement by Marx:

The mode of production of material life determines the general character of social, political and spiritual processes of life. At a certain stage of their development, the material forces of production in society come into conflict with the existing relations of production, or—what is but a legal expression for the same thing—with the property relations within which they had been at work before. From forms of development of the forces of production these relations turn into their fetters. Then comes the period of social revolution. With the change of the economic foundation the entire immense superstructure is more or less rapidly transformed. (Marx, [1859] 1904: 11–12)

Marx considered technological progress and capital accumulation decisive in determining the productive capacity of society and denied the importance of natural resources relative to population. In this respect, our perspective differs from Marx's and is closer to that of new institutional historians in emphasizing the influence of changes in relative resource endowments and prices due to population growth and other factors (North and Thomas, 1973; North, 1981). We also consider that institutions are not quite as inflexible as to make violent revolution inevitable for major institutional changes. There is considerable historical evidence to support the hypothesis that the basic institutional framework, including property relations, changed through cumulative adjustments by such means as informal agreements and reinterpretations of laws and codes (Davis and North, 1970).

However, there is no guarantee that such cumulative adjustments are sufficiently rapid and responsive to emerging social needs. The cost of incremental change in one institution can be prohibitively high as this particular institution is inseparably intertwined with others. Its change thereby demands a change in the total institutional framework that has been historically determined (see Section 1.2.4 on this historical path dependency). Due to fear of social sanctions, such as ostracism, against the deviation by individuals from established norms and conventions, even obviously inefficient institutions like castes are often difficult to change (Akerlof, 1984). Because a future gain from an institutional reform is uncertain, and its distribution among various social groups is difficult to predict relative to the obvious loss to a specific group, opposition to reform tends to be strongly organized, while support is only weakly so (Fernandez and Rodrik, 1991), in terms of the logic of the political market (Section 1.2.3). It is therefore not uncommon to observe that a society continues to be trapped in economic stagnation and poverty under a dysfunctional system bound by strong social inertia for the preservation of established institutions (Basu *et al.*, 1987).

Thus, it is likely that changes in institutions and, more so, in culture lag significantly behind changes in the material production base, and that the

resulting contradictions may create strong social and political tension, culminating in major disruptions, as Marx and Engels envisioned.

1.2 The Theory of Induced Innovation*

The theoretical framework developed in the previous section is general but
not very operational for economic analysis in the sense that the implied
hypotheses are too broad for empirical testing. In the following section
we will construct an operational economic model by extracting some elements from the general model, on which development economics must
focus. For this purpose it is necessary to use technical terms specific to
economics.

1.2.1 Induced technological innovation

First, our focus will be placed on a causal relationship within the economic
subsystem in Figure 1.1, in which changes in resource endowments induce
changes in technology. A standard economic theory on this relationship is
called the theory of 'induced technological innovation' in the tradition of
John R. Hicks (1932).

The Hicksian theory presupposes a mechanism in which, as the endowment of one factor (e.g. capital) becomes more abundant relative to another
factor (e.g. labour), a change in technology is induced towards using more
capital and saving labour for given relative factor prices (for a more exact
definition, see Section 6.4.2). Such a biased change in technology stems from
the efforts of profit-seeking entrepreneurs to reduce production costs by
substituting relatively more abundant (hence cheaper) resources for scarcer
(hence dearer) resources. The induced innovation theory within the framework of neoclassical economics has assumed a competitive market by which
relative abundance and scarcity of factors are reflected in factor prices used
as data for entrepreneurs' production plans. However, this theory can be
applicable to subsistence-oriented non-market economies also, if it is
assumed that relative resource scarcities are recognized by producers, even
very roughly, in terms of shadow prices reflecting the social opportunity
costs of the resources.

Based on such assumptions, Figure 1.1 is a model explaining the process
of transition from the hunting-gathering economy to the agricultural economy, as well as subsequent advances in the technology of agricultural
production. With some modification, this model can be used to explain a
transition to the industrial economy also.

---

* Readers not accustomed to the technical analysis of economics may wish to skip this section.

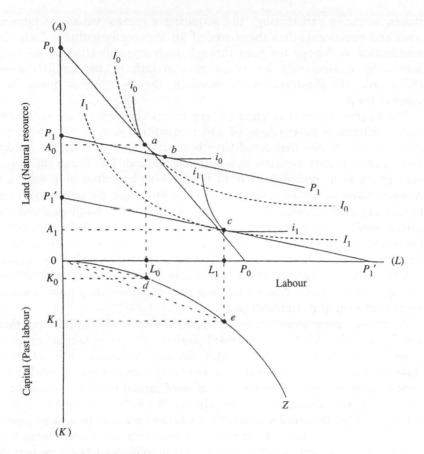

FIG. 1.2 *A model of induced innovation*

Figure 1.2 represents the production relation (production function) of producing a single commodity (e.g. food) from inputs of three factors: labour (L), capital (K), and land (A) representing natural resources. Capital is here assumed to be produced mainly by past labour input.

The upper A–L quadrant in Figure 1.2 represents the substitution between land and labour in terms of isoquant for producing one unit of product (unit isoquant). On the other hand, the O–L line in the lower L–K quadrant represents the complementary relationship of capital with labour in the event of substituting labour for land. For example, as long as a farmer engages in slash-and-burn shifting cultivation, he can cultivate a large area using his own labour with very little capital consisting of such small items as a hatchet, a digging stick, and a stock of seeds. However, if he attempts to shift to a more labour-intensive, land-saving system under settled agriculture, he must build up large capital by improving farmlands (removing roots and stones, terracing and fencing) and acquiring a greater variety of farming tools and implements than those needed for shifting agriculture. Thus, the substitution of labour for land through such intensification of land-use should be accompanied by exponential growth in the capital–labour (K/L) ratio. To illustrate this relationship, the O–L line is drawn in a concave form.

The I-curve in the A–L quadrant represents the 'innovation possibility curve', defined as an envelope of unit isoquants corresponding to all the possible technologies that could have been developed with the knowledge and human capacity available at a particular period. This curve shifts over time (from I_0 in period 0 to I_1 in period 1 as indicated in Figure 1.2) corresponding to the accumulation of knowledge and the improvement in human capacity. According to the theory of induced technological innovation, a particular technology as represented by i_0 is developed and adopted for period 0, because it is this technology that minimizes the cost of production for the price ratio between land and labour (P_0), reflecting relative scarcities of these factors in this period. In other words, i_0 is developed through the effort of producers to reach the cost-minimizing point a within an available set of possibilities (I_0).

Assuming complementarity between labour and capital in their substitution for land, as explained earlier, the land–labour ratio at point $a(OA_0/OL_0)$ corresponds with the capital–labour ratio at point $d(OK_0/OL_0)$. Since in this particular case it is assumed that capital is the product of past labour alone and, the price of capital relative to the price of land can be considered to move largely parallel with the labour-land price ratio (P_0). This assumption of complementarity between labour and capital is adopted for the sake of simplicity to represent the three-dimensional relation in a two-dimensional diagram. This simplification might be permissible as an approximation to facilitate understanding the characteristics of technological progress in pre-industrial economies. For the analysis of industrial economies in Chapter 6, the substitution between labour and capital as well as the substitution between tangible and intangible capital will be treated as a central problem.

Assume that, as time passed from period 0 to period 1, relative scarcity of land increased with the result of lowering the relative price of labour to land from P_0 to P_1. Meanwhile, the innovation possibility curve would have shifted towards the origin from I_0 to I_1, reflecting the increased capacity of society to produce a unit of food with a smaller input of factors. Corresponding to these changes, it now becomes optimum for producers to reach point c by choosing a technology represented by i_1, over other possibilities embraced by I_1.

However, until the new i_1 technology is actually developed, producers will have to continue using the old i_0 technology and, hence, can move only from point a to b. It is through producers' efforts in repeated trial and error, as well as organized scientific research and development (in the case of modern society) that the new i_1 technology will become available. The basic premiss in the theory of induced technological innovation is that the expected gain (or reduction in cost) for producers, as measured by the distance between P_1 and P'_1, in the move from point b to c, will induce them to make efforts for technological development with the result of changing technology from i_0 towards i_1.

The move from hunting and gathering to agriculture may be explained in terms of this theory as follows: When the availability of usable land appeared to be limitless relative to sparse population and, therefore, the relative scarcity of land to labour (P_0) was very low, collection of foods from wild animals and plants (i_0) could well have been an optimum technology in the sense that it produced food at a minimum cost. Even if population grew, and the relative scarcity of land rose (P_0 to P_1), there would have been little scope to increase food supply by applying more labour to limited land (a to b) as long as hunting and gathering were the sole option for food production. However, if farming technology (i_1) became available, people would be able to produce much more food from given land resources (b to c) at a lower cost. This possibility would have worked as a driving force for primitive hunters and gatherers to search for ways to increase reproduction of useful animals and plants.

1.2.2 Induced institutional innovation

The theory of induced technological innovation is explained above in terms of producers' cost-minimizing behaviour in the tradition of neoclassical economics. Such a theoretical structure appears to be relevant to modern market economies in which technological innovations are carried out mainly by large firms with research and development capacities, though theory has been a subject of heated theoretical discussion.[4] Major modifications are needed to apply the theory to the analysis of transformation within subsistence-oriented economies and transition from subsistence-oriented to market-oriented economies.

The reason is not, as once commonly thought, because small subsistence-oriented producers in premodern economies are ignorant and bound by tradition, and therefore, unable to search for and adopt profitable crops and cultural practices. On the contrary, accumulated evidence shows that subsistence-oriented small farmers in developing economies allocate resources rationally and respond effectively to profitable economic opportunities (Schultz, 1964; Hopper, 1965; Yotopoulos, 1968; Barnum and Squire, 1979; Rosenzweig, 1984; Tiffen and Mortimore, 1994). This trait would be shared not only by farmers but by hunters and gatherers as well.

It is not reasonable, however, to assume that they anticipate a wide range of innovation possibilities along the *I*-curve and move linearly towards point *c* in response to changes in relative factor scarcities and/or innovation possibilities. It is more reasonable to assume an evolutionary process of the Nelson–Winter (1982) type, namely as food production per capita decreased for hunters and gatherers, corresponding to growing population pressure on natural resources, they were forced to search for ways to increase food supply through trial and error. Only those who happened to reach the i_1 curve (agriculture) were able to survive. With this modification, induced technological innovations are thought to produce technological change in the direction that the traditional theory predicts. However, some economies may not be able to survive because they continue to be trapped in the old technology (i_0).

A major modification required for the theory to cover both primitive and high stages of development would be to combine the theory of technological innovation with the theory of institutional innovation. For whatever high profit a technological innovation may be expected to produce, and however rational a producer may be, it may not be possible for him alone to carry out the innovation. As explained earlier, the development from hunting and gathering to agriculture involves the process of capital accumulation in the form of livestock, standing crops, and prepared farm fields, for which property rights need to be established. However, assignment and protection of property rights can hardly be achieved by individual efforts but need collective action by people in the society. Collective action is required not only to create institutions for promoting private investment incentives, but also to undertake large-scale investment in social overhead capital, such as flood control of rivers and building of gravity irrigation systems. Appropriate institutions must be prepared to organize people effectively for such collective action.

Then what mechanism should we assume to organize collective action to facilitate technological progress and capital accumulation in a socially optimum direction? The most naïve model would be to assume that collective action is organized when aggregate social profit from the move from point *b* to *c* (Figure 1.2) exceeds the cost of organizing the collective action to enable such a move. This naïve model could well be valid in broad terms of progress in human history in which property rights have been strengthened and institutions to mobilize collective action for building infrastructure (such as irrigation) corresponding to growing population pressure on natural resources.

However, if such a naïve mechanism of induced institutional innovation always operated, all the economies would have grown smoothly and no great income gap would ever have emerged between developed and developing economies. Thus, to understand the causes of the poverty and underdevelopment versus the wealth and development of nations in today's world it is necessary to understand the conditions under which the mechanism of induced institutional innovation fails to operate effectively.

1.2.3 Logic of political market

The supply of public goods in response to social needs is determined through political process at equilibria between demands for and supplies of those public goods from various interest groups, which might be called 'political markets' in analogy with economic markets for ordinary goods and services. The problem is that the mechanism of the political market does not guarantee the optimum supply of public goods in terms of economic well-being in society. As Mancur Olson (1965) predicted, collective action is usually much less organized than a socially optimum level, because only part of its profit accrues to those who shoulder the cost of organizing the action. This is the basic cause of a general undersupply of public goods.

Social rules (such as property rights) and social overhead capital (such as roads) bear the properties of 'non-rivalness' and 'non-excludability' common to public goods. Non-rivalness is the property of a good to be utilized jointly by many, and non-excludability is the property of a good where utilization by those who do not pay for the cost of its supply is possible (Musgrave, 1959). For example, once an irrigation canal is dug by the collective work effort of villagers, all those who engage in farming along this canal can utilize its water jointly. The problem is that it is difficult and costly to prevent someone from using (or stealing) water who did not contribute labour for the construction of the canal. For this latter property (non-excludability), temptation is high for anyone to become a free-rider in the use of public goods; this applies equally to the enforcement of social rules, such as property rights, as explained in the previous section.

For the supply of public goods someone must take charge of organizing collective action. Collective action is organized at various levels, including voluntary co-operation in the local commuity and the religious group. For the supply of 'global public goods' widely applicable to a large number of people in society, however, it often becomes necessary to set up a mechanism of coercion in the form of 'state'. The collective action aimed to form and manipulate the coercive power of state is called 'politics' or 'political movements'. The organizer of political movements is called a 'political leader' or 'politician', whether from small local communities, nation states, or international arenas. The leader must apply major efforts to bring people together in an agreement on collective action and enforce it with persuasion, intimidation, bribery, or violence. Economic benefits expected from the public good produced by organized collective action for society may far exceed the cost paid. This benefit is not usually appropriated by the political leader. For example, the stipulation and protection of property rights on livestock may enable primitive hunters to engage in agriculture (as represented by a move from point b to c in Figure 1.2). However, the economic benefit from this provision of public good, as measured by $P_1 P_1'$, is appropriated by individual producers who shifted from hunting to agriculture.

Returns to the leader for his cost of organizing collective action for the supply of a public good (e.g. property-rights protection) would be the strengthening of his power base due to increased support from people who capture economic gains from the public good. Unless the increment in his utility arising from his strengthened political power was expected to exceed his cost, he would not attempt to organize the collective action.

Such behaviour of the political leader is modelled in Figure 1.3, in the tradition of public choice theory on the economics of politics (Downs, 1957; Buchanan and Tullock, 1962; and Breton, 1974). Line MR represents decreasing marginal revenue of the leader for increasing the supply of a public good. Marginal revenue for the politician is defined as the marginal increase in his utility from the strengthening of his power base (increased votes in the case of parliamentary democracy) expected from a unit increase in the public good provision. Line MR is drawn as a downward slope since it seems reasonable to assume that the marginal social productivity of a public good tends to decrease as its supply increases, with a resulting decrease in the marginal gain in political support from the beneficiaries.

On the other hand, the leader's marginal cost (MC) is defined as the marginal disutility of his time and effort in organizing the collective action. Line MC is upward-sloping because the cost of preventing 'free-riders' rises progressively as a greater number of people will have to be organized for an increased supply of the public good.

Because the vertical distance between MR and MC measures the marginal net utility or marginal profit (revenue minus cost) of the political leader, his profit will be maximized by the level of public good supply at the intersection

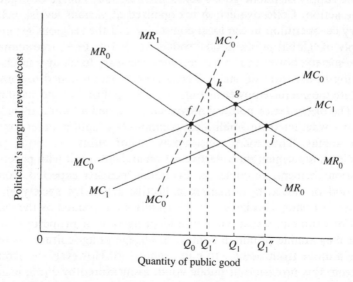

FIG. 1.3 *A model of political market for a public good*

of these two lines. There is no guarantee at all that this optimum for the politician coincides with the optimum for society. In general, it is probable that the supply of public good is below the social optimum because only a fraction of social benefits will accrue to the politician.

If the political leader's marginal revenue and cost are located in an initial period (0) at MR_0 and MC_0, OO_0 is the optimum supply of the public good for the political leader. If, towards the next period (1), changes occur in relative resource scarcities and in technological possibilities (as represented respectively by P_0 to P_1 and I_0 to I_1 in Figure 1.2), a shift from the old to the new technology (i_0 to i_1) would become profitable for a large number of producers in the society. Then these potential beneficiaries from the new technology would render stronger support for the politician who would act to provide the public good (such as the protection of property rights) that is needed for the adoption of the new technology. The result would be the moving up of the politician's marginal revenue curve from MR_0 to MR_1. The mechanism of induced innovation in technology and institution would thus work through such an inducement mechanism for the supply of public goods in the 'political market'.

The problem lies in how efficiently this inducement mechanism would work in terms of the economic welfare maximization criteria for the society. How much the supply of a public good would increase in response to an increase in social demand depends, in part, on how efficiently the increased social demand is translated into the upward shift in the politician's MR curve. This efficiency tends to be low, especially for the type of public good whose social benefit is large in aggregate but is distributed thinly over a large number of private producers, and, hence, not visible enough to mobilize political support (or lobbying) activities. This is the basic dilemma that results from major under-investment in the public goods with high social pay-offs (Olson, 1965).

Another factor determining the efficiency of the political inducement mechanism is the slope of the MC curve. The increase in the supply of public good in response to a given shift in the marginal revenue curve from MR_0 to MR_1 is larger for a relatively flat marginal cost curve such as MC_0 than for a sharply rising curve such as MC_0'. A major determinant of the location and shape of the MC curve is people's value system. For example, the marginal cost of strengthening property rights would be high in a society in which the theft of animals had not been recognized as a major crime.

Conflict of interests among various groups in a society would also sharpen the slope of the MC curve. For example, the establishment of property rights on land should produce major benefits to those undertaking the change to settled agriculture. It would be opposed, however, by hunters and nomads who would be excluded from the use of the land to which property rights are assigned. If this opposition is well organized, the marginal cost of strengthening property rights on land would rise sharply so that the supply of this public good would be severely limited relative to increased social need.

How can the efficiency in the translation of social demand to the politician's marginal revenue curve be improved? How can his marginal cost curve be lowered? To a large extent, these tasks were facilitated in premodern societies by the religious developments that changed people's moral perceptions. What ideologies would be an effective substitute for this role of religion in modern societies? How can modern education and information media promote efficiency of the induced innovation mechanism involving political processes? This problem is one of the most difficult and most important agendas in development economics (to be discussed in detail in Chapters 8, 9, and 10).

1.2.4 Historical path dependency

A major constraint on the effective working of the induced innovation mechanism would be scale economies in an institutional set-up corresponding to a particular technological regime. Such scale economies would make incremental changes difficult in an economic system that was historically formed. For example, in the process of transition from nomadism to agriculture, it may have been difficult for a small number of farmers to establish arable farming with their collective action, even if they agreed to respect each others' property rights on lands and crops. They could hardly prevent nomads from grazing animals on their croplands because of the customs of nomadic society. Thus, the transition to settled agriculture induced by population pressure on land resources could have been disrupted by the binding power of traditional nomadic culture and institutions. However, if for some historical reason (such as a large-scale migration of agriculturalists like homesteading in the US West) a majority of land happened to be enclosed, nomads may have found it difficult to continue their traditional way of life and would have been compelled to move to settled agriculture, thereby eliminating the nomadic system.

This example illustrates the possibility of multiple equilibria (e.g. domination of nomadism versus domination of settled agriculture) for a society to reach in a manner similar to the world of 'new growth theory' with the assumption of increasing returns based on externality (Romer, 1987; Murphy *et al.*, 1989; Krugman, 1991; Grossman and Helpman, 1991), which is discussed later (Sections 8.4.2 and 8.5.3). To which equilibrium a society will move depends to a large extent on its 'historical path' (David, 1985; Arthur, 1988; North, 1990, ch.1).

A good example of a multiple equilibrium can be found in the histories of England and Spain. In England, private property rights of land were gradually strengthened from the late medieval period until 'commons' or grazing land for communal use by villagers were enclosed by landlords into large private farms in the eighteenth century. Enclosure prepared the way for significant increases in land productivity based on the change from the traditional three-field system to modern crop rotation including fodder crops such as clover and turnips—the so-called 'Agricultural Revolution' (North and Thomas, 1973:16 and 150–1). This traditional paradigm on the Agricultural Revolution in eighteenth century England through landlords' enclosure has recently been challenged by Robert Allen (1992). He demonstrated that the major increase in land productivity was brought about by yeomen (small independent farmers) in the seventeenth century, based on their secured land tenurial rights in the sixteenth century.

Therefore, both the old and the new paradigms have identified secure property rights in land as the necessary condition for major agricultural productivity growth in England. In contrast, Spain failed to protect private rights on croplands because of the opposition of politically powerful sheepgrazers. Consequently, arable farmers were not able to prevent grazing animals from encroaching on their standing crops. This was identified as one of major factors underlying stagnation of Spain's agriculture and economy relative to England's in modern history (North and Thomas, 1973: 130; Nugent and Sanchez, 1989). It is likely that the contrast between England and Spain was rooted in the different cultural-institutional subsystems that had been historically formed in each country.

This historical example seems to show that, even if the importation of advanced technology from developed countries were economically profitable for developing countries, the importation of foreign institutions for the use of this technology without due regard to differences in cultural values and social conventions may not serve its intended purpose but only create social disorder. Effective policy effort should be directed to the creation of an economic system that can best exploit new economic opportunities by making good use of deeply rooted traditional norms and conventions (Chapter 9 and 10).

1.3 Developing Economies in the Light of the Theoretical Framework

From this theoretical perspective it can be seen that a major problem for developing countries today is the speed with which resource endowments and technology change. Twentieth-century population growth has been extremely rapid, with rates two to three times that of developed economies in their initial phase of modern growth in the nineteenth century (Chapter 3). This explosive growth rate has been very rapidly raising the scarcity of natural resources, especially land, relative to labour. In many developing economies, the endowment of arable land per agricultural worker decreased significantly, resulting in pauperization of the rural population. As the favourable farming area has become relatively smaller and incapable of sustaining subsistence for the increased population, some farmers have been forced to open fragile lands in hills and mountains for cultivation, with the result of serious environmental degradation such as soil erosion and flooding. Alternatively, many have been forced to migrate to urban slums seeking subsistence from various informal activities (Chapter 7).

Such a crisis situation could be overcome by the effort of substituting labour and capital for natural resources and using appropriate technology, as has been repeated in history since the transition from hunting and gathering to settled agriculture. Development of appropriate agricultural technology, though difficult, is possible with investment in adaptive research for exploiting the backlog of scientific and technological knowledge accumulated in developed economies (Chapter 4). Also, with appropriate technology borrowing, developing countries should in theory be able to achieve rapid industrialization with the creation of major non-farm income and employment opportunities (Chapter 6). Yet, in reality, foreign technologies imported to developing economies are often highly capital-intensive since they were developed in high-income, labour-scarce economies. Their importation tends to result in aggravation of labour surplus and unemployment in developing economies (Chapter 7).

To exploit the great opportunities in technology borrowing, and adjust foreign technologies to the economic and social environments of developing economies, institutional innovations are called for in areas such as market structure, industrial organization, labour management and regulation, research, training, and education systems. However, appropriate adjustments to rapidly changing economic forces are not easy. Institutions are slow to change, as they are strongly constrained by cultural traditions and social customs. In some cases, importation of foreign ideologies aggravates the contradiction between the economic subsystem and the cultural-institutional subsystem. For example, based on international diffusion of humanitarianism and respect for human rights, a tendency has emerged in developing economies to introduce social welfare and labour laws such as minimum wage and labour union regulations. These regulations provide limited benefits to a relatively small number of employees in the formal sector consisting of large modern enterprises and government agencies. As effective wage rates are raised in this sector, the substitution of capital for labour is encouraged with the result of decreased employment, and as well as increased unemployment and underemployment outside the sector (Chapter 7).

Foreign influences tend to heighten this contradiction in developing economies partly because culture, institutions, and technology change separately, rather than evolving through dialectic interactions within each society. However, a more basic reason appears to be that changes in resource endowments and technology happen too fast for people's value system and organizational principles to adjust. For example, when the population was sparse, and people made their subsistence living in isolated villages and tribes, many of these small communities were able to manage 'common-property resources' or 'common-pool resources', such as forests, pasture lands, and communal irrigation systems, which are subject to the danger of exhaustion due to overexploitation but for which it is difficult to charge the cost to the resource-users. The strong personal ties binding community members together as well as traditional moral codes and conventions, including religious taboos, were largely effective in preventing people from becoming free-riders.

However, as the population grew and interlocational interdependencies increased, co-ordination of people over a wide area covering many villages would have been required. To the extent that social organization and institutions to cope with this situation lagged behind the emerging need, it is well known that, while forests were relatively well preserved and grazing animals were adequately controlled to allow for reproduction of pasture within each village, the surrounding public forests were destroyed by shifting cultivation and pasture lands were turned into deserts by overgrazing (Chapters 7 and 9).

The same problem has been emerging at the state level. In general, people in developing countries have a stronger sense of belonging to communities such as tribes and villages than to the state. This tendency is especially strong in some countries (particularly those in Africa), which were originally sub-divided into colonies by Western powers with little consideration for the social integrity of native people. These countries later achieved independence with few adjustments to the colonial boundaries. In these countries it is only natural for politicians to place a high priority on the policies that benefit the communities to which they belong rather than on policies that promote a nationwide benefit. People there also tend to consider such behaviour by politicians to be natural and legitimate. As a result, an oversupply of negative public goods (or more appropriately called 'public bads') tends to prevail that benefit a small group at the expense of the majority (Chapter 8).

Such a contradiction or mismatch between the economic subsystem and the cultural-institutional subsystem is likely to become especially critical for the economies characterized by rapid changes in resource endowments and technology, probably culminating in the Marxian solution of revolution and civil war. Yet, hasty reforms of institutions without due consideration for historical path dependency can only aggravate the crisis.

A wide gap exists in technology and institutions between developing and developed economies. This gap could be a potential source of rapid economic development for developing economies. The key to exploiting this potential is to establish a feedback mechanism whereby changes in resource endowments and technology evolve institutions that incorporate cultural tradition appropriately, thus promoting the speed of induced innovation while also avoiding the tragic mismatch between infrastructure and superstructure.

Where is such mechanism operating in developing economies? Who are the carriers of this mechanism? What means may promote it? Understanding the total interdependency among all the components in the social system will be necessary for an answer. However, we will only be thwarted if we try to understand the entire complex system from the beginning. To move toward this understanding, the only option is to start with the analysis of partial relations between population and natural resources, resources and technology, technology and institutions, etc. Then we should try to develop a global perspective on the results of the partial analyses. The theoretical framework outlined in this chapter is designed to serve as an integrating device for the partial analyses that follow.

NOTES

1. A somewhat similar model is developed in Hayami and Ruttan (1985: 111).
2. There have developed many theories concerning the origin of agriculture that took place around 10,000 BC. Some have determined that the desiccation in West Asia and North Africa corresponding to the retreat of glaciers from the end of the Pleistocene forced human and animal inhabitants to concentrate in river valleys and oases, and was therefore a prime pressure on domestication (Childe, 1928). Others have emphasized as a decisive factor the cultural and religious changes, in addition to accumulation of knowledge on animals and plants (Sauer, 1952). There has also been a theory identifying the exhaustion of wild animals due to the innovation of bow-and-arrow hunting technology as the major factor inducing the development of agriculture (V. L. Smith, 1975). These theories have their own truths. They are not inconsistent with the general hypothesis that a shift to agriculture was induced by a decline in the endowment of natural resources per capita. There is little doubt that population growth for given natural resource endowments was one of the most fundamental factors, if not the only factor, to have induced the change to agriculture.
3. Marx's view was typically advanced in the famous preface to *A Contribution to the Critique of Political Economy* ([1859] 1904) to be quoted later. His interpretation of historical processes were expressed in various works, e.g. Marx ([1939–41] 1953). It was Engels ([1884] 1953) who developed a systematic treatise of Marxian interpretation of human history.
4. As for the debates on whether the Hicksian bias in technological changes is induced by changes in relative factor prices, see Fellner (1961), Samuelson (1965), and Ahmad (1966). For more detail, see Hayami and Ruttan (1985: 84–6).

2

A Comparative Perspective on Developing Economies

Before proceeding to detailed analyses of various aspects of economic development, this chapter will present a bird's-eye view of developing economies' current economic level and growth potential, using condensed international comparative statistics.

A major problem in an exercise of this nature is the limited comparability of national account statistics across countries in different stages of economic development. According to conventional national accounts, goods and services produced in households—such as yarn spun and cloth woven by a housewife—are not included in the national product when consumed at home, but are counted as components of it when sold outside the household. Even when they are sold outside the home, these household products often fail to be covered in official data collection by statistical agencies. Similarly, the use of family labour by small peasants to plant trees and improve pasture are activities that are theoretically considered investment, but are difficult to measure for inclusion in national account statistics. Therefore, the more subsistence-oriented economies are, the stronger the tendency is for their national incomes and investments to be underestimated relative to market-oriented economies.

Another major problem is how to convert national incomes measured in local currencies into comparable units. The commonly used procedure—conversion by exchange rates into US dollars—tends to underestimate the level of economic welfare in developing economies relative to that of developed economies. The reason is that market exchange rates are supposed to reflect purchasing power parities with respect to tradable goods. Because the prices of non-tradables, such as services and real properties, are usually low (relative to tradables) in developing economies as compared with developed economies, market exchange rates tend to underestimate the purchasing power of local currencies in developing economies for a wide range of goods and services, including both tradables and non-tradables. On the other hand, official exchange rates in developing economies are often overvalued for the sake of promoting certain domestic industries (Section 8.2.4).

The undervaluation in market exchange rates and the overvaluation resulting from government interventions may cancel each other to some extent. However, experimental estimates using purchasing power parities indicate that the use of exchange rates tends to result in major underestimation of real national product for less developed economies.[1]

Considering the large statistical errors and biases in international comparisons, analysis in this chapter will not go beyond identification of very broad patterns. For such broad comparisons, the most convenient set of statistics are the World Development Indicators in the Appendix of the World Bank's *World Development Report* (annual). International comparisons presented here are for the year of 1990 based on data drawn from the 1992 edition of this World Bank publication, supplemented by the 1991 and 1993 editions.

The World Development Indicators in this Appendix represent a handy summary of international comparative statistics. Yet, data enumerated in more than thirty statistical tables (thirty-three tables in the 1992 edition) are excessive for the purpose of this chapter and, therefore, are condensed into only four tables. The countries (120 plus) compared in World Development Indicators are too numerous for our purpose. Therefore, three countries from Sub-Saharan Africa (Tanzania, Nigeria, and Kenya), two countries from South Asia (Bangladesh and India), four countries from East Asia (China, Indonesia, Thailand, and the Republic of Korea), three countries from Latin America (Argentina, Mexico, and Brazil), and four countries representing OECD members (the UK, France, the USA, and Japan) were selected. Comparative analyses were made with both individual country data and regional averages.

The countries selected have relatively large populations and high economic weights in respective regions, and were chosen to represent respective stages of development in each region. For example, from East Asia, China was selected because of its dominant weight in world population, and to represent the transition from a centrally planned to a market economy. Indonesia, Thailand, and Korea were selected to represent relatively low-income, middle-income, and newly industrializing economies (NIEs) respectively. Convenience in interregional comparison was also considered. For example, Nigeria, Indonesia, and Mexico were selected for the purpose of comparison among oil exporters in different regions.

Yet, it is difficult to select the countries that satisfy the objective criteria of both regional representiveness and convenience in interregional comparisons. Admittedly the choice of such a small number of countries from the world is bound to be arbitrary. Much of the useful information contained in the World Bank statistics, especially pertaining to the Middle East and the ex-Soviet Union bloc, had to be discarded with great reluctance. This choice is necessary, however, as a strategy to convert a large body of data into systematic knowledge through condensation of information. Yet, the possibility cannot be ruled out that the knowledge obtained may in some way be biased. It is hoped that readers will make an effort to correct for this possible bias by comparing the condensed summary in this chapter with the original tables in World Development Indicators.

2.1 Economic Growth and Structural Change

Table 2.1 summarizes international comparisons on macroeconomic growth and changes in industrial structure. In this table and the three following tables, countries are arranged in descending order by gross national product (GNP) per capita in 1990, converted to US dollars by exchange rates (column 1). For simplification, hereafter, Sub-Saharan Africa is referred to as 'Africa', 'East-Asia' includes Pacific countries, and 'Latin America' includes Caribbean countries. Unless otherwise stated, Korea refers to the Republic of Korea in the South.

2.1.1 Per capita GNP and its growth

The range of per capita GNP in the sample, from $110 in Tanzania to $25,430 in Japan, is indeed very wide. In terms of regional averages, the OECD level of about $20,000 was almost sixty times higher than Africa's $340 and South Asia's $330. Despite any adjustments made for coverage in GNP statistics and for purchasing power parities, a very large gap in per capita income will remain between low-income and high-income economies.

That growth in per capita GNP in low-income economies has been slower than that of high-income economies is alarming (Table 2.1, column 2). While the average per capita GDP for OECD members increased at a compound rate of 2.4 per cent per year in real terms from 1965 to 1990, it was less than 2 per cent for South Asia and was nearly stagnant at only 0.2 per cent for Africa. Obviously the wide income gap between high-income economies and the poorest economies (with per capita GNP of less than $300) has been widening further. There is little doubt that these low-income economies are far from joining 'the club of convergence' consisting of relatively advanced industrial economies, in which laggard economies tend to grow faster by closing their productivity gap with the advanced through technology borrowing (Baumol, 1986; Barro, 1991; Maddison, 1991).

East Asia represents a sharp contrast to this situation, with a regional average growth rate twice that of OECD members. Especially dramatic was the case of Korea with its per capita real GDP growth as high as 7 per cent per annum from 1965 to 1990. With this extraordinary increase, Korea (which prior to 1960 was ranked as one of the poorest nations along with Sub- Saharan and South Asian countries) climbed to a level of per capita GNP over $5,000 in 1990, and is now approaching the ranks of high-income economies. Rapid convergence of Korea and other high-performing East Asian economies towards the level of advanced economies suggests a critially important role of technology borrowing in achieving successful development. It is the major theme of this book to explore the conditions of

TABLE 2.1 *Economic growth and structural change in selected economies*

	(1)	(2)	(3)	(4)	(5)	(6)	(7)	(8)
	GNP per capita $	Average annual growth rate of GNP per capita (%)	Share of GDP (%) Agriculture		Industry		Share of manufactures in merchandise export (%)	
	1990	1965-90	1965	1990	1965	1990	1965	1990
Africa(Sub-Saharan)	**340**	**0.2**	**40**	**32**	**20**	**30**	**7**	**8**
Tanzania	110	-0.2	46	59	14	12	13	11
Nigeria	290	0.1	55	36	12	38	3	0
Kenya	370	1.9	35	28	18	21	10	11
South Asia	**330**	**1.9**	**44**	**33**	**21**	**26**	**37**	**70**
Bangladesh	210	0.7	53	38	11	15	—	73
India	350	1.9	44	31	22	29	48	73
East Asia (and Pacific)	**600**	**5.3**	**37**	**21**	**32**	**45**	**32**	**69**
China	370	5.8	38	27	35	42	65	73
Indonesia	570	4.5	51	22	13	40	4	35
Thailand	1,420	4.4	32	12	23	39	3	64
Korea, Rep.	5,400	7.1	38	9	25	45	59	94
Latin America (and Caribbean)	**2,180**	**1.8**	**16**	**10**	**33**	**36**	**7**	**32**
Argentina	2,370	-0.3	17	13	42	41	6	36
Mexico	2,490	2.8	14	9	27	30	16	44
Brazil	2,680	3.3	19	10	33	39	9	53
High-income(OECD)	**20,170**	**2.4**	**5(6)[a]**	**(3)[a]**	**43(42)[a]**	**(34)[a]**	**69**	**81**
UK	16,100	2.0	3	2[c]	46	37[b]	84	81
France	19,490	2.4	8	4	38	29	71	77
USA	21,790	1.7	3	2[b]	38	29[b]	65	78
Japan	25,430	4.1	10	3	44	42	91	98
World	**4,200**	**1.5**	**10**	**—**	**41**	**—**	**69**	**81**

[a] Sample average of four countries are shown in parentheses while averages of all OECD members are shown outside.
[b] 1989 value
[c] 1988 value

Source: World Bank , *World Development Report 1990, 1991, and 1992.*

technology borrowing for developing economies, which will be discussed in detail in Chapters 6, 8, 9, and 10.

In comparing Africa, South Asia, and East Asia, a tendency appears to exist in which the higher the level of per capita GNP, the faster the rate of growth. However, this rule does not seem to apply when Latin America is added to the comparison. While the average per capita GNP in Latin America was as high as $2,000 in 1990, its growth rate from 1965 to 1990 was about the same as for South Asia with the average GNP only a little over $300. Mexico and Brazil—which represented NIEs in the 1970s, ahead of Korea and Taiwan—now lag significantly behind their East Asian counterparts.

The country representing relative stagnation in Latin American economies is Argentina. In the 1920s and during the period immediately after World War II, Argentina ranked among the wealthiest nations in the world. However, with subsequent slow growth (negative growth for 1965–90), its per capita GNP declined by 1990 to below one-tenth of the OECD average. These growth records in Latin America show that there is no guarantee that developing economies will sustain accelerated growth once they reach a certain threshold level of per capita income, as was assumed in some development doctrines of the early post-World War II years (Section 5.2).

2.1.2 Changes in industrial structure

Such differences in economic growth across regions and across income groups correspond to differences in changing industrial structures. Columns 3 through 6 in Table 2.1 show how the shares of agriculture and industry in gross domestic product (GDP) changed from 1965 to 1990.[2] Except in Tanzania and Argentina (where negative growths in per capita GNP were recorded), developing economies experienced decreases in agriculture's share and increases in industry's share. In high-income economies, both the agricultural and the industrial sectors reduced their GNP shares, implying major expansions in the service sector.[3] These changes are consistent with the so-called Petty-Clark Law which predicts that the centre of gravity in economic activities shifts from the primary to the secondary sector and, further, to the tertiary sector as average per capita income continues to rise. Such shifts occur through market adjustments in intersectoral resource allocations as demands increase rapidly for industrial commodities in an early stage of economic growth, followed by accelerated growth in demand for services, with relative saturation in the consumption of industrial commodities (Clark, 1940; Kuznets, 1966; Syrquin and Chenery, 1988).

If increases in per capita income are the major force inducing changes in industrial structure, why did the industrial sector expand its share in African economies at a comparable pace with Asian economies, despite much lower rates of growth in per capita GNP? This puzzle seems to be explained by the development strategy commonly shared among newly independent nations that placed high priority on the promotion of industrialization. Under colonialism these economies were imposed upon to act as a supplier of primary commodities as well as a market for manufactured commodities from Western powers. It was natural that, for both repulsion against colonialism and an ardent desire to catch up with advanced economies, they adopted policies geared to transform their economies from those heavily dependent on primary production into those centred on industrial activities (Section 5.2.4).

Industrialization in these developing economies was promoted by the use of various policies, including targeted allocations of government subsidy and credit, among which the so-called 'import-substitution industrialization policy' was commonly adopted. This policy was designed to secure domestic markets for domestic manufacturers by suppressing foreign competition with tariffs, import quotas, and foreign exchange licensing. Such protection policies were considered indispensable for establishing viable industries in developing economies handicapped with low accumulations of capital, less-skilled labourers, and lower entrepreneurial and managerial capacities (Section 8.2.4).

Were these protective policies successful in fostering viable domestic industries in developing economies? An answer may be found from changes in the share of manufactured commodities in total commodity exports (equal to the sum of manufactured and primary commodity exports). If domestic industries had been fostered to a viable level, their competitive position in international markets should have been upgraded, resulting in increased exports of manufactured commodities. The speed with which the export structure changes relative to changes in the domestic industrial structure, depends largely on the structure of comparative advantage based on relative resource endowments. For example, in countries such as China and India—characterized by high population density relative to natural resource endowments—the export share of manufactured commodities tends to be high relative to the GDP share of industry, while the reverse holds in Latin American countries endowed with abundant natural resources.

In general, however, since capital, skilled labour, and management abilities specific to industrial production accumulate in the course of industrialization, it is expected that the export share of manufactured commodities increases parallel to increases in the GDP share of industry over time. This parallelism holds largely for Asia, as shown in Table 2.1. In contrast, in African economies the export share of manufactured commodities did not rise significantly despite increases in the GDP share. This observation seems to indicate failure of their industrial protection policies to foster domestic industries towards a viable form that could withstand international competition. This failure of protection policies in building competitive industry may have promoted economic stagnation in Africa.

A more concrete image can be obtained on the problem of African economies in contrast to Asia, especially East Asia, by comparing Indonesia and Nigeria. Both countries are large in population and area. Both are significant oil exporters and are richly endowed with natural resources. However, their economic growth records are sharply contrasting. Until the 1960s, Indonesia had been behind Nigeria in per capita income level. Yet, subsequent high economic growth raised Indonesia's per capita GNP to twice that of Nigeria by 1990. Meanwhile, both countries experienced oil booms from the 1970s to the early 1980s, with major windfall gains in government revenue and foreign exchange earnings, with which governments undertook ambitious development plans to promote modern industries such as petrochemicals.

Upon the collapse of the oil boom, capital-intensive industrialization in Nigeria based on the import-substitution policy was interrupted and its economy slid into stagnation. Indonesia, by contrast, changed gears to supporting labour-intensive manufactures by such means as currency devaluation, and liberalization in imports and direct foreign investment. This policy reorientation was successful in promoting production and export of labour-intensive industries, for which Indonesia has a comparative advantage, resulting in a major increase in the export share of manufactured commodities from 4 per cent in 1965 to 35 per cent in 1990. This performance in Indonesia represents a dramatic contrast to Nigeria, in which the export share declined from 2 to zero per cent during the same period (Section 4.4.3).

2.2. Investment, Saving, and Prices

A major task of development economics is to identify the factors underlying differential economic growth performances among regions and countries. To prepare for this endeavour in later chapters, the next three sections will postulate some hypotheses through intercountry cross-section comparisons between per capita GNP growth, and the possible determinants for which data are readily available.

2.2.1 Investment and saving in economic growth

Generally speaking, growth in average income or product per capita results from increases in the endowment of 'broadly defined capital', including not only tangible capital (such as machinery, factories, and inventory of products and materials for processing), but also intangible capital (such as forms of human knowledge and capacity enhanced by investments in education and training, health care, research and development, etc.). 'Capital' conventionally defined in national accounts consists of tangible capital alone, and 'investment' is measured as an increment in this form of capital for a given period (usually a year).

Columns 1 and 2 in Table 2.2 compare the 1965–90 average compound rates of real growth in gross domestic investments in total and per capita, conventionally measured in national accounts. These are not the rates of growth in capital stock but the rates of acceleration in capital accumulation. However, because these rates are calculated as long-term averages for twenty-five years, errors involved would be relatively minor by assuming that the larger the growth rates of investment, the larger the growth rates of capital stock, except in cases of especially large differences in the capital stock growth rates for the initial years.

High positive correlation between the growth rates of per capita GNP (Table 2.1, column 1) and per capita investment (Table 2.2, column 2) are

TABLE 2.2 *Investment, saving, external debt, and inflation in selected economies*

	(1)	(2)	(3)	(4)	(5)	(6)	(7)
	Average annual growth rate of domestic investment (%) 1965–90		Ratio of domestic saving to GDP (%)		Ratio of total external debt to export		Average annual rate of inflation (%)
	Total	Per capita	1965	1990	1980	1990	1980–90
Africa(Sub-Saharan)	**3.5**	**0.6**	**13**	**16**	**1.0**	**3.2**	
Tanzania	3.8	0.8	16	–6	3.2	10.7	26
Nigeria	4.7	1.9	10	29	0.3	2.4	18
Kenya	4.1	0.4	15	18	1.7	3.1	9
South Asia	4.3	2.0	14	19	1.6	2.8	
Bangladesh	–0.2	–2.7	8	2	3.5	4.5	10
India	4.6	2.4	15	20	1.4	2.8	8
East Asia (and Pacific)	**10.9**	**8.9**	**22**	**35**	**0.9**	**0.9**	
China	11.9	10.0	25	43	0.2	0.8	6
Indonesia	12.5	10.4	8	37	0.9	2.3	8
Thailand	8.3	5.9	19	34	1.0	0.8	7
Korea, Rep.	14.5	12.9	8	37	1.3	0.4	5
Latin America (and Caribbean)	**4.1**	**1.8**	**22**	**22**	**2.0**	**2.6**	
Argentina	–5.6	–7.1	22	16	2.4	4.1	395
Mexico	3.7	1.0	19	19	2.6	2.2	70
Brazil	6.9	4.6	22	23	3.0	3.3	284
High-income(OECD)	**3.6**	**2.9**	**24**	**22**			
UK	3.3	3.1	19	17			6
France	3.0	2.4	27	22			6
USA	3.0	2.0	21	15			4
Japan	6.4	5.4	33	34			2
World	**3.9**	**1.7**	**23**	**23**			

Source: World Bank, *World Development Report 1992*.

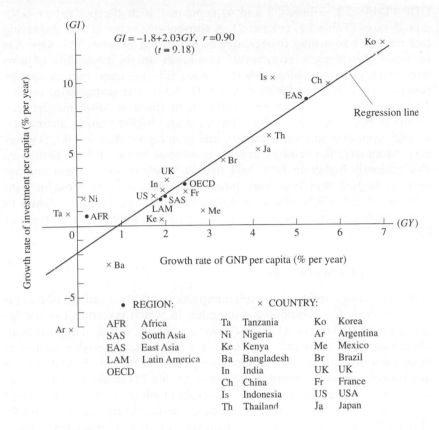

FIG. 2.1 *International comparison of the average annual growth rates of GNP and gross domestic investments per capita, 1965–90 averages*
Sources: Table 2.1 (col. 2) and Table 2.2 (col. 2).

evident in Figure 2.1. Indeed, their correlation coefficient is as high as 0.9 per cent. However, it cannot be concluded from this correlation that growth in investment is a major determinant of GNP growth. There is little doubt that a causal relationship works for investment growth to contribute positively to GNP growth. At the same time, however, a reverse causality of high-income growth that results in high investment is likely to operate, since expected returns to investment are usually so high in fast-growing economies that much of the incremental income above the 'permanent income' in the Friedman (1957) sense would turn into savings.

These two-way causal relationships have reinforced each other to create a virtuous circle in Asia, while they seem to have operated in a vicious circle in Africa. Indeed, the hypothesis that a high rate of income growth promotes the rate of saving is supported by the ratios of gross domestic savings to

GDP (Table 2.2, columns 3 and 4) compared with the per capita GNP growth rates (Table 2.1, column 2). A conventional view is that the saving rate increases according to increases in per capita income. This view has underlain development economists' pessimism on the possibility of low-income economies escaping from the low-equilibrium trap characterized by poverty and stagnation (Section 5.2.3). However, the saving rates in East Asian economies were not only higher than those in lower-income economies in South Asia and Africa, but were also higher than in the middle-income economies in Latin America, and even higher than in OECD members. Moreover, the rates of growth in savings from 1965 to 1990 were also distinctly higher in East Asia than in other regions. These findings seem to suggest that even very poor economies, such as those in Sub-Saharan Africa, will be able to invest sufficiently large domestic savings to achieve high economic growth once these economies are set on the track of high growth.[4]

2.2.2 External debt and inflation

Domestic savings and foreign capital imports are the two sources of domestic investment. For developing economies, in which investment needs for development tend to exceed domestic saving capacities, capital imports from abroad represent a possible escape from a vicious circle of slow economic growth and low saving. The role of foreign capital imports in bridging the gap between domestic investment (I) and saving (S) could be quite significant, as illustrated by the case of Tanzania in which domestic investment increased despite a sharp decline in the domestic saving rate for 1965–90 (Table 2.2, columns 2, 3 and 4). However, the danger exists that capital imports may accumulate to the point of insolvency at a national level, such that the borrowing country will become unable to meet debt-service obligations. In Tanzania, for example, the outstanding external debt which used to be about three times its total export value in 1980, rose to more than ten times that in 1990 (columns 5 and 6). Such multiplying debt accumulation was common among many developing economies during the 1980s. The problem became especially serious in that decade because the high interest rates, which resulted from the economic policy of the Reagan administration, and the slump in international markets of primary commodities following the collapse of the second oil boom in 1981, added much to the burden of debt service in developing economies.

In theory, it is not wrong for developing economies to rely on external credit to finance their domestic investment. If borrowed funds could be utilized effectively to install production facilities, commodities produced therefrom would contribute to reduction in imports, and, further, to expansion in exports. If external debt could be paid back by foreign exchange thus saved or earned, no serious accumulation of external debt would arise. In fact, fast-growing economies in East Asia, especially Korea, borrowed heavily in their development process. Nevertheless, the debt–export ratio on average did not rise for East Asia and decreased for Korea. This occurred not so much because outstanding debt decreased, but more because export increased faster than the speed of debt accumulation. Such a rapid increase in total exports was led by expansion in the export of manufactured commodities as observed in Table 2.1 (columns 7 and 8). These relationships seem to indicate a virtuous circle operating in fast-growing economies in East Asia, where domestic investment augmented by external credits bore the fruits of increased production and export capacity that produced sufficient foreign exchange earnings to meet increased debt service. In contrast, in low-income economies, such as those in Africa, it is likely that external credits were not so effectively invested as to create such production and export capacities.

Ex post, domestic investment is always equal to the sum of domestic saving and net capital imports from abroad.[5] However, foreign capital does not automatically flow into a country to close the gap between domestic investment (I) and domestic saving (S). How much capital may be imported depends, *ex ante*, on the difference in the expected rates of return to investment between domestic and foreign capital markets. In many cases, expected returns to investment in developing economies are discounted by investors abroad for such factors as country risk and regulations on foreign enterprise activities. Where country risk is high, capital inflows to developing economies are discouraged and capital flights are encouraged. If net capital inflow from abroad fails to close the domestic (I–S) gap, the difference works as an inflationary pressure. The inflation could be avoided if the government undertook fiscal and financial policies to curb effective demands. However, such deflationary policies are not easy to implement by governments in developing economies for fear of increases in unemployment and bankruptcy which would undermine their political basis. Instead, they are often tempted to finance excess investment by means of printing money, which leads to high rates of inflation.

A typical example can be found in the records of hyperinflation in Latin America during the 1980s. Governments in Latin America were inclined to practise deficit financing under the pressure of populism (Section 8.3.4). Large government consumption and investment had been a major source of the (I–S) gap operating secularly as a pressure on inflation. From the 1970s to the early 1980s, resource-rich economies in Latin America experienced a major economic boom when the prices of oil and other primary commodities were elevated to an abnormally high level. Sharp increases in government revenue and foreign exchange earnings due to this commodity boom induced governments to undertake ambitious development projects, together with further increases in government consumption. Investment needs for these development projects were easily financed by the foreign capital that was attracted by high expected returns during the boom period.

However, with the fall in commodity prices following the collapse of the second oil boom, the budget deficit increased and the foreign capital inflow stopped and the (I–S) gap widened progressively. When governments tried to close this gap with increased money printing, it became inevitable that inflation would progress at a galloping pace.

Inflation does not necessarily cause harm to real economic growth so long as its speed is moderate and stable. However, hyperinflation of the order of several hundred per cent per year makes future prediction difficult for entrepreneurs, who are induced to use available funds for short-run specu-lation rather than for long-term investment in fixed production facilities, causing a serious negative effect on real economic growth. Furthermore, as the rate of inflation rises, the risk increases for foreign investors of incurring loss from devaluation of local currency. This should result in a reduction in foreign capital inflow, and, thereby, increase the need for governments to print more money. In this way hyperinflation tends to be reinforced in a vicious circle.

Such experience in resource-rich economies in Latin America were in sharp contrast to resource-rich Indonesia in South-east Asia. Indonesia, which had relied heavily on its government revenue and foreign exchange earnings from oil, had to face the same crisis as Mexico and Brazil with the downfall of primary commodity prices in the 1980s. In response to this crisis, Indonesia tried to maintain macroeconomic stability by curtailing govern-ment expenditure, and also by facilitating foreign capital inflow with liberal-ization in trade and foreign direct investment. With these policies Indonesia was successful in shifting its economic base from natural resource exploita-tion to labour-intensive manufacturing, resulting in extensive employment creation. In a sense Indonesia took advantage of the crisis from the collapse of the oil boom by reorientating its economy towards sustainable economic development. This comparison between resource-rich economies in Latin America and East Asia suggests that policies matter more than resource endowments in determining economic performance (Section 4.4.3).

Observations in this section are clearly inconsistent with the pessimism that low-income economies will not be able to escape from poverty and stagnation because their savings and, hence, investment are bound to be low due to their low-income level. According to the experience in East Asia, it is possible for low-income economies to mobilize sufficient domestic savings and foreign capital imports to initiate the virtuous circle of development in which growth in income and investment reinforce each other. On the other hand, as the Latin American experience in the 1980s indicates, even if an economy reaches a high level of income, it remains subject to the danger of stagnation or retardation, depending on the policies chosen. There is a truth in the statement that 'once development has started, the circle is likely to become an upward spiral' (Hirschman, 1958: 5). However, it is only with an adequate policy that the upward spiral can be sustained.

2.3 Accumulation of Human Capital

In the previous section economic growth performances were compared across countries in relation to investment conventionally defined in national accounts. This section will focus on non-conventional investment to enhance the ability of human beings, commonly called 'investment in human capital'.

2.3.1 Improvements in education and health

Such activities as education and health care contribute to growth in national product through improvements in people's productive capacitiy, such as higher skills and better health. Since expenditures for these activities have the same effect on economic growth as investment in tangible capital, it is appropriate to call them investment in human capital. However, in economics these expenditures have traditionally been treated as a part of consumption and have not been counted as investment in national accounts. The critical importance of human capital in economic development has recently been recognized (as to be fully discussed in Chapter 6). Yet, preparation of statistics regarding human capital is still at a rudimentary stage. Direct measures of human capital investment are not available for international comparison over a wide range of countries.

Therefore, this section involves cross-country comparison based on two indirect measures which are considered to reflect changes in human capital. The first measure is the average school enrolment ratio (in per cent), shown in Table 2.3 (columns 1 and 2). This ratio is a simple average of school enrolment ratios for primary and secondary levels of education. Both are calculated by dividing the number of enrolled students by the number of children of formal schooling ages. Because some children are enrolled in schools before and after formal schooling ages the ratio could exceed 100 per cent, as in the case of France. The school enrolment ratio can be considered a proxy for investment in education, since expenditure for education is normally used to raise the enrolment ratio.

The second measure is average life expectancy at birth, or average number of years from birth to death, as shown in Table 2.3 (columns 4 and 5). The average life expectancy should be a reflection of health, and, therefore, should reflect the level of investment in health care including medical and hygienic activities.

High positive correlations of these two measures of human capital with per capita GNP are shown in Figure 2.2. These observations reflect the relationship in which investment in education and health care promotes human productivity, resulting in higher output per person. At the same time, a reverse causal relationship must be operating in which higher per capita incomes induce people to spend more on education and health

TABLE 2.3 *Improvements in education and health in selected economies*

	(1) (2) (3)=(2) – (1) Average school enrolment ratio[a] (%)			(4) (5) (6)=(5) – (4) Average life expectancy at birth (years)		
	1965	1990	increase	1960	1990	increase
Africa(Sub-Saharan)	**23**	**43**	**20**	**43**	**52**	**9**
Tanzania	17	34	17	42	49	7
Nigeria	19	46	17	47	49	2
Kenya	29	59	30	46	59	13
South Asia	**46**	**64**	**18**	**(47)[b]**	**(57)[b]**	**10**
Bangladesh	31	45	14	46	56	10
India	51	71	20	47	58	11
East Asia (and Pacific)	**53[c]**	**88(83)[c]**	**35(30)[c]**	**(49)[c]**	**(67)[c]**	**18**
China	57	92	35	43	69	26
Indonesia	42	81	39	46	59	13
Thailand	46	59	13	52	68	16
Korea,Rep.	68	98	30	53	72	19
Latin America (and Caribbean)	**60**	**78**	**18**	**54**	**70**	**16**
Argentina	65	93	28[d]	67	72	5
Mexico	55	84	29	56	70	14
Brazil	62	72	10	52	66	14
High-income(OECD)	**84**	**99**	**15**	**70[e]**	**76[e]**	**6**
UK	87	96	9	71	76	5
France	95	105	10	70	77	7
USA	—	99	—	70	76	6
Japan	91	99	8	68	79	11
World	**58**	**79**	**21**	**53**	**62**	**9**

[a] Average of school enrolment ratios in primary and secondary levels
[b] Simple averages for two countries are shown in parentheses.
[c] Simple averages for four countries are shown in parentheses while regional averages are shown outside.
[d] 1989 value
[e] Average of 'established market economies' in *World Development Report 1993* (Table A.3)
Source: World Bank, *World Development Report 1992 and 1993*.

care. As consumption goods (or services), education and health care must have high income elasticities of demand, especially at a high level of income. Also, relative advantages of education and health care as investment activities should rise with an increase in per capita income and a corresponding decrease in the future discount rate, because these are the activities that increase people's income-earning capacity over an extended time period. Therefore, the high positive correlations observed in Figure 2.2 should reflect the two causal relationships between economic growth and human capital accumulation, operating in a mutually reinforcing manner.

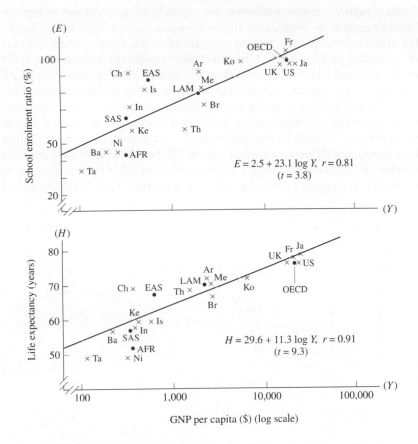

FIG. 2.2 *International comparison of the average annual school enrolment ratios for primary and secondary levels of education and average life expectancies at birth, 1990 Sources*: Table 2.1 (col. 1) and Table 2.2 (cols. 2 and 5).

2.3.2 Regional differences in the level of education

In Figure 2.2 it is evident that East Asian economies (except Thailand) diverge significantly upward from the regression line. This suggests a tendency for East Asian economies to invest in education more heavily than normal, relative to their income levels.[6] In 1990, the regional average GDP per capita in East Asia was less than one-third that of Latin America, whereas the average school enrolment ratio in the former was more than 10 per cent higher than in the latter. It is reasonable to hypothesize that the high rate of investment in education underlies the excellent economic growth performance in East Asia relative to the other regions, even though factors underlying the high educational investment are yet to be identified.

   Despite high correlations between per capita GNP and the two indicators
of human capital in 1990, correlations between growth rates in per capita
GDP and increases in these human capital indicators from 1965 to 1990 are
low, as shown in Figure 2.3. The correlation coefficient between the GNP
growth rates and increases in the school enrolment ratio is only 0.37, which
is statistically not significantly different from zero. A major reason for the
low correlation appears to be the inadequacy of using the average enrolment
ratio for primary and secondary schools as a proxy for the level of education. Especially in high-income economies, where primary and secondary
school enrolments have approached nearly 100 per cent, these changes have
not reflected improvements in education as much as other indicators, such as
the number of students per teacher and the enrolment ratio for colleges and

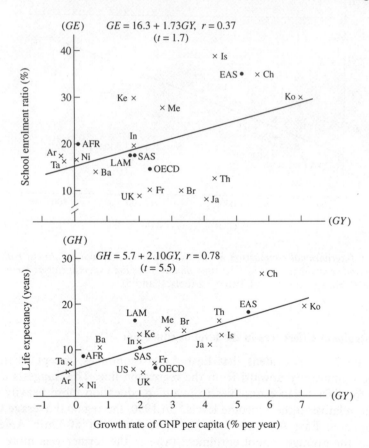

FIG. 2.3 *International comparison of the average annual growth rates of per capita
GNP, 1965–1990 and: (a) percentage increases in average school enrolment ratios for
primary and secondary levels of education from 1965 to 1990; (b) average life expectancy at birth, from 1960 to 1990*
Sources: Table 2.1 (col. 2) and Table 2.3 (cols. 3 and 4).

universities. Such inadequacy of our proxy variable especially for high-income economies is considered the factor underlying the divergence of OECD members below the regression line. In fact, a correlation coefficient (0.49) statistically significant at the 5-per cent level can be calculated from the sample by excluding OECD members.[7]

An interesting observation in the upper diagram of Figure 2.3 is that major increases in school enrolment were recorded by low-income economies in Africa, despite almost zero growth in GNP per capita; this implies that educational investment has so far failed to produce significant growth dividends in Africa. This may reflect low quality and inappropriate orientation of education in Africa. It may also suggest a possibility that Africa made 'overinvestment' in education for the purpose of maximizing economic growth, if short-run growth is considered. In general, improved skill and knowledge due to education and training can contribute relatively little to productivity growth, unless appropriately combined with tangible capital. For example, education would not raise productivity in simple manual work (such as digging a ditch with a shovel or spade), but it would significantly increase efficiency in the operation of modern sophisticated earth-moving machinery. It could well be that low GNP growth rates, relative to major advances in the school enrolment ratio in Africa, reflect such a relative shortage of tangible capital. This tendency might be augmented by bias in technological change towards a tangible capital-using direction, which typically emerges in the early phase of industrialization based on borrowed technology (Sections 6.1 and 6.2).

However, the policy of allocating resources disproportionately to education at such a low-income stage as in Africa may not be counterproductive to the goal of promoting economic growth in the long run. First of all, the problem in Africa was not that investment in education increased too fast but that investment in tangible capital increased too slowly. As discussed in the previous section, it should be possible, with appropriate policies, to increase investment incentives to mobilize sufficient domestic savings and foreign capital inflows so that investment in tangible capital could be increased without sacrificing investment in intangible capital, especially education.

Further, if African economies are to be set on the track of sustained economic growth with appropriate policies, human capital created by prior education investment—which may appear to have produced relatively small economic returns so far—may turn out to be the basis for immense productivity growth, since it might enable the effective use of rapidly accumulating tangible capital thereafter.

Probably a more basic role of education should be to transform people's value system by improving their knowledge of their own position in wider national and international perspectives. Without this transformation, the institutional and organizational reforms needed for modern economic development are unlikely to be forthcoming (Chapter 10). Indeed, cases can be found in the history of modern economic growth that less developed nations, aiming at catching up with advanced industrial economies, have attempted what appeared to be 'overinvestment' in education relative to their economic capacity, but which later proved to be the key to their successful development, as was the case in Japan (Japanese Ministry of Education, 1962).

The above-mentioned are conjectural hypotheses based on casual observations. It is of the utmost importance to the agenda of development economics to investigate the relationships between conventional investment in tangible capital and non-conventional investment in intangible capital (such as education) at different stages of development (Chapter 6).

2.4 Population, Natural Resources, and Foods

Production activities by human beings are the activities of processing natural resources with the application of labour and capital. In a sense, progress in civilization has been the process of substituting man-made capital for natural resources under the pressures of population growth. This substitution has been facilitated by technological and institutional innovations, as explained in the previous chapter.

2.4.1 Population pressure on natural resources

Limited endowments of natural resources should not be a major constraint on economic growth in the long run if they are effectively supported by increases in man-made capital. In the absence of more appropriate indicators, the average number of persons per square kilometre of surface area may be used as a rude proxy for relative scarcity of natural resources. When the data of this variable (Table 2.4, column 1) are compared with those of GNP per capita (Table 2.1, column 1), no systematic relationship can be observed when the correlation coefficient is calculated to be only 0.008.

Of course, land area is such a poor proxy for natural resource endowments which consist not only of physical area but also of many other factors, including soil fertility, rainfall, mineral deposits, etc. Considering the fact that Japan (with much poorer natural resource endowments than the USA by any standard) was able to reach about the same per capita income level as the USA and that resource-poor Korea was able to surpass the income levels of resource-rich economies in Latin America, it can hardly be argued that endowments of natural resources represent an overriding constraint on economic growth. In history, though rather exceptional, some economies

TABLE 2.4 *Population, land, and food production in selected economies*

	(1)	(2)	(3)	(4)	(5)
	Population per square kilometre of territorial area 1990	Average annual population growth rate (%)		Average annual growth rate of agricultural land (%) 1965–89	Percentage increase in food production per capital from 1979–81 to 1988–90 (%)
		1965–80	1980–90		
Africa(Sub-Saharan)	**21**	**2.7**	**3.1**	**0.7**	**–6**
Tanzania	26	2.9	3.1	0.9	–12
Nigeria	125	2.5	3.2	0.3	6
Kenya	42	3.6	3.8	1.0	6
South Asia	**223**	**2.4**	**2.2**	**0.2**	**16**
Bangladesh	741	2.6	2.3	0.1	–4
India	258	2.3	2.1	0.2	19
East Asia (and Pacific)	**101**	**2.2**	**1.6**	**0.3**	**27**
China	119	2.2	1.4	–0.3	33
Indonesia	94	2.4	1.8	0.9	23
Thailand	109	2.9	1.8	2.4	6
Korea,Rep.	432	2.0	1.1	–0.4	6
Latin America (and Caribean)	**21**	**2.5**	**2.1**	**1.3**	**6**
Argentina	12	1.6	1.3	0.7	–7
Mexico	44	3.1	2.0	0.3	2
Brazil	18	2.4	2.2	2.1	15
High-income(OECD)	**25**	**0.8**	**0.6**	**0.2**	**1**
UK	234	0.2	0.2	–0.3	5
France	102	0.7	0.5	–0.1	3
USA	27	1.0	0.9	0.2	–8
Japan	327	1.2	0.6	–1.0	1
World	**40**	**2.0**	**1.7**	**0.3**	**12**

Source: World Bank, *World Development Report 1992 and 1993.*

were able to achieve a high income level through exploitation of natural resources, but their growth was temporary and not sustainable if they continued to rely solely on natural resource exploitation (Chapter 4, Section 4).

However, for low-income economies today, the growing relative scarcity of natural resources, under the pressure of explosive population growth, represents a very serious problem since these economies relied so heavily on natural resource-based activities such as agriculture and mining for both production and export Table 2.1 (columns 3, 4, 7, and 8). Demographic changes in developing economies will be examined in detail in the next chapter. However, a cursory look at Table 2.4 (columns 2, 3, and 4) reveals the tendency towards faster population growth in low-income economies. Some Asian economies, notably China, were successful in significantly curtailing population growth rates from the 1965–80 to the 1980–90 period. Yet, Africa maintained a growth rate of 3 per cent per year even in the 1980s. This rate is a doubling of population every quarter of a century.

It is not easy to achieve substitution of capital for natural resources at a speed to maintain per capita income under rapidly decreasing natural resource endowments per capita, corresponding to such explosive population growth. Financing of needed investment is not an easy task. The more difficult problem, however, is how to accelerate technological and institutional innovations to achieve the needed substitution of capital for natural resources.

2.4.2 Population growth vs. food supply

Increased population pressure on natural resources, which makes low-income economies unsustainable, can be inferred from trends in agricultural land area and food production in Africa (Table 2.4, columns 4 and 5). Traditionally, developing economies have responded to population growth by opening new lands for cultivation. The speed of agricultural land expansion has been high in Africa and Latin America, with their lower population density and larger capacity for new land opening than in Asia. Yet, expansion in agricultural land area has failed to keep up with rapid population growth. Especially in Africa, the average population growth rate for 1965–90 was about 3 per cent per year while agricultural land increased at less than 1 per cent, with the result that agricultural land endowment per capita decreased at the rate of over 2 per cent per year. Correspondingly, domestic food output per capita decreased by 6 per cent during the 1980s.

Decreases in per capita food production in Africa indicate a failure to compensate for the negative effects of decreases in per capita endowments in natural resources, by increasing capital and improving technology. This failure was not the inevitable consequence of high population growth. In fact, low-income economies in Asia, especially China and India, were able to achieve significant increases in food production per capita in the 1980s despite decreases in agricultural land area per capita of about the same magnitude as in Africa.

In low-income economies in which the agricultural sector has a dominant weight, stagnation in agricultural production as expressed by decreases in per capita food production has had a major adverse effect on overall economic development. This difficulty may be seen in Figure 2.4, which compares the growth rates of per capita food output (Table 2.4, column 5) with those of per capita GNP (Table 2.1, column 1). Divergence of OECD members and Korea below the regression line in this diagram should reflect

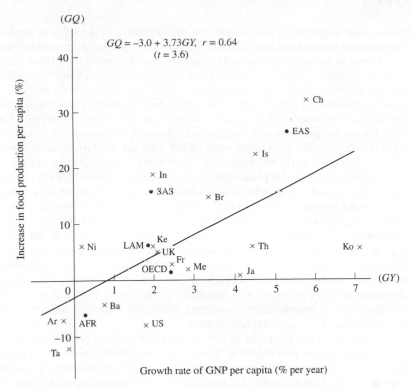

FIG. 2.4 *International comparison of the average annual growth rates of GNP per capita, 1965–90, and percentage increases in food production per capita from 1979–81 to 1988–90*
Sources: Table 2.1 (col. 2) and Table 2.4 (col. 5).

little dependence of economic growth performance on agriculture in industrialized economies. By removing OECD members and Korea from the example, the correlation coefficient increases from 0.64 to 0.84. The high correlation for the sample of developing economies (except Korea) seems to indicate that it is necessary for low-income economies to overcome the constraint of land resources on food production by raising agricultural productivity in the process of industrialization until they reach the NIEs stage of development. The failure of Africa in this regard appears to be a major factor underlying economic stagnation in this region.

Through what process has Asia been able to achieve food production increases at a higher pace than population increases under the severe constraint of land resources? What kinds of technological and institutional innovations have underlain this process? These questions will be dealt with in the next two chapters.

NOTES

1. For example, estimates of real product per capita relative to the USA by the UN International Comparison Programme (ICP) based on purchasing power parities, were higher in low-income economies—three to six times more than those based on exchange rates in 1990. See World Development Indicators (Tables 1 and 30) in the World Bank's *World Development Report 1992*. For the approach and results of ICP, see Summers and Heston (1988, 1991). For the more fundamental question of how appropriate it is to use conventional national income statistics such as GNP for assessing relative well-being in low-income economies, see Sen (1992).
2. GDP is defined as the total gross value added from the production factors used within a country's territorial boundary, while GNP is conceptually defined as gross value added from the production factors owned by nationals of the country irrespective of locations of these factors within or outside its territory. In practice, the difference between GDP and GNP is net factor income from abroad, which is normally negligible for broad comparisons, such as those in this chapter.
3. Even today's high-income countries experienced relative expansion in the industrial sector until the middle of this century (Kuznets 1966, ch. 3). Significant shrinkage in the share of the industrial sector, corresponding to relative expansion in the service sector for the past half-century, may be interpreted as a quantitative expression of the coming of post-industrial society (Bell, 1973) for developed countries. In this interpretation developing economies including NIEs may still be in the stage of classical 'industrialization'.
4. In order to assess the influences of the absolute level and the growth rate of per capita income on the rate of saving, a regression equation to explain the ratio of domestic saving to domestic income (*s*) in 1990 by per capita GNP (*Y*) and its growth rate (*GY*) is estimated on intercountry cross-section data in Table 2.1 (cols. 1 and 2) and Table 2.2 (col. 4) by the least ordinary least-square method as follows:

$$s = 9.96 + 0.229 \log Y + 4.647\, GY, \quad \bar{R}^2 = 0.611.$$
$$ (0.10) (5.59)$$

Judging from the *t*-statistics (shown in parentheses), the absolute level of per capita GNP has no significant effect, while the influence of its growth rate is highly significant. The coefficient of determination adjusted for the degree of freedom $\bar{R}^2$ indicates that about 60 per cent of intercountry variations in the rate of gross domestic savings are explained by this regression equation.
5. Gross domestic product (*Y*) on its demand side is defined as the sum of private consumption (*C*), government consumption (*G*), gross domestic investment including inventory change (*I*) and export (*X*) minus import (*M*) as follows:

$$Y = C + G + I + (X - M).$$

From the side of income appropriation gross national product, which is the sum of GDP (*Y*) and net factor income from abroad (*N*), is defined as the sum of private and government consumption and savings (*S*), neglecting transfers namely

$$Y + N = C + G + S.$$

From the above two equations, the equality between domestic saving minus investment and the current account balance of payments can be derived:

$$S - I = (X - M) + N.$$

Since the current account balance is equivalent to net increase in external assets or net capital exports to abroad (F), the above equation can be transformed to an identity between domestic saving and the sum of domestic investment and net investments abroad (or net capital exports), i.e.

$$S = I + F,$$

which can be arranged to

$$I = S + (-F)$$

representing an *ex post* identity between domestic investment (I) and the sum of domestic savings (S) and net capital imports from abroad ($-F$).

6. The regression equation used to explain the school enrolment (E) in 1990 by per capita GNP (Y) and a dummy variable (D) with the assignment of 1 for East Asian economies and 0 for others, is estimated by the ordinary least-square method based on cross-country data in Table 2.1 (col. 1) and Table 2.3 (col. 2). The result is:

$$E = -5.25 + 24.4 \log Y + 15.7 D, \quad \bar{R}^2 = 0.727.$$
$$\quad\quad\quad (7.3) \quad\quad\quad (2.7)$$

The coefficient of D is positive and statistically significant at the 5% level in terms of the t-statistics shown in parentheses, which is consistent with the hypothesis that East Asian economies invested in education more heavily than other economies.

7. Another possibility is that the level of education instead of its growth rate is the major determinant of a country's capability for borrowing external technology, and hence, the country's economic growth rate. A regression analysis by Barro (1991) based on a sample of ninety-eight countries for 1960–85 shows that the growth rate of real per capita GDP was positively related with the primary school enrolment ratio and inversely related to the initial level of per capita GDP. These relationships were not found to be statistically significant from our data, possibly because of the small sample size. For literature on economic returns to education, see T. P. Schultz (1988).

3

Population Growth and the Constraint of Natural Resources

When low-income economies try to escape from stagnation and set out for modern economic development, the first problem that they normally face is acceleration in population growth and consequent relative exhaustion of natural resources. As observed in the previous chapter, the rates of population growth in developing economies, especially those belonging to low-income groups, are explosive. Correspondingly, the endowments of natural resources per capita decrease at a rapid pace. In general, the lower the level of income per capita, the higher the dependency of economies on natural resources, as evident from cross-country comparisons in shares of agriculture in GDP as well as in commodity exports (Table 2.1). It is easy to imagine how serious the problem of decreasing natural resource endowments per capita would be in these low-income economies.

This chapter gives a historical and theoretical perspective for the future in developing economies that are experiencing a population explosion today. Further, we will develop an understanding of how the relative exhaustion of natural resources due to rapid population growth may constrain the development of low-income economies, in terms of development theories pertaining to this problem.

In this chapter and the next, 'natural resources' are often abbreviated as 'resources' in contrast with the broader concept of 'factors of production' in general (including labour, capital, and natural resources, as used in Figure 1.2).

3.1 Population Growth in Economic Development

When compared to the problem experienced by developed economies during their modern economic growth, the population problem which developing economies face today can be characterized by the following two points.

First, the speed of population growth in developing economies today is incomparably faster than it was in advanced industrial economies during their early phase of development. In the initial stage of industrialization (which ranged country by country from the late eighteenth century to the early twentieth century), today's advanced economies experienced major acceleration in population growth rates relative to the premodern rates. Yet, their population growth in the modern era was only about 1 per cent per year on average, rarely exceeding 2 per cent, in contrast to the average of about 2.5 per cent for today's developing economies, and as much as 3 per cent or even higher for low-income economies (Table 2.4).

Second, compared with the history of advanced economies— in which the acceleration in population growth was essentially an endogenous phenomenon induced by accelerated economic growth—that of developing economies today has largely been exogenous in nature. Acceleration in the former was based on increased employment and income that were supported by major productivity growth in the newly established industrial economies, whereas acceleration in the latter was, to a large extent, given exogenously through importation of health and medical technologies from advanced economies (Wrigley, 1969; Birdsall, 1988). Indeed, Sub-Saharan Africa recorded significant increases in life expectancy and decreases in infant mortality rates for the quarter century from 1965 to 1990, despite declines in per capita calorie intake (Thorbecke, 1995*b*). This implies that high population growth in Africa (as observed in Table 2.4) was not supported by improved income and level of living, but resulted from imported public health and medical technologies. When such exogenous population growth is explosive and not paralleled by increases in employment and income, developing economies are destined to face the serious problem of relative resource exhaustion, economic degradation, and destitution.

3.1.1 Historical changes in world population

For future prediction it is important to recognize that the major acceleration in population growth, commonly called 'population explosion' in developing economies today, is not a new phenomenon, but began to take place within a couple of decades after World War I.

Table 3.1 characterizes this population explosion in developing economies in terms of long historical changes in world population. The data in this table are those selected by Simon Kuznets from various estimates, supplemented by UN estimates. Naturally, the earlier the period, the less accurate the population estimates are, such that the figures for AD 1,000 may more properly be called 'guestimates' rather than estimates.[1]

Yet, there be little doubt from the data that a major acceleration in world population did occur with the beginning of 'modern economic growth' in the Kuznets sense, marked by the Industrial Revolution (1966, ch. 1). (For characterization of modern economic growth, see Chapter 6, Sections 1 and 2.) As the first column in Table 3.1 shows, the growth rate of world population increased about three times from before the years after 1750, which is considered the eve of the Industrial Revolution in England. Starting from the premodern rate of only about 0.1 per cent per year before 1750,

TABLE 3.1 World population, 1000 to 2025

	World	Area of European settlement	Other Area		
			Total	Asia	Africa
	..........................10 million (%)..........................				
1000	28(100)	6(21)	22(79)	17(60)	5(19)
1750	73(100)	16(22)	57(78)	47(64)	10(14)
1800	91(100)	22(24)	69(76)	60(66)	9(10)
1850	117(100)	33(28)	84(72)	74(63)	10(9)
1900	161(100)	57(35)	104(65)	92(57)	12(7)
1930	202(100)	79(39)	123(61)	107(53)	16(8)
1960	301(100)	107(36)	194(64)	168(56)	26(9)
1990	528(100)	129(24)	399(76)	345(65)	54(10)
2025 Projection	830(100)	168(20)	662(80)	518(62)	144(17)
Average growth rate per year...............................%...........................					
1000–1750	0.13	0.13	0.13	0.14	0.09
1750–1800	0.44	0.64	0.38	0.49	–0.21
1800–1850	0.50	0.81	0.39	0.42	0.21
1850–1900	0.64	1.10	0.43	0.44	0.37
1900–1930	0.76	1.09	0.56	0.50	0.96
1930–1960	1.34	1.02	1.53	1.52	1.63
1960–1990	1.89	0.63	2.43	2.43	2.47
1990–2025	1.30	0.76	1.46	1.17	2.84

Sources: 1000–1960 from Kuznets (1966: 35–8). 1990–2025 from World Bank, *World Development Report* 1992, by assuming the area of European settlement to consist of OECD members (except Japan), low-and middle-income Europe and Latin America.

world population growth continued to accelerate until it reached nearly 2 per cent in the latter half of the twentieth century.

An important observation in Table 3.1 is the difference in the pattern of population growth between the area of 'European settlement' and the 'other' area, according to Kuznet's classification. The European settlement area includes, in addition to Europe itself, North and South America and Australasia where descendants of migrants from Europe predominate. The 'other' area consists mainly of Africa and Asia including the Middle East. Even though this classification is different from that of developed versus developing economies, it will not produce much bias in our conclusion in treating this 'other area' as largely equivalent to developing economies, considering the dominant weight of Asia and Africa in the population of developing economies.

By comparing these two areas the impacts of modern economic growth on population growth can be clearly observed. While there was no difference in the population growth rate between the European settlement and the other areas in the premodern era, the growth rate accelerated much faster in the former and reached the peak of about 1.1 per cent per year in the latter half of the nineteenth century and the first decade of the twentieth century, a level twice that of the latter. Correspondingly, the share of the European settlement area in world population, which was about 20 per cent in 1750 and before, increased to as much as 40 per cent by 1930.

This accelerated growth of the population from Europe with the initiation of modern economic growth, as compared to Asia and Africa, is consistent with the hypothesis that the acceleration in population growth in the history of advanced economies today was an endogenous phenomenon induced by economic growth. It cannot be denied that the large-scale shipment of slaves from Africa to the American continents underlay the especially slow growth (negative growth for 1750–1800) in Africa, compared with fast growth in the European settlement area. Yet, the observation that growth in the European settlement continued to accelerate during the latter half of the nineteenth century (when the slave shipment was reduced) seems to imply that modern economic growth itself was the major factor underlying the population growth acceleration in the early phase of industrialization in Europe and North America.

Such a lead in population growth in the European settlement over the other area began to be reversed from the 1920s and 1930s. From the 1900–30 to the 1960–90 period population growth rate in the European settlement area declined approximately by half from 1.1 to 0.6 per cent per year, and increased four times, from about 0.6 to 2.4 per cent, in the other area. Consequently, the population share of Asia and Africa, which went down from 80 to 60 per cent during the 1750–1930 period, recovered to 75 per cent by 1990.

The explosive population growth in developing economies (represented by Asia and Africa) since about the 1920s began to decelerate from the 1970s, and their population is expected to reach a stationary state sometime during the twenty-first century. Meanwhile, however, the growth in the European settlement will be exceeded by that of the other area, with the result that the latter's share will approach 80 per cent in 2025, of which 60 and 20 per cent will be in Asia and Africa, respectively, according to the UN estimation. These predicted population shares are exactly the same as those that prevailed in the premodern period. It is highly intriguing to see that the inter-area distribution of world population is returning to the premodern structure after almost 300 years of modern economic growth. The internal mechanism causing this is beyond our speculation at this moment.

If the data in Table 3.1 are compared with those in Table 2.4, it is evident that the population growth being recorded by today's developing economies is much faster than was experienced by advanced economies in the past. Also, the poorer the economies are, the faster their population growth is. This observed tendency is consistent with the hypothesis that their population explosions are not endogenous—that is, not supported by fruits of their economic development.

3.1.2 Demographic transition

To promote our understanding of the mechanism underlying the population explosion in developing economies, it is useful to conceptualize the natural rate of population growth (NR) as equivalent to the birth-rate (BR) minus the death-rate (DR). The rate of population growth in an economy is this natural rate with adjustments for migrations to and from other economies (the so-called 'social change' in population). These population movements over space played an important role in the past, such as in the development process of new continents, but their role is unlikely to be very significant in the world today where new frontiers for settlement are largely closed. Therefore, we will proceed with our analysis with the terms of NR as a good proxy for the population growth rate.

The 'theory of demographic transition' defines changes in NR in terms of changes in BR and DR. The conventional form of this theory assumes the following sequences in the course of modern economic growth (Kirk, 1968; Birdsall, 1988; *World Development Report 1984*): both the birth- and the death-rates are high in premodern societies with the natural rate remaining at a very low level; with the start of modern economic growth the first phase of demographic transition begins in which the death-rate begins to decline while the birth-rate remains largely constant, resulting in acceleration of the natural rate; in the second phase the death-rate stops decreasing further, but the birth-rate is maintained at a high level with sustenance of the high natural rate; then comes the third phase, in which the birth-rate begins to decline at a faster rate than the death-rate towards the low rate of natural population growth. After going through the three phases, the premodern pattern of demographic change—characterized by slow population growth with high birth- and death-rates–is transformed into the modern pattern that is also characterized by slow population growth, but with the low birth- and death-rates.

It was believed (in the absence of official statistics before 1838) that this demographic transition took place in England (e.g. Griffith, 1926; Hicks, 1960, ch. 5). However, this presumption does not seem to stand up in the face of recent developments in demographic history, especially the definitive work by Wrigley and Schofield (1981) based on parish register records. In Figure 3.1 the official series of birth- and death-rates for the UK are spliced with the Wrigley and Schofield series for England for the period before 1840. A major modification of the conventional assumption is indicated for Phase 1, which corresponds to the period of industrial revolution from the 1780s to the 1820s. This shows that the acceleration in the natural rate of population growth during this phase was equally contributed to by the decrease in the death-rate and the increase in the birth-rate.

This deviation of the demographic pattern from the conventional assumption is not such an anomaly if it is examined in terms of theory. It seems

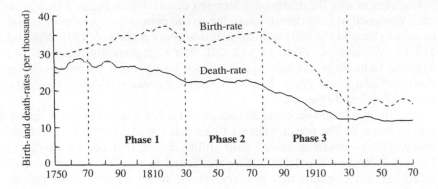

FIG. 3.1 *Changes in the birth and death rates in the UK, 1750–1970, nine-year moving averages*
Sources: 1842–1971 series for UK from Mitchell (1980); 1750–1841 series for England from Wrigley and Schofield (1981), spliced to the UK series by multiplying the 1838–46 average ratio (0.901).

rather reasonable to hypothesize that increased employment and income-earning opportunities arising from the beginning of modern economic growth would have contributed not only to reductions in the death-rate through improvements in nutrition (especially of mothers), clothing, and housing, in addition to public health infrastructure such as water supply and sewage systems but, also, to increases in the birth-rate through reductions in the age of marriage. In the histories of England, other European countries, and Japan, it was common to observe that major reductions in population and the labour force due to famines and pests (such as the Black Death) raised the real wage rates, resulting in both increased birth-rates and decreased death-rates. The subsequent recovery of population worked to depress the wage rates relative to food prices with the effect of curbing further growth in population (Birdsall, 1988).

In this historical perspective the observed increase in the birth-rate for Phase 1 in England may be considered a continuation of the demographic response in premodern society to increased employment and income-earning opportunities. However, the elevation of the natural population growth rate—from a level of 2 to 4 per thousand before the beginning of the Industrial Revolution to a level as high as 15 per thousand about fifty years later—is likely to have been supported by large expansions in economic activities due to the progress of industrialization. Moreover, it is reasonable to assume that the birth-rate was maintained at a high level for Phase 2, despite accelerated population growth since Phase 1, because increased population was adequately absorbed by the expanded industrial activities that prevented real wage rates from decreasing, unlike the population growth cycles during the premodern era.

One reason why the death-rates stopped decreasing in Phase 2 may have been worsened hygienic conditions, due to the concentration of population in urban slums in the early industrialization process (Levine, 1978: 504 and 513–14; Williamson, 1990: 14 and 22). More importantly, medical and hygienic technology had not been developed to prevent major epidemics from spreading until Phase 3 when bacteriology was established (with the lead by Koch and Pasteur).

Why did the birth-rate begin to decrease at a faster speed than the death-rate in Phase 3? The reason appears to be that the cost for parents to have many children began to exceed their utility during that period. First, the Factory Acts were stipulated and strengthened to regulate employment of infant labour. Concurrently, primary school systems began to be propagated. To the extent that the age of children entering into the labour market was delayed due to labour legislation and education, parents' cost of rearing children increased and their income from children's work decreased (Hicks, 1960, ch. 5).

The utility for parents to have children as a means for old-age security also declined since it was replaced by personal savings and insurance with the development of financial markets. Further, the development of social security systems reduced the role of family as a security institution. More basic were the decreased infant mortality rates since the previous period, which reduced the need to bear a large number of children for the sake of the family's sustenance (Wrigley, 1969: 190–202; Heer, 1972: 106–9; Birdsall, 1988: 517–18).

Historical patterns of demographic transition differ country by country. The British case of birth-rate acceleration during Phase 1 was probably unique. The Scandinavian countries, typically Denmark, appear to have followed a 'classical pattern' with no such initial acceleration (McKeown and Brown, 1955: 137; Simon, 1992: 25–7). In countries such as France and the USA, the birth-rate began to decline with little time lag behind the decrease in the death-rate. In general, the later a country started industrialization, the faster the process of demographic transition was completed—often with a shift from Phase 1 to Phase 3, skipping over Phase 2, as observed for Japan, Russia, and South and East European nations (Yasuba, 1980: 50–6). It appears that the population explosion in developing economies today follows this trend.

3.1.3 The case of India

As a representative example, the demographic transition in India will be examined. India has the longest continuous series of population censuses among developing countries, which began in 1871 (much earlier than Japan's first census in 1908). The Indian census population data, as shown in Table 3.2, indicate that growth acceleration began in the period from

TABLE 3.2 *Population in India, 1871 to 1991*

	Population (million)	Average annual growth rate per year for the preceding decade (%)
1871	209	—
1881	211	0.10
1891	231	0.91
1901	238	0.30
1911	252	0.57
1921	251	−0.04
1931	279	1.06
1941	319	1.35
1951	361	1.24
1961	439	1.98
1971	548	2.24
1981	683	2.23
1991 (provisional)	844	2.14

Sources: Cassen (1978: 7) and Government of India (1994).

1921 to 1931, which coincided with the acceleration in Asia and Africa in Table 3.1.

This acceleration resulted from a sharp, continuous decline in the death-rate from about 40 per thousand in the 1920s to less than 20 per thousand in the 1960s, while the birth-rate remained relatively stable at a level around 40 per thousand (Figure 3.2). In this pattern India in the 1920–60 period is considered to have been at Phase 1 in the classical transition process. The difference of India from the experience of advanced economies was the speed

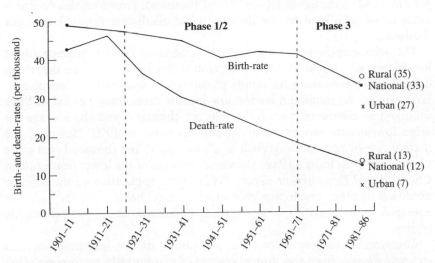

FIG. 3.2 *Changes in the birth and death rates in India, 1901–86, ten-year averages*
Source: Economic Intelligence Service (1990).

of transition. The decrease in the death-rate by more than 20 per thousand points within only forty years was not only twice as large as UK's 10 per cent decrease in Phase 1 but also larger than the decrease for the entire period (over 150 years) of British demographic transition. Such a precipitous drop in the death-rate would not have been possible without importation of modern medical and hygienic technology from advanced countries.

In the Indian case a phase comparable to the UK's Phase 2 is not observed. It appears that Phase 1 engulfed Phase 2 as the death-rate continued to decline (unlike the UK case) presumably because of importation of modern medical technology. Phase 1 shifted directly to Phase 3 (skipping over Phase 2), as characterized by parallel declines in both the birth- and the death-rates. In Phase 3 the birth-rate went down relatively rapidly, presumably reflecting the effects of education (especially of women) and family planning promoted by the Indian government. Since the death-rate also continued to decline at a high pace, the natural rate of population growth remained relatively stable in a way similar to Phase 2 in the UK.

The death-rate in India reached 12 per thousand in 1981–6 and 11 per thousand in 1990. Since this level is largely comparable with that of developed economies (9 per thousand in 1990), it is unlikely that the death-rate will continue to decline as fast as in the past four decades. Therefore, to the extent that the birth-rate is likely to continue decreasing, a considerable deceleration in population growth may be expected. Yet, this deceleration is likely to be slow, judging from the differences in the birth- and death-rates between the rural and urban areas for 1981–6, as indicated in Figure 3.2. With the elevation of education and the diffusion of hygienic knowledge among rural people, it is likely that their rural birth-rate will decline from 35 per thousand to the urban level of 27 per thousand. However, this decline is likely to be paralleled by the decline in the death-rate from 13 to 7 per thousand.

The demographic pattern of India is considered fairly representative of low-income economies. A major exception to this is China, where the strong drive by the government for family planning was successful in reducing its birth-rate to the minimum among low-income economies, i.e. only 22 per thousand as compared with India's 30 per thousand and the average for other low-income economies of 38 per thousand in 1990. However, the natural rate of population growth in China was 15 per thousand, not quite so different from India's 19 per thousand, because of the lower death-rate in China (*World Development Report 1992*). Also, application of the Chinese approach to other developing economies is improbable since they are not equipped with as strong a government command as in the communist regime.

Considering these situations, the probability of low-income economies escaping quickly from the strong pressure of exogenously given population growth appears to be relatively slim within the next couple of decades.

3.2 Economic Theories of Population Growth

In this section the demographic transition process observed in the previous section will be examined in terms of economic theories.

3.2.1 The Malthus model

Thomas Robert Malthus (1766–1832) is known as a pioneer in the economic theory of population. His *Principle of Population* ([1798] 1926) was a reflection of England's premiere entrance into the process of modern demographic transition.

His population theory may be summarized as follows: as with other animals, human beings have a natural instinct to bear children to a physical maximum; under this 'fixity of passion' people tend to multiply in an exponential rate; where the production of food is constrained by the fixed endowment of natural resources, especially land, and can increase only arithmetically, whatever slack of food supply per capita beyond a subsistence level may exist will eventually be used up by increased population; further increases in population are bound to be checked by famines, pests, and wars of desperate competition for limited food supply; thus, it is not possible that the levels of living and income per capita for the majority of people can remain beyond a subsistence minimum in the long run.

This theory may be expressed by line *GG* in Figure 3.3, which represents a relationship between the wage rate (*W*) or an average income per labourer and the growth rate of population ($\Delta N/N$) where N and ΔN denote

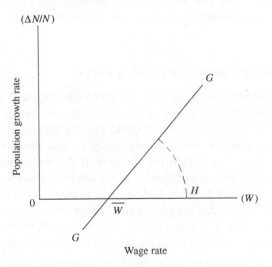

FIG. 3.3 *The Malthusian population theory and its revision*

respectively, population and its absolute increase. Line *GG* cuts through the horizontal axis at $\bar{W}$. The wage rate measured by the distance between O and $\bar{W}$ is defined as the subsistence wage rate that is barely sufficient for a labourer and his family to subsist, and, hence, keeps average family size and total population constant.

Line *GG* is upward-sloping to indicate a relationship by which any increase in the wage rate beyond $\bar{W}$ (due to an increase in labour demand or a decrease in labour supply) results in a positive rate of population growth. The exponential growth in the labour force that is implied from the positive population growth rate will eventually close any excess labour demand and thereby drive the wage rate back to $\bar{W}$.

On the other hand, as continued growth in population and the labour force creates excess labour supply, the wage rate is pushed down below the subsistence level so that the population would decrease via the Malthusian check to recover the labour demand–supply equilibrium at the subsistence wage rate. Thus, in the Malthus model the sustained divergence of the wage rate from $\bar{W}$ never occurs.

While Malthus is known as a heretic in the English Classical School, his population model has been accepted widely, even by opponents such as David Ricardo. However, Malthus's prediction has not stood the test of subsequent history. Indeed, according to the commonly observed pattern of demographic transition, both the birth-rate and the natural rate of population growth decrease in Phase 3, which corresponds to the period character-ized by sustained increase in the real wage rate. This association of population growth deceleration with sustained increases in the wage rate indicates that the relationship between $\Delta N/N$ and W is not linearly rising as represented by line *GG*, but turns to be downward-sloping towards H after a certain threshold is reached, as indicated by the dotted line in Figure 3.3.

3.2.2 The household utility maximization model*

Even though the Malthus model did not stand the empirical test for the later stage of development, it was relevant to English economy in the 1770s and 1780s when the theory was developed. During this period employment opportunities expanded with the beginning of the Industrial Revolution following the Agricultural Revolution. Even if the wage rate per hour may not have increased very significantly, the household income level increased from increased working hours and employment of females and children. Such a condition induced people in the labour class to marry earlier and produce more children. When this tendency coincided with decreases in the death-rate (owing to improved living conditions) the first population explo-

---

* Readers not interested in the technical analysis of economics may skip this section.

sion in the epoch of modern economic growth took place in England. Indeed, the way that the birth-rate responded positively to increased income per capita was consistent with Malthus's theory. Such a positive response through adjustments in the marriage age and rate can be universally observed in premodern societies, e.g. Wrigley and Schofield (1981) for England, and A. Hayami (1992) for Japan. The rising trend of the birth-rate for Phase 1 in England seems to reflect the premodern response to the early phase of industrialization.

To predict the future course of demographic changes in developing economies, a more general model should be envisaged that is able to explain both the empirical relevance of the Malthus theory for the early phase and its divergence from reality in the later phase of development. Attempts to build such a model have used an approach of maximizing the utility function common to household members (Leibenstein, 1957; Easterlin, 1975; Becker, 1976). Figure 3.4 presents a model that follows the Liebenstein approach, in consideration of its relative ease in understanding, even though the Becker model is a little more general in incorporating an explicit choice among consumption goods, and the number and quality of children in parents' utility function.

The model in Figure 3.4 assumes that parents have sole decision-making power within a household and that a husband and wife have the same utility function. Their marginal utilities and marginal disutilities from having an additional child are represented by lines MU and MD respectively. The vertical difference between MU and MD measures net marginal utility of parents.

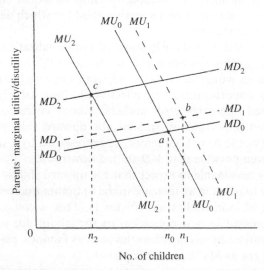

FIG. 3.4 *A household utility maximization model on the determination of the number of children*

Parents' utility for having children may be derived from (*a*) instinctive pleasure, such as love of children and satisfaction of having heirs; (*b*) expected income from children for the household; and (*c*) security for parents during old age. It is reasonable to assume that utilities from these sources increase at decreasing rates, corresponding to increases in the number of children.

On the other hand, the disutility of having children may be generated from (*a*) physical and psychological hardships in bearing and rearing children; (*b*) costs paid for child-bearing and rearing; and (*c*) opportunity costs of parents' labour used for child-bearing and rearing. While the marginal disutility from the first element is likely to increase in response to an increased number of children, both increasing and decreasing effects are conceivable from the second and third elements. In Figure 3.4, MDs are drawn in moderately upward-sloping forms, but the theoretical conclusion would be unchanged with the assumption of horizontal or moderately downward-sloping forms.

Assuming that in the initial period the marginal utility and disutility had been located at MU_0 and MD_0 respectively, parents' net utility would have been maximized by the number of children measured by $\underline{On_0}$. In the beginning of industrialization, employment and income-earning opportunities may have increased without accompanying significant developments in financial and insurance markets and social security systems for the majority of households. In such an institutional environment, any marginal increase in household income would result in an expansion in the demand for children as represented by a shift from MU_0 to MU_1. This shift might not be so small since an increased number of children would enhance old-age security that is considered to be a superior good for which demand tends to increase faster than income.

On the other hand, in the early stage of industrialization, when labour laws and primary school systems had not been established, expected earnings from children would have increased from increased employment and income-earning opportunities. This effect could have largely compensated for the increased opportunity of mothers' labour corresponding to their increased market opportunities. In sum, the upward shift in the marginal disutility curve would have been minor, as represented by a shift from MD_0 to MD_1. It is even possible that MD shifted downwards.

Anyway, it is reasonable to expect that the upward shift in MU exceeded the shift in MD to result in an increase in the optimum number of children in the early stage of industrialization (Phase 1). This is considered the same response to increased income opportunities for labour due to reductions in labour supply caused by major calamities such as famines, pests, and wars in the premodern era as Malthus contemplated.

However, as modern economic growth continued, major changes in social and economic systems emerged. As mentioned earlier, with the introduction of school systems, the cost of children increased. This paralleled the increased opportunity cost of mothers' labour under expanded labour markets. Progress in birth control technology decreased the marginal cost of reducing the number of children, which implied an increased marginal cost of increasing their number. All these factors combined, the marginal disutility of increasing the number of children should have experienced a major upward shift, as represented by MD_1 to MD_2, in the late stage of industrialization (Phase 3).

More importantly, the marginal utility curve that had shifted upwards in the early stage began to shift downwards in the late stage. The utility of having children for old-age security decreased with development of social security systems and private insurance markets. With increased social mobility, the probability of children staying with and taking care of parents decreased. Most decisively, the reduced death-rate reduced the utility of having many children for parents in terms of both instinctive pleasure and future security. Thus, when modern economic growth reached a stage at which social and economic systems were completely modernized, further increases in the wage rate and per capita income would have had the effect of shifting parents' utility curve downwards from MU_1 to MU_2 with the result of reducing the number of children from On_1 to On_2.

In this way, the premodern response of demography to economic growth, as theorized by Malthus, and the contrary response in advanced modern society can be understood within one theoretical framework. The difficulty in developing countries today is that, through a sharp decline in the death-rate from exogenous causes the response of the birth-rate to economic growth has not yet transformed into the modern pattern because of an adjustment lag in social institutions and value systems. A major question is how soon institutions and value systems will be adjusted and how effectively such programmes as education for women and extension of family planning will be able to promote the adjustments in low-income economies in the short to medium run.

3.3 Theories of Resource Constraint on Economic Growth

Although the speed of population growth in developing economies has been decelerating since the 1970s, it will continue to be 'explosive' in low-income economies, at least for a couple of decades. Is it possible that the low-income economies (characterized by high dependency on natural resources) will be set on the track to sustained growth in per capita income with decreasing availability of natural resources per capita? A clue to answering this question may be found in the theories that have analysed how fixed endowments of natural resources may constrain economic development under growing population.

3.3.1 From Malthus to the Club of Rome

As explained previously, it was Malthus who first pointed out the possibility of the growing relative scarcity of natural resources as a binding constraint on economic growth. The Malthus theory based on the fixity of both human passion and natural resources has had great influence on public opinion because of its simplicity and intuitive appeal.

Although the famine that Malthus predicted as an inevitable consequence of population growth was largely eradicated from industrialized economies during the nineteenth century, fear of the Malthusian crisis has never been erased. Indeed, the Malthus prediction has been publicized repeatedly on the occasions of food supply shortages and price increases in the world market due to crop shortfalls, wars, and other reasons. For example, towards the end of the nineteenth century India (previously an exporter of wheat) turned into an importer of wheat, and crop failure in the USA caused international wheat prices to rise. At that time Sir William Crookes (a leading scientist in England, known for his discovery of the element thallium) preached on the danger of a Malthusian food crisis (Crookes, 1899).

A dramatic reappearance of the Malthus theory in a somewhat different form was presented in a report to the Club of Rome by Meadows *et al.* (1972), titled *The Limits to Growth*. This report was not only concerned with the population–food crisis, but also with the crisis of natural resource exhaustion and environmental degradation due to overexploitation and waste of resources resulting from the exponential growth in economic activities. It predicted that, if this exponential growth was not curbed, industrialization would stop and economic activities would begin to shrink by the first two decades of the twenty-first century due to resource exhaustion. Then, world population would be curtailed because of an increase in the death-rate due to food shortage and environmental pollution.

This report had exceptionally strong public appeal, because in 1973, a year after its publication, a so-called 'World Food Crisis' due to world-scale crop failure and the first oil crisis triggered by the OPEC embargo in response to the fourth Middle East War did occur. A several-fold increase in food and energy prices resulted. However, as the crisis passed and commodity prices declined, the effect of this report on the public diminished and its theoretical and statistical basis became subject to criticism.[2]

A major limitation of the simulation analysis is the assumption that exponential increases in population, industrial production, and other economic activities at the average rates in the past (1900–70) will remain unchanged in the future with proportional increases in food and raw material consumption. The analysis does not consider the rational response of economic agents to save the increasingly scarce resources. Mechanical extensions of past trends, with no consideration of possible changes in production coefficients, are bound to lead economic growth into collision with the fixed endowment of natural resources. In this regard, the 'systems dynamics' analysis based on a large equation system is essentially the same approach as Malthus's exponential extrapolation of population under the 'fixity of passion' that eventually collides with the fixed endowment of land resources.

This type of mechanistic approach has merit in showing a magnified picture of a potential danger implied in present trends, and, thereby, spurs the public to take action to prevent the danger from materializing. For example, Crookes (1899)—who pointed out the danger of the approaching Malthusian food crisis—proposed the concept of a new technology to extract ammonium from air, then considered a dream. However, his dream came true with the development of an aerial ammonium-fixation method developed by Haber and Bosch during World War I, which later proved to be a key invention for avoiding the materialization of the Malthusian crisis.

Irrespective of its scientific credibility and predictive power, the contribution of the Club of Rome report in drawing public awareness to the need for saving and conserving the environment and natural resources must be duly recognized. However, it is inevitable that simple extrapolations of past trends will produce future predictions that will widely diverge from actual outcomes.[3]

3.3.2 The Ricardo model*

As explained in Chapter 1, the development of human society has been realized through developments in technology and institutions that facilitated substitution of man-made capital for natural resources. The Malthus theory that focused on the side of human behaviour driven by animal instincts without due regard for capital formation activities could be a theory of population, but could hardly be called a theory of economic development.

It was David Ricardo (1772–1823) who clarified the mechanism on how economic growth is constrained by natural resource endowments, by building the genuine theory of economic development. His *Principles of Political Economy and Taxation* was published in 1817, towards the completion of the Industrial Revolution in England. This was the period when population growth reached its peak (see Figure 3.1).

Ricardo's development theory identified capital accumulation in modern industries, which emerged from the Industrial Revolution, as the driving force of economic growth. 'Capital' in his view was the 'wage fund', defined as the sum of payments to labour in advance of sale of commodities produced by the labour applied, as well as payments for the purchase of tools and structures complementary to the use of labour. Therefore, the demand for labour increases proportionally with the increase in the wage

---

* Readers not interested in the technical analysis of economics may skip explanations with the use of Figure 3.5 in this section.

fund. On the other hand, the supply of labour is determined by the number of labourers existing who are willing to work full time regardless of the wage rate. This implies that labour supply is constant in the 'short run' (defined as the period within which population is constant). Therefore, as new investment is added to the wage fund, labour demand increases by raising the wage rate along the inelastic supply in the short run. If the wage rate is raised above the subsistence wage rate in the Malthusian sense ($\bar{W}$ in Figure 3.3), however, population begins to increase with subsequent increases in the labour force. Therefore, the supply of labour is considered infinitely elastic in the long run (defined as the sufficiently long period in which population and labour force are allowed to change), under which the wage rate always tends to be pushed back to the subsistence level. Thus, in the long run the wage cost to industry does not rise, and profit increases proportionally with the increase in capital. Since the rate of profit does not decline, incentive is maintained to reinvest profits so that production and employment continue to increase in the modern industrial sector.

However, the subsistence wage for industrial workers depends on food prices. Unlike industrial production, agriculture cannot escape from decreasing returns in production since it is constrained by the endowments of the land. To the extent that food demand is met by production using the most fertile 'superior' land, its marginal cost remains constant. However, if increased food demand (corresponding to population growth) exceeds the output produced on the most superior land, the next superior land must be brought into cultivation, resulting in an increased marginal cost, since more labour and capital must be applied to produce the same amount of food per unit of inferior land. Thus, as more inferior lands are opened for food production, the marginal cost will increase progressively. In this process demands for superior lands increase since it is more profitable to cultivate superior lands. Consequently, higher rents must be paid to the landlords for using superior lands up to the difference between production costs on superior lands and those of the 'marginal land' (the most inferior land being used in production).

As food prices rise corresponding to the cost hikes, nominal monetary wages paid to industrial workers need to be raised to maintain their subsistence living. As the wage cost rises, profit does not continue to increase proportionally with the increase in capital. Thus, as food demand continues to increase corresponding to capital accumulation and employment growth, food prices will eventually be raised to a level at which the rate of profit will become so low as to provide no incentive for further investment. Economic growth will stop at this point.

The Ricardo theory, summarized above, is reconstructed as a model in modern economics in Figure 3.5. The left-hand diagram represents a labour market for the modern industrial sector, in terms of the Marshallian partial equilibrium model. Line *DD* represents a labour demand curve, which is assumed to correspond to a schedule of the marginal value product of labour for a given stock of capital in use.[4]

While the diagram is structured in a neoclassical fashion, the classical characteristic of the Ricardo theory is represented by the shape of labour supply. Adopting the Malthusian law (line GG in Figure 3.3), Ricardo assumed a horizontal supply of labour at the subsistence wage rate ($O\bar{W}$) in the long run, as represented by line LS. However, because labour force remains constant in the short run and, because the marginal disutility of labour relative to the marginal utility of income is considered negligibly small for workers living at a near- subsistence level, the short-run supply of labour can be assumed to be inelastic to the wage rate, as represented by the vertical line SS.

Assume that at the beginning of industrialization the labour demand schedule is given as DD_0 corresponding to the stock of capital K_0 owned by industrial capitalist- entrepreneurs, and that the long-run equilibrium in the initial period is established at point A with labour employed by OL_0 at the subsistence wage rate. Then, total value product in the industrial sector is represented by area $ADOL_0$ of which area $A\bar{W}OL_0$ is paid to workers and the remaining area $AD\bar{W}$ becomes profit or return to capital.

As a common assumption of both Classical and Marxian economics, labourers who are at the subsistence level consume their entire wage incomes, and wealthy capitalists (always seeking increased profits) reinvest nearly all the profits they receive, so that capital stock increases from K_0 to K_1 (K_0 + area $AD\bar{W}$). Correspondingly, labour's marginal products shift upwards, resulting in a shift to the right of the labour demand curve from DD_0 to DD_1, and the wage rate increases beyond $O\bar{W}$ to OW_S.[5] However, as the wage rate rises above the real wage rate, Malthus's law will begin to operate (with increases in population and labour force). Therefore, with a lapse of time, the short-run labour supply curve SS will shift rightwards to pull down the wage rate along the labour demand curve DD_1 to point B, at which the new long-run equilibrium level of employment OL_1 is determined.

If scale neutrality of production and Say's law of production to create demand are assumed according to the theory of Ricardo, product, capital stock, and labour employment will increase at the same rate in the long run under the constant subsistence wage rate as measured by product unit.[6] Then, total wage payment (wL) and total profit ($Y - wL$) increase at the same rate as total output (Y) and capital (K), so that the rate of profit or return to capital [$(Y - wL)/K$] remains constant. Thus, the horizontal supply of labour (supported by the Malthus law of population) prevents the profit incentive of capitalist-entrepreneurs for investment from decreasing and, thereby, guarantees continuation in capital accumulation and output growth in the modern industrial sector.

The constraint to such growth of the modern sector is decreasing returns in food production that operate in the agricultural sector. The right-hand

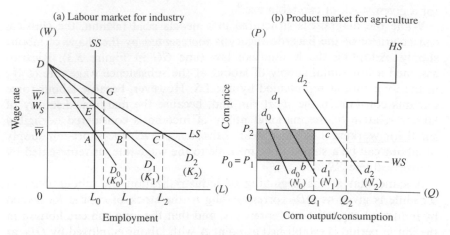

FIG. 3.5 *The Ricardo model of economic development*

diagram of Figure 3.5 presents a market for food represented by 'corn' (grain), where the horizontal axis measures corn output/consumption and the vertical axis measures its price. Line *HS* represents the supply schedule of corn determined by its marginal costs. According to Ricardo, this schedule rises stepwise, because land is distributed from the most superior to the most inferior category and the area belonging to each category is fixed. The marginal cost of corn production remains constant at $OP_0(=OP_1)$ up to the maximum output that can be produced by the best land category (OQ_1), but jumps up to OP_2 as output exceeds this limit and the second-class land is brought into cultivation. The stepwise increases continue as the land of more inferior qualities is brought into production.

Because corn is consumed mostly by labourers and because their per capita income is constant in the long run at the subsistence wage rate, a shift in its demand curve *dd* occurs in response to population growth alone. Assume that d_0d_0 in the right-hand diagram represents a corn demand curve corresponding to employment in the industrial sector represented by OL_0. As this employment increases to OL_1, and then to OL_2, population growth proportional to the growth in employment shifts the corn demand to d_1d_1, and then to d_2d_2 respectively. To the extent that corn demand is met by production using only the best land category, as in the case of d_1d_1, the price of corn stays at $OP_0(=OP_1)$. As the corn demand is expanded to d_2d_2, however, the corn price rises to OP_2; corresponding to the marginal cost of production using the second grade of land. Here it is assumed that the increase in the marginal cost of increasing corn output by means of bringing the second-grade land into cultivation is the same as applying more capital and labour to production in the first-grade land.

As the corn price rises from OP_0 to OP_1, the subsistence wage rate of $O\bar{W}_0$ which used to be sufficient for labourers to purchase corn in a sufficient quantity for their subsistence at OP_0, becomes less sufficient. Therefore, the wage rate in the industrial sector will have to be raised in the long run to $O\bar{W}'$, which enables labourers to purchase sufficient corn for their survival. Then, the profit in the industrial sector, with the application of capital by K_2, decreases from area $CD\bar{W}$ to GDW'. Therefore, the rate of profit to capital in the industrial sector will decline progressively as lower-grade lands are opened for cultivation. This will have the effect of depressing the income of capitalist-entrepreneurs and their investment incentives.

On the other hand, as the corn price rises from OP_1 to OP_2, corn producers using the first-grade lands can capture excess profit by $\underline{P_1P_2}$ per unit of output. Since excess profit is obtainable by using the first-grade instead of the second-grade land, competition among producers to use the first-grade land will raise its rent to $\underline{P_1P_2}$, with the landlords' revenue amounting to the shadowed area. Thus, landlords capture windfall gains from capital accumulation in the industrial sector through expansions in population and food demand.

The Ricardo theory predicts that, under given natural resource endowments in terms of fixed land areas by grade, food-price increases resulting from population growth will drive the economy into a 'stationary state' where the rate of profit is so low that it provides no incentive for additional investment and labourers' real wage rates do not diverge from a subsistence minimum, while landlords alone receive enlarged rent revenue. This mechanism of fixed land resource endowments that constrain economic growth in the early stage of industrialization is commonly called the 'Ricardian trap', or alternatively called the 'food problem' by T. W. Schultz (1953).

The policy that Ricardo proposed for unbinding the British economy from the trap of land resource constraint was liberalization of grain imports, or more specifically, repeal of the Corn Laws that had imposed a tariff barrier on the import of cheap grain from abroad as part of the mercantile system. Ricardo argued that superior lands should be available in infinite amounts not within Britain, but in the world including new continents. Therefore, if trade was liberalized, total corn supply from both domestic and external sources would become horizontal at a low price (OP_0), as represented by line WS. Then, labour supply in the modern industrial sector could continue to be horizontal at the wage rate $O\bar{W}$ on which capital accumulation and economic growth in the modern sector could be sustained. The repeal of the Corn Laws was a necessary condition to sustain modern economic growth that began with the Industrial Revolution. As such, Ricardo provided to the emerging bourgeois class a theoretical edge to fight the vested interests of landed aristocracy and gentry.

The Ricardo model sets out clearly the problem of natural resource constraints that low-income economies will have to face when they undertake industrial development when agriculture is stagnant. If rapid population growth in the early industrialization stage is not paralleled with increases in food supply, food prices will rise sharply to pull up the cost of living to low-income people characterized by the high Engel coefficients. This would produce strong pressure for wage hikes through organized bargains as well as food riots. Resultant wage increases would imply a serious blow to industries in the early stage, which are dependent on labour-intensive technologies.

This Ricardian trap faced by low-income developing economies today cannot be solved by liberalization of food imports alone. Ricardo's advocacy for free trade was relevant to England in the early nineteenth century, when its population was only a small fraction of world population and its supremacy in industrial productivity made it easy to earn sufficient foreign exchange for food imports. It is not easy for developing economies today to earn sufficient foreign exchange from the export of industrial products during the early stage of industrialization. Also, if many populous developing economies compete for food imports, the international price would rise so much that the domestic price could hardly remain stable.

For them, there appears to be no other way to escape the Ricardian trap but to advance agricultural technology concurrently with industrialization. Ricardo did not deny the possibility of improving agricultural technology, but considered that it was too limited to overcome decreasing returns in agricultural production in the long run. This idea was created when technological advances in agriculture were mainly based on the experiences and trials of farmers. History has proved that, with the organized application of science to the problem of agricultural production (which began in late nineteenth century), technological progress in agriculture has accelerated so that the growth rate of agricultural productivity has exceeded that of industrial productivity in advanced industrial economies (Table 4.1). It is obvious that the escape from the Ricardian trap for developing economies is to follow the pattern of agricultural productivity growth of advanced industrial economies in the past.

3.3.3 The dual economy model*

It was W. Arthur Lewis (1954) who built upon the thrust of the Ricardo model a new two-sector model as a theory of economic development in developing economies today. His model analyses the process of development through interactions between the traditional sector (represented by agriculture) and the modern sector (represented by industry), which have different behavioural principles. In the modern industrial sector the wage rate is supposed

---

* Readers not interested in the technical analysis of economics may skip explanations with the use of Figure 3.6 in this section.

to be established at the equation with marginal productivity of labour, as dictated in neoclassical economics, whereas that of the traditional agricultural sector is considered to be institutionally determined at a subsistence level along the tradition of classical economics, including Ricardo's theory.

Lewis's model is the same as Ricardo's at the point that labour supply to the industrial sector is characterized by infinite elasticity, which ensures parallel increases in capital accumulation and profit. The two models differ on the mechanism of producing the horizontal labour supply schedule. While Ricardo based this mechanism on the Malthusian population law, Lewis based it on surplus labour existing in the traditional sector.

According to Lewis, excess labour is employed in rural communities in developing economies because of their customs of mutual help and income-sharing within family, tribe, and/or village, so that labour's marginal product is much lower than the institutional wage rate, if not zero. Labourers, whose marginal contributions to agricultural output are below the institutional wage rate, should be willing to migrate to the industrial sector if employment there is offered at the fixed institutional rate. Accordingly, labour supply to the industrial sector would remain horizontal up to the point when all the surplus labour finishes migrating from the agricultural sector. Until then, the Ricardian process of parallel increases in capital and profit will continue.

Once all the surplus labour in agriculture is absorbed into industry, the wage rate in the agricultural sector will rise along its marginal product curve, corresponding to further absorption of labour by industry. As this point marks the transition from the traditional economy (subject to the classical principle) to the modern one (subject to the neoclassical principle), it is called the 'turning-point'. After the turning-point is reached, the dual nature of the economy is lost, and agriculture becomes a part of the modern economy in which the wage rate and per capita income continue to rise along the upward-sloping labour supply curve. In this way, Lewis pointed out that the mechanism to achieve economic modernization is latent in the traditional economic system characterized by poverty and surplus labour.

Lewis himself did not recognize the danger that the dual economic growth process could be stopped by the Ricardo–Schultz food problem before reaching the turning-point. This possibility is clearly indicated in the Ranis–Fei model that extended and formalized the Lewis theory (Ranis and Fei, 1961; Fei and Ranis, 1964).

Figure 3.6 is a simplified representation of the Ranis–Fei model. Horizontal axis $O_1 O_2$ represents the total labour force, with the industrial labour force measured from O_1 to the right and the agricultural labour force measured from O_2 to the left. For example, point S implies the distribution of labour force between $O_1 S$ to industry and $O_2 S$ to agriculture. The upper portion of the diagram represents the market demand and supply relationships for industrial labour that are essentially the same as in the left-hand

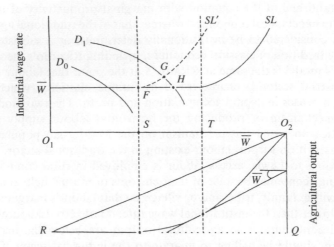

FIG. 3.6 *The dual economy model of the Lewis–Ranis–Fei type*

diagram in Figure 3.5. The lower portion represents a production response to labour input (production function), in the agriculture sector in an inverted shape. Concave curve O_2R represents the relationship where agricultural output increases at a decreasing rate corresponding to increases in labour input from origin (O_2) until point S, beyond which labour's marginal product becomes zero.

A purely traditional economy before industrialization is represented by point O_1 at which all labourers are engaged in agricultural production. It is assumed at this point that labour's marginal productivity in agriculture is zero, but output is shared equally among labourers according to the principle of mutual help and income-sharing in rural communities. Income per worker is, therefore, represented by the tangency of a straight line connecting O_2 and R. This average productivity ($\bar{W}$) is considered the determinant of the cost of living, hence the institutionally determined subsistence wage rate.

Starting from point O_1 the agricultural labour force migrates to the industrial sector as the demand curve for industrial labour shifts to the right in response to capital accumulation in the industrial sector. It may appear that the supply price of labour to industry remains constant until industrial labour employment reaches point T (the Lewis turning-point) because agricultural labour's marginal product continues to be lower than the institutional wage rate offered by industry. If so, the turning-point will be reached through parallel increases in capital stock and profit supported by the infinitely elastic labour supply.

However, once industrial employment exceeds point S, agricultural labour's marginal product becomes positive. Further labour migration to industry results in an absolute decline in total (and per capita) food output, so that food prices rise relative to industrial product prices. Point *S* is called the 'shortage point' as it marks the beginning of a food supply decrease.

Beyond this shortage point, the wage rate (measured in industrial product units) needs to be increased so that industrial labourers can purchase the same food basket for their subsistence. Correspondingly, the labour supply curve to industry becomes upward-sloping from point *S*. This curve's slope could well be sharp, because rises in food prices and cost of living for labourers are likely to be sharp in response to reduction in the production of foodstuffs characterized by low demand elasticities. If so, the rate of profit in the industrial sector may decline sharply from point *S*, so that capital accumulation stops before reaching point *T*.

The shortage point in the Ranis–Fei model represents another formulation of the Ricardian trap in which developing economies may be caught when they try to achieve economic modernization by forcing resource reallocation from agriculture to industry, while neglecting the efforts to increase agricultural productivity. This danger is more strongly advocated by Dale W. Jorgenson (1961) in his two-sector model which is similar to the Ranis–Fei model except that no surplus labour is assumed to exist in agriculture and the wage determination in the agricultural sector is based on the neoclassical marginal principle. In the absence of surplus labour in agriculture, industrialization must be supported from its very beginning by technological progress in agriculture to prevent food prices and the cost of living from rising sharply.[7]

It has been the subject of major academic debate whether surplus labour exists in the rural sector of developing economies and whether its wage determination is based on the classical or the neoclassical principle (Hayami and Ruttan, 1985, ch. 2). Irrespective of which theory is adopted, the same conclusion pertains—that successful industrialization cannot be expected without the parallel effort of increasing food production to avoid the danger of being caught in the Ricardian trap.

It must also be pointed out that the contribution of agriculture to industrialization is not only in the supply of food and labour but in many other areas, such as provision of domestic markets for industrial commodities, earning of foreign exchange through exports of agricultural products, and transfer of savings through taxation and financial markets. Industrialization and modern economic growth can hardly be successful without healthy developments in the agricultural sector, which is so dominant in the early stage of development (Mellor, 1966; Johnston and Kilby, 1975; Hayami and Ruttan, 1985).

NOTES

1. Further back to about the beginning of the first millennium, world population is guestimated within a range from 200 to 300 million, considering the estimates of

210 to 250 million by Woytinsky and Woytinsky (1953), about 250 million by Berelson (1974), and about 300 million by the World Bank in its *World Development Report 1984.*

2. For a major study in support of the advocacy of the Club of Rome, see the joint report to President Carter by the Council on Environmental Quality and the US Dept. of State (1980). For a criticism, see Simon and Kahn (1984).

3. The same comment may be applied to a recent prediction by Brown and Kane (1994) on the arrival of the Malthusian food crisis within a couple of decades, advocating strengthening of population control. However, the possibility cannot be denied that a major surge in world food prices may occur in the relatively near future. The reason is not so much continued population growth as deceleration in the productivity of major food staples, such as rice and wheat, since the mid-1980s, due to a decline in public investment in agricultural research and irrigation systems since the late 1970s. This applies not only to food but to energy as well. Considering the fact that high investments induced by high food and energy prices during the 1970s resulted in oversupply and low prices in the 1980s, high prices may well emerge for a decade to come. It must be recognized that both governments and international agencies tend to overly respond to short-run price fluctuations by neglecting long-run investment in research and development geared to increasing food production as well as saving energy. Unless such myopic behaviour of public agencies is corrected, recurrent food and energy crises will continue to be repeated.

4. Unlike the neoclassical (Marshallian) presentation of the labour market in Figure 3.5, labour demand in the theory of Ricardo and the English Classical School in general is determined by the wage fund e.g. long-run employment is determined by dividing the wage fund by the subsistence wage rate, and short-run employment is equal to existing the labour force, while the long-run wage rate is equal to the subsistence wage rate and the short-run wage rate is given by dividing the wage fund by the existing labour force. While the same conclusion can be derived from the wage fund theory, it is more precise and easier for readers trained in neoclassical economics to understand the nature and significance of the Ricardian model in terms of neoclassical representation as in Figure 3.5. To further understand Ricardo's original theory as well as Marx's theory (discussed in the next chapter), see Negishi (1989).

5. The shift in the labour supply curve from DD_0 to DD_1 in a rotational manner with point D being fixed is a very special case. The reason this special shift is assumed is because it is the only way to present the Ricardian case of constant factor shares by using linear demand curves. A more general case can be drawn with the use of non-linear curves including both increasing and decreasing returns to labour. However, this cannot be done without complicating the diagrammatic presentation.

6. Say's law precludes the possibility of any product price declining in the long run. Under the assumption of constant returns to scale, the production function of relating output (Y) to labour (L) and capital (K) inputs,

$$Y = F(L, K)$$

is linear homogeneous and, hence, labour productivity ($y = Y/L$) can be expressed as the function of the capital–labour ratio ($k = K/L$) alone as

$$y = f(k).$$

At the profit-maximizing equilibrium the profit rate (r) and the wage rate (w) can be expressed, respectively, as

$$r = f'(k) \quad \text{and} \quad w = f(k) - kf'(k).$$

Therefore, for given $\bar{w}$, $\bar{k}$ and $\bar{r}$ are constant, implying that K and L change proportionally with the rate of profit to remain constant. The assumption of constant returns in industrial production could well be a fairly close approximation of technology in the days of early industrialization. Imagine a case in which a workshop employing ten weaving workers with ten looms invests in the purchase of two additional looms and an increase in the wage fund equivalent to two additional weavers' advance payments, with no possible increase in average output per worker and per loom.

7. Jorgenson's neoclassical model assumed a Malthusian mechanism in which population grows as per capita food availability exceeds a minimum subsistence level resulting from agricultural productivity increases. As Birdsall (1988) points out, the neoclassical one-sector growth model of the Solow–Swan variety (Solow, 1956; Swan, 1956) is also Malthusian because it predicts that capital and consumption per capita will decrease with higher rates of population growth, even though this model has little relevance to the development of developing economies.

4

Breaking the Resource Constraint

As aptly pointed out by the classical theories of development, a condition for low-income economies to attain sustained growth is to achieve food production increases at a speed exceeding explosive population growth. Failure in this endeavour is evident in Sub-Saharan Africa where food output per capita declined parallel to decreases in per capita availability of farmland (Table 2.4). At the same time, the desperate effort to maintain subsistence under severe land resource constraint has forced people in developing economies to push cultivation towards agriculturally unsustainable areas, resulting in environmental degradation such as soil erosion and desertification.

A similar problem was also encountered by today's industrial economies in their early stage of development. Nevertheless, they were able to escape the trap of natural resource exhaustion by means of capital accumulation and technological progress supported by institutional innovations. By comparing these different historical experiences this chapter explores the means of overcoming the problem of mounting population pressure on limited natural resources in developing economies.

While this problem also applies to minerals, water, forests, and other environmental resources, the first three sections of this chapter will strongly focus on the constraint of land resources for agricultural production, since it is the most pervasive and binding constraint in the way of economic development in its early stages, as advanced by great economists since Malthus and Ricardo (Chapter 3, Section 3). Merits and demerits of rich natural resource endowments for development will be discussed in more general terms in Section 4.

4.1 Potential of Science-Based Agriculture

Within the last half century, the world population has increased about 2.5 times, while farmland has increased less than 30 per cent. Despite the fact that per capita availability of farmland declined to nearly half, grain output per capita increased about 30 per cent. This long-term trend has continued in recent years. Food production per capita increased by 10 per cent during the 1980s (Table 2.4). According to the projection of the Food and Agriculture Organization (FAO, 1993), the rate of increase in grain production will slow down towards 2010, but due to the deceleration in the population growth rate per capita grain output is expected to increase moderately, with a slightly downward trend in international grain market prices.

How have such increases in food production become possible under the severe limitation of land resources? The key answer to this question is the development of 'science-based agriculture' that coincided with the beginning of the population explosion in the first three decades of this century. Until this development, the biological process of agricultural production could not escape the basic constraint of natural fertility in soil. Agricultural output per unit of land area, therefore, remained low compared with modern standards, even though some significant developments in farm mechanization had been achieved, especially in the USA in the nineteenth century.

The traditional approach to increasing land productivity in agriculture had been to design a farming system for more intensive cropping without causing depletion in soil fertility. A renowned example was a change from the two-field system (rotation between cereal crop and fallow) to the three-field system (two successive cereal crops followed by fallow) in medieval Europe (Slicher Van Bath, 1963). Another example was the change from the three-field system to the so-called 'Norfolk crop-rotation system' in England in the seventeenth to eighteenth centuries, in which lands hitherto left fallow were planted with forage crops such as turnip and clover. Increased forage production enlarged the capacity to carrying livestock, which increased the supply of stable manure to crop fields. Increased land productivity from this new husbandry, often called the 'Agricultural Revolution' in England, prepared a condition of sufficient food supply for industrial workers in the succeeding Industrial Revolution, thereby preventing food prices from rising sharply, as feared by Malthus and Ricardo (Timmer, 1969). According to the conventional theory, the shift to the Norfolk system was brought about by innovative landlords in the eighteenth century (Chambers and Mingay, 1966). However, a recent iconoclastic study by Robert Allen (1992) has demonstrated that the major yield-increasing innovation was accomplished mainly during the seventeenth century by yeomen (i.e. small independent farmers).[1]

Although such developments in 'resource-based agriculture' (based on the recycling of plant nutrients) could well meet food demand increases corresponding to a population growth rate of less than 1 per cent per year, they were not capable of sustaining adequate long-term production increases when population growth was more than 2 per cent per year. In developing economies today, the effect of high population growth rate augmented by the effect of per capita income growth often amounts to a rate of growth in per capita food demand as fast as 4 per cent per year. Such a high growth rate of demand could hardly be met without the application of chemical fertilizers and improvements in crop varieties based on scientific research. This approach to increasing land productivity in agriculture beyond the constraint of natural soil fertility by means of scientific knowledge and industrially produced inputs is what we call 'science-based agriculture'.

A revolutionary increase in the potential of agricultural production due to the change to science-based agriculture is clearly visible in the trends in yields per acre and real domestic prices (deflated by the consumer price index) of corn and wheat in the USA (Figure 4.1). Since the USA has been the leading exporter of grain, changes in its domestic prices are considered to largely parallel international market prices. Even though real grain prices have at times fluctuated wildly—shooting up during the two World Wars and then slumping in the World Depression period—they have shown no overall upward trend, despite the closure of Western frontiers for new land opening since the latter part of the nineteenth century. Instead, the real price of corn even declined from the pre-1920s to the post-1930s time-period. This

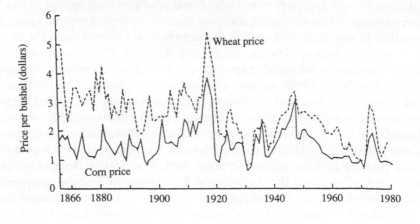

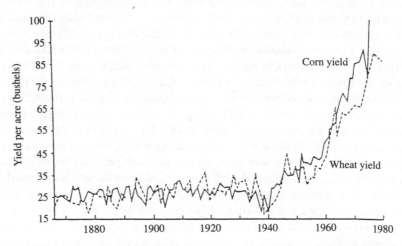

FIG. 4.1 *Long-term changes in real prices (deflated by CPI) and yields per hectare of corn and wheat in the USA*
Sources: Prices from Martin and Brokken (1983: 159); yields from Luttrell and Gilbert (1976: 527).

occurred despite the fact that the 1920s and 1930s were the period when the developing countries' population explosion began and world population growth accelerated (Section 3.1.1).

Why did real grain prices not rise when closure of open land frontiers in the USA and other countries coincided with the acceleration in population growth? The reason was quantum leaps in yields per acre, which rose to almost three times their original value within four decades from the end of the 1930s (lower section of Figure 4.1).

In the USA, the major effort to develop agricultural production technology from the mid-nineteenth century to the early twentieth century involved mechanization (first using horses and later using tractors) geared towards cultivating larger areas with less labour. However, as farmland area expansion decelerated from the turn of the century, agricultural research and experiments for varietal improvements were strengthened in land-grant colleges and the US Department of Agriculture in response to farmers' demands for yield increases. These efforts bore fruits with a significant time-lag in the form of high-yielding varieties, as represented by hybrid corn. The principle of hybrid vigour was discovered at the beginning of the twentieth century, but systematic research for its application was not organized until the 1920s, and the supply of commercial hybrid seeds to farmers began in the 1930s (Hayami and Ruttan, 1985: 208–22).

Modern varieties, represented by hybrid corn, are characterized by their high capacity to absorb plant nutrients and transform them into grain. This capacity could not be fully realized when the supply of nutrients was based solely on natural soil fertility. The constraint on the nutrient supply was removed by developments in fertilizer industries, including innovations in the manufacturing process such as aerial nitrogen fixation, as well as in mining and transportation. These industrial innovations were effective in lowering the price of chemical fertilizers relative to the price of agricultural commodities by about 40 per cent during the 1900–30 period, while the price of farm land increased approximately 200 per cent relative to farm product prices (Hayami and Ruttan, 1985: 482–3). The development of science-based agriculture induced by this sharp decline in chemical fertilizer prices relative to farmland prices is considered a typical case of induced technological innovation (Section 1.2.1). With the success of induced innovation, the world could escape from the Malthusian crisis despite acceleration in population growth and deceleration in farmland area expansion.

It must be emphasized that such developments in science-based agriculture could not be achieved by the profit-seeking efforts of farmers and private entrepreneurs in fertilizer supply industries alone. Because it is often difficult to set and protect patents on inventions in biological technology, it is difficult to mobilize sufficient investment from the private sector for agricultural research on the improvement of plant varieties and cultural practices. For this reason, advanced industrial economies such as the USA

TABLE 4.1 *The average annual growth rates of real labour productivities in agriculture and manufacturing in selected countries, 1960 to 1990[a] (%)*

| | | Average growth rate per year of labour productivity | | Rate of change in comparative productivity |
		Agriculture (1)	Manufacturing (2)	(1)–(2)
Developed economies	USA	3.6	3.3	0.3
	UK	3.9	3.2	0.7
	France	5.7	3.6	2.1
	Germany (FR)	5.9	3.4	2.5
	Japan	5.1	5.5	–0.4
Developing economies	Korea	3.4	7.1	–3.7
	Philippines	1.7	6.4	–4.7
	India	1.6	3.2	–1.6

[a] Average growth rates calculated between 1958–62 averages and 1988–92 averages, except for agriculture in Germany and manufacturing in all countries in 1990 for which 1989–91 averages are used.

Sources: UN, *Yearbook of Industrial Statistics*; FAO, *Production Yearbook*; ILO *Yearbook of Labour Statistics*.

have spent large sums of money to build public-supported agricultural research and extension systems. Development of these systems to supply biological technologies with public-good attributes are an example of the induced institutional innovations that enabled provision of new land-saving technologies in response to farmers' demand (as represented by a shift from i_0 to i_1 in Figure 1.2).

The huge productivity potential of science-based agriculture may be seen in the fact that the rates of increase in real labour productivity in agriculture were higher than in manufacturing in advanced industrial economies (except Japan) which were successful in establishing science-based agriculture (Table 4.1). The reverse was true for Japan, not because its agricultural productivity growth was slow, but because its manufacturing productivity growth was unusually fast. In contrast, the rates of agricultural productivity growth in developing economies such as India and the Philippines—relative to both the productivity growth rates of their manufacturing sectors and the agricultural productivity growth rates in developed economies—indicate a lag in their change from resource-based to science-based agriculture.

4.2 A Perspective on the Green Revolution

Considering the large potential of science-based agriculture, the effective transfer of this mechanism to low-income economies should release them from the Ricardian trap no matter what population pressures they might be subjected to. A condition of this shift is the appropriate supply of public goods, such as roads for efficient transportation and laws for efficient market transactions of farm products and inputs, as well as publicly supported agricultural research and extension systems. The lower the level of development of an economy, the more difficult it is to prepare such infrastructure.

However, developing economies have their own advantage towards achieving high rates of agricultural productivity growth by utilizing the backlog of advanced technologies accumulated in developed economies. This 'technology borrowing' in the sense of Alexander Gerschenkron (1962) is not easy, especially in agriculture. As agriculture is strongly constrained by environmental conditions, it is difficult to transfer advanced technologies developed in the temperate zone to the tropical zone. For example, high-yielding rice varieties in Japan often yield much less than local varieties in tropical Asia, since they are susceptible to exotic pests and insects. Because of this decisive influence of environmental factors on agricultural production, the international transfer of agricultural technology is more difficult than that of industrial technology. However, the environmental difference is not an insurmountable barrier. With appropriate adaptive research, agricultural technology transfers across different environments can be made possible. A dramatic example was the diffusion of modern rice and wheat varieties in tropical Asia from the late 1960s, commonly known as the 'Green Revolution'.

4.2.1 Development and diffusion of modern varieties

Modern varieties of rice and wheat have 'semi-dwarf' characteristics, with short and stout stems for sustaining heavier grain yields and with pointed leaves for better reception of solar radiation. They are characterized by higher grain yields at higher levels of fertilizer input. In contrast, traditional tropical varieties are tall with droopy leaves. Heavy application of fertilizers promotes plant growth but results in little increase (or some decrease) in grain yield.

Despite their similarities and fertilizer responsiveness, the modern varieties that began to diffuse in the tropics from the late 1960s were not the varieties developed in advanced economies. Rather, the improved varieties in the temperate zone provided a prototype for the modern varieties suited to the environmental conditions of the tropics. For example, so-called 'Mexican dwarf wheats', which were propagated widely over the Indian subcontinent, were crosses between traditional varieties in Mexico and short-statured *Gains* wheats in the western states of the USA. Their development, which was originally undertaken by the Maize and Wheat Breeding Program of the Rockefeller Foundation in Mexico, was further strengthened by the establishment of the International Center for the Improvement of Maize and Wheat (CIMMYT). In their propagation in India and other

Asian countries, the Mexican dwarf varieties were assimilated to the new environments through crosses with local varieties (Hayami and Ruttan, 1985: 264–74).

Rice-breeding for modern varieties was strongly promoted by the International Rice Research Institute (IRRI), established in the Philippines in 1962. IRRI was successful in developing an epoch variety, *IR8*, through a cross between Taiwan's dwarf variety (*Dee-Geowoo-Gen*) and an Indonesian variety (*Peta*). *IR8* had the potential to yield over eight tonnes per hectare under ideal cultural practices and field conditions, compared with less than three tonnes per hectare for traditional varieties in the tropics (Herdt and Capule, 1983; Barker and Herdt, 1985). Although *IR8* was modelled after the high-yielding Japanese varieties, it was not a *Japonica* variety, but an *Indica* variety with long and thin grains, commonly consumed by the population of tropical Asia. Similar to the case of Mexican dwarf, *IR8* and other *IR* varieties of rice were propagated over South and South-East Asia through crosses with local varieties.

Diffusion of the modern semi-dwarf varieties was very rapid. By the early 1980s, as much as 60 per cent of the rice area and 50 per cent of the wheat area in developing economies was planted with the modern rice varieties. As a result, India and Indonesia, which had been major importers of food grains, were able to achieve self-sufficiency from the 1970s to the 1980s. The fact that small subsistence-orientated farmers ('peasants' who mainly use family labour) adopted the new biological technology at a dramatic speed supports the hypothesis of T. W. Schultz (1964) that they are rational and efficient in resource allocation and are responsive to new profit opportunities arising from changes in technology and market demands.

Diffusion of the modern varieties was often interrupted by natural calamities. For example, a rapid diffusion of *IR8* after 1966 had enabled the Philippines to achieve rice self-sufficiency during 1968–70, but a subsequent outbreak of tungro virus disease forced the Philippines to return to importing until the mid-1970s. A similar setback was experienced in Indonesia where the diffusion of *IR5* was interrupted by a major outbreak of brown planthopper. However, the momentum of the Green Revolution was not destroyed by these calamities. As the plant-breeding efforts to incorporate pest and insect-resistant genes into modern varieties materialized, rice yield increases in these economies began to accelerate again in the late 1970s, culminating in the re-establishment of self-sufficiency in the 1980s.

The relationship between varietal improvements and yield increases is clearly visible in the Indonesian case, shown in Figure 4.2. Average rice yield per hectare in Indonesia began to rise sharply corresponding to the initial diffusion of *IR5* (called *PB5* in Indonesia) in the late 1960s, but its increase decelerated with the outbreak of brown planthopper biotype I in the early 1970s. The varieties resistant to this pest such as *IR26*. and *IR30*, were

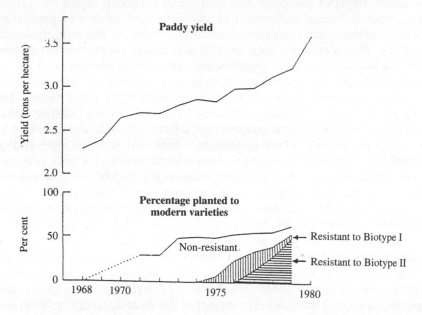

FIG. 4.2 *Increases in paddy yield per hectare corresponding to diffusion of the modern varieties with different characteristics of resistance to brown planthopper Biotypes I and II*
Source: Bernsten, Siwi, and Beachell (1981).

released during the mid-1970s but were severely damaged again as the brown planthopper transformed from biotype I to biotype II. Later, with the development of *IR36* and *IR38* resistant to biotype II, yields increased with the result that Indonesia—which had been the world's largest importer of rice, accounting for as much as 10 million tonnes per year in the 1960s—was able to achieve self-sufficiency by the late 1980s.

These experiences in the Philippines and Indonesia show that the 'Green Revolution' was not a one-shot development and diffusion of the 'miracle rice' variety. Instead, it was a continuous process of technological improvement through application of science to biological problems, in competition against natural counteracting forces. In this sense, the Green Revolution marked an epoch of science-based agriculture in developing economies.

4.2.2 Conditions of technology transfer[2]

In a historical perspective the Green Revolution can be viewed as a transfer of the mechanism for developing land-saving technologies to tropical Asia from Japan where this mechanism was initiated.[3]

Unlike the USA and other new continental countries, Japan was subject to a severely limited endowment of cultivable land relative to population from the beginning of modern economic growth in the late nineteenth century. With almost no open land frontier except on the northern island of Hokkaido, agricultural development efforts were concentrated on increasing output per unit of arable land area. Application of commercial fertilizers (such as fish meals and soybean cakes) began much earlier than the practical use of chemical fertilizers. Crop varieties with characteristics similar to those of modern varieties were selected through trial and error by experienced farmers. These indigenously improved varieties were further tested and improved by agricultural experiment stations for wide propagation. The publicly supported system of scientific crop breeding was developed in a relatively early stage, so that such varieties as *Norin No. 10*, a primogenitor of Mexican dwarf wheats, was developed in the 1930s (Hayami and Ruttan, 1985: 231–49; Hayami and Yamada, 1991, chs. 2 and 3).

Consequently, rice yield per hectare in Japan began to show an upward trend before the turn of the century, more than three decades ahead of the crop yield spurt in the USA. Yet, the increased production in Japan was not quite sufficient to meet the increased demand due to population growth and per capita income increases. The danger of the Ricardian trap in Japan was keenly felt in 1918 when a major urban riot was triggered by a sharp rise in the price of rice under the economic boom during World War I. This crisis prompted the Japanese government to transfer their rice production technology to Korea and Taiwan, which were then the overseas territories of Japan. As a result, rice yields in Korea and Taiwan began to increase sharply after the 1920s, as if to catch up with the yield level of Japan (Figure 4.3).

The success of the rice technology transfer was first attained in Taiwan. Since Taiwan is located in the semi-tropical zone, direct transfer of the temperate-zone Japanese varieties was not possible. Agricultural research efforts to adopt the Japanese varieties to Taiwan's semi-tropical environment resulted in the development of the *Ponlai* varieties. The *Ponlai* varieties were higher yielding than Taiwan's traditional (*Chailai*) varieties by 20 to 30 per cent with higher levels of fertilizer application. The *Ponlai* varieties commanded higher market prices because they were preferred by Japanese consumers. The high yields required a good water-control system in the paddy-fields. Irrigation systems that had been constructed by the colonial government to expand sugar cane production provided a precondition for the success of rice production in Taiwan.

As observed in Figure 4.3, the spurt of rice yield per hectare in Korea lagged almost a decade behind Taiwan's. This may seem anomalous considering the greater similarities in climatic conditions between Japan and Korea than between Japan and Taiwan. In fact, rice varieties used in northern Japan could be planted in Korea without local adaptation. Why then did the yield spurt in Korea lag behind Taiwan?

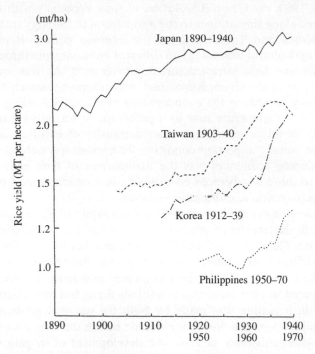

FIG. 4.3 *Changes in rice yield per hectare (in brown rice) in Japan, Taiwan, and Korea, five-year moving averages, semi-log scale*
Source: Kikuchi and Hayami (1985: 73).

As noted in the literature on Korean agriculture, the lack of irrigation was identified as the critical cause of low productivity and stagnant yields, as represented by the following statement:

The first technical condition of rice production is nothing but water control. But paddy field in Korea is so-called 'rain-fed paddy field', . . . accordingly marshy paddy field with drainage difficulty, which is considered of low quality in Japan, is considered good paddy field . . . Who would dare to apply fertilizers under such conditions? (Tobata and Ohkawa, 1937: 2–3)

Because of the precarious water supply, the Japanese varieties introduced into Korea in the early stage of the colonial rice production development programme were not the high-fertilizer-responsive varieties. Therefore, a major share of the colonial government's development budget in the 1920s was allocated to the construction of irrigation systems. As the irrigation infrastructure was improved, more fertilizer-responsive and higher-yielding varieties were brought from Japan or selected from experiment stations established in Korea. With diffusion of these varieties over the irrigated fields, rice yields in Korea rose sharply in the 1930s.

Since the 1960s the Green Revolution in Asia, especially with respect to rice, occurred along similar lines to the agricultural technology transfer from Japan to Korea and Taiwan during the interwar period. It involved a transfer of agricultural technology to different environments through adaptive research and land infrastructure improvements. As was emphasized earlier, the core of the Green Revolution was adaptive research to develop the technology suitable to the environments of the tropics, using advanced technology in the temperate zone as a prototype. It was more a transfer of the capacity of adaptive research than a transfer of existing technology. However, an equally important condition for agricultural technology transfer to developing economies was the assimilation of their environmental conditions to those of advanced economies—investment in land infrastructure such as irrigation and drainage systems.

Indeed, the transfer of rice technology from Japan to Korea and Taiwan involved both the transfer of adaptive research and the assimilation of land infrastructure. This was also the case in the Green Revolution. For example, the rapid diffusion of modern varieties in the Philippines was not only because IRRI was located in the Philippines and modern varieties were especially suited to environmental conditions there, but also because heavy investment in irrigation was made by both the national government and international aid agencies during the decade before the Green Revolution.

For wet rice cultivation, at least, the development of irrigation systems represented a precondition for the diffusion of modern varieties and the application of fertilizers. If population pressure on limited land resources were to induce both private and public efforts towards increasing land productivity, the rate of irrigation investment would have been inversely correlated with the rate of expansion of cultivable land area. Such a relationship can be observed from the histories of Japan and the Philippines, as shown in Figure 4.4.

The case of the Philippines in the lower diagram may be examined first. Even though similar to other developing economies, when population growth began to accelerate from around the 1920s, cultivated land expanded more rapidly than the agricultural labour force on open frontiers that existed in Mindanao, Visayas, and Luzon until the late 1950s. After this point, however, the growth rate of the cultivated area decelerated, and the land–labour ratio declined. In contrast, irrigation development accelerated, resulting in increases in the ratio of irrigated area. A decade later the ratio of area planted to modern varieties rose sharply.

The case of Japan in the upper diagram may seem anomalous because the rise in the ratio of the area covered by land infrastructure development projects was preceded by an increase in the ratio of area planted to improved varieties. This lag of infrastructure can be attributed to feudal heritage. By the beginning of the modern era, the irrigation and drainage systems in areas such as Kinki (the region centred on Kyoto and Osaka) and Northern

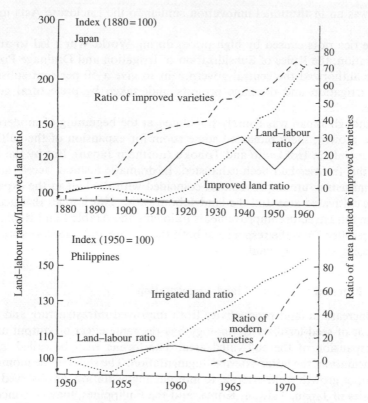

FIG. 4.4 *Changes in farmland area per worker, percentages in area improved by land infrastructure development projects, and area planted to improved rice varieties in Japan and the Philippines*
Source: Kikuchi and Hayami (1985: 77).

Kyushu had been developed sufficiently to introduce fertilizer-responsive high-yielding rices. Those varieties were selected mostly by veteran farmers and were further tested and improved by government experiment stations. As the diffusion of the technology approached the limit of the area having adequate water-control facilities, infrastructure became the major constraint.

When this happened, anxiety over the food supply induced public investment and institutional innovations, in addition to colonial rice development programmes. As early as 1899, public concern about national security, arising from Japan's position turning to a net importer of rice after the Sino-Japanese War (1894–5), resulted in the enactment of the Arable Land Replotment Law (revised in 1905 and 1909). The law stipulated compulsory participation of everyone within the land-improvement project area upon consent of the landlords who jointly owned two-thirds of the project area.

This was an institutional innovation similar to the Enclosure Acts in England.

The rice riots caused by high prices during World War I led to another innovation, the Rules of Subsidization of Irrigation and Drainage Projects. These authorized the central government to give a 50 per cent subsidy to large irrigation and drainage projects undertaken by prefectural governments.

Although Japan was densely populated at the beginning of modern economic growth, there remained some room for expansion of the cultivated area, mainly in Hokkaido and Tohoku (northern Japan). But by the 1910s, even this frontier had been exhausted. In dramatic fashion, acceleration in land-infrastructure improvements coincided with the halt in the expansion of the cultivated area and the land–labour ratio. This implies that acceleration in infrastructure improvements following the Arable Land Replotment Law resulted from the response of both the private and public sectors to the increasing scarcity of land.

4.2.3 External and internal land augmentation

The increase in land productivity from improved infrastructure and development of seed-fertilizer technology has the same effect on output as does the expansion of the cultivated area. The former may be called internal augmentation, the latter external augmentation. The shifts in the momentum of output growth from external to internal augmentation, as observed in the histories of Japan, Taiwan, Korea, and the Philippines, may be conceptualized as follows.

As population pressure pushes the cultivation frontier on to inferior land, the marginal cost of increasing production through expansion of the cultivated area rises relative to the marginal cost of intensification. Eventually, internal augmentation becomes less costly. This is illustrated in Figure 4.5.

The marginal cost of increasing output by opening new land is represented by curve A, and by constructing irrigation facilities, by curve I. With abundant land, curve A is horizontal and below curve I, indicating a relative advantage for external augmentation. As the cultivation frontier moves to inferior land, curve A rises, and crosses curve I at P, at which point irrigation (internal augmentation) becomes a more profitable method.

As the area under irrigation expands, construction moves from relatively less costly to more costly projects, which means the marginal cost of irrigation has a rising trend. This eventually chokes off the incentive to invest in land infrastructure. However, improvement in irrigation permits the introduction of new seed-fertilizer technology. Due to their high complementarity, fertilizers and improved seeds have the effect of reducing the cost of irrigation required to produce a unit of additional income, as illustrated by

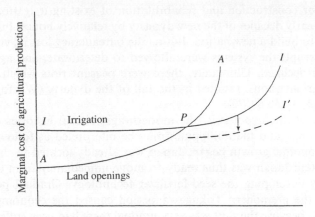

FIG. 4.5 *Relationship between marginal costs of agricultural production from new land openings and from irrigation construction*

the shift of the irrigation cost curve downward from *I* to *I'*. This downward shift increases the incentive to invest in infrastructure rather than to expand the cultivated area. These relationships emerge in the transition of momentum from the expanding cultivated area to increasing land productivity.

It may appear anomalous to assume that the marginal cost of production using irrigation construction diverges downwards from the marginal cost of opening land, because the optimum resource allocation by private producers is supposed to establish an equality in the marginal rates of returns among investment alternatives. This can be explained by the time-lag involved in adjusting the supply of public goods to the economic opportunity represented by the cross-over point. Typically, private individuals settle new areas, either as legal homesteaders or as illegal squatters; they open the new land using their own labour and capital. In contrast, irrigation systems, especially of the gravity type used in monsoon Asia, are characterized by indivisibility and externality requiring public investment by government or collective action by farmers which requires leadership and discipline. The indigenous capacity to organize large-scale public work projects cannot be developed immediately the need arises; rather, their development may require several generations. Thus, the marginal cost of building irrigation systems tends to diverge downwards because of underinvestment in irrigation due to slow development in rural organization.

It is possible for the government to fill this gap, but government investment in irrigation cannot be expected to quickly re-establish equality in the marginal rates of returns of the two alternatives. A government response of investing in infrastructure depends on the condition of political market, as modeled in Figure 1.3. That is determined by social and political climates. The dynastic cycle, in China in particular, can be cast in these terms. There was a major construction and rehabilitation of existing irrigation systems during the early decades of the new dynasty by relatively honest bureaucrats motivated to build a new nation. But as the bureaucracy lost its vitality and became corrupt, the systems were allowed to deteriorate, and agricultural production declined. Ultimately, there were peasant riots which, together with foreign invasions, resulted in the fall of the dynasty (Wittfogel, 1957: 171; Perkins, 1969: 60–70).

In terms of this hypothesis, the modern agricultural histories of Japan, Taiwan, Korea, and the Philippines may be interpreted as follows. Before modern economic growth began, Japan was already located to the right of point *P*. Meiji Japan was thus ready to move immediately from curve *I* to curve *I'* by developing the seed-fertilizer technology. Gradual population growth in the premodern Tokugawa period caused the economy to pass point *P*, but because the shift was very gradual there had been sufficient time for village communities to develop the organizational capacity for mobilizing communal labour to build and maintain local irrigation facilities (Section 9.2.2). Feudal lords had also taken the responsibility of controlling rivers and major irrigation systems. The decentralized power structure of the feudal system might have contributed to this response to local needs.

It appears that Korea was also located to the right of *P* before modern agricultural growth began. However, partly due to the incapacity of the Yi dynasty at the end of the nineteenth century, and partly due to the highly centralized, despotic structure of the government, irrigation systems were not extensive (Kim, 1987). Therefore, initial large-scale investment in irrigation was required before the shift from curve *I* to *I'* could begin.

Taiwan, in contrast, seems to have reached *P* in the late 1910s. The increase in the Japanese colonial government's investment in irrigation during this period played a large role. But an even more basic factor appears to have been the increase in the relative advantage of irrigation over the opening of new lands. Government investment provided the condition for shifting from *I* to *I'* in the 1920s and 1930s.

The Philippines seems to have reached *P* only in the late 1960s. The nation's desire to achieve self-sufficiency in food, together with foreign-exchange considerations, helped focus public attention on the need to invest in irrigation, which had become a relatively less costly means to increase rice output. The way for the shift from *I* to *I'* in the mid-1960s was thus prepared.

4.3 Barriers to Induced Innovation

In a broad perspective the Green Revolution is considered an innovation in agricultural production technology induced by population pressure on limited land resources. In terms of our basic model in Figure 1.2, it can be represented by a move from point *b* to point *c*, corresponding to a major inward shift in the innovation frontier (I_0 to I_1) owing to the availability to developing economies of scientific knowledge accumulated in developed economies, as well as to growing scarcity of land relative to labour and capital (P_0 to P_1). However, this shift was not possible with the effort of private farm producers alone, but initially hinged on institutional innovations such as public-supported agricultural systems (including international agricultural research centres) and land-infrastructure development organizations (Hayami and Ruttan, 1985: 264–74).

If such institutional innovations are to be effectively induced so that needed public goods (such as adaptive research and irrigation infrastructure) can be appropriately provided, even low-income economies under high population pressure should be able to produce sufficient food and escape from the Ricardian trap during this early industrialization process. Their opportunity to borrow technology, as represented by the distance between I_0 and I_1 (Figure 1.2) is extremely large.

Indeed, the great potential for productivity gain from borrowed technology may be seen in the rapid rice yield increase in Figure 4.3 Compared with the yield growth rate of only about 1 per cent per year in Japan—at the time of its yield spurt around the turn of the century—those of Taiwan and Korea in the interwar period reached about 2 per cent per year. The yield growth rate in the Philippines during the Green Revolution period was as high as 4 per cent, which exceeded its population growth rate of about 3 per cent. A pattern of agricultural productivity convergence was clearly indicated in East Asia. If this trend is extended further, low-income economies such as those in Sub-Saharan Africa—which have been suffering from explosive population growth and stagnant agricultural productivity—should be able to overcome the constraint of natural resources on their agricultural and economic developments.

So far, the modern varieties of rice and wheat developed by IRRI and CIMMYT have been high-yielding under irrigated or favourable rainfed conditions. To upgrade productivity in drought-prone rainfed areas and in flood-prone areas in major river deltas, varietal improvements should be promoted on different principles and methodologies from those semi-dwarf varieties using the varieties in developed economies as a prototype. Also, the yield ceiling imposed by developed economies' prototypes must be raised to meet rapidly expanding food demands in developing economies (Kush, 1995).

Further, the Green Revolution must be expanded beyond rice and wheat. Few technological breakthroughs have been achieved in the production of tropical subsistence crops such as millets, pulses, roots, and tubers. Research on these crops has lagged, partly because usable knowledge has not accumulated on these tropical food crops in temperate zones, and partly because a relatively low economic value for each individual crop lowered the expected rate of return to investment in their research.

However, institutional infrastructure for research on agricultural production in unfavourable environments and on tropical food crops has begun to be laid out. The initial success of IRRI and CIMMYT prompted the creation of the Consultative Group on International Agricultural Research (CGIAR), a consortium consisting of developed countries' aid agencies and international aid agencies, such as the World Bank, for supporting international agricultural systems. Under CGIAR, eighteen international agricultural research centres including IRRI and CIMMYT, have been established for the mandates of both specific crops and livestock (e.g. International Potato Centre in Lima, Peru) and climatic zones (e.g. International Crops Research Institute for the Semi-Arid Tropics in Hyderabad, India). A network of national agricultural research institutes has also been strengthened, especially from the 1970s to the mid-1980s, by collaboration with the international centres.

By urging institutional innovation in the form of national and international research systems on subsistence food production in the tropics, the Green Revolution, which has been limited to particular areas and crops, could be expanded globally so that the constraint of natural resources on development of low-income economies could be removed. A disquieting aspect is that, partly because of general 'aid fatigue' of developed countries after the demise of the cold war, partly because increased food production in developing economies is inconsistent with agricultural interests within donor countries, and partly because of low food prices in the world market since the 1980s—due to the very success of the institutional innovation on agricultural research and land infrastructure development—international support as well as national governments' investment have been waning since the mid-1980s (Von Braun *et al.*, 1993). Unless this trend is reversed, recurrence of a perceived Malthusian crisis (akin to the World Food Crisis of 1973–4) might be unavoidable.

In a broader perspective, however, the major impediment to a change to land-saving production systems appears to be the social-institutional complex that was created under the land-abundant regime. For example, in Africa, especially East Africa, population density has traditionally been lower than in Asia, so that shifting cultivation and nomadic grazing have commonly been practised. Much farmland has remained in communal possession of tribes, and, therefore, the development of private property rights as a means of facilitating long-term investments in land infrastructure has lagged.

The lag in the shift to settled agriculture underlies the lag in the formation of overhead capital such as roads and irrigation systems. According to a survey on the humid and subhumid tropics in Africa covering eighteen countries, the percentage of cropland irrigated in 1987–9 was only 2.5 per cent (3 per cent in both Tanzania and Nigeria). This ratio was only one-tenth of India's 25 per cent in 1950 when India's population density was about the same as in this part of Africa today. Also, the extension of roads per 1,000 square kilometres in this area was 53 kilometres, less than 20 per cent of India's 388 kilometres in 1950 (36 per cent in Tanzania and 14 per cent in Nigeria) (Spencer, 1994).

Such underdeveloped infrastructure is hardly sufficient to support the Green Revolution of the Asian type critically based on irrigation and the supply of commercial inputs such as chemical fertilizers. This difficulty is especially pronounced since African economies, which had traditionally been characterized by an abundance of natural resources, suddenly became resource-scarce economies of the Asian type. There is strong evidence that individual peasants in Africa have been making significant efforts in switching to intensive agricultural production systems by investing in land infrastructure, such as terracing and the introduction of high-valued commercial crops. Yet their efforts have not adequately been supported in complementary investments by governments (Tiffen and Mortimore, 1994). The crisis situation in Africa, as reflected in the decrease in per capita food supply (Table 2.4), has stemmed from the intrinsic difficulty of creating state and local community institutions for the supply of public goods to overcome the newly emerged constraint of natural resources under explosive population growth within a short span of time.

Such a social disequilibrium can be considered in Figure 1.2 as a situation of private producers being trapped at point *b* under the inadequate supply of public goods despite their potential optimum point having shifted to point *c*. In terms of Figure 4.5, the situation may be conceptualized as the inability to shift from the *A*-curve to the *B*-curve despite the cumulative divergence between them after the economies pass through point *P*.

What makes this situation especially serious appears to be governments' propensity to intervene in the markets of private goods rather than to make efforts to provide public goods of high social demand. Because of repulsion against the private marketing system dominated by foreign middlemen (such as Indians) as a colonial legacy, many African states after independence adopted the socialist mode of economic management characterized by strong regulations on markets. Policies frequently used to eliminate private traders from the marketing channels of agricultural commodities involved governmental monopoly organizations called 'marketing boards' or 'parastatal'.

These government interventions into markets not only fostered inefficiency and corruption, but also were a means of exploiting agriculture for the sake of promoting industrialization. The monopoly purchase of agricultural products and the monopoly sale of farm inputs by these governmental marketing agencies worked as a mechanism to exploit farmers through lower product prices and higher input prices than border prices. This exploitation mechanism was augmented by other policies for industrial protection, such as overvalued exchange rates, tariffs on manufactured commodities, and export duties on agricultural commodities (for details, see Section 8.2.4).

However, exploitation of agriculture to promote industrialization was not a strategy unique to African states but rather universal to developing countries, especially during the first three decades after World War II (Anderson and Hayami, 1986; Krueger *et al.*, 1991). Even in Taiwan, known for its success in achieving the world's highest land productivity in agriculture as a basis of healthy industrial development, the government monopolized the supply of fertilizers and forced farmers to barter rice for fertilizers at much less favourable terms than those in the international market from the early development stage until the 1960s. It is also well known that Thailand used the export duty (called 'export premium') on rice as an important source of government revenue. However, although these Asian states exploited agriculture, they did not neglect to make necessary investments in irrigation and agricultural research to increase land productivity.

In contrast, there has been a tendency among politicians in Africa to compensate for agricultural exploitation by distributing subsidized credits and inputs to particular rural élites instead of providing public goods. According to Robert Bates (1981, 1983) the selective distribution of such private goods ('divisible inputs' in Bates's terminology) to specific rural élites was more advantageous for politicians interested in maximizing the probability of their keeping office than supplying public goods which benefit a large number of farmers indiscriminately. Serious underinvestment in public goods has been inevitable from such political behaviour.

A relevant question to ask is why the appropriate supply of public goods was realized in Asia as a compensation for agricultural exploitation when the dominant mode of compensation in Africa has been selective distribution of private goods. A partial explanation may be that the exceedingly rapid shift from land-abundant to land-scarce economies in Africa has not allowed enough time for rural communities to develop traditions and customs to build irrigation and other local infrastructure through their collective effort, or to lobby for state provision of large-scale infrastructure. Moreover, territorial boundaries of many African nations were determined through competition and compromise of colonial powers with little regard for the social integrity of the indigenous population. It is natural that, even after independence, both politicians and citizens continued to have a stronger sense of belonging to their local and tribal communities than to their nation. What prevails there is a 'limited group morality' applicable to close acquaintances and relatives rather than a 'generalized morality' applicable to wide society (Platteau, 1992, 1994). Under such a traditional norm, politicians put high priority on profits for the communities they belonged to than for the social welfare of the whole nation. Therefore, it is no surprise to see that politicians were motivated to allocate resources in their control to élites in their own tribes.

Overcoming this incompatibility between political motivation and achieving new social optima is a key requirement for low-income economies (such as those in Africa) to escape from the Ricardian trap created by population pressure on limited natural resources.

The major controversies that surround the Green Revolution—whether the diffusion of modern varieties with heavy application of fertilizers and other chemical inputs might widen income inequality and degrade natural environments in rural areas—will be dealt with in Chapter 7 (Sections 3 and 4).

4.4 Development via Natural Resource Slack

Economic activities, especially exports, in developing economies are characterized by a high dependency on natural resources (Table 2.1). Even though the scarcity of natural resources has been rapidly increasing, some developing economies are still endowed with significant slack in mineral, forest, and other natural resources for the production of primary commodities. Several historical examples are available from countries such as Australia, Canada, and the USA, in which economic growth in the early stage of development was primarily based on exploitation of natural resources. Is it possible today that some developing economies with relatively favourable endowments of natural resources might achieve economic take-off through exploitation of their resource slack? This possibility will be examined here with reference to theories pertaining to the development process of resource-rich economies.

4.4.1 Colonialism and the vent-for-surplus theory

The so-called 'vent-for-surplus theory' by a Burmese economist, Hla Myint (1971, ch. 5) focused on the process of development in 'empty lands' with low population density, large tracts of unused land, and abundant natural resources, typically found in South-east Asia and Africa at the outset of Western colonization. When these economies were integrated into international trade under colonialism, unused natural resources (hitherto having had no value to indigenous people) began to command market value since they were found useful to produce primary commodities of high external demand. These natural resources, when exploited by foreign capital and entrepreneurship, became a new source of income. A typical example is the development of Malaysia as a major exporter of primary commodities through the exploitation of tin-mines and the conversion of jungle to rubber plantations by migrant labourers from China and India, mobilized by British capital.

Such vent-for-surplus development, however, did not bring about significant increases in the levels of income and living of the native people. According to Hla Myint, this was because colonial government and foreign enterprises in collusion suppressed education and skill formation of native workers to preserve the source of cheap labour. Another underlying factor was identified as the monopolistic exploitation of small peasants by foreign traders (Hla Myint, 1965, chs. 3 and 5). A similar perspective prevailed on the regressive effects of foreign entrepreneurs' activities in mines and plantations to create enclaves in indigenous economies and consume large resource rents for the import of luxurious goods from abroad. This argument was once widely accepted to explain poverty and underdevelopment in former colonial economies (Singer, 1950; Boeke, 1953; S. Lewis, 1989).

This theory, together with 'dependency theory'—advancing the neo-Marxist perspective that poverty in the Third World is bound to be reproduced in order to maintain the high rate of return to capital in advanced economies (Baran, 1957; Furtado, 1963; Frank, 1967)—provided an ideology in support of import-substitution-industrialization policies and nationalization of foreign-owned enterprises and resources (see Section 8.2.4).

However, a strong criticism of these theories was made by Jamaica-born W. A. Lewis (1970, ch. 1). He insisted that it was not large plantations but small peasants that made a major contribution to increased export of tropical crops in the late nineteenth to the early twentieth century. Peasants' income, if not the wage rate, did increase in this process through more intensive use of their family labour and land resources. Further, he maintained that incomes produced from mines and plantations also had the effect of inducing local industrialization. Although he recognized that some colonial policies had repressive effects on the development of local economies, the meagre supply of public goods such as education and roads was not intended by colonial governments to suppress local development. The governments failed to undertake major public investment simply because their financial basis was very weak at that time. Thus, he conjectured that if the tropical export boom from the 1880s had not been interrupted by the World Depression in the 1930s, many tropical economies would have been able to switch gradually from natural resource-based economies to industrial economies.

Thus, interpretation of the intentions and consequences of colonial policies differs sharply between Hla Myint and Lewis. However, these two great economists, both born in the Third World, are in complete agreement that whether economic growth based on exploitation of natural resource slack could lead to sustained economic growth and increased welfare of indigenous people depended critically on mobilization of resource rent for investment in human capital and on improvements in both physical and institutional infrastructure for efficient functioning of the market mechanism.

4.4.2 The staple theory

The 'staple theory', originally developed by Canadian economic historians (Innis, 1933; Watkins, 1963), has the same theoretical structure as the vent-for-surplus theory for explaining the development process of empty lands under the impact of international trade. However, this theory, based on the historical experience of developed economies, focused on the transition pattern in the economic development of empty lands from exploitation of natural resource slack for export to growth in domestic commerce and industry.

'Staple' here means a major primary commodity which plays a leading role in expansion of exports from the empty lands. As population increases owing to employment and income opportunities created from the staple export, domestic consumption as well as the processing and transportation activities related to staple production and export would increase, inducing developments in domestic commerce and industry. However, it takes time before a local population can reach a threshold beyond which scale economies operate for commerce and industry. If unused slack of resources for the production of a staple is exhausted before this point is reached, sustained economic growth cannot be achieved.

Therefore, the successful transition from development based on natural resource exploitation to that based on expansion in commercial and industrial activities would require switching from one staple to another based on different natural resources until the economy reaches a threshold of industrial and commercial development. In Canada, this switching took place from cod and fur on the East Coast to timber in inland forests, and further to wheat in the Great Plains. Through this process the domestic market was expanded with developments in commercial and transportation networks accompanied by developments in timber and wheat mills as well as manufactures for domestic consumption demands.

Such switching among staples was carried out by the private profit-seeking motives of farmers, traders, and mining entrepreneurs. However, effective switching to sustain the growth momentum of a resource-based economy must be supported by the supply of public goods. The switching from coastal marine products to timber and wheat could not have been possible without public investment in inland transportation infrastructure such as canals and railways. Institutional infrastructure such as land registry and homesteading had been developed to push the cultivation frontiers to the West. As the frontiers began to be closed, development of agricultural research and extension systems was required to maintain the vigour of wheat exports (North, 1955). Many kinds of physical, human, and institutional infrastructure had to be laid out for developments in commerce and industry.

Development mechanism, as described by the staple theory, was successful in transforming empty lands in North America and Australasia into economies of sustained growth resulting in major gains in the economic welfare of the resident population (albeit at the expense of the aboriginal population). No comparable outcome has yet been achieved from the vent-for-surplus growth in Asia and Africa. The failure in the latter to reach sustained economic growth may be explained by colonial exploitation policies, a late start in development interrupted by the World Depression, or other factors. Yet, it is certain from comparisons between the staple theory experienced and the vent-for-surplus growth that the simple exploitation of natural resources alone can neither sustain economic growth nor improve the living standards of indigenous populations. The problem for the developing economies that are still endowed with relatively abundant natural resources is to find a way to mobilize rent produced from the exploitation of natural resources for investment in human capital and social overhead capital needed for shifting to sustainable economic development.

4.4.3 The Dutch disease

While the endowment of abundant natural resources is a large asset for economic development, it sometimes harbours a pitfall leading to economic retardation. This phenomenon is called the 'Dutch disease', after the experience of the Netherlands on its discovery of a rich natural gas deposit in the North Sea in the late 1950s. Exploitation of this new resource base brought about a major improvement in the balance of trade for the Netherlands, but ironically resulted in declines in domestic industries with increased unemployment. Appreciation in the real rate of exchange for local currency resulted from increased trade surplus, which undermined the international competitive position of agriculture and industry (Cordon and Neary, 1982).

In general, the shrinkage in value added in the agricultural and manufacturing sectors in resource-rich economies due to the resource export boom is more than compensated for by increased income in the resource sector. However, because the mining of gas and oil as well as minerals is characterized by high capital intensity (Bairoch, 1975, ch. 3), the increase in employment in the mining sector is not sufficient to absorb workers laid off from agriculture and industry.

A part of this employment loss may be compensated for by increased employment in the production of non-tradables, such as construction and services, for which expanded demand is derived from the booming resource sector. This intersectoral labour reallocation, however, usually involves a significant time-lag.

The danger for resource-rich economies is that the resource-export booms, such as those experienced in the first and the second oil crisis in 1973–5 and 1979–81 respectively, vastly increase export prices and earnings but are also abrupt and short-lived. Sharp appreciation in the exchange rate of the local currency in the boom period tends to seriously damage domestic agriculture and industry, resulting in an irreversible loss in fixed facilities, and labour and management skills for the production of non-resource tradables. As a result, recovery of these sectors will become difficult. Meanwhile, with the collapse of the resource boom, derived demand for non-tradables will decline precipitously. A major economic slump with a high unemployment rate will then become inevitable. If some key manufactures (or agriculture) having strategic complementarities with other industries are destroyed by the natural resource boom, the economy may not only be unable to return to the former development path but might even be trapped at a low-level equilibrium (Krugman, 1987, 1991; Matsuyama, 1991).

This pathology of the Dutch disease can be observed in Nigeria. As a major oil exporter, this country benefited from a major export boom during in the two oil-crisis periods. Similar to other developing economies, the official exchange rate was fixed. However, because much of increased oil revenue was spent for conspicuous development projects and government consumption, excess effective demands were created that resulted in inflation. The real rate of exchange sharply appreciated under the fixed official exchange as the domestic price level increased faster than the international level. Consequently, the sectors producing non-oil tradables, especially agriculture, were severely damaged. Rural villages were deserted, and urban slums were inflated by migrants seeking employment in service sectors. This process was aggravated by the government's construction of modern large-scale, capital-intensive industries, based on large oil revenues and foreign credits attracted by high solvency of Nigeria in the expectation of continued high oil prices. After the collapse of the second oil boom in 1981, Nigeria was left with desolated rural villages and swarms of unemployed workers in cities—a situation resembling the low-equilibrium trap in the strategic complementarity theory.

This Nigerian experience was commonly shared by many other oil exporters such as Mexico (Gelb *et al.*, 1988; Little *et al.*, 1993). However, an example of escape from the Dutch Disease is found in the case of Indonesia (Pinto, 1987). Like Nigeria, Indonesia had a high dependency on oil for both government revenue and export earnings. However, during the two oil booms, the Indonesian government increased assistance to agriculture through investment in irrigation and agricultural research as well as giving subsidies for fertilizers and other farm inputs, so that the productive base of domestic agriculture was strengthened. This was demonstrated by their achievement of self-sufficiency in rice. Also, a disciplined fiscal policy prevented galloping inflation. Repeated devaluations in the exchange rate (1978, 1983, 1986), together with liberalization in international trade and foreign direct investment, were successful in supporting the development of labour-intensive manufacture in which Indonesia's comparative advantage lay (Koguro and Kohama, 1995).

Major differences in the economic growth performance of Nigeria and Indonesia can be observed in Tables 2.1 and 2.2. The contrast between Nigeria and Indonesia was not unique but was rather general between Sub-Saharan African and East Asia (Thorbecke, 1995*a*). This shows that a rich endowment of natural resources is not necessarily a good support for economic development, but can instead be a stumbling-block. It also clearly demonstrates that such a trap for resource-rich economies can be avoided with the application of appropriate policies.

NOTES

1. Allen argued that landlords' innovation did not increase yields much but reduced labour inputs significantly. His view is consistent with Marx's that enclosure of smallholders' plots into large estates by landlords contributed to the formation of an industrial reserve army (ch. 5, sect. 1). According to Allen, however, not many labourers displaced from agriculture in the eighteenth century were able to find productive employment in manufacturing.
2. This section draws heavily on Kikuchi and Hayami (1985). For a comprehensive treatment of international agricultural technology transfer, see Hayami and Ruttan (1985, chs. 9 and 10).
3. Interregional diffusion of agricultural technology has always been a major source of productivity growth in agriculture since prehistoric times (Sauer, 1952). In the case of rice, the transfer of drought-resistant and short-maturing varieties from the state of Champa in central Indo-China to central and south China resulted in major increases in rice production during the Sung, Yuang, and Ming Dynasties (the twelfth to the seventeenth centuries), as these varieties permitted the practice of double-cropping (Ho, 1956; Barker and Herdt, 1985: 17). However, such premodern technology transfer was typically very slow relative to technology transfer in the era of scientific agriculture, as it was not speeded up by organized adaptive research and extension.

5

Capital Accumulation in Economic Development

The previous chapter demonstrated that even low-income economies suffering from depletion of natural resources because of strong population pressure should be able to achieve modern economic development by mobilizing the efforts of numerous small countryside producers if they are supported by an adequate supply of public goods. The major problem that low-income economies have to face in their early development stage is how to promote substitution of natural resources by labour with complementary growth in labour and capital (as shown in Figure 1.2). Once these economies successfully become industrialized, their dependency on natural resources will decline rapidly. At that stage, sustained economic growth hinges critically on how to promote the accumulation of capital and facilitate its substitution for labour.

Of course, the effort to increase the productivity of labour by applying more capital has progressed since the beginning of human history. However, at the stage when natural resource endowments were the binding constraint on people's living, the primary concern would have been how to increase the productivity of natural resources by applying more labour and capital. It has been under the new technology regime since the Industrial Revolution that the substitution of capital for labour is seen as the central issue in economic development.

Many developing economies are trying to achieve rapid industrialization under high population pressure and severe natural resource constraints. A strategy commonly adopted has been to maximize the rate of capital accumulation under the government's directive. In this strategy, capital tends to be conceived as large-scale modern machinery and factories embodying the labour-saving technology advanced in high-income economies, while due consideration is often not paid to the use of scarce capital relative to abundant labour by making efforts to adjust technologies to relative resource endowments. The inefficiency of this approach has now become evident as revealed by the stagnation of the economies that tried to achieve high rates of saving and investment for the promotion of industrialization under central planning and command by government.

There is no doubt that the accumulation of capital is a necessary condition of industrial development. Whether the accumulated capital can be effectively utilized depends on human capacities and social organization. Developments in technology and human capacity are resource-using activities aimed at increasing productive power in the future, similar to investment in tangible capital such as machinery and factories. The rate of economic growth depends not only on the rate of capital accumulation but also on its allocation among various investment opportunities, especially between tangible and intangible capital. What is the optimum level and allocation of investment to set developing economies on the track to sustained industrial development? What institutions and organizations are needed to mobilize and allocate investible funds in a manner compatible with the development goal?

This chapter and the next aim to undertake theoretical and empirical preparation in seeking an answer to this basic question in development policy. First, a historical perspective is developed on how the strategy geared to strengthening capital accumulation under government control and guidance became predominant among developing economies after World War II. Then, the theory underlying this strategy is tested by the method of growth accounting.

5.1 From Adam Smith to Marx

A strong tradition in economics since Adam Smith has been to identify capital accumulation as the engine of economic growth. The tradition assumes that the mechanism of achieving a high rate of capital accumulation is inherent in capitalistic market economies, and therefore, by fostering this mechanism, high economic growth can be realized.

5.1.1 Capital in Adam Smith

In his advocacy of *laissez-faire* and small government, Adam Smith (1723–90) stands opposite to the model of high accumulation under government directives. However, with his argument that a condition of economic growth is increased investment by suppressing consumption, he was a forerunner of the models of capitalist development based on high saving and high investment, including the model of Karl Marx.

Smith's *Wealth of Nations* ([1776] 1937) was a comprehensive treatment on how social and economic systems should be structured to maximize the wealth (or income) of Britain (among other nations) on the eve of its Industrial Revolution. In his theory, it is labour engaged in 'useful and productive' work that produces value to society. The number of 'useful and productive' workers employed as well as their productivity depends on the stock of capital accumulated, as stated in his words:

The number of useful and productive labours, it will hereafter appear, is every where in proportion to the quantity of capital stock which is employed in setting them to work, and to the particular way in which it is so employed. (A. Smith [1776] 1937: lviii)

Adam Smith considered the increase in capital stock critically important in raising the productivity of labour as it advances the division of labour. In his famous example of pin manufacturing, he argued that a worker can hardly produce more than twenty pins in a day if he alone has to cover the entire production process; however, if the production process can be sub-divided into eighteen distinct operations, each assigned to a specialized worker, such that one man draws out the wire, another straightens it, a third cuts it, a fourth points it, and a fifth grinds it at the top, and so on, then more than four thousand pins per worker can be manufactured.

This great increase of the quantity of work, which in consequence of the division of labour, the same number of people are capable of performing, is owing to three different circumstances; first to the increase of dexterity in every particular workman; secondly to the saving of the time which is commonly lost in passing one species of work to another; and lastly to the invention of a great number of machines which facilitate and abridge labour, and enable one man to do the work of many. (A. Smith [1776] 1937: 7)

In order to execute this division of labour, both the funds to purchase workshops, tools, and materials, and the funds for payments to labourers in advance of the sale of pins (wage fund) must be available to a capitalist-entrepreneur. The sum of these is Adam Smith's stock of capital. As this stock usable by capitalist-entrepreneurs increases, the division of labour can be advanced by employing more labourers for more differentiated operations.

According to Smith, this stock of capital in society accumulates through 'parsimony' and 'frugality' of industrious entrepreneurs in manufacturing and it diminishes through 'prodigality' and 'misconduct' of absolute mon-archs, landed aristocrats, and privileged merchants. Therefore, the depletion of capital can be prevented by reducing the incomes of those spendthrifts, such as cutting pensions to courtiers, removing tax exemptions to landlords, and abolishing monopoly trade licences to merchants. The accumulation of capital can be promoted by removing undue regulations and taxation on industrial capitalist-entrepreneurs.

Removal of government regulations on production and marketing activities not only contributes to increased income of the entrepreneur class and, thereby, increased rate of social savings, but also contributes to expansion in markets. The size of markets, together with the stock of capital, is a critical determinant of progress in the division of labour. For example, even if it is possible to produce hundreds of thousands of pins a day in a factory, such a mass production system (based on advanced division of labour) would not be adopted if market demand is too small to absorb the output. Therefore, unification of local markets into a national market through removal of regulations on domestic transactions greatly facilitates progress in the division of labour. Further, if trade monopolies and protective measures in the Mercantile System are broken, the domestic market is integrated into a large international market where major advances in the division of labour are expected. For Smith, since 'the division of labour arises from a propensity in human nature to exchange' (A. Smith [1776] 1937: 13), creation of a free and wide market by removal of undue regulations is the sufficient condition for progress in the division of labour, assuring sustained increases in the wealth of nations.

While Adam Smith strongly advocated free market competition, he recognized the importance of public goods for the support of the market mechanism, such as national defence, police and judicial systems, public infrastructure construction, and education. However, his strong repulsion against the Mercantile System led him to argue that the supply of public goods should be privatized as much as possible (e.g. private schools and toll-roads). It must be recognized, however, that his plan for small government was made after Britain had been unified into a nation with a wide domestic market based on military force and bureaucracy of the absolute monarch, and decent public infrastructure such as roads and canals had been constructed, based on government revenue derived from Mercantilism. If his theory had been formed earlier in the transition period from feudalism to absolutism, his proposed policies would no doubt have been different.

5.1.2 Ricardo revisited

The proposition that a mechanism of suppressing conspicuous consumption and increasing investment in 'useful and productive' activities is necessary for promoting economic growth is but one important pillar of Adam Smith's theory. In subsequent developments of the English Classical School, this mechanism is used as a central pillar of economic growth theory.

A representative example is Ricardo's model as explained earlier (Section 3.3.2). In his model, consumption of labourers—the majority of the population—is in the long run reduced to a minimum subsistence level under the ruthless force of the Malthusian population law. Surplus of industrial product above labourers' subsistence accrues to capitalists who have a high propensity to save and invest. This mechanism guarantees that high rates of capital accumulation and output growth will be sustained.

One force that would stop this growth process was identified by Ricardo as increases in food prices due to population pressure on limited land resources resulting in increased nominal wage rates. If this force were allowed to increase, social surplus (total product minus labour and capital costs) would be captured by the class of landlords who are prone to conspicuous consumption. In order to sustain the high rates of capital accumulation and economic growth, Ricardo advocated liberalization of cereal food imports as a means to prevent social surplus from being monopolized by 'prodigal' landed élites.

5.1.3 The Marx model of capitalist development*

Karl Marx (1818–83) created a unique theory of capitalist economic development. As he had initially learned economics from the English Classical School, the structure of his theory, laid out in *Das Kapital* ([1867–94] 1909–12), is similar to Ricardo's, even though underlying assumptions and policy implications are diametrically oppposed.

The basic similarity of Marx's model to Ricardo's is that labour supply to the modern industrial sector is infinitely elastic at an institutionally determined subsistence wage rate, which works as a basic support for rapid capital accumulation. However, Marx rejects the Malthusian population law as the mechanism for producing the infinitely clastic labour-supply curve. Instead, Marx based his explanation on the existence of the 'surplus' labour force beyond productively employed workers in the industrial sector, called the 'industrial reserve army'. The reserve army consists of lumpenproletariat in urban slums who stake out a bare living from various informal activities (from petty trade to pilferage), while seeking formal employment in the industrial sector. As such, they are readily available to accept employment at the subsistence wage rate upon recruitment by industrial employers. Therefore, as long as this reserve army exists, the industrial wage rate is prevented from rising above the subsistence level.

The basic assumption of the Marxian model is that the industrial reserve army will never be exhausted, as it is reproduced in the capitalistic development process. The original sources of the reserve army were small peasants and self-employed manufacturers using traditional production methods who were overcome by modern capitalistic enterprises and were compelled to seek employment in the labour market. The number of people ousted from traditional occupations continued to increase as the capitalist sector expanded, replenishing the industrial reserve army. On the other hand, capitalists always try hard to substitute capital for labour through large-scale mechanization. As a result, employment in the modern industrial sector increases more slowly than the speed of capital accumulation and output growth. This slow employment growth in the modern sector is sufficiently counteracted by additional entries to the reserve army from the traditional sector. Thus, Marx considered that the horizontal labour supply

* Readers not interested in technical analysis of economics may skip explanations with the use of Figure 5.1 in this section.

curve to capitalist entrepreneurs is not the product of natural population law, but the consequence of capitalism incessantly reproducing the industrial reserve army.

Even though the underlying mechanisms are thus different, both Marx and Ricardo shared the common view that the infinitely elastic labour supply at the subsistence wage rate is the basic mechanism supporting high capital accumulation and economic growth in the modern industrial economy. However, because strong motivation on the part of capitalists to save labour by means of increased use of capital is assumed by Marx, the income share of capital increases at the expense of labour's share, implying an inherently inequalizing tendency in the capitalist economy.

The Marxian model is reconstructed in the terms of modern economics in Figure 5.1. This figure corresponds to the left-hand diagram of Figure 3.5 which models Ricardo's theory. It represents the labour market for the modern capitalist sector ('industry' in Figure 3.5) in terms of a Marshallian partial equilibrium model, with the vertical and horizontal axes measuring the wage rate and employment respectively. In both figures, line DD represents a labour demand curve, corresponding to a schedule of labour's marginal value product for a given stock of capital.

The above assumptions are the same for Figures 5.1 and 3.5. Further, the labour supply curve (S') drawn horizontally at the subsistence wage rate ($\bar{W}$) in Figure 5.1 is similar to the long-run labour supply curve (LS) in Figure 3.5. However, while Ricardo's labour supply is assumed to be indefinitely horizontal in the long run owing to the Malthusian population law, Marx's

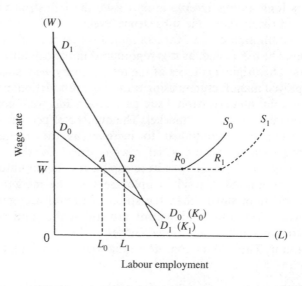

Labour employment

FIG. 5.1 *The Marx model of capitalist economic development*

begins to rise from a certain point (R_0) which represents exhaustion of the industrial reserve army.

Assume that in an initial period (0) a labour demand curve for the modern capitalist sector is located at line D_0D_0 corresponding to capital stock (K_0). The initial equilibrium is established at point A with labour employed by OL_0 at the subsistence wage rate $O\bar{W}$. However, according to Marx's assumption, the number of labourers seeking employment in the modern industrial sector measured by $\bar{W}R_0$ is larger than OL_0. Those unable to find employment stake out bare subsistence on informal activities in urban slums, awaiting the opportunity to be employed in the capitalist sector. This population, as measured by AR_0, is the industrial reserve army of Marx's definition. Therefore, increases in labour demand corresponding to capital accumulation do not result in an increase in the wage rate until point R_0 is reached.

Unlike Ricardo's long-run labour supply curve, which is indefinitely horizontal, Marx's curve begins to rise from point R_0 implying that capitalists have to offer higher wage rates to attract labourers when the reserve army is exhausted. However, in his model the reserve army is never drained. First, in the process of capitalist development, small self-employed producers in traditional agriculture and cottage industries are overcome by modern capitalist enterprises and fall to the rank of industrial reserve army. In terms of Figure 5.1, corresponding to an increase in capital stock from K_0 to K_1, as capitalists invest a major portion of their initial profit area ($AD_0\bar{W}$), the output of their enterprises expands from area AD_0OL_0 to BD_1OL_1. Outcompeted by this expansion in capitalist production, traditional self-employed producers and their family members are forced to seek employment in the capitalist sector, resulting in the elongation of the horizontal portion of labour supply curve to R_1.

Also, unlike Ricardo's case, Marx assumes the growth of industrial employment to be slower than the speed of capital accumulation. Ricardo had developed his theory in the late eighteenth century during the Industrial Revolution when automation (based on new power sources such as the steam engine) had not yet been highly developed. In his image, capital invested in the development of a factory production system was mainly used as the wage fund. Therefore, at a fixed subsistence wage-rate, employment was considered to increase parallel to increased capital stock.

In contrast, by the mid-nineteenth century when Marx developed his theory, automatic steam-powered machines were in common use, and a share of such fixed capital items in total capital stock increased. As a result, relative to rapid capital accumulation and output growth, employment increased rather slowly. This labour-saving effect of machine capital embodying new industrial technology is represented by a shift in labour demand from line D_0D_0 to D_1D_1. A change in the labour demand curve to a more steeply sloping one implies a technical change biased towards the labour-saving and capital-using direction in the Hick's definition (see Chapter 6, Section 4). With this bias the technological progress embodied in new machinery, the increase in employment from OL_0 to OL_1 became slower than the growth of output from area AD_0OL_0 to BD_1OL_1.

Thus, Marx envisioned that, with the ability of the modern capitalist production system to ruin traditional self-employed producers, together with the labour-saving bias in industrial technology, the industrial reserve army would never be exhausted. High rates of profit and capital accumulation in the capitalist economy are guaranteed by maintenance of low wage rates under the pressure of the ever-existing reserve army. In his view, the industrial reserve army is bound to be reproduced since it is the supporting arch for development of the capitalist economy.

The process of capitalist development, as described by Marx, necessarily involves rapid increases in inequality of income distribution. Unlike Ricardo's case—where the wage rate can rise in the short run (along SS in Figure 3.5) until the population adjusts to demand increases in the process of capital accumulation—no such possibility exists for industrial workers in Marx's world since they are under the constant threat of being replaced by reserve army constituents. Labourers' income is reduced relative to capitalists' by the labour-saving effect of modern industrial technology. This tendency is illustrated in Figure 5.1, in which the labourers' wage share income in total savings output decreases from $A\bar{W}OL_0/AD_0OL_0$ to $B\bar{W}OL_1/BD_1OL_1$, while the share of capitalists' profit rises from $AD_0\bar{W}/AD_0OL_0$ to $BD_1\bar{W}/BD_1OL_1$.[1]

Marx predicted that the increasing inequality in the capitalist economy would fuel hostility between the labourer and capitalist classes, eventually leading to a violent revolution in which capitalism based on private ownership of capital by a few would be transformed into socialism based on public (or the people's) ownership.[2] This prediction did not materialize in the history of advanced industrial economies. In Western Europe and North America, real wage rates have risen and the income share of labour (labour's share of total national income) has increased since the late nineteenth century (Section 6.1).

However, the Marxian model gives an important insight into the problem faced by today's developing economies. Many developing economies have attempted to achieve rapid development by concentrating investment in the modern industrial sector. In some cases, significant success has been recorded in the growth of industrial production. However, increases in employment have typically been much slower than output growth owing to concentration of investment in modern machinery and equipment embodying labour-saving technologies developed in high-income countries. On the other hand, the rate of increase in the labour force has been high under explosive population growth. Where labour absorption in the agricultural sector reaches the saturation point under the rapidly closing land frontiers, labour tends to be pushed from rural to urban areas. The swollen urban population beyond limited employment in the modern industrial sector of high-capital intensity has accumulated as lumpenproletariat in urban slums. Growing inequality and social instability visible in these economies are similar to the situation observed by Marx in mid-nineteenth century Europe. How to overcome this problem in developing economies during their early phase of industrialization is a question that needs to be resolved before they can advance to higher phases of development (Chapter 7).

A comment may be added on Marx's neglect of the possibility of the 'food problem' of the Ricardo–Schultz type (or 'the Ricardian Trap' in Chapter 3, Section 3). He did not envisage the problem of food supply shortage to result in increases in the cost of living and the wage rate of workers, presumably because he assumed that advanced industrial economies like England could obtain a cheap supply of food and materials from overseas. Also, Marx assumed that, while small peasants may be outcompeted by large-scale capitalist farms to drop out into urban slums, their holdings would be combined in larger and more efficient farms under management by capitalist entrepreneurs leading to increases in the domestic food supply.

As Marx had observed increased food imports in England after the repeal of the Corn Laws (1840) and the establishment of large-scale commercial farming, he would have felt no need to worry about the food problem. Absence of concern about the food problem in Marx's theory of capitalist development seems to reflect the decline in its importance as industrialization advanced. Alternatively stated, it reflects the tendency of successful industrial development to free the economy from the constraint of natural resources.

5.2 Development Theories and Policies after World War II

Both Classical and Marxian economics identified the mechanism of suppressing consumption as a basis of high rates of capital accumulation and economic growth inherent in capitalist market economies. In contrast, in the development theories that became dominant during the quarter century following World War II, this market mechanism was considered insufficient for achieving high accumulation and growth in newly independent developing economies, because they were too poor to mobilize sufficient savings. This view was based on the classical assumption that the saving rate is zero at the subsistence income level and rises exponentially in response to increases in income per capita.

Under this assumption, poor developing economies at a near-subsistence income level can hardly expect to escape from the vicious circle between low saving and low income if resource allocations are left to the free market. The policy prescription envisaged then was to use government orders and regulations to suppress consumption, or to require that investible funds be set aside before consumption (Srinivasan, 1990; Krueger, 1995). Such a theoretical perspective was influential in inducing many developing economies to adopt development strategies inclined towards the socialist model (based on central planning and directives).

5.2.1 The theory of balanced growth

A theory which had a major impact on this policy was the 'theory of balanced growth' by Rosenstein-Rodan (1943) and Ragner Nurkse (1952, 1953). This was based on the recognition that newly independent economies after World War II could not expect economic growth, based on rapid increases in primary commodity exports, as experienced from the nineteenth century until the start of the World Depression in 1929. This export pessimism led to the conclusion that there was no other option for these economies but to undertake development by manufacturing hitherto imported industrial commodities. It was feared, however, that this industrialization strategy would be so hampered by small domestic markets that large-scale production of any commodity from a modern industrial plant would produce more than its market could absorb. Therefore, for modern industrial development to be viable, various industries should be simultaneously promoted so that they would create markets for each other (e.g. employees of the shoe manufacturer would purchase shirts while those of the shirt manufacture would purchase shoes)—a perspective recently being renovated as the theory of 'strategic complementarity' among various industries (Murphy *et al.*, 1989; Bardhan, 1995: 2292–6), which will be discussed later in Section 8.4.2.

This 'balanced growth' or simultaneous development of many industries would require mobilization of large amounts of resources at one time. According to Rosenstein-Rodan and Nurkse, poor developing economies were characterized by a large surplus of labour employed at zero marginal cost in the traditional sector (similar to the assumption of the dual economy model in Section 3.3.3). Under this assumption of disguised unemployment, the labour supply would create no major bottleneck to a 'great leap forward' in industrialization.

The key to the success of the balanced growth strategy would, of course, be to mobilize sufficient funds for simultaneous development of many industries. Large-scale capital imports from advanced economies, as experienced in the era of colonialism for the purpose of development in primary commodity production, could not be expected after independence. At the same time, the domestic saving rate was typically low in poor developing economies. Thus, the theory of balanced growth left no alternative for development in newly independent nations other than to establish a mechanism of forced saving under government command.

5.2.2 Application of the Harrod–Domar model*

A similar prescription was also derived from the Harrod–Domar model. In the 1940s Roy Harrod (1948) and Evsey Domar (1946) separately developed a macro-dynamic model through an extension of Keynes's theory. The model's original intent was to identify the source of instability in the growth of developed economies where effective demand is normally exceeded by supply capacity. In the 1950s and 1960s this model was applied to economic planning in developing economies. The basic equation in the Harrod–Domar model is very simple, as expressed by:

$$g = s/c, \tag{5.1}$$

where $g = \Delta Y/Y$ is the growth rate of national income Y, $s = S/Y$ is the ratio of saving S to income, $c = \Delta k/\Delta Y$ is the marginal capital–output ratio (or capital coefficient) which measures additional capital investment required to produce one additional unit of national income. In the model c is assumed to be a technologically given constant and, therefore, equal to average capital–output ratio (K/N). It can easily be verified that equation 5.1 holds under the assumption of Keynesian equilibrium between saving (S) and investment $(I = \Delta K)$.

Under the assumption of constant c, g increases proportionally with s. Because s is considered to increase proportionally with income per capita, s is bound to be low and, hence, g will be low in low-income economies if savings and investment are left to private decisions in the free market. The model implies, therefore, that the promotion of investment by government planning and command is needed to accelerate economic growth in low-income economies. In fact, the Harrod–Domar model provided a framework for economic planning in developing economies, such as India's Five-Year Plan (Mahalanobis, 1955; Srinivasan, 1990).

5.2.3 The model of low-equilibrium trap*

These models, which consider economic growth to be totally dependent on investment in tangible capital, were combined with the population theory to produce a model of a vicious circle between low per capita income and low saving in low-income economies, alternatively called the models of the'low-equilibrium trap', 'critical minimum effort', and 'great leap forward' (Leibenstein, 1954; Nelson, 1956). A model of this type is structured in Figure 5.2 to be consistent with the Harrod–Domar model.

The upper section of Figure 5.2 shows the relationship between the population growth rate $(\Delta N/N)$ and income per capita (Y/N). Since per

---

* Readers not interested in the technical analysis of economics may skip this section.

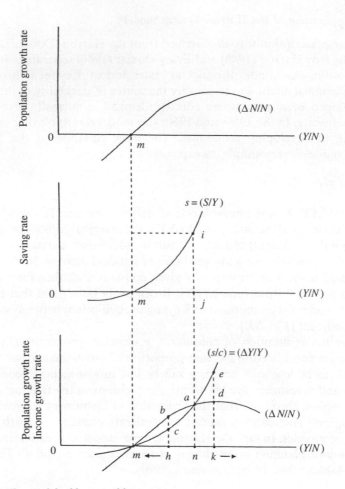

FIG. 5.2 *The model of low-equilibrium trap*

capita income is largely proportional to the wage-rate, the curve of $(\Delta N/N)$ in Figure 5.2 corresponds to the $G\bar{W}H$ curve in Figure 3.3, and m in Figure 5.2 corresponds to $\bar{W}$ in Figure 3.3, with $\underline{om}$ measuring the subsistence level of per capita income at which the population growth rate is zero.

The middle section depicts the relationship between the saving rate $(s = S/Y)$ and per capita income (Y/N). As conventionally assumed, s rises exponentially as Y/N increases. The saving rate curve is drawn to cut the horizontal axis through m, implying that people consume all their income at the subsistence level. The conclusion will be little affected by assuming that the cut-through point slightly deviates from m.

The lower section analyses the determination of income per capita and its growth-rate by combining the relationships in the upper and the middle sections. In this diagram, the population growth curve $(\Delta N/N)$ is moved down after being divided by the capital–output ratio (c). The value of s/c is equivalent to the income growth-rate $(\Delta Y/Y)$ according to the basic equation in the Harrod–Domar model.[3]

Point m in the lower diagram represents a stable equilibrium. If Y/N declines below *om*, population decreases faster than total income, so that per capita income will be pushed back towards point m. On the other hand, even if per capita income rises above point m to point h for some reason (e.g. bumper crops or increased foreign aid), the population growth-rate (*hb*) becomes higher than the income growth rate (*hc*), so that income per capita will be pulled down to point m. Thus, economies located at point m would not be able to escape this subsistence income level with modest increases in investment that they may be able to mobilize because any growth in per capita income from such modest efforts will be eaten up by increased population, and thereby pushed back to the subsistence level. This vicious circle between low-income level and economic stagnation is aptly called the 'low-equilibrium trap'.

Escape from this trap is not possible with cumulative increases in modest investment over an extended period. In order to achieve sustained growth, investment large enough to push the economy beyond point n must be attempted at one time. Once the economy goes beyond the threshold (n) to reach point k, the income growth rate (*ke*) becomes higher than the population growth rate (*kd*) so that growth in income per capita becomes self-sustainable.

In order to escape from the low-equilibrium trap to sustained economic growth, it is necessary to mobilize a high saving rate, as represented by *ji* at the subsistence income level (*om*), in which no saving is generated if left to the market mechanism. This extraordinary jump in the mobilization of saving and investment is a 'critical minimum effort' for low-income economies to accomplish. The model implies that, if large-scale capital imports as experienced during the colonial era are unlikely to be forthcoming to newly independent economies, no development alternative is left for them but to set aside necessary investible funds from meagre income by forcing people to tighten their belts on hungry stomachs.

5.2.4 Development theories and policy choice

It is not certain how much these development theories (with heavy emphasis on capital accumulation) influenced policy choice in developing economies. Yet, many newly independent nations adopted policies to expand the sector producing investment goods—at the expense of the production of consumption goods and services—by such means as direct investment by state enterprises, government-directed credits, regulations on marketing, and discriminatory taxation. The agricultural exploitation policy (as explained in Chapter 3, Section 3) was a part of this strategy. Export tax on agricultural commodities and high marketing margins of farm products by state monopoly procurement were an important source of government revenue for industrial investment. Lowered agricultural product prices caused by these policies suppressed farmers' income and consumption. At the same time, lowered food prices kept the cost of living and the wage rate of industrial workers low and thereby kept capital profit and investment incentives high.

In the former Soviet Union and other socialist economies the strategy of high capital accumulation by government command and planning was strongly and thoroughly executed. That the Soviet economy appeared relatively successful in achieving a high rate of growth until the 1960s had attracted developing countries to the socialist system. Another factor had been a rejection in developing economies of market economies, which had been imposed upon them by colonial powers and viewed as a mechanism of exploitation, especially where market channels had been controlled by ethnic minorities (such as Indians in Africa and Chinese in South-East Asia). Among economic professionals, too, high regard for Keynesian intervention policies, coupled with the classical and Marxian traditions, made the postwar development theories (with heavy emphasis on capital accumulation under the government's directive) easier to accept.

The nature and consequences of such policies will be examined in Chapter 8. However, to briefly state the conclusion, enforcement of capital accumulation by government command and planning did not yield high economic growth rates in developing economies. The failure of this strategy became evident with the collapse of the centrally planned economies in the 1980s. In general, for three to four decades since World War II, economic growth performances has been poorer in developing countries, such as India, Nigeria, and Ghana, that leaned more strongly towards socialist systems.

5.3 Growth Accounting Test*

Failure of the development strategy geared to mobilizing high domestic saving by government command has cast a doubt on the traditional view that capital accumulation is the key to economic growth and that a weak supply of savings is the major constraint on the growth of developing economies. A crude but robust method to resolve this question on empirical grounds is called 'growth accounting'.

* Readers not interested in technical detail may skip this section.

5.3.1 The growth-accounting equation

Growth accounting assumes an aggregate production function relating an economy's output to the inputs of labour and capital (and natural resources if separated from capital). Using this production function, contributions of increased inputs to output growth are measured, and any residual not explained by input increases is considered a measure of growth in the productivity of factor inputs. This residual, called growth in 'total factor productivity' (abbreviated as 'total productivity'), is a measure of technological progress broadly defined as output growth when inputs are being held constant.

In practice, however, it is difficult to measure labour and capital accurately. In terms of its contribution to output, the number of work hours is a more direct measure of labour input than the number of workers, but data for the former are more difficult to obtain. It is more difficult to adjust labour inputs of different quality due to age, sex, and education into a single homogeneous labour variable. Likewise, the measurement of capital is subject to many problems, such as rate of utilization, vintage, and depreciation, etc. Moreover, if economies of scale operate, contributions to output growth are not proportional to input increases. Also, aggregate output can rise with no increase in inputs if factors of production are reallocated more efficiently across regions and across industries. Specification of the form of production function for empirical analysis also involves a multitude of problems (Jorgenson and Griliches, 1969; Jorgenson *et al.*, 1972).

Since it is difficult to accurately measure the contributions of input increases to output growth, growth in total productivity measured as a residual is not free from large observational and approximation errors. In attempting to reduce these errors, the growth-accounting analysis necessarily becomes highly complex and sophisticated (see Chapter 6, Section 3). In this section, however, analysis will be based on the most simplified accounting equation to produce robust conclusions on the determinants of modern economic development. For non-technical readers it is not necessary to understand the mathematical derivations that follow. It is sufficient to understand the formal structures of the derived equations (Equations 5.3, 5.7, and 5.8) used for empirical analysis.

First, an aggregate production function of the following form is assumed:

$$Y = AF(L, K), \tag{5.2}$$

where national product (Y) is produced from labour (L) and capital (K). A specific assumption here is that $F(L, K)$, which represents the output produced from given L and K for the initial period, increases A-times with technological progress. Specification of the multiplicative shift in the production function implies the neutral technological change in Hicks's definition, by which marginal productivities of labour and capital change in equal rates for a given capital–labour ratio (see Chapter 6, Section 4).

In addition, another simplifying assumption of linear homogeneity or constant return to scale is adopted. Then, taking total derivatives of equation 5.2 with respect to time (t) and dividing all term by Y yields:

$$G(Y) = G(A) + \alpha G(L) + \beta G(K),\qquad(5.3)$$

where $G(\ )$ represents the growth rate of any variable specified inside the parentheses, e.g. $G(Y) = \Delta Y/Y$, and α and β are production elasticities of labour and capital respectively, which are expressed by

$$\alpha = (\partial Y/\partial L)/(Y/L) \quad \text{and} \quad \beta = (\partial Y/\partial K)/(Y/K)\qquad(5.4)$$

which present percentage increases in output relative to 1 per cent increases in labour and capital respectively. Under the assumption of linear homogeneity, the sum of elasticities is equal to one ($\alpha + \beta = 1$).

Since $G(L)$ and $G(K)$ are the growth-rates of labour and capital, multiplying them by α and β estimates the contributions of increases in L and K to growth in Y, as represented by the second and third terms in the right-hand side of equation 5.3. If time-series data are available for Y, L, and K, $G(A)$ can be calculated by subtracting measured $\alpha G(L)$ and $\beta G(K)$ from the measured $G(Y)$ according to the relation of equation 5.3. Since $G(A)$ is a residual in the growth of Y after the effects of L and K are subtracted, it estimates the growth of output where the inputs of labour and capital are held constant.

Statistical estimation of production elasticities from input–output data are possible but subject to major technical difficulties.[4] A widely used convention is to regard the income shares of labour and capital as equivalent with α and β under the assumption of competitive equilibrium in factor markets. The income shares of labour and capital are the shares of returns to labour (labour income) and to capital (capital income) in total income, respectively. If the input of labour is denoted by L and the rate of return to labour (wage rate) by w, labour income is given as wL. Similarly, capital income is given as rK, with K and r denoting, respectively, the input of capital and the rate of return to capital (profit rate). National income (Y) defined as value added in a national economy is the sum of labour and capital incomes, i.e. $Y = wL + rK$. The income shares of labour and capital are represented by wL/Y and rK/Y respectively, which add up to one.

Under the assumption that labour and capital markets are competitive, in equilibrium the wage rate (w) should be equal to labour's marginal productivity ($\partial Y/\partial L$) and the profit rate (r) equal to capital's marginal productivity ($\partial Y/\partial K$). Then, α and β in Equation 5.4 can be expressed as

$$\begin{aligned}\alpha &= (\partial Y/\partial L)/(\partial Y/L) = wL/Y, \\ \beta &= (\partial Y/\partial K)/(\partial Y/L) = rK/Y\end{aligned}\qquad(5.5)$$

to establish the equivalence between factors' production elasticities and income shares. However, to the extent that the real economy diverges from competitive equilibrium, errors in the results of growth-accounting analysis are inevitable from the use of factor shares in lieu of production elasticities.

Growth in total national income or product can be accounted for by increases in factor inputs and total productivity with the use of equation 5.3. However, a more relevant analysis for economic development might be identification of the sources of growth in income per capita or income per unit of labour input (labour productivity). The accounting equation for growth in per capita income (Y/N) can be obtained by subtracting the growth rate of population $G(N)$ from the left-hand side of equation 5.3 and $(\alpha + \beta)G(N)$ from the right-hand side (where $\alpha + \beta = 1$) as follows

$$G(Y) - G(N) = G(A) + \alpha[G(L) - G(N)] + \beta[G(K) - G(N)]. \qquad (5.6)$$

For infinitely small differential changes, the difference between two variables' growth rates is equal to the growth rate of their ratio. Therefore, equation 5.6 may be approximated by

$$G(Y/N) = G(A) + \alpha G(L/N) + \beta G(K/N) \qquad (5.7)$$

which can be used as the growth-accounting equation for income per capita.

Similarly, by subtracting $G(L)$ from both sides of equation 5.3, the growth-accounting equation for labour productivity can be approximated by

$$G(Y/L) = G(A) + \beta G(K/L). \qquad (5.8)$$

In the world of differential calculus with respect to infinitely small time changes, the same estimates of $G(A)$ can be obtained from the use of equations 5.3, 5.7, and 5.8. However, because empirical analysis must be based on observations for discrete time-units (such as years), approximation errors may produce slightly different estimates for different equations. However, these errors are likely to be minor relative to errors arising from such simplifying assumptions as constant returns to scale and competitive factor market equilibrium as well as from observational errors in variables. Considering the possibility of major errors, the growth-accounting analysis could only be effective to identify very broad trends.

5.3.2 The relation with the Harrod–Domar model*

Before proceeding to empirical application, it would be useful to clarify the relationship between the growth-accounting equation (5.3) and the basic equation of the Harrod–Domar model (5.1).

---

* Readers not interested in technical detail may skip this section.

Because g in equation 5.1 is the same as $G(Y)$ in equation 5.3, and $s = S/Y$ is equivalent to $\Delta K/Y$ under the equilibrium between S and $I(= \Delta K)$, equation 5.1 can be expressed as

$$G(Y) = [(\Delta Y/\Delta K)/(Y/K)](\Delta K/K). \tag{5.9}$$

This growth equation for discrete time change may be considered an approximation of

$$G(Y) = \beta G(K). \tag{5.10}$$

However, the Harrod–Domar model assumes constancy in the capital–output ratio. Under this assumption, β equals one because the marginal and the average capital–output ratios are the same. Therefore, the Harrod–Domar basic growth equation boils down to

$$G(Y) = G(K). \tag{5.11}$$

Namely, the Harrod–Domar equation is a special case of equation 5.3, in which both α and $G(A)$ are zero, and β equals one.

The assumption of $\alpha = 0$ stems from the assumption that labour and capital are not substitutable in production, and hence output does not increase by applying more labour for a given stock of capital. Harrod's original theory dealt with the short-run situation in which designs of factories and machinery were fixed in a certain optimum combination with labour. However, in the long-run process of development, where major technological advances are expected, fixed factor proportion does not seem to be a relevant assumption.

The assumption of $\alpha = 0$ might be relevant to developing economies if disguised unemployment exists as assumed in the theory of balanced growth. However, empirical evidence casts doubt on the existence of surplus labour at zero marginal productivity (Schultz, 1964; Hopper; 1965; Kao *et al.*, 1964; Yotopoulos, 1968).

More irrelevant to long-term development analysis is the assumption of no technological progress, though it could be appropriate in dealing with the problem of short-run economic fluctuations. Harrod considered the possibility that technological progress would keep the capital–output ratio constant at a given interest rate (the 'Harrod-neutral' technological change equivalent to the 'Hicks-capital-using' technological change). However, in applying the Harrod–Domar model to the design of development policies, it appears only natural to incorporate efforts to reduce the capital–output ratio (c) by means of technological advancement.

The reason why a model assuming fixed capital–output ratio and no factor substitution was popular among planners and policy-makers in developing economies may be explained partly by the underestimation of developing economies' capacity to carry out technological innovations, as well as overestimation of disguised unemployment. Another reason may be based on the misunderstanding by economic theorists of the historical trend of capital–output ratio. For example, Nicholas Kaldor argued in his influential paper (1961) that constancy in the capital–output ratio is one of the stylized facts common in the growth processes of advanced economies, with which the economic growth theory must be consistent.

However, it has become evident from the accumulation of long-term economic statistics that the capital–output ratio declined in advanced economies from the late nineteenth century to at least the mid-twentieth century, though it is most likely that it increased before then. These trends will be observed through the empirical analysis of growth accounting that follows.

5.3.3 Sources of modern economic growth

We will now review the results of simple growth accounting with the use of equations 5.3, 5.7, and 5.8, or slight modifications thereof.

Application of this analysis to US economic growth was pioneered by Moses Abramovitz (1956) and Robert Solow (1957), followed by many other studies on the growth process of advanced industrial economies within the past 100 years. Results of these studies presented a major challenge to the conventional view that capital accumulation is the engine of economic growth.

The central message of growth-accounting analysis is illustrated by the following calculation by Kuznets (1966: 79–85). He summarized that in advanced industrial economies (in Western Europe and North America) for fifty to 100 years (ending in the middle of this century), the average growth rates of real income per capita ranged mostly from 1 to 2 per cent per year with an average of about 1.5 per cent. Meanwhile, the average number of work hours per capita decreased by about 0.3 per cent per year. The capital–output ratio declined by about 30 per cent for the whole period. This means that the per capita rate of growth in capital should have been 70 per cent of the per capita income growth rate, namely about 1 per cent per year (1.5 per cent × 0.7). The income shares of labour and capital in advanced economies are typically 0.75 and 0.25, respectively. If those average figures are applied to equation 5.7, the contribution of capital to growth in per capita income is given as

$$\beta G(K/N) = 0.25 \times 1.0 = 0.25\%$$

which is only 17 per cent of the average growth rate of income per capita (1.5 per cent). On the other hand, labour's contribution calculated as

$$\alpha G(L/N) = 0.75 \times (-0.3) = -0.23\%$$

takes a negative value. Adding both contributions together estimates a contribution of growth of 'total input' (or aggregate of labour and land

TABLE 5.1 *Growth rates of output, input, and productivity in selected developed countries*

	Average rates of growth per year (%)							Contribution of total productivity (%)	
	Product[a] (1)	Labour[b] (2)	Capital[c] (3)	Total input (4)	Total productivity (5)=(1)−(4)	Product per capita (6)	Labour productivity (7)=(1)−(2)	(8)=(5)/(6)	(9)=(5)/(7)
United Kingdom (GDP)									
1855–1913	1.8	0.7	1.4	1.0	0.8	0.9	1.1	89	73
1925/29–63	1.9	0.8	1.8	1.1	0.8	1.4	1.1	57	73
France (GDP)									
1913–66	2.3	−0.5	2.0	0.2	2.1	1.9	2.8	111	75
Norway (GDP)									
1879–99	1.7	0.7	1.9	0.9	0.8	0.9	1.0	89	80
1899–1956	2.8	0.3	2.5	0.7	2.1	2.0	2.5	105	84
Canada (GNP)									
1891–1926	3.0	1.8	2.7	2.0	0.9	1.0	1.2	90	75
1926–57	3.9	0.8	2.9	1.2	2.7	2.1	3.1	129	87
United States (GNP)									
1889–1929	3.7	1.7	3.8	2.4	1.2	2.0	2.0	60	60
1929–57	2.9	0.5	1.0	0.6	2.3	1.7	2.4	135	96

[a] Definitions of product shown in parentheses in the left column
[b] Work hours
[c] Producible capital

Source: Kuznets (1971: 74).

inputs) to total income growth of only 0.02 per cent. This means that 99 per cent of real per capita income growth resulted from growth in total productivity. Thus, this calculation illustrates the dominant role of technological progress in economic growth relative to that of capital accumulation. A similar calculation using equation (5.8) shows that only about 20 per cent of labour productivity growth was accounted for by the growth of the capital–labour ratio and the 80 per cent balance was contributed by total productivity growth.

Results of such calculations differ across countries and over time. However, the basic conclusion remains the same: that the contribution of total productivity to real income growth was far more important than that of factor inputs. This is evident in the cases of five advanced economies as summarized by Kuznets (shown in Table 5.1). In this table, the average growth rates per year of real income (column 1), labour in work hours (column 2), and capital stock (column 3) are shown. From these data common trends in advanced economies are observable: real income grew faster than labour input, implying increases in labour productivity, and capital stock grew faster than labour input but slower than real income, resulting in decreases in the capital–output ratio.

Labour (column 2) and capital (column 3) are aggregated with factor share weights into total productivity (column 4), which is subtracted from real income (column 1) to produce total productivity (column 5) according to equation 5.7. The growth rates of total productivity relative to those of income per capita are found to exceed 90 per cent on the average (column 8). Also, contributions of total factor productivity growth to real labour productivity growth, as calculated according to equation 5.8, are estimated to be nearly 80 per cent on the average (column 9). Both are consistent with the illustrative calculations by Kuznets mentioned above.

Such results urged a major shift in development paradigm. If the major underlying force of economic growth is not the accumulation of tangible capital as conventionally measured, but technological progress (broadly defined in terms of total productivity), then even poor economies with low-saving capacities might be able to achieve high rates of growth by borrowing technologies from advanced economies. It could be more effective for them to invest in education, research, and development (in support of private entrepreneurs' innovative activities, including borrowing foreign technology) to accelerate their economic growth than to merely try to increase their stock of tangible capital through command and planning by the government.

5.4 Changes in the Pattern of Economic Growth

Based on the review of growth-accounting studies as summarized in the previous section, Kuznets characterized the 'modern economic growth' of

Western economies since the Industrial Revolution as predominantly dependent on sustained improvements in technology rather than capital accumulation, due to the 'extended application of science to the problems of
economic production' (Kuznets, 1966: 9). It is only reasonable to expect
that, with this rapid technical progress, decreasing returns to increased
application of capital were overcome, resulting in decreases in the capital–
output ratio.

A major question, however, is whether it is possible for developing economies to immediately enter into the process of economic growth characterized
by a relatively minor reliance on capital accumulation. The growth-accounting studies, such as those summarized by Kuznets in Table 5.1, are mostly
based on data of Western economies since the fourth quarter of the nineteenth century, when those economies had already progressed to an
advanced stage of industrialization. Recent attempts to extend growth-
accounting analysis back to the period of the Industrial Revolution and
earlier suggest that a markedly different pattern of economic growth had
existed before emergence of the pattern dominated by growth in total
productivity.

5.4.1 A historical extension of growth-accounting

Existence of an economic growth pattern heavily based on capital accumulation rather than on technological progress in the early stage of industrialization was suggested by Abramovitz (1993) from his extension of the
growth-accounting analysis back to the beginning of that century. Results
of his accounting for labour productivity growth based on equation 5.7 are
summarized in a simplified form in the upper section of Table 5.2. For the
two early periods (1800–55 and 1855–90), contributions of growth in total
productivity to growth in labour productivity were smaller than those of
growth in the capital–labour ratio; this finding is coupled with the observation that the growth rates of real labour productivity were exceeded by those
of the capital–labour ratio, implying increases in the capital–output ratio.
Moreover, the income share of capital increased significantly from 0.34 in
Period 1 to 0.45 in Period 2. Such a growth pattern is akin to Marx's theory
of capitalist economic development (explained in the first section of this
chapter).

If we tentatively assume that the Industrial Revolution emerged in the
USA around the 1840s and 1850s, Period 1 and Period 2 in Abramovitz's time
demarcations may correspond with a transition to 'take-off' and a 'drive to
maturity' in the terminology of Rostow (1960). Alternatively, Period 1 might
be called 'a transition to initial industrialization', and Period 2 'a transition
to the advanced stage of industrialization'. The Abramovitz results suggest
that a growth pattern analogous to the Marx pattern did emerge in the US
economy before the newly born industrial economy reached 'maturity'.

TABLE 5.2 *Accounting for long-term growth in labour productivity in the USA and Japan*

	Income share of capital β (1)	Average growth rate per year (%)		Contribution of capital βG(K/L) (4)=(1)×(3)	Total productivity G(A) (5)=(2)−(4)	Contribution of total productivity (%) (6)=(5)/(2)
		Labour productivity G(Y/L) (2)	Capital-labour ratio G(K/L) (3)			
USA (Private (GDP))						
1. 1800–1855	0.34	0.4	0.6	0.2	0.2	50
2. 1855–1890	0.45	1.1	1.5	0.7	0.4	36
3. 1890–1927	0.46	2.0	1.3	0.6	1.4	70
4. 1929–1966	0.35	2.7	1.7	0.6	2.1	78
5. 1966–1989	0.35	1.4	1.8	0.6	0.8	57
Japan (Non-primary private GDP)						
1. 1888–1900	0.33	2.1	5.7	1.9	0.2	10
2. 1900–1920	0.39	2.7	6.1	2.4	0.3	11
3. 1920–1937	0.43	2.3	2.8	1.2	1.1	48
4. 1958–1970	0.33	8.2	11.6	3.8	4.4	54
5. 1970–1990	0.28	3.8	7.4	2.1	1.7	45

Notes: Y: Defined in parentheses in the left column
L: Work hours
K: USA in total fixed capital. Japan in reproducible capital (adjusted for utiltzation rate)

Sources: USA from Abramovitz (1993, Table 1, p. 223) using the 'Frame 1' data for 1800–27. Japan from Hayami and Ogasahara (1995, Table 2).

Further, Abramovitz's data indicate that the Marx pattern was replaced by the pattern of modern economic growth as summarized by Kuznets (henceforth called the Kuznets pattern) after the economy reached the advanced stage of industrialization. Indeed, from Period 3 (1890–1927) to Period 4 (1929–66) both the income share of capital and the capital–output ratio decreased. The contribution of total productivity growth jumped from 36 per cent in Period 2 to 70 per cent in Period 3, and further to 78 per cent in Period 4—typical of advanced industrial economies.

The hypothesis that the Marxian pattern did apply in the early stage of industrialization is also supported by the results of growth accounting for Japan as summarized in the lower section of Table 5.2. This study by Hayami and Ogasahara (1995) represents a renovation of a pioneering study by Ohkawa and Rosovsky (1973) for the private non-primary sector in Japan. This sector coverage is similar to Solow's (1957) but narrower than Abramovitz's (1993) for the total domestic economy in the USA. Because of this difference, the results for Japan are not comparable with those of the USA in absolute magnitudes. Yet, the estimates for the non-primary sector of Japan should be useful for identifying changes in basic growth trends, especially in modern industry and commerce. Time demarcations for the Japanese economy in Table 5.2 were made to be comparable with Abramovitz's for the US economy, albeit based on rather arbitrary judgements.

It seems reasonable to assume that the Industrial Revolution, or the first spurt of industrialization in Japan, took place around the turn of the century, from the Sino-Japanese War (1893–4) to the Russo-Japanese War (1903–4) (Nishikawa and Abe, 1990; Shimbo, 1995). If so, Period 1 (1888–1900) and Period 2 (1900–20) may be presumed to correspond with a transition to initial industrialization and a drive to the advanced stage of industrialization, respectively. In this early phase covering the first two periods, the rates of growth in real labour productivity were exceeded by those of the capital–labour ratio implying increases in the capital–output ratio. Meanwhile, the income share of capital increased, and only about 10 per cent of the labour productivity growth is explained by the total productivity growth, with the rest contributed by increases in the capital–labour ratio.[5]

As in the US case, the Marx pattern that prevailed in Periods 1 and 2 began to shift to the Kuznets pattern in Period 3, as the gravitation of the manufacturing sector shifted from light to heavy industries. Above all, the relative contribution of total productivity jumped to about 50 per cent. Capital's share, which reached a peak in this period, declined in the following period. Unlike the US case, the rate of growth in the capital–labour ratio continued to exceed that of labour productivity for Period 3 (1920–37).

Period 4 (1958–70) was the so-called 'High Economic Growth' period during which Japan recorded unprecedented high rates of economic growth, closing the gap in per capita income and labour productivity *vis-à-vis* advanced industrial economies in Western Europe and North America. Nevertheless, this rapid growth in labour productivity was outpaced by the growth in the capital–labour ratio to imply increases in the capital–output ratio, though the absolute magnitude of this coefficient was smaller in Period 4 than in Period 3. The increases in the capital–output ratio in Period 4 corresponded to a relatively modest contribution of total productivity, explaining only about 50 per cent of labour productivity growth, as compared with about 80 per cent in the USA for Period 4. In this respect, the Japanese economy in the High Growth period did not follow a typical Kuznets pattern but followed a mongrel pattern between the Marxian and the Kuznets types.

This mongrel pattern was common to both the USA and Japan for Period 5. In fact, the slow-down in output and productivity growths since the 1970s has been rather universal among advanced industrial economies (Maddison, 1991, 1995). This apparent return from the Kuznets to the Marx pattern for the most recent period might reflect the entrance of advanced industrial economies to a new epoch of human history, such as 'the post-industrial society' (Bell, 1973). This is a problem of far-reaching significance to advanced economies. However, since it has relatively small bearing on the problems of developing economies, we will not undertake further investigation here.

While some divergence from the Kuznets pattern was observed for recent years, what we have observed so far is consistent with the hypothesis that the Marx pattern did emerge in the early phase of industrialization in Japan as well as in the USA. A major question is how typical this sequential change in the growth pattern observed for the USA has been been amongst the modern histories of advanced economies. As for the capital–output ratio, a review of empirical evidence in industrial economies supports the hypothesis that the capital–output ratio changed in an inverted-U shape, with a rising trend until a certain threshold of per capita income and a decreasing trend thereafter (Bicanic, 1962). Further accumulation of empirical evidence on the trends of factor shares and the contribution of total productivity growth to product growth might confirm that Marx did develop a theory of economic development highly consistent with the stylized facts in the economies of his age.

5.4.2 A trap in the Marx-type growth

As the data in Table 5.2 show, both the USA and Japan were able to shift from the Marx pattern of growth based on capital accumulation toward the Kuznets pattern based on improvements in productivity. With this pattern change, the share of growth dividend paid to capital became smaller and the share to labour became larger, implying increased equality in income distribution.

Such a change in the growth pattern is not necessarily guaranteed to all economies. A sharp contrast with the USA and Japanese cases can be found in the experience of the former Soviet Union. Table 5.3 accounts for growth in gross national product (GNP) in the Soviet Union in a comparable format to the USA and Japanese accounting in Table 5.2. Estimates of GNP and other statistics used in the calculation in Table 5.3 were prepared by Abram Bergson and other Western scholars so as to be consistent with the standard concepts of national accounts. National income in the Soviet Union and other socialist economies was measured as 'net (or gross) material product', which excluded value added from many service activities. Growth accounting, based on the data of net material product, produced essentially the same conclusion as that based on the GNP estimates (Yoshida, 1990). In the absence of factor markets in the central planning system, a constant weight applied to capital is considered a kind of informed guess on the production elasticity of capital

The economic planning of the Soviet Union can be regarded as a polar case for pushing forward the economy by maximizing capital accumulation under the directive of government. Reflecting this drive, the rates of increase in the capital–labour ratio were much higher than in advanced market economies (e.g. compare USA and Soviet Union, Tables 5.2 and 5.3, column 3). The rates of labour productivity growth were also quite high from the interwar period to the 1960s. However, the growth in labour productivity was exceeded by increases in the capital–labour ratio over a wide margin, implying major increases in the capital–output ratio. Contributions of total productivity to labour productivity growth had been modest, ranging from about 30 to 40 per cent. This pattern of Soviet economic growth until the 1960s was similar to those of the USA and Japan in their early industrialization phase.

TABLE 5.3 *Accounting for growth in labour productivity in the Soviet Union*

	Capital's weight	Average growth rate per year (%)				Contribution of total productivity
		Labour productivity	Capital labour-ratio	Contribution of capital	Total productivity	
	β (1)	G(Y/L) (2)	G(K/L) (3)	βG(K/L) (4)=(1)×(2)	G(A) (5)=(2)–(4)	(%) (6)=(5)/(2)
1. 1928–40	0.38	2.5	4.7	1.8	0.7	28
2. 1950–60	0.38	4.5	7.5	2.9	1.6	36
3. 1960–70	0.38	3.5	5.3	2.0	1.5	43
4. 1970–80	0.38	1.7	5.0	1.9	−0.2	−12
5. 1980–5	0.38	1.3	4.7	1.8	−0.5	−39

Notes: : Sum of capital's weight (0.33) and land's weight (0.05) used by Abram Bergson for input aggression
    Y: Bergson's estimates of gross national product
    L: Labour force adjusted for changes in work hours
    K: Aggregation of fixed capital and land with weights of 0.35 and 0.05 respectively
Source: Ofer (1987: 1778–79).

However, in contrast with the US and the Japanese cases in which total productivity growth increased both absolutely and relatively to labour productivity growth in the later periods (except for the most recent period), in the Soviet Union it dropped sharply to negative levels during the 1970s and 1980s. These data clearly show that Soviet economic growth failed to shift from the Marx to the Kuznets pattern. It appears that the Soviet economy was trapped by severe decreasing returns to capital while rapidly accumulating capital was applied to the production process with little technological progress. Why have centrally planned economies such as the Soviet Union been captured by such a trap of Marx-type growth? How could this trap be avoided?

This question is pertinent to policy choice in middle- income economies which have accomplished the initial industrialization and are now striving to reach the advanced stage of development. In fact, according to a recent study by Jong-Il Kim and Laurence Lau (1994), the dramatic rise of the newly industrializing economies (NIEs) in East Asia (including Korea, Taiwan, Hong Kong, and Singapore) appear to follow the Marx pattern. Kim and Lau used a translog production function with the assumption of a

TABLE 5.4 *Comparisons in the growth rates of labour productivity and total productivity between newly industrializing economies (NIEs) and developed industrial economies*

		Production elasticity of capital	Average growth rate per year (%)			
			Labour productivity	Capital-labour ratio	Total productivity	
		β (1)	G(Y/L) (2)	G(K/L) (3)	G(A) (4)=(2)- (1)×(3)	Kim–Lau estimates (5)
NIEs						
Korea	1960–90	0.45	5.1	8.9	1.1 (21)	1.2 (24)
Taiwan	1953–90	0.49	6.2	9.6	1.5 (24)	1.2 (19)
Hong Kong	1966–90	0.40	5.2	6.1	2.8 (54)	2.4 (46)
Singapore	1964–90	0.44	4.5	6.6	1.6 (36)	1.9 (42)
Average		**0.45**	**5.3**	**7.8**	**1.8 (34)**	**1.7 (33)**
Developed Economies						
France	1957–90	0.28	3.8	4.7	2.5 (66)	2.6 (68)
Germany (FR)	1960–90	0.25	3.6	4.9	2.4 (67)	2.2 (61)
UK	1957–90	0.27	2.3	3.0	1.5 (65)	1.5 (65)
USA	1948–90	0.23	1.5	1.6	1.2 (80)	1.5 (100)
Japan	1957–90	0.30	6.0	9.7	3.1 (52)	2.9 (48)
Average		**0.27**	**3.4**	**4.8**	**2.1 (66)**	**2.1 (68)**

Notes: (1) Average of estimates using the translog production function
(2) Real GDP per work hour
(3) Reproducible capital (excluding residential buildings) per work hour, adjusted for utilization rates.
(4)–(5) Relative contributions to the growth rate of labour productivity in percentages are shown in parentheses.
(5) Estimated using the translog production function with the assumption of capital-augmenting technological progress
Source: Kim and Lau (1994, Tables 3–1, 6–3 and 7–1).

capital-augmenting technological progress for their growth-accounting analysis. However, for the sake of comparison with the US and the Japanese
cases (Table 5.2) and the Soviet case (Table 5.3), the Kim–Lau data were
transformed into a conventional growth-accounting form as shown in columns (1) through (4) in Table 5.4, while their original econometric estimates
are shown in column (5). Results of the conventional accounting and the
econometric analysis are largely the same.

The growth patterns of Asian NIEs for the past three decades, shown in
the upper section of Table 5.4, contrast sharply with those of developed
economies in the lower section. While the production elasticities of capital
were much higher for NIEs than developed economies, the reverse was the
case in the relative contributions of total productivity growth to labour
productivity growth, as shown in parentheses in columns (4) and (5). Among
the developed economies, Japan's pattern was closest to that of NIEs. These
observations are consistent with the hypothesis that the Marx pattern in the
early phase of industrialization tends to emerge more typically and persist
longer among late starters of industrialization, whose development is more
heavily dependent on borrowed technology[6]

Will Asian NIEs be able to sustain their economic growth and eventually
shift from the Marx to the Kuznets pattern of economic growth? Or will they
be trapped in the stalemate of Marxian-type growth, as feared by Paul
Krugman (1994)? This will be a major concern not only for the 'four tigers'
in East Asia, but for all the developing economies as they accomplish initial
industrialization and strive towards the advanced stage of development.

Answers to these questions will be explored in the next chapter.

NOTES

1. This explanation represents a reinterpretation of the Marxian model by modern
   economics. In Marx's original concept, capital consists of 'variable capital', which
   is the fund for advance wage payment to labourers (wage fund), and 'constant
   capital', which is the fund for the purchase of capital goods and intermediate
   products (Marx, [1867–94] 1909–12). According to Marx, the use of 'constant
   capital' by a capitalist does not produce 'surplus value' or profit because, endowed
   with no better bargaining power than other capitalists, he has to purchase
   machinery and materials at prices equal to the values that those constant capital
   items will produce On the other hand, because his bargaining position is much
   stronger than labourers, he can impose wage rates that are lower than the values
   that labourers produce. Therefore, it is only the use of variable capital that
   produces surplus value in the capitalist production process. Marx considered it a
   law in capitalist development that the ratio of constant to total capital (so-called
   the 'organic composition of capital') rises, and hence, the rate of profit or the ratio
   of surplus value to total capital stock value declines.

2. Marx believed that social instability would also be intensified through recurrent depressions. He considered the decrease in the rate of profit an unavoidable tendency in the capitalist development process where the share of constant capital necessarily increases. When the profit rate decreases below a certain level, investment incentives are so lowered as to trigger depression. The economy may recover as capital is depleted by depression. However, continued increases in the share of constant capital create more severe and frequent depressions, with labourers suffering more.

3. The model of the low-equilibrium trap is not necessarily constructed on the Harrod–Domar model. For example, the model by Nelson (1956) is based on the neoclassical production function. However, the binding force of the trap is especially strong and clearly visible under the Harrod–Domar assumption. Therefore, it is common to use the Harrod–Domar production function for illustration of the low-equilibrium trap model, e.g. Hla Myint (1965, ch. 7).

4. Unless technological progress is measured in advance, it is not possible to estimate a production function from time-series data for one economy. It is possible to estimate it from cross-section data among regions or countries. However, it is questionable whether such cross-section estimates of production elasticities are relevant for accounting for growth in an aggregate economy over time. A commonly used econometric method to minimize this problem is to pool time-series and cross-section data, e.g. Kim and Lau (1994), referred to in the next section.

5. Along the long-term increasing trend the capital share fluctuated, rising in boom periods and falling in slump periods (Minami and Ono, 1978)

6. The results of the Kim–Lau study may appear inconsistent with the large contributions of total productivity to economic growth estimated by World Bank (1993: 56). In the World Bank's study a single set of production elasticities was estimated from pooling the 1960–90 series data for eighty-seven countries to growth accounting for all economies. High rates of total productivity growth in economies in East Asia were derived from the use of capital's elasticity as small as 0.178. If this elasticity is applied to the NIEs' average in Table 5.4, $G(A)$ turns out to be 4.1%, and its contribution to labour productivity growth, $G(A)/G(Y/L)$, becomes 75%—a magnitude comparable with those of advanced economies. Considering the larger income shares of capital in earlier stages of industrialization, as observed in Table 5.2, application of the same set of production elasticities to the analysis of economies in different stages of development does not seem appropriate.

6

Patterns and Sources of Technological Progress

Simple growth-accounting analysis in the previous section demonstrated that technological progress, broadly defined (including the effects of improvements in input quality), made a predominant contribution to economic growth relative to the accumulation of tangible capital in the advanced stage of industrialization. However, it is likely that in the earlier phase when economies began modern industrial development through the process of 'industrial revolution' or 'take-off', economic growth depended more heavily on capital accumulation. Moreover, economic growth in the earlier phase appears to have been associated with increased inequality in income distribution, as represented by increases in the income share of capital at the expense of labour's share, in contrast with the equalizing tendency in the later phase. Historical data suggest that the pattern of economic growth experienced by advanced economies in their early industrialization stage was akin to the description of capitalist economic development by Marx, characterized by high saving and investment through concentration of income in the hands of capitalists.

Will this be the pattern that developing economies have to follow in the course of their industrialization? Will the newly industrializing economies (NIEs) be able to shift away from this Marx pattern to the advanced stage pattern of developed economies? These questions will be explored in this chapter through identification of the forces underlying the major shift in the growth pattern in the process of modern economic development.

6.1 The Marx vs. the Kuznets Pattern of Economic Growth

The previous chapter (Section 4) indicated that the pattern of economic growth in the initial stage of industrialization was similar to Marx's theoretical prediction (hence called the 'Marx pattern'), whereas the pattern in the advanced stage was abstracted by Kuznets from accumulated empirical data for advanced economies mainly since the last quarter of the nineteenth century (hence called the 'Kuznets pattern'). In this section these two patterns will be characterized more comprehensively and confirmed by additional data.

6.1.1 Stylization of the two patterns

Table 6.1 summarizes characteristics of the Marx pattern that appear in the initial stage of industrialization (Phase I) and the Kuznets pattern in the advanced stage (Phase II) in terms of 'stylized facts' or common trends in the major economic indicators of the growth process. The stylized facts for the Kuznets pattern were those outlined by Kuznets (1966, 1971) as characteristic of modern economic growth and were popularized among economists, as represented by Samuelson's textbook (Samuelson and Nordhaus, 1985: 793-6).

On the other hand, presumed common trends in major economic indicators for Phase I were those implied in Marx's theory of capitalist economic development (see Chapter 5, Section 1), except row (6) on the interest rate. Marx considered that the rate of return to capital will decline in the course of capitalist development with the faster accumulation of 'constant capital' (the fund to purchase non-labour inputs) relative to 'variable capital' (the fund to purchase labour inputs), since profit or 'surplus value' is derived only from the exploitation of labour. Yet, the decreasing returns to total capital input are not an inevitable consequence of rising 'organic composition of capital' (ratio of 'constant capital' to total capital). The profit rate can be constant if the rate of surplus value can be increased due to technological progress or for other reasons, so as to counteract the rising organic composition. Moreover, if the rate of return to capital were to decrease very fast, Marx's prediction of the increasing income share of capital (row 4) could be violated. In the neoclassical interpretation of Marx's theory advanced in Figure 5.1, capital-using bias in technological progress can maintain, or even increase, the rate of return to capital under rapid increases in the capital–labour ratio. Because of the theoretical implication of Marx's model, as well as some empirical evidence to be advanced later, the interest rate is assumed

TABLE 6.1 *Stylized facts in the two phases of modern economic growth*

		Phase I (Marx Pattern)	Phase II (Kuznets Pattern)
(1) Income per capita	Y/N	Increase	Increase
and Labour productivity	Y/L	Increase	Increase
(2) Capital per capita	K/N	Increase	Increase
and Capital–labour ratio	K/L	Increase	Increase
(3) Capital–output ratio	K/Y	Increase	Decrease
(4) Capital's share in income	rK/Y	Increase	Decrease
(5) Saving rate	S/Y	Increase	Constant
(6) Interest rate r		Constant	Constant
(7) Wage rate	w	Constant	Increase
(8) Relative contribution	$G(A)G(Y/N)$	Small	Large
of total productivity	$G(A)G(Y/L)$	Small	Large

Note: (1), (2), (3), (6), (7), and (8) are defined in real terms.

to be constant in the Marx pattern. For this reason our Marx pattern stylized in Table 6.1 may be called the 'revisionist' instead of the 'orthodox' Marxist pattern.

However, our revisionist Marx pattern does not rule out the possibility of a moderate decrease in the rate of return to capital. Likewise, the revisionist pattern allows the possibility of a moderate increase in the real wage rate (w), even though it is stylized as being constant in row (7) according to the original Marx model, which assumes the wage-anchoring mechanism of the 'industrial reserve army'. In our revisionist Marx pattern, however, the rate of decrease in the wage–rental ratio (w/r), if any, must be smaller than the rate of increase in the capital–labour ratio (K/L) so that the income share of capital (rk/Y) increases (row 4). If w/r increases faster than K/L so that rK/Y decreases, it belongs to the world of the Kuznets pattern.

As shown in rows (1) and (2), both the Marx and the Kuznets patterns are characterized by the rising trends in national income per capita (Y/N) and per worker (Y/L) as well as in capital stock per capita (K/N) and capital–labour ratio (K/L). However, the commonality ends at this point.

In the Marx pattern, K/N and K/L increased faster than Y/N and Y/L respectively, to result in increases in the capital–output ratio (K/Y), whereas the reverse is the case in the Kuznets pattern as indicated in row (3). This implies that decreasing returns to capital set in with increased applications of capital per worker for a fixed or small shift in production function underlying the Marx pattern. In contrast, in the Kuznets pattern, the decreasing returns were overcome by a large shift in production function. Different assumptions on production function shifts are shown in row (8) in the form of small versus large contributions of total factor productivity growth to growth in per capita and per-worker outputs between the Marx and the Kuznets patterns.

In the Marx pattern, despite increases in the K/L ratio, the income share of capital (rK/Y) increased, implying that technical progress during Phase I was biased toward the capital-using and labour-saving direction in the Hicks definition (if the elasticity of substitution is less than one). It is considered that because of this bias, the rate of return to capital, as reflected in the interest rate (r), was prevented from decreasing sharply relative to the wage-rate (w). The capital-using bias in technical progress is consistent with the small contribution of total factor productivity to product growth in Phase I, because increases in the income share of capital tend to make capital's contribution to product growth larger, with the consequence of a small residual in conventional growth accounting.

In the Kuznets pattern, the income share of capital decreased, while the wage-rate increased and the interest rate remained unchanged. These trends are consistent with the hypothesis that the technical change was biased towards the labour-using and capital-saving direction, even though the less-than-unitary elasticity of substitution should have also contributed to the decreases in capital's share, corresponding to increased K/L ratio.

Marx's theory predicted an increase in the rate of saving relative to national income (S/Y) in the capitalist development process because income tends to be concentrated in the hands of wealthy capitalists who have a higher propensity to save. In our interpretation, however, the high saving propensity could not have been maintained unless technology was developed towards the capital-using direction so that the rate of return to capital was maintained at a decently high level. The largely stable rate of saving in the Kuznets pattern under the increased income share of labour, due to sharp rises in the increased wage rate relative to the interest rate, reflects the high propensity of the middle-income working class to save as their wage incomes continued to rise—the situation diametrically opposite to Marx's assumption of no saving by labourers.

Demarcation between Phases I and II in actual history is, of course, an empirical question, which varies widely among countries depending on how early or late they entered the epoch of modern economic growth and advanced to a higher stage of industrial development. Our approach is to make the interphase demarcation in terms of empirically observed trends in major economic indicators.

6.1.2 Trends in the rates of saving, interest, and wages

Results of long-term growth-accounting analysis in the previous chapter (Table 5.2) were consistent with the hypothesis that the Marx pattern preceded the Kuznets pattern in the course of modern economic growth in the USA and Japan with respect to stylized facts (1), (2), (3), (4), and (8) in Table 6.1. Here, we will try to see if trends in (5) saving rate, (6) interest rate, and (7) wage rate were also consistent with the hypothesis in the case of Japan.

Long-term changes in the saving rate (S/Y) in terms of both national and domestic savings relative to GNP and GDP respectively in Japan are plotted in Figure 6.1; these two series do not appear to imply different conclusions for the purpose of broad trend comparisons. For the period before World War II, if we adjust for a sharp rise during the World War I boom period and a subsequent slump during the World Depression period, a basic rising trend in the saving rate from about 5 to 10 per cent could be observed. This observation is consistent with the argument by Rostow (1960), and by W. A. Lewis (1954), that investment rises in the 'take-off' period from about 5 to 10 per cent or more of national income. For the post-World War II period the saving rate remained relatively stable at a high level within the 25–35 per cent range. Such a change is consistent with the characteristics of the Marx and the Kuznets patterns respectively, as specified in Table 6.1 (column 5).

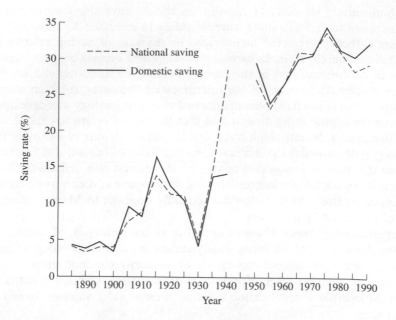

FIG. 6.1 *Movements in the ratios of national saving to GDP and domestic saving to GNP in Japan. Five-year averages centring on the shown for 1890–1940 and ending with the years shown for 1950–90*
Sources: Ohkawa *et al.*, *LTES*, vol. 5, *Savings and Currency* (1988: 44), supplemented for 1970–90 by Japan Economic Agency, *National Accounts* (annual issues).

Figure 6.2 plots changes in both the nominal and the real rates of interest for lending by banks. Throughout the whole period the nominal rate remained relatively stable, but the real rate (as calculated by subtracting from the nominal rate the rate of change in the wholesale price index) shows highly volatile fluctuations. However, neither an upward nor downward trend can be observed from the real interest series for either the earlier or the later phases of industrialization in Japan. Thus, a stylized fact established for advanced industrial economies since the beginning of this century, namely that the real interest rate oscillated violently with no systematic trend (Samuelson and Nordhaus, 1985: 794–5) seems also to be applicable to the earlier phase in Japan.

For the wage rates, a somewhat different picture emerges from the series of manufacturing and agricultural sectors as shown in Figure 6.3. The real wage rate in manufacturing began a rising trend with the World War I boom, whereas that of agriculture increased during the boom period but returned to the prior level with the post-war recession. Such a contrast is commonly explained in terms of the emergence of a 'dual' economic structure during the interwar period. As industrialization progressed to a stage

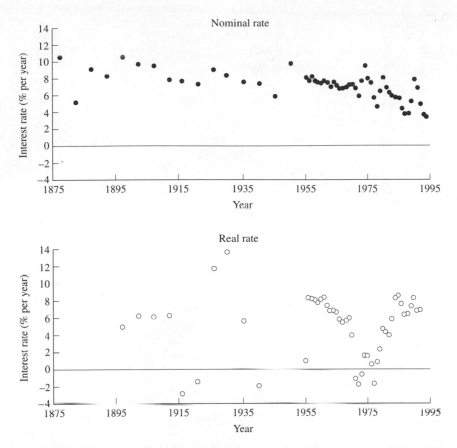

FIG. 6.2 *Movements in nominal and real rates of interest in Japan, 1877–1990*
Sources: Nominal rates are averages of the highest and the lowest bank lending rates
from Bank of Japan (1966: 260–4) for 1877–1940; all banks' average lending rate
from Bank of Japan, *Keizai Tokei Geppo* (Economic Statistics Monthly). Real rates
are nominal rates minus the rates of change in the wholesales price index in 7-year
moving averages from Bank of Japan (1966: 76–7) and *Bukka Shisu Geppo* (Price
Indexes Monthly).

centring on heavy and chemical industries, large-scale enterprises using
capital-intensive high technologies preferred to employ better-educated
labourers in a long-term contract with relatively favourable terms so as to
internalize investment in the skill formation of their workers (Odaka, 1984;
Nakamura and Odaka, 1989). On the other hand, small and medium-scale
enterprises tended to specialize in labour-intensive production by employing
labourers who were excluded from large enterprises. When uneducated
labourers in agriculture sought employment in non-agriculture, they had
no option but to enter the lower stratum of the dual structure as unskilled

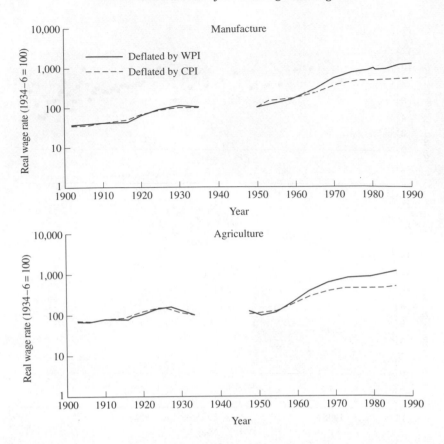

FIG. 6.3 *Movements in the real wage rate in Japan (1934–6=100), 1896–1994, seven-year averages, semi-log scale*
Sources: Nominal wage rates for manufacturing from Ohkawa *et al.*, *LTES*, vol. 8, *Prices* (1967: 246), and Japan Ministry of Labour, *Maigetu Kinro Tokei Chosa* (Monthly Labour Survey); for agriculture from *LTES*, vol. 9, *Agriculture and Forestry* (1966: 107) and Japan Ministry of Agriculture, *Noson Bukka Chingin Chosa* (Survey on Rural Prices and Wages). WPI from Bank of Japan (1966: 76–7) and *Bukka Shisu Geppo* (Price Indexes Monthly). CPI from Ohkawa, *et al.*, *LTES*, vol. 8, *Prices* (1967: 135–7) and Japan Management and Coordination Agency, *Shohisha Bukka Shisu Geppo* (Monthly Report on the Consumer Price Index).

workers in small and medium enterprises who were easily laid off in recession.

Thus, the wage rates in agriculture and small/medium industries moved together in a flexible manner in response to business fluctuations, whereas those of capital-intensive, large-scale industries were characterized by downward rigidity. Average wage rates in manufacturing, which did not decline in the post-war recession, are considered to include increased payments to more highly educated and skilled workers employed in the rapidly expanding capital-intensive sector. On the other hand, the agricultural wages are considered to reflect the supply price of unskilled labour to the non-agricultural sector. Thus, it seems reasonable to assume that the real wage rate for raw labour was characterized by a largely stable trend. After World War II, in contrast, both the agricultural and manufacturing wage rates showed sharply rising trends, as Japanese industries caught up with the level of advanced economies in Western Europe and North America.

Overall, changes in the trends of savings rate as well as the real wage and interest rates in Japan are consistent with the characterization of the growth patterns for the earlier and later phases of industrialization specified in Table 6.1 (rows 5, 6, and 7).

6.2. Technological Conditions of the Two Growth Patterns

What mechanism would have underlain the shift from the Marx to the Kuznets pattern? Two possible explanations advanced here are: (*a*) a shift in the regime of industrial technology from visible to invisible technology, and (*b*) a shift in people's demand from standardized to differentiated products. These together change the speed and the direction of technological progress.

6.2.1 The shift in the industrial technology regime

There should be little doubt that the major factor underlying the shift in the growth pattern was acceleration in technological progress as measured by growth in total productivity. If the rate of technological progress in Phase II had remained as small as in Phase I, decreasing returns to capital would have prevailed so that the capital–output ratio continued to increase in Phase II also.

What, then, would have underlain the acceleration in technological progress? The answer appears to be what we call 'institutionalization of scientific research and education'—establishment of scientific research and educational systems geared towards improvements in industrial technology—in Phase II. This may sound similar to Kuznets's 'epochal innovation' characterizing his 'modern economic growth'. Kuznets considered modern economic growth since the Industrial Revolution one of the major epochs in human history. In his view each epoch was characterized by its own epochal innovation; e.g. the epoch of 'merchant capitalism' from the mid-fifteenth to mid-eighteenth century, in which overseas trade played a strategic role in the economic growth of the time, was supported by 'improvements in science and technology, bearing upon navigation, ships, and weapons, and of advances in domestic production and political organization' (Kuznets,

1966: 2). Then, 'the epochal innovation that distinguishes the modern economic growth epoch is the extended application of science to problems of economic production' (Kuznets, 1966: 9). Systematic application of science was identified by Kuznets as the factor making technological progress in modern economic growth much faster and steadier than in premodern epochs, when advances in technology had been intermittent and sporadic as they were based on accidental flash of genius as well as trial and error by artisans.

Kuznets considered the systematic application of science the engine of modern economic growth since the time of the Industrial Revolution. However, as elucidated by Rosenberg and Birdzell (1986, Chapter 8), until about the 1870s, advances in industrial technology in Western Europe and North America had largely originated with artisans in the areas of 'visible' mechanic arts such as levers, gears, shafts, and cranks; it was the last quarter of the nineteenth century when the frontier of technology began to move to the invisible world of atoms, molecules, electron flows, and magnetism. In this new technology regime organized research by teams of scientists who received advanced formal education and training became the major source of Western industrial technology.

For the effective operation of new invisible technologies the calibre of workers had to be changed also, from those equipped with manual dexterity through on-the-job training to those who developed the potential for decoding scientific and engineering manuals through formal education. Corresponding to this need, a wide diffusion of primary and secondary education has been paralleled with the establishment of advanced education and research institutions with practical orientation, such as land-grant colleges in the USA and *Technische Hochschulen* in Germany, since about the 1870s (Landes, 1965; 1969)[1]. Japan quickly followed this pattern with the establishment of an engineering college in 1886 within the newly founded Tokyo Imperial University and a network of technical high schools modelled after the German system in subsequent decades (Japanese Ministry of Education, 1962). There seems to be little doubt that sharply expanded investment in intangible capital, such as education and research in the new 'invisible technology' regime, underlay the much larger contribution of total productivity relative to the contribution of tangible capital to product growth in conventional growth accounting for Phase I than for Phase II.

6.2.2 The shift in the demand structure

The shift in the technology regime may be considered a shift in the orientation of technical progress from facilitating substitution of tangible capital for labour to facilitating substitution of intangible for tangible capital. Alternatively stated, the bias in technological progress changed from the tangible-capital-using and labour-saving direction to the intangible-capital-using and tangible-capital-saving direction.

As argued strongly by Marx, technical progress in the early phase of industrialization was orientated towards replacing labour by capital. Take an example of draining water from coalmines, which used to be a major problem at the time of Industrial Revolution in England. If water was lifted up by manpower using buckets, the marginal product of one additional bucket beyond the number equal to the number of water-lifting workers would have declined sharply, probably close to zero. Therefore, profit-seeking entrepreneurs would not have invested in the purchase of more than one bucket per worker (in addition to a few spares). Suppose that a water-pump run by James Watt's steam engine was invented, which could drain with only five operators the same volume of water lifted by one hundred workers with buckets. If this pump set costs equivalent to one hundred buckets, the entrepreneur would have been willing to invest up to twenty times more capital per worker with no fear of decreasing marginal productivity. Such a capital-using and labour-saving bias appears to be characteristic of mechanization in the early industrialization phase, as exemplified by Arkwright's jenny and Hargreaves's spinning-machine. With this bias in technical progress, any hike in the wage rate (w) was suppressed to a moderate rate; the rate of return to capital (r) was prevented from decreasing sharply despite rapid increases in the capital–labour ratio (K/L), so that the income share of capital (rK/Y) increased.

Such labour-saving mechanization would have been effective, especially for the mass production of standardized commodities for which demand expanded rapidly in the early phase of industrialization, when per capita incomes had been near subsistence level for the majority of people. Water lifting, for example, can be easily mechanized, because water to be drained is economically homogeneous and, therefore, a perfectly standardized product. However, as per capita incomes rose further and people's basic needs were satisfied, demands tended to shift from standardized to differentiated products which are less susceptible to mechanization.

For example, at a low-income stage the shirts of a standard make at a cheap price may be demanded in a large quantity. For the mass production of such a shirt, the use of large-scale automatic machinery can be efficient. But at a high-income stage, demands would shift towards fashionable shirts differentiated by colour and design. For the economic production of such differentiated commodities each demanded in a small quantity, large-scale mass production facilities are not relevant. Instead, the human ability of developing attractive designs to affluent people in response to capricious changes in fashion becomes critically important.

In this new regime the marginal productivity of human ability and knowledge rose sharply relative to that of tangible capital, as typical of information industries today. Correspondingly, the measured wage rates which include returns to human capital acquired through education and training in addition to returns to raw labour, rose sharply relative to the rate of return to tangible capital. The consequent increase in the wage–rental ratio (w/r) would have exceeded the increase in the capital–labour ratio (K/L) resulting in decreased capital's share (rK/Y).

It must be true that increases in the labour wage rates in Phase II were also accelerated by deceleration in the growth in labour supply owing to both a slow-down in population growth rates and increased preference for leisure corresponding to per capita income rises. Yet, if the product demand structure had remained the same, and human capital had not accumulated so fast in Phase II, the traditional labour-saving and capital-using technical progress of the Phase I-type would have continued to advance at a sufficiently rapid speed so that the effect of labour supply reduction could have been counteracted, resulting in no appreciable increase in the wage rate. Thus, the shift from the Marx to the Kuznets pattern can be explained consistently in terms of both the shift from a visible technology regime to the invisible technology regime and the shift in the product demand structure from standardized to differentiated products. Both shifts together increased the rate of technical progress and also changed the bias in technical progress from the tangible-capital-using to the intangible-capital-using direction.

6.2.3 Borrowed technology and the Marx-type growth

A major question remaining unsolved in the previous chapter with respect to Table 5.2 was why the growth of the Japanese economy did not make the same shift to a typical Kuznets pattern as observed in the US case. Especially in Period 4 (1958–70) when Japan was able to catch up with the level of the advanced industrial economies in the West, the percentage contribution of total productivity to labour productivity growth was smaller than 60 per cent. Moreover, the capital–output ratio did increase under the extremely rapid increase in the capital–labour ratio, even though the income share of capital approached a level similar to that of other industrial economies.

It is possible that this Marx–Kuznets mongrel pattern tends to emerge rather universally among newly industrializing economies on the track of catching up with advanced economies based on borrowed technology. As argued by Alexander Gerschenkron (1962), latecomers to industrialization tend to borrow from their predecessors the advanced technologies of high capital intensity and labour-saving effect. This capital-using and labour-saving bias in borrowed technology for recipient economies could be strengthened by international trade and foreign direct investment.

According to the theory of product cycle by Raymond Vernon (1966), multinational corporations locate their product development base in high-income economies which are characterized by large markets for new products as well as abundant endowments of high-calibre human resources for research and development. After a product is developed in this R & D base through a series of market tests, and its production process is standardized, its mass production is typically transferred to developing economies, such as Korea and Taiwan up to the 1970s, where cheap but relatively well-educated labour is abundantly available. From this mass production base products are exported to advanced economies. Through this cycle, advanced industrial economies tend to specialize in R & D and product development activities with intensive use of high human capital, whereas newly industrializing economies (NIEs) tend to specialize in standardized mass production based on automatic machinery and cheap labour. This process could well be driven not only by multinational firms but also by domestic entrepreneurs in NIEs.

Indeed, the process of industrialization in Japan as a latecomer was similar to that described in the product cycle theory, even though the roles of domestic entrepreneurs and domestic markets played a much more important role than implied in the Vernon theory (Shinohara 1966; Yamazawa, 1984; Shimbo, 1995). The High Economic Growth period from the mid-1950s up to the early 1970s, corresponding to Period 4 in Table 5.2, was essentially the process of very rapid technology borrowing based partly on a widened technology gap during the World War II *vis-à-vis* the USA, and partly on the prior establishment of human resources and R & D organizations that facilitated the technology borrowing. Capital-using bias inherent in borrowed technology could well explain why Japan's economic growth in Period 4 diverged from a typical Kuznets pattern as observed for the USA.

It is, therefore, likely that the Marx pattern tends to emerge more typically and persist longer in rapidly industrializing economies based on borrowed technology. This hypothesis is consistent with the experience of Asian NIEs, including Korea, Taiwan, Hong Kong, and Singapore, as observed in Table 5.4. If this hypothesis is accepted, the Marx pattern experienced by Japan since the end of last century and by Asian NIEs for the past three decades cannot be considered a symptom of unsustainability, with economic growth primarily based on resource accumulation instead of improved efficiency, as argued by Paul Krugman (1994). In fact, the Abramovitz data in Table 5.2 show clearly that the USA also experienced this pattern in its early phase of industrialization. Is there any strong reason to suspect that Asian NIEs will not be able to shift to the Kuznets pattern after their technology borrowing is completed?

6.3 Searching for the Sources of Technological Progress

So far it has become clear that technological progress is the major determinant of the speed and the pattern of economic growth and that the source of technological progress is investment for improvements in human knowledge and capability. A major question remains in regard to the kinds of investment that are effective relative to others in enhancing technological progress. A more basic problem is what kind of institutional framework is conducive to efficient investment allocations for promoting technological progress. These will be discussed in this section.

6.3.1 Accounting for total productivity growth*

Growth in total productivity, measured by simple growth accounting in the previous chapter (Sections 5.3 and 5.4), were residual in output growth left unexplained by increases in conventional inputs (such as labour measured in work hours and capital in tangible capital stock) under the assumption of linear homogeneous production function. This residual is called 'technological progress broadly defined'. It includes not only technological progress narrowly defined as a shift in production function, but also the effects of many other factors such as scale economies, more efficient resource allocations, and better input quality. Quantitative assessments on how much each of these factors contributed to economic growth are critically important for the design of development policy. Various efforts have been undertaken to explain this 'unexplained residual' or 'measure of ignorance'. Here, as an illustration, a well-known study by Edward Denison will be outlined. Results of his analysis for five advanced economies are summarized in Table 6.2.[2]

Row (3) through (7) in Table 6.2 presents the procedures of simple growth accounting based on equation (5.7). However, in this analysis, growth in real income per person employed was accounted for using the number of employees instead of total population as the denominator of national income. Row (7) enumerates conventional estimates of total productivity obtained by subtracting aggregate contributions of labour and capital (row 4) from growth in income per employee (row 3). The results confirm the characteristic of advanced economies that relative contributions of total productivity growth to growth in income are predominant, ranging from 70 to 100 per cent.

Denison's major contribution was to decompose total productivity growth measured in row (7) into factors of rows (8) through (12).

Row (8) estimated changes in efficiency in labour owing to changes in the age and sex composition of workers. The estimation assumed equality between the wage rates and the marginal value productivities of labour. Under this assumption, the indices of average wage rates were calculated each year across the groups of employees in different sex and age brackets (with males from 20 to 60 years equal to 100). These were aggregated into an annual average labour quality index using the numbers of employees in

* Readers not interested in technical detail may skip this section.

TABLE 6.2 *Sources of growth in national income per person employed in selected developed economies*

	1950–62				1948–69	1953–71
	UK	France	Germany (FR)	USA	USA	Japan
Growth rate per year (%)						
(1) National income[a]	2.38	4.70	6.27	3.36	4.00	8.81
(2) Employment	0.65	0.11	2.43	1.17	1.55	1.46
(3) Income per employee	**1.73(100)**	**4.59(100)**	**3.84(100)**	**2.19(100)**	**2.45(100)**	**7.35(100)**
Contribution to the income growth rate per employee[b]						
(4) Total conventional input	**0.21(12)**	**0.74(16)**	**0.20(5)**	**0.40(18)**	**0.20(8)**	**1.99(27)**
(5) Work hours	0.15(–9)	–0.02(0)	–0.27(–7)	–0.17(–8)	–0.21(–9)	0.21(3)
(6) Capital[c]	0.36(21)	0.76(16)	0.47(12)	0.57(26)	0.41(17)	1.78(24)
(7) Output per unit of conventional input	**1.52(88)**	**3.85(84)**	**3.64(95)**	**1.79(82)**	**2.25(92)**	**5.36(73)**
(8) Age-sex composition	0.04(–2)	0.10(2)	0.04(1)	–0.10(–4)	–0.10(–4)	0.14(2)
(9) Education	0.29(17)	0.29(6)	0.11(3)	0.49(22)	0.44[d](18)	0.36[d](5)
(10) Improved allocation of resources	0.12(7)	0.95(21)	1.01(26)	0.29(13)	0.30(12)	0.95(13)
(11) Economies of scale	0.36(21)	1.00(22)	1.61(42)	0.36(17)	0.42(17)	1.94(26)
(12) Residual (Advances of knowledge)	0.79(45)	1.51(33)	0.87(23)	0.75(34)	1.19(49)	1.97(27)
(13) Education(9)+Residual(12)	**1.08(62)**	**1.80(39)**	**0.98(26)**	**1.24(66)**	**1.63(67)**	**2.33(32)**

[a] Net national product at the factor cost adjusted for irregularities in weather and resource utilization rates
[b] Relative contributions in percentages with the growth rate of income per employee set as 100 are shown in parentheses.
[c] Total national assets including inventory, land, and external assets
[d] Includes 'unallocated'

Sources: Denison and Chung (1976: 98–9) except: employment from Denison (1967: 48–50) and Denison and Chung (1976: 88 and 106); USA (1950–62) from Denison (1967: 298).

respective groups as weights. Growth rates of this index are those reported in row (8).

The same procedures were applied to estimation of the effects of labour quality improvement due to education, reported in row (9). Employees were grouped according to the number of formal school years completed. The indices of average wage rates by group (with males with eight school years equal to 100) were aggregated, using group sizes as weights, into a single annual index, from which the rates of increase in labour efficiency due to education were calculated. In this procedure, adjustments were made to reduce intergroup differences in the wage rates from the base group by two-fifths to remove the effects of non-educational factors such as native intelligence (as measured by IQ), which are supposed to correlate with accomplishments in schooling. In other words, it was assumed that three-fifths of the differences in the wage rates result solely from the differences in formal education.

Row (10) estimates the contributions of improved allocation of resources, including the effects of labour reallocation from the lower to the higher productivity sectors and of improved income-earning capacity due to trade liberalization. The former was measured as the sum of increased remuneration to workers who moved from self-employed activities (such as agriculture) to other occupations. The latter was measured by increased national income from increases in export prices and decreases in import prices.

Row (11) measures the effect of scale economies as 15 per cent of growth in national income. Row (12) presents residuals left unexplained by the factors specified in rows (8) through (11). These residuals accounted for 30 to 50 per cent of growth in total productivity. In other words, one-half to two-thirds of unexplained residuals in the ordinary growth accounting were explained by the factors of row (8) through (11).

Denison's estimates were based on many arbitrary assumptions, such as assuming the effect of scale economies to be 15 per cent of national income growth. As such, they are more 'guesstimates' than estimates. Yet, due credit should be given to his contribution in producing the best 'informed guess' for the causes of total productivity growth, based on the exhaustive use of available information.

Among the many interesting findings by Denison, the most relevant to the theme of this chapter are the estimates of education's contributions (row 9) and residuals (row 12). Denison claimed that these residuals represent the effects of 'advances in knowledge', since the effects of all the conventional and non-conventional factors, other than unquantifiable stock of knowledge were subtracted from growths in national income per person employed. If we accept this argument, row (13), which is the sum of rows (9) and (12), can be considered the estimates of production function shifts due to increased human capacity and knowledge from investment in education and research. By comparing row (13) with row (6), which measures contributions of conventional capital, it can be concluded that investment in intangible capital, such as education and research, made contributions to economic growth two to three times larger than accumulations of tangible capital.

This conclusion is likely to be robust and will remain broadly intact even if major improvements in data and methodology for growth accounting arise in the future. It must be noted that the results reported in Table 6.2 pertain to the post-World War II period before the first oil crisis, when advanced economies experienced relatively high growth rates typical of the Kuznets pattern. The policy implication appears to be that a basic condition for developing economies in the initial phase of industrialization to transform themselves into advanced industrial economies is increased investment in the infrastructure of education and research. High priority in the study of development economics should, therefore, be placed on how institutions and policies should be structured so as best to promote investment in intangible capital (Jimenez, 1995; Evenson and Westphal, 1995).

6.3.2 Schumpeter and centrally planned economies

Why then were the centrally planned economies, such as the former Soviet Union, not able to sustain economic growth? In general, ex-socialist economies invested heavily in education and research. Their rates of diffusion in primary and secondary education were normally higher than those of capitalist market economies at comparable levels of income per capita. Public investment in advanced education and research systems was also high. For example, the ratio of expenditure for scientific research and development to national income in the Soviet Union during the 1960s and 1970s exceeded 4 per cent, significantly higher than the 2 to 3 per cent in advanced market economies. Also, the number of scientists and engineers engaged in research and development in the Soviet Union was higher than in the USA (Japan Science and Technology Agency, *White Paper on Science and Technology*). With such strong national efforts to advance scientific education and research, the Soviet Union was able to rival the USA in the development of space technology throughout the 1960s and 1970s.

Nevertheless, contributions of total productivity to the growth of the Soviet economy were relatively low and declined over time, as observed in the previous chapter (Table 5.3). These observations seem to indicate that investment in education and research is necessary, but not sufficient, for a shift from the Marx to the Kuznets pattern. What then is the sufficient condition? The answer to this question may be found in *The Theory of Economic Development* ([1912] 1961) by Joseph Schumpeter (1883–1950).

Unlike the tradition from the Classical School to Marx who identified capitalist economic development as being led by capital accumulation, Schumpeter considered 'innovation' the engine of development in capitalist economy. His definition of innovation is not scientific discovery and invention, but the process by which new ideas are utilized by entrepreneurs to create a new combination of production resources to increase their profit. Innovations can take various forms such as (1) the introduction of a new good or a new quality of good, (2) the introduction of a new method of production, (3) the opening of a new market, (4) the conquest of a new source of supply of raw materials, and (5) the designing of the new organization of any industry. Concrete examples might be (1) the introduction of the transistor to replace the vacuum tube, (2) development of a low-cost mass production system for transistors, (3) exploitation of overseas market for transistors, (4) utilization of new materials such as silicon, and (5) organizational developments such as industrial parks and venture capital markets (such as NASDAQ in the USA).

According to Schumpeter, in the absence of innovation, competition in the market will eventually eliminate excess profits from all the economic sectors and bring the economy to a stationary state at the long-run equilibrium which equates revenue and cost (where the lowest point in average cost curve equals the market price). However, he considered incessant occurrence of innovations a basic trait of the capitalist economy, in which profit-seeking entrepreneurs always try to increase profits by introducing new goods and new production methods in response to changes in both demand and production possibilities. Once this mechanism of incessant creation of innovations stops, the economy will no longer be capitalist but would be transformed to a non-capitalist economy (Schumpeter, 1942).

The entrepreneurs who accomplished an innovation first could capture a large excess profit. However, inherent to innovations is risk. It is very possible that entrepreneurs will incur a loss when a good, expected to meet high market demand, commands low sales, or when a new machine happens to operate at a much lower efficiency than originally anticipated. The entrepreneurs who undertake innovation are the economic agents who bear the risk in seeking excess profit.

Undertaking innovation entails the capital fund to employ workers and to purchase equipment and materials for production. In the world of the Classical economists and Marx, this capital was supposed to be provided by entrepreneurs themselves, implying an identity between capitalists and entrepreneurs. In Schumpeter's world, an entrepreneur would have the ability to perceive profitable innovation opportunities, and the courage to shoulder risk, but need not be a 'capitalist' himself. The required funds could be obtained by credit from banks if he was able to persuade bankers of the profitability of the new investment he planned to undertake.

Suppose additional purchasing power is handed to entrepreneurs through a bank's credit creation in a stationary equilibrium characterized by full employment of resources. As this credit is spent by entrepreneurs and added to effective demand, market prices rise, resulting in declines in real income and, hence, in consumption by ordinary citizens. Thus, the inflation caused by a bank's credit creation depresses consumption that results in 'forced savings' and, thereby, transfer of resources from consumers to entrepreneurs for their investment in innovations. Thus, in Schumpeter's theory, the major force underlying economic development is not the accumulation of capital based on savings by capitalists, as assumed by Adam Smith through Marx. Instead, the prime engine is innovation, and it is through innovation that savings needed for investment can be mobilized. In undertaking an innovation, an entrepreneur has to bear major risk. However, once the new good or new method introduced by him proves successful, the risk associated with its introduction declines precipitously. Then it is natural for other entrepreneurs to imitate this new business. As those 'followers' to the 'innovator' increase cumulatively in number, supply of the new good (or a new good produced by the new manufacturing method) expanded, pulling down its market price. Concurrently, increased demands for production factors associated with increased product supply would pull up input prices. Through squeezes in product price declines and input price hikes, excess profit would continue to decrease until the point at which the trough of the new product's average cost curve is equal to its market price.

It is consumers who gain in this process of restoring the new equilibrium as they become able to consume the product at a reduced price. Thus, innovation imposes sacrifice (or forced saving) on ordinary citizens at the outset, but in the end their real income increases through reduced product prices, as long as the market is competitive. On the other hand, entrepreneurs in Schumpeter's world are induced to maximize their efforts to best utilize new technological opportunities (advanced by scientific education and research) for service to consumers, as they are both attracted by the carrot (excess profit) and chased by the whip (market competition).

Critically lacking in centrally planned economies was this market mechanism of mobilizing entrepreneurs' efforts for innovations of high social demand. In centrally planned economies, those who were supposed to carry out innovations were bureaucrats in a hierarchy ranging from the central planning committee to ministries in charge of individual industries, and further down to managers of state enterprises. In principle, they were responsible to best utilize advanced scientific knowledge for the people's well-being. But, it was inevitable that their efforts were slackened and/or diverted from the goal of benefiting people in the absence of profit incentive and the whip of market competition.

In centrally planned economies, the major incentive scheme for enhancing work efforts was to set quantitative targets on output to be produced at various levels, from industrial ministries to managers and workers in state enterprises (Ofer, 1987). Those who were able to produce more than the target volumes were rewarded with bonuses and promotions and those who failed to meet the targets were penalized. Under this scheme, it was inevitable that the quantitative targets became the supreme goal while little consideration was paid to improvements in the quality of products. Unlike private entrepreneurs in market economies, who are penalized by a loss of customers when their products are of low quality, state enterprises under state procurement and distribution were subject to no such penalty.

Moreover, this incentive scheme promoted managers' and workers' efforts to procure as much capital and other inputs to achieve quantitative output targets. This tendency was further induced by low (zero in principle) rates of interest in accord with Marx's theory of value and the 'soft-budget constraints' (no danger of bankruptcy to state enterprises for uneconomical production and investment plans). Under such a system, both managers and workers of state enterprises had little incentive to improve efficiency in the use of capital goods and intermediate products. Instead, their major efforts concentrated on maximizing quota allocation of those inputs to their shops through connections, bribery, and intimidation. It was no wonder that the Soviet economy had to face sharply decreasing returns to capital, as increasingly more capital was applied per worker with little innovation towards the capital-using and labour-saving direction, as attested by several empirical studies (Weitzman 1970; Desai, 1976; Ofer, 1987; Easterly and Fisher, 1994). The low and the decreasing contributions of total factor productivity to Soviet economic growth, as observed in Table 5.3, are a reflection of the unsustainable nature of this economic system (see Chapter 8, Section 3 for more detailed account about the rise and fall in centrally planned economies).

Viewed from Schumpeter's theory, decay in centrally planned economies, which culminated in their collapse in the 1980s, represents strong evidence in support of the hypothesis that investment in scientific education and research is a necessity, but is not a sufficient condition to accelerate technological progress. While education and research play a critically important role in expanding technological opportunities for innovations, an institutional mechanism must be prepared for effective exploitation of the opportunities created. Competitive markets should be the core of such mechanism. It must be recognized, however, that an effective market mechanism cannot be created by *laissez-faire* alone. The effective working of a competitive market must be supported by institutions such as civil codes, commercial and contract laws, and police and judicial systems to protect property rights and enforce contracts. One important condition for the promotion of innovation within the framework of the market economy is the establishment of a patent system and other means for protection of intellectual property rights (as touched upon in Chapter 1, Section 1). Innovative activities could be maximized if public investment in basic scientific research was expanded and, at the same time, effective institutions established to support efficient market transactions of inventions and other forms of intellectual property rights in the applied end of technology.

6.3.3 Conditions of borrowing technology

A major source of technological progress for developing economies is importation of advanced technologies from developed economies. Gerschenkron (1962) observed a tendency in the history of industrialization in Europe for late starters to achieve higher rates of industrial growth because of their advantage in borrowing advanced technologies from early starters. This catching-up mechanism resulting in convergence in productivity among industrial countries has continued to operate until today (Baumol, 1986; Maddison, 1987, 1991; Nelson, 1991). An important contribution of Gerschenkron was to clarify that establishment of appropriate institutions was necessary for late starters to achieve high rates of industrial growth based on borrowed technology.

Among various institutions Gerschenkron focused on banking systems. At the beginning of industrialization, capital that accumulated in the hands of domestic entrepreneurs was usually small, whereas capital requirements were larger for late starters introducing advanced technology of high capital intensity from abroad. In order to meet this requirement, development of financial institutions became necessary to mobilize savings from a wide range of citizens. Since this need was not so compelling in England, the earliest starter of industrialization, the so-called 'merchant banks' prevailed that engaged mainly in short-term production loans through discounting of bills, while long-term investment in fixed equipment and facilities was financed mostly by equity capital provided by capitalist-entrepreneurs themselves and a small number of wealthy people.

However, as France began industrial development in the middle of the nineteenth century under Napoleon III, the supply of equity capital was found grossly insufficient to meet the enlarged fixed capital requirement necessary to introduce the most advanced technologies from England. This financial constraint for technology borrowing was mitigated through development of a savings bank called *Crédit Mobilier*, which accepted savings from a wide range of citizens for lending to industrialists for their fixed capital investment.

Still later, when Germany advanced to industrialization in the late nineteenth century, with a strong bent toward the heavy and chemical industries from a relatively early stage of industrialization, fixed capital requirement became much larger. In response to this demand, large banks were developed in Germany which had the form of a 'universal bank', engaging in all financial transactions from bill discounting to long-term loans for fixed capital investment as well as issuance and brokering of bonds and stocks. These banks, equipped with multiple means of financial mobilization and diversified portfolios, were able to meet the enlarged capital requirement for industrial technology borrowing in Germany.[3]

Such developments in the banking system emphasized by Gerschenkron make up only one example out of many institutional conditions needed for effective borrowing of advanced technologies by developing economies. In broader terms, economic backwardness creates an opportunity for faster growth but the actual catch-up depends on a nation's ability or 'social capability' to exploit this opportunity (Abramovitz, 1986). A major challenge in development economics is to identify how to strengthen the social capability of achieving institutional innovations critically needed to exploit the great potential of technology borrowing for developing economies.

6.4 Theoretical Supplements to Technological Progress*

This supplement aims to give diagrammatical and mathematical expositions of the shift from the Marx pattern in Phase I to the Kuznets pattern in Phase

* Readers not interested in technical detail may skip this section.

II in the course of industrialization, along the neoclassical theory of economic growth.[4]

6.4.1 Increases in the capital–labour ratio and shifts in production function

The change in the contribution of technological progress to economic growth is the prime factor underlying the change in the growth pattern. Technological progress is defined in modern economics as an upward shift in the production function. The production function to produce output (Y) from the inputs of labour (L) and capital (K) is expressed as

$$Y = F(L, K), \tag{6.1}$$

where F is differentiable with respect to L and K with positive first derivations ($F_L, F_K > 0$), negative second derivatives ($F_{LL}, F_{KK} < 0$), and a positive cross-derivative ($F_{LK} > 0$).

Assuming that F is linear homogeneous, labour productivity ($y = Y/K$) can be expressed as a function of the capital–labour ratio ($k = K/L$) alone:

$$y = f(k). \tag{6.2}$$

As long as technology is constant, f is expressed as a single convex curve in Figure 6.4 with the horizontal and the vertical axes measuring k and y

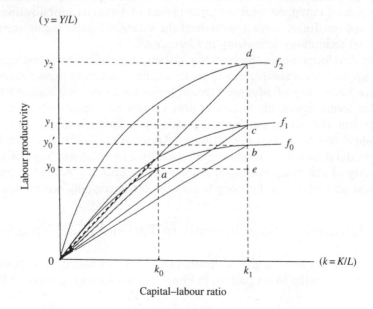

FIG. 6.4 *Elements of growth in labour productivity*

respectively. Assume that in the initial period (0) production function and the capital–labour ratio are f_0 and k_0 respectively, so that labour productivity is determined at $y_0 = f_0(k_0)$. In this case the productivity of capital (Y/K), which is the inverse of capital–output ratio, is given as the slope of line Oa. If the production function remains at f_0 and the capital–labour ratio alone increases from k_0 to k_1 in the next period, capital productivity decreases from the slope of line Oa to that of line Ob. It is then inevitable that the capital–output ratio (K/Y) increases if more capital is applied per unit of labour for constant technology, as long as the production function has normal characteristics defined with respect to equation (6.1).

In fact, even in Phase I technology did not remain constant. However, it appears reasonable to assume that during this phase the shift in production function (f_0 to f_1) was small relative to the increase in the capital–labour ratio (k_0 to k_1), so that the contribution of production function shift (<u>cb</u>) to the growth of labour productivity (<u>ce</u>) was smaller than the contribution of increased capital–labour ratio (<u>be</u>). Correspondingly, the slope of line Oa became less steep than that of line Oc, implying the increase in the capital–output ratio in Phase I.

On the other hand, in Phase II the shift in production function (f_0 to f_2) was large relative to the increase in the capital–labour ratio (k_0 to k_1), so that the contribution of the production function shift (<u>db</u>) to the growth of labour productivity (<u>de</u>) became larger than the contribution of increased capital–labour ratio (<u>be</u>). Correspondingly, the slope of line Od became steeper than that of line Oa, resulting in the decrease in capital–output ratio.

6.4.2 The classification of technological change

It is bias in technological change, together with the elasticity of substitution, that determines the relationship between the capital–labour ratio (K/L) and the wage–rental ratio (w/r), thereby determining the income shares of labour and capital.

Technological change is usually classified according to the bias in the use of production factors. The classification by John Hicks (1932), which is relevant to the problem concerned here, is based on the direction of change in the marginal rate of substitution between labour and capital for a given capital–labour ratio.[5] Three categories of technological changes according to the Hicks definition in the two-factor economy are illustrated in Figure 6.5. Each of the *i*-curves in this diagram is a unit isoquant representing a schedule of input combinations between labour (L) and capital (K) for producing a unit of output. With the use of equation (6.1) it is defined as

$$1 = F(L, K). \tag{6.3}$$

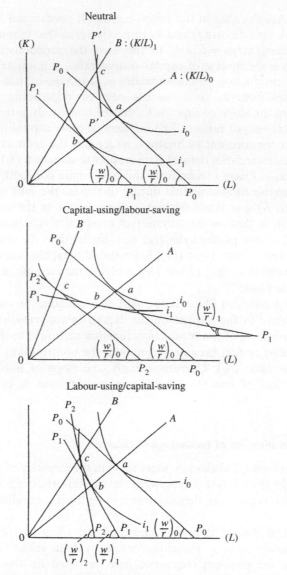

FIG. 6.5 *Classifications of technological progress and substitution between labour and capital*

(F_L/F_K) for a given K/L ratio. This technological progress is represented by a shift from i_0 to i_1 in the upper diagram of Figure 6.5. Since the ratio of marginal productivities between L and K is the marginal rate of substitution $(\partial K/\partial L = F_L/F_K)$, it can be measured by the slope of a line tangent to the i-curve, while the K/L ratio is the slope of a straight line from the origin. A parallel shift in the unit isoquant illustrated as i_0 to i_1 is 'neutral', because slopes of tangent lines to i_0 and i_1 at points a and b respectively, on line OA corresponding to a fixed K/L ratio, are the same. Assuming competitive equilibrium in factor markets, the marginal rate of substitution between (L) and (K) is equal to the wage–rental ratio (w/r). Therefore, for a given wage–rental ratio represented by $(w/r)_0$, the capital–labour ratio remains as (K/L_0) for a parallel shift from i_0 to i_1. Thus, the definition can be restated that technological progress is *neutral* if it does not alter the K/L ratio for a given w/r ratio. Therefore, under this type of technological progress, the ratio of labour income (wL) to capital income (rk) is unchanged, implying no change in the income shares between labour and capital.

Capital-using and labour-saving technological progress is defined as the technological progress that increases the marginal productivity of capital (F_K) relative to the marginal productivity of labour (F_L) for a given K/L ratio. This type is illustrated by a non-parallel shift in the i-curve in the middle diagram of Figure 6.5. It is characterized by larger shift to the origin for the region of higher K/L ratio. As a result, the slope of a tangent line (P) to i-curve at the point crossed by line OA, corresponding to a fixed K/L ratio, decreases upon the shift from i_0 to i_1 (a move from point a to point b). This reflects the decrease in F_L/F_K for a given K/L ratio. If this type of technological progress occurs, the K/L ratio increases for a given w/r ratio (a move from point a to point c in the middle diagram). Thus, the alternative definition of capital-using (and labour-saving) technological progress can be stated as the technological progress that induces the K/L ratio to increase for a given w/r ratio. It is easy to see that under such technological progress the income share of capital increases at the expense of labour's share.

Labour-using and capital-saving technological progress is defined as the technological progress that increases the marginal productivity of labour (F_L) relative to the marginal productivity of capital (F_K). This type is illustrated in the lower diagram of Figure 6.5. Contrary to the capital-using bias in the middle diagram, the labour-using bias is characterized by a larger shift in the origin for the region of lower K/L ratio. As a result, the slope of a tangent line to i_1 at point b becomes larger than that of i_0 at point a on line OA. This reflects the increase in F_L/F_K for a given K/L ratio. If this type of technological progress occurs, the K/L ratio decreases for a fixed w/r ratio. The alternative definition of labour-using and capital-saving technological progress is the technological progress that induces the K/L ratio to decrease for a given w/r ratio. Under such technological progress the income share of labour tends to increase at the expense of capital's share.

6.4.3 Changes in the trends of factor prices and factor shares

How can changes in the trends of factor prices and factor shares between Phases I and II be understood in terms of factor-using (or factor-saving) bias in technological progress illustrated in Figure 6.5?

The two phases shared a common rising trend in capital–labour ratio. This stylized fact may be represented by a shift in the factor ratio line from *OA* to *OB*. It is highly likely that, if technology were to remain constant, rapid decreases in capital's marginal productivity would result from the increase in the capital–labour ratio, as previously explained (the case of lifting water by bucket in Section 2 of this chapter).

This possibility is represented in the upper diagram by a sharp increase in the marginal rate of substitution of capital for labour, corresponding to an increase in the K/L ratio (from line *OA* to *OB*) for i_0 remaining unchanged (a move from point *a* to point *c*). As such, the decline in capital's marginal productivity would proceed, and the rate of return to capital would eventually decline below capital's supply price (consisting of such factors as risk premium, transaction costs, and discount rate of future consumption), so that further capital accumulation would stop.[6] This could have been the case, even with modest technological progress, if this progress were neutral.

In Phase I, stylized facts like rapid increases in the capital–labour ratio, relative stability in the wage–rental ratio, and increases in the income share of capital, can be consistently explained by capital-using technological progress illustrated in the middle diagram. These stylized facts are consistent with the hypothesis that rapid increases in the capital–labour ratio (*OA* to *OB*) coincided with capital-using technological progress (i_0 to i_1); this biased technological progress was effective in preventing the marginal productivity of capital from declining sharply and, thereby, preventing the wage–rental ratio from rising despite major increases in the capital–labour ratio, represented by parallel tangent lines at points *a* and *c*. The income share of capital increased. Constancy (or moderate rise) in the wage rate may have also been supported by fast population growth in Phase I, but the labour-saving effect of capital-using technological progress would have been equally significant.

In contrast, increases in the wage rates and decreases in the income share of capital associated with increases in the capital–output ratio in Phase II can be explained in terms of labour-using and capital-saving technological progress. This type of technological progress is represented by a shift from i_0 to i_1 in the lower diagram of Figure 6.5, which should have occurred concurrently with the rise in the capital–labour ratio (*OA* to *OB*). As the production point moved from *a* to *b*, the marginal rate of substitution of capital for labour rose sharply, with a corresponding increase in the wage–rental ratio from $(w/r)_0$ to $(w/r)_2$. This increase was larger than the increase in the capital–labour ratio so that the labour income increased relative to the capital income. The reason that bias in technological progress shifted from the capital-using to the labour-using direction was explained earlier (Section 2), namely the shifts in the technology regime (from visible to invisible technology) and in the demand structure (from standardized to differentiated products) together increased productivity of intangible human capital relative to that of tangible capital. Correspondingly, there was increased incentive for people to invest more heavily in education, research, and development. Observed increases in the wage rates in Phase II, therefore, can be considered remuneration to accumulated human capital per person in addition to remuneration to raw labour power.

6.4.4 Possibilities for induced innovation

As explained in Section 2 of this chapter, developing economies which try to promote industrialization based on borrowed technology are likely to experience increases in the income share of capital due to rapid progress in technology biased towards capital-using and labour-saving.

To avoid the danger of growing inequality, it is necessary to make efforts to adjust imported technologies to the conditions of relative resource endowments in developing economies. This issue will be discussed in detail in the next chapter (Section 2). Here it will be made clear that development of 'appropriate technology' to relative resource endowments does not necessarily sacrifice economic efficiency, but can promote both efficiency and equity. A theoretical framework for understanding this possibility is the theory of induced innovation (Chapter 1, Section 2).

Figure 6.6 is essentially the same as the middle diagram of Figure 6.5. It represents a typical pattern of economic growth based on borrowed technology, in which capital-using technological progress (i_0 to i_1) coincided with an increase in the capital–labour ratio (OA to OB). Correspondingly, equili-

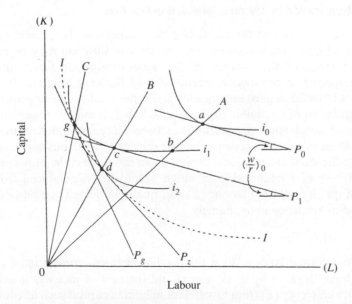

FIG. 6.6 *Possibilities for induced technological innovation*

brium moved from point *a* to point *c* in such a way as to leave the wage-rental rate unchanged at $(w/r)_0$. We assume that i_1 represents a borrowed technology by developing economies that was originally developed in advanced economies as an appropriate technology for their relative resource scarcities. In other words, i_1 was a unit isoquant chosen out of many unit isoquants enveloped by an innovation possibility curve *I* because it minimized production cost for the high wage–rental ratio in advanced economies (P_g).

If this assumption is valid, developing economies should be able to minimize their production cost by developing an isoquant such as i_2 which is tangent to *I* at point *d*. The wage–rental ratio to be established in equilibrium at this point is the slope of line P_2 which is larger than that of line P_1. Therefore, the labour income increases relative to the capital income as technology changes from i_1 to i_2. Thus, if developing economies would extend major efforts to correct the strong capital-using bias in technology borrowed from advanced economies, both efficiency and equity could be promoted.

According to the traditional theory of induced innovation within the neoclassical theory of the firm, i_2 should be developed through innovative efforts of private entrepreneurs since it represents a more efficient technology than i_1. However, it is difficult to expect that a frontier technology such as i_2 in developing economies could be developed by the efforts of private entrepreneurs alone, who are not well endowed with funds and human resources for research and development. The policies needed to close this gap will be discussed in the next chapter.

6.4.5 Interpretation by the meta-production function

The theory advanced so far to explain the changes in the growth pattern from the initial to the advanced stage of industrialization may be reinterpreted in terms of the concept of the 'meta-production function'. This function specifies a production relationship in the very long run in which the effects of technological innovations and input quality improvements due to accumulation of intangible capital are included. It may be regarded as an envelope of neoclassical production functions (Hayami and Ruttan, 1985: 133–7). Meta-production function can be specified in various ways, such as including the stock of intangible capital as an input variable. However, it is specified here as a relationship in which output (*Y*) is produced from the inputs of quality-adjusted labour (*X*) and quality-adjusted capital (*Z*), both measured in efficiency units, namely

$$Y = M(X, Z). \tag{6.4}$$

Quality-adjusted labour (*X*) is the product between conventionally measured labour (such as by work hours) and the rate of increase in labour's productive efficiency (*E*) from investment in human capital such as education and health care. If a person can produce twice as much output with increased skill, due to training for example, efficiency is doubled ($E = 2$). Quality-adjusted capital (Z) is the product of conventionally measured capital (K) and the rate of increase in capital's efficiency (H). For example, if a new model of a pump at the same price as the old model can lift up to three times more water within one hour, capital's production efficiency is tripled ($H = 3$).

E and H are often called 'augmenters' or 'augmenting coefficients' of labour and capital respectively. It is relatively common in the mathematical analysis of economic growth to use a production function with EL and HK included as input variables (e.g. Phelps, 1966). However, M in equation 6.4 is defined for the very long run, in which technology can adjust to changes in resource mix. For example, when E rises as the result of education investment so that $X(= EL)$ increases relative to $Z(= HK)$, M is defined for a sufficiently long period in which technological innovation geared to prevent X's marginal productivity from declining will exert its full effect. Thus, elasticity of substitution between X and Z in M must be very large.

The elasticity of substitution between X and Z is not the ratio between the rate of change in the input ratio $G(Z/X)$ and the rate of change in the wage–rental ratio $G(w/r)$. The wage rate conventionally measured (w) is considered to be a product between return to raw labour (v) and its efficiency (E). Similarly, the observable interest rate (r) is the product between return to efficiency unit of capital (q) and its efficiency (H). Thus, the elasticity of substitution between X and Z is given as

$$\sigma G(Z/X)/G(v/q) = \{[G(K) + G(H)] - [G(L) + G(E)]\}/[G(v) - G(q)]. \tag{6.5}$$

Figure 6.7 draws a unit isoquant m of the meta-production function in the X–Z quadrant. As inputs are measured in efficiency units, m remains unchanged for any technological change. Investments for the purpose of technological progress and human capital enhancement are considered to have the effect of changing the input ratio (Z/X), as represented by a straight line from the origin, through changes in E and H.

Now, assume that in the initial period the input ratio was given as $(Z/X)_0$, represented by line OA, for which the input price ratio was determined as $(v/q)_0$, corresponding to the marginal rate of substitution at point a.

What happened in Phase I can be interpreted as follows: K accumulated rapidly, and, also, H increased rapidly because of the bias in technological progress towards increasing the efficiency of capital, resulting in very rapid growth in $Z = HK$. In contrast, human capital investment was still relatively modest so that increases in E were much smaller than those of H, with the result that the Z/X ratio increased, as represented by a shift from line OA to OB. Corresponding to a shift in equilibrium from point a to point b, the input price ratio became less favourable to capital from $(v/q)_0$ to $(v/q)_1$. However, because H increased faster then E, the wage–rental ratio ($w/r = rE/qH$) remained relatively stable.

In contrast, in Phase II increased human capital investment resulted in a major increase in Z relative to increases in K and H, so that the Z/X ratio decreased, represented by a shift from line OB to OC. The decrease in the v/q ratio was more than compensated for by the increase in E relative to H, so that the wage–rental ratio (w/r) increased in Phase II.

As a basic characteristic of the meta-production function the elasticity of substitutions is very large. Under the assumption of an elasticity of substitution greater than one, the rate of change in the v/q ratio is smaller than that of the Z/X ratio. Therefore, in Phase I when Z/X increases, $q = vZ/qX$ increases, implying increases in the income share of capital. In Phase II when Z/X decreases, vZ/qX also decreases, implying decreases in the income share of capital.

Thus, theoretical predictions of the change in the growth pattern from Phase I to II under the assumption of the meta-production function turned out to be the same as those under the assumption of different biases in technological progress using the ordinary production function.

6.4.6 Mathematical analysis of changes in factor shares

Finally, we try to confirm by mathematics the mechanism of change in factor shares explained in terms of Figure 6.7.

Assume equation (6.4) has the same properties as equation (6.1); e.g. M is differentiable with respect to X and Z with positive first derivatives

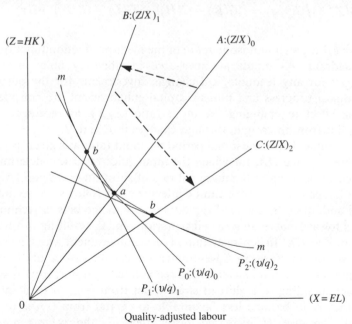

FIG. 6.7 *Factor substitution along meta-production function*

($M_x M_z > 0$), negative second derivatives (M_{xx}, $M_{zz} < 0$), and a positive cross-derivative ($M_{xz} > 0$). Assuming competitive equilibrium in factor markets, the income share of capital ($\beta = rK/Y = qZ/Y$) is given as:

$$\beta = M_z Z / Y \tag{6.6}$$

which can be expressed in terms of growth rates as

$$G(\beta) = G(M_z) + G(Z) - G(Y). \tag{6.7}$$

Since M is assumed to be linear homogeneous, the following relations hold:

$$\begin{aligned} M_x X + M_z Z &= Y \\ M_{xx} X + M_{xz} Z &= 0 \\ M_{zx} X + M_{zz} Z &= 0. \end{aligned} \tag{6.8}$$

The elasticity of substitution can be expressed as

$$\sigma = (1/Y) \cdot (M_x M_z / M_{xz}). \tag{6.9}$$

Since $(1 - \beta) = M_x X / Y$, equations (6.8) and (6.9) produce

$$G(M_z) = [M_{xz} dX + M_{zz} dZ]/M_z = [(1 - \beta)/\sigma] \cdot [G(X) - G(Z)]. \tag{6.10}$$

Similarly, the following equation can be derived:

$$G(Y) = (1 - \beta)G(X) + \beta G(E). \tag{6.11}$$

Substituting equations (6.10) and 6.11) for equation (6.7), we obtain

$$\begin{aligned} G(\beta) &= (1 - \beta)[(\sigma - 1)/\sigma] \cdot [G(Z) - G(X)] \\ &= (1 - \beta)[(\sigma - 1)/\sigma] \cdot \{[G(K) - G(H)] - [G(L) + G(E)]\} \end{aligned} \tag{6.12}$$

which determines the income share of capital.

If, as the basic characteristic of the meta-production function, the elasticity of substitution in M is sufficiently large so that $\sigma > 1$ the income share of capital (β) increases for

$$G(K) + G(H) > G(L) + G(E).$$

This corresponds to the pattern in Phase I represented by a shift from line *OA* to *OB* in Figure 6.7. In contrast, β decreases for

$$G(K) + G(H) < G(L) + G(E),$$

which corresponds to the pattern in Phase II represented by a shift from line *OB* to *OC*.[7]

NOTES

1. Public investment in scientific research and education lagged in England, partly because of high accumulation of skill among workers developed through on-the-

job training and partly because of Smithian *laissez-faire* tradition. It was in 1883 that the Finsburg Technical College was opened as the first advanced engineering school with the support of the City of London, which was incorporated in the University of London as late as 1908. Establishment of new universities, such as Birmingham, Liverpool, and Manchester, with orientation towards applied science and technology was also after 1900. France pioneered in the area of military engineering with the establishment of École Polytechnique for training military engineers under Napoleon. This French model was transferred to the USA with the first chair of engineering established in West Point in 1802, more than half a century before the opening of the Massachusetts Institute of Technology in 1861.

2. Denison's major contributions are an analysis of the US economy (Denison, 1962) and a comparative study of nine advanced economies (Denison, 1967). Findings summarized in Table 6.2 are based on revised estimates reported in Denison and Chung (1976). There have been several other attempts to investigate sources of growth in total factor productivity, among which a contribution by Christensen and Jorgenson (1970) is especially important.

3. Gerschenkron's thesis has been criticized for its overly heavy emphasis on the role of banks, neglecting the role of equity capital market (Cameron *et al.*, 1967).

4. The central issue in the neoclassical theory of growth is to identify the conditions and properties of economic growth at a steady rate in final equilibrium ('steady-state growth'). However, that is not the concern of this section. Utilizing the tools of the neoclassical growth theory, we try to develop a formal analysis on the technological conditions for the shift in the economic growth pattern which were explained in the text of Section 3. For an overview of the neoclassical growth theory, see Solow (1970) and Wan (1971).

5. There are other classifications used in economics. The classifications by Harrod (1948) are based on changes in the capital–output ratio (K/Y) for a given marginal productivity of capital (r), i.e. neutral if K/Y remains constant, capital-using if K/Y increases, and capital-saving if K/Y decreases. On the other hand, the classifications by Solow (1970) are based on changes in the labour–output ratio (L/Y) for a given wage rate (w), i.e. neutral if L/Y remains constant, labour-using if L/Y increases, and labour saving if L/Y decreases. Harrod-neutrality is capital-using and labour-saving in terms of Hicks's criteria, and Solow-neutrality is capital-saving and labour-using in Hicks's criteria.

6. This statement applies to the case of market economy in which investment decisions are based on profit calculations by private entrepreneurs. However, it is possible that in the centrally planned economies capital accumulation was promoted much beyond the equilibrium between the marginal return and the marginal cost of capital, as evidenced by the estimate of capital's marginal productivity decline to nearly zero towards the end of the Soviet regime in Russia (Easterly and Fischer, 1994).

7. Therefore, when $\sigma > 1$, technological progress is capital-saving and labour-using if $G(H) > G(E)$ and labour-using and capital-saving if $G(H) < G(E)$ in the Hicks definition. On the contrary, when $\sigma < 1$, technological progress is labour-saving and capital-saving if $G(H) > G(E)$ and capital-using and labour-saving if $G(H) < G(E)$.

7

Income Distribution and Environmental Problems

If the Marx pattern of economic growth tends to emerge in the early phase of industrialization, as the analysis in the previous chapter shows, developing economics are likely to experience increasing inequality in income distribution. Inequalization is not desirable by the criteria of social justice. From the point of view of economic growth also, increased inequality provokes dissatisfaction and frustration among the poor, which may culminate in disruption and civil war, destroying the social and political basis of economic activities.

Another major difficulty that developing economies will have to face is the environmental problem. Due to explosive population growth in the early phase of industrialization, demand for arable land expands rapidly, so that cultivation frontiers are pushed to ecologically fragile lands in hills and mountains (which would be better preserved as forests and pasture lands), resulting in serious soil erosion and flood incidence. On the other hand, in its early stage, industrialization tends to proceed without due investment in pollution control and energy-saving, with the danger of escalating air and water pollution to unbearable levels.

In this chapter we will discuss the effects of economic growth on income distribution and environment in developing economies and search for possible solutions.

7.1 Economic Growth and Income Distribution

First, we will observe how income distribution changes in the process of economic development.

7.1.1 Personal distribution and functional distribution

The problem of income distribution is commonly understood as the problem of 'personal income distribution'—how incomes are distributed among people. The units of living for most people are families. Children of rich parents, for example, can enjoy affluent lives even if they themselves earn no income.

Therefore, comparison among households rather than individuals is usually an appropriate way to assess equality (or inequality) in society.

Income equality among households is usually measured by the distribution of incomes according to the size (or level) of income per household (or household member). This distribution across income-size classes is commonly called the 'size distribution of income'. The lower the income share of high-income classes and the higher the share of low-income classes, the more equal income distribution is considered to be. Thus, the size distribution is an intuitively appealing concept of income distribution.

However, in economics, income distribution has more often been analysed in terms of the income shares of factors (factor shares) for production. Because factor shares measure relative incomes accruing to production factors, such as labour and capital, according to their contributions to value added, they are called the 'functional distribution of income'.

Indeed, analysis of the functional distribution has been one of the central issues in development economics. Among the Classical economists, Ricardo classified national income into three categories, i.e. wage as return to labour, profit as return to capital, and rent as return to land. His analysis focused on how national income is distributed among the three major classes in society—labourers, capitalists, and landlords—through the functional distribution among the three factors. His analysis predicted that inequalization will progress in the process of economic growth based on capital accumulation in modern industries because the progressively larger share of income will go into the hands of wealthy landlords—traditional élite in England—as long as food supply relies on domestic production (Chapter 3, Section 3).

A half-century later, Marx predicted growing inequality in the capitalist development process. Corresponding to a reduction in the importance of land through further progress in industrialization from Ricardo's time, Marx analysed how national income is divided between the two categories, i.e. wage and profit, and predicted increases in the latter relative to the former, resulting in the concentration of income in the hands of capitalists and the pauperization of labourers (Section 5.1.3).

In general, the size distribution of income is determined by both the distribution of income between labour and capital assets (functional distribution) and the distribution of the assets across the income-size classes. Ricardo and Marx discussed the issue of income distribution among social classes based on the analysis of functional distribution, under the assumption that all the land and capital assets are owned by landlords and capitalists respectively, and labourers had no means of production other than their own labour. This assumption might have been a reasonable approximation in their day. However, in advanced economies today, assets owned by employees are very significant. They own not only tangible assets, but also intangible assets such as knowledge and skill accumulated through human capital investment. Therefore, changes in income distribution in the process of economic development cannot be judged appropriately through the analysis of functional distribution alone.

We have already analysed changes in factor shares in the previous two chapters. In this section we will try to analyse changes in social equality through direct observations on size distribution of income among households.

7.1.2 Indicators of inequality

There are many possible measures of equality (or inequality) in the size distribution of income. The most simple is to take a percentage of total income accruing to households belonging to the high-income class (e.g. the top 20 per cent of households) or that of the low-income class (e.g. the bottom 20 per cent). Of course, the higher the share of the high-income class and the lower the share of the low-income class, the greater the inequality. Another measure may be the ratio of the income share of the top group to that of the bottom group, which equals the ratio of average income in the highest-income group to that of the lowest-income group.

These simple measures are both easy to understand intuitively and also easy to calculate. However, they are subject to shortcomings, such as partial use of information pertaining only to the top and the bottom groups and arbitrariness in the demarcation of the income classes.

Among several measures intended to overcome those defects, the mostly widely used is the Gini coefficient. Geometrically, the Gini coefficient is expressed by the Lorenz curve that draws cumulative percentage distributions of household incomes (in the vertical axis) corresponding to cumulative distributions of the numbers of households (in the horizontal axis) ranked according to household incomes from the bottom to the top. For illustration, the Lorenz curves of India, Brazil, and Japan based on data classified into quintile household groups are compared in Figure 7.1 (data in Table 7.1). The degree of inequality in income distribution is higher when the Lorenz curve arches more strongly downward. In terms of this criterion, inequality is about the same in India and Japan, but their inequality is substantially lower than in Brazil. Such a relationship can be easily understood from the observations that the income received by the bottom 20 per cent of households is 8.1 per cent in India, 8.7 in Japan, but only 2.4 per cent in Brazil, and that the income received by the bottom 40 per cent is 20.4 per cent in India, 21.9 per cent in Japan, but only 8.1 per cent in Brazil. The Gini coefficients are estimated as 0.31 for India, 0.54 for Brazil, and 0.27 for Japan.

The Lorenz curve coincides with the diagonal line *OB* in the case of perfect equality in which all the households receive the same income. At the other extreme, the case of perfect inequality in which one household monopolizes all the income while the other households receive no income, the Lorenz curve

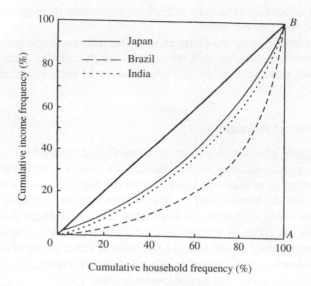

FIG. 7.1 *Lorenz curves for Japan, Brazil, and India*
Source: World Bank, *World Development Report 1992*, World Development Indicators, Table 30.

would follow the right-angled line OAB. Thus, inequality can be judged to be larger if the area between line OB and the Lorenz curve is larger.

The Gini coefficient is measured by this area to the area of triangle $\underline{OAB}$. It measures inequality within the range from 0 for perfect equality to 1 for perfect inequality. This coefficient can be calculated mathematically,[1] but can also be obtained graphically in the case of broad classifications (such as quintile breakdowns of households).

TABLE 7.1 *Cumulative shares of household incomes, by quintile class of households, India, Brazil, and Japan*

Income-Size Class	Cumulative frequency from bottom (%)		
	India 1983	Brazil 1983	Japan 1979
I (Top)	100	100.0	100.0
II	80	58.7	37.4	62.5
III	60	36.7	18.8	39.4
IV	40	20.4	8.1	21.9
V (Bottom)	20	8.1	2.4	8.7
	0.31	0.54	0.27

Source: World Bank. *World Development Report 1992*, World Development Indicators, Table 30.

The following analysis on the effects of economic growth on income distribution will be based on estimates of the Gini coefficient.

7.1.3 The inverted-U-shape hypothesis

Relative to the theory of factor shares, economic theory has been under-developed for the analysis of size distribution. No more than conjecture exists on how the size distribution changed in the early phase of industrialization (Phase I in Table 5.1), because household survey data in industrial economies have been available only since the late nineteenth century when those economies had already reached the advanced stage (Phase II).

Based on available data, Kuznets concluded that inequality in income distribution in advanced economies decreased from the 1920s, especially with large reductions from the period before to the period after World War II (Kuznets, 1966: 206–17). Further, in the absence of reliable data, he considered it possible that inequality increased in the earlier period (Kuznets, 1955). According to his conjecture, if historical data are available to draw the measures of inequality (such as the Gini coefficient) in the vertical axis in association with average income per capita in the horizontal axis, the relationship would be curved in an inverted-U shape with an initial phase of increasing inequality succeeded by a phase of decreasing inequality.

Despite several efforts to test this hypothesis, it has not yet been confirmed by historical data of Western Europe and North America (Paukert, 1973). However, for Japan in which organized statistical collection began early relative to its start of industrialization, some data exist for estimating changes in income distribution from the early phase of industrialization. The Gini coefficients estimated from these data are compiled in Table 7.2.

TABLE 7.2 *Estimates of the Gini coefficient in Japan, 1890 to 1980*

	Ono-Watanabe (1976)	Otsuki-Takamatsu (1978)	Minami et al. (1993)	Wada (1975)	Mizoguchi et al. (1978)
1890		0.31			
1900		0.42			
1910	0.36	0.42			
1920	0.42	0.46	0.51[a]		
1930	0.43	0.45	0.51		
1940	0.47	0.64	0.54[b]		
1956				0.31	
1962				0.38	0.38
1968					0.35
1974					0.34
1980					0.33

[a] 1923 value
[b] 1937 value

Source: Mizoguchi (1986: 152) except Minami et al. (1993).

These estimates before World War II are likely to involve significant errors, as they were based not on household survey data but on other indirect sources such as taxation statistics (estimates by Ono and Watanabe, 1976) and national account statistics (estimates by Otsuki-Takamatsu, 1978). Yet, all the estimates unanimously show that inequality increased from the beginning of industrialization until World War II, and declined to a large extent during the post-war period.

Such movements in the Gini coefficient in Japan are apparently consistent with the inverted-U-shape hypothesis. The Japanese data in Table 7.2 can be considered a significant evidence for the phase of increasing inequality to have existed in the early period. However, it is doubtful if the data support the hypothesis that equalization began operating in the later phase as an endogenous mechanism of economic growth. The reason is that the major declines in inequality estimated for the post-war period resulted from the *ad hoc* event of the major defeat in the war that destroyed the assets of rich city dwellers and forced institutional reforms such as land reform and property tax, which were unlikely to have been instituted in a peacetime setting. Future research is needed to determine how much of this equalization was due to the shock of the war and how much was due to the internal mechanism of growth.

Thus, it is difficult to confirm the inverted-U-shape pattern by time-series data. However, it is relatively easy to observe it by intercountry cross-sectional data (Paukert, 1973; Alhuwalia, 1976; Fields, 1980, ch. 4), although significant counter-evidence also exists (Anand and Kanbur, 1993; Fields, 1995). Figure 7.2 plots in a double logarithmic diagram the observations for nineteen countries of the Gini coefficients estimated during the 1970s and 1980s in relation to GNP per capita in 1990. The figure shows a smooth bell shape with a peak at per capita GNP around $US 2,000 to $US 3,000. Goodness of data fit to a quadratic curve is also high.[2]

If low-income economies have to experience rising inequality in the early phase of industrialization as indicated in Figure 7.2—such as a rise in the Gini coefficient for Bangladesh from the present level (0.25) to the level of Malaysia (0.42)—social tension is likely to loom large, endangering political stability.

It is worth noting that, although not shown in the figure, income distributions in former socialist economies were significantly more equal than in market economies. For example, the Gini coefficient of Poland was 0.24 for its per capita GNP of $1,690, which was very low compared with Colombia's 0.44 for $1,260 and Botswana's 0.50 for $2,040. Likewise, the Gini coefficient of Hungary was 0.21 at a per capita GDP of $2,780, which was low compared with Malaysia's 0.42 at $2,320 and Brazil's 0.54 for $2,680.

Comparatively low inequality thus observed demonstrates a merit of the socialist system despite its other shortcomings. However, as those economies pursue the transition to market economies, a danger may arise for the Gini

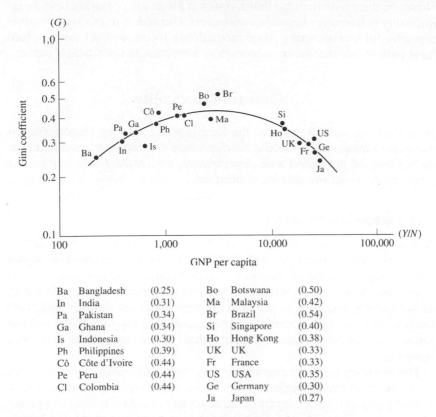

(G)

Gini coefficient

GNP per capita

(Y/N)

Ba	Bangladesh	(0.25)	Bo	Botswana	(0.50)
In	India	(0.31)	Ma	Malaysia	(0.42)
Pa	Pakistan	(0.34)	Br	Brazil	(0.54)
Ga	Ghana	(0.34)	Si	Singapore	(0.40)
Is	Indonesia	(0.30)	Ho	Hong Kong	(0.38)
Ph	Philippines	(0.39)	UK	UK	(0.33)
Cô	Côte d'Ivoire	(0.44)	Fr	France	(0.33)
Pe	Peru	(0.44)	US	USA	(0.35)
Cl	Colombia	(0.44)	Ge	Germany	(0.30)
			Ja	Japan	(0.27)

FIG. 7.2 *International comparison of the Gini coefficients, double-log scale*
Notes: Numerical values of the Gini coefficients shown in parentheses are calculated from quantile distributions. GNP per capita pertains to 1990. The Gini coefficients are based on household surveys conducted in the 1970s and 1980s.
Source: World Bank, *World Development Report 1990*, World Development Indicators, Tables 1 and 30.

coefficient to move upward so that it will approach the inverted-U-shape curve observable from international comparative data. An important agenda in the market-orientated transition, therefore, is to prevent inequality from rising too sharply or to prepare a safety net of social security for those people who might drop down to poverty.

Although former socialist economies represent major deviations from the cross-country inverted-U curve, there are many significant deviations—economies in Latin America are generally located above and those in East Asia below the curve. Since the inverted-U relationship has not been confirmed by time-series data, it should not be taken as the route that developing economies cannot avoid following in their development process.

However, there is no denying that significant forces are operating to increase inequality in the early phase of development. Our task is to examine possible measures for counteracting those inequalizing forces, so that the development path of low-income economies may not simulate the Kuznets curve.

7.2 Causes of Inequality

In this section we will examine the factors which may be responsible for increases in inequality in income distribution in developing economies in the early phase of their economic development, and explore possibilities for reversing the trend towards inequalization.

7.2.1 Changes in factor shares

A major inequalizing force that developing economies are likely to face in their early developmental phase is increases in the income share of capital (which means decreases in labour's income share). As observed in the previous two chapters, a general tendency exists in which the later the start of industrialization, the more capital-using and labour-saving technology tends to be borrowed. Therefore, it is possible that capital's share will rise faster in developing economies today than in the histories of advanced economies.

This tendency has been aggravated by policies commonly adopted by the governments in developing economies to promote heavy and chemical industries of high capital intensity from the beginning of industrialization with the aim of catching up with advanced economies at maximum speed. Frequently used for this end have been policies favouring large-scale industries based on capital-intensive technology—at the expense of small and medium enterprises based on labour-intensive technology—by such means as import restrictions, foreign exchange allocations, and overvalued exchange rates. These policies will be examined in detail later (Section 8.2.4). Here, it is pointed out that the policy bias towards promoting introduction of capital-using technology should be corrected to prevent capital's share from rising sharply in developing economies.

Further, a major effort must be devoted to adjust borrowed technology to the underlying resource endowments in developing economies. Since the technology being used in advanced economies was developed as an optimum (minimum cost) technology under the condition of low capital costs relative to labour costs, reductions in both production cost and capital's share can be achieved by adjusting it in the labour-using direction (as represented by a shift from i_1 to i_2 in Figure 6.6).

It could be difficult to develop the optimum technology on the frontier of innovations (i_2 in Figure 6.6) by R & D resources available in developing economies. Yet, significant room exists for promoting both efficiency and equity through relatively simple adjustments, such as the removal of sophisticated automation devices from an original machine design and purchase of second-hand machines (Stewart, 1977). These adjustments are by nature minor, but cumulative in effect, making formal means of protection such as patents difficult to establish. Moreover, firms in developing economies, especially those engaged in labour-intensive manufacturing, are usually too small as operational units to internalize major gains from innovation to pay for the costs. Because of this externality, it is unlikely that sufficient innovative activities can be mobilized for the development of 'appropriate technology' (defined as optimum technology under relative resource endowments in developing economies) if left solely to private entrepreneurs. Governments in developing economies must assist not only in basic research, but also in applied-end technology development. The assistance may extend from development and demonstration of new machines and production layouts in industrial experimental stations and trade fairs to technical training and managerial consultancy centring on small and medium enterprises, which could well be left to private consulting firms in developed economies (Pack and Westphal, 1986). The need for public investment in applied research and extension in development of labour-intensive manufacturing in developing economies is similar to the case of the development of biological technology for agriculture (Sections 4.1 and 4.2).

7.2.2 The dual economic structure

If large-scale industries with high capital intensity are promoted at the stage in which labour supply is relatively abundant, differentials in labour productivity and the wage rate arise. This so-called 'dual structure' emerged in Japan during the interwar period in response to increased demand for better-educated and trained workers by large-scale industries (Chapter 6, Section 1). It is highly possible that the dual structure will become a much more serious source of inequality in developing economies today than it was in Japan.

Unlike Japan before World War II, developing economies have imported the institutions to protect labourers, such as labour unions, minimum wage laws, and regulations on work hours, which were especially strengthened in developed economies after the war under the slogan of 'welfare states'. However, application of these labour protection measures in developing economies has been limited largely to large-scale enterprises in which unions are organized. In the so-called 'formal sector', consisting of large enterprises and government agencies, stable employment is guaranteed and the wage rates are high since workers are protected by labour laws. To the extent that workers in the formal sector enjoy their prestigious employment, entry to this sector is closed to labourers in the 'informal sector', who earn subsistence as employees in small enterprises, casual labourers on a daily employment contract, petty traders, and self-employed manufacturers.

With the barriers of labour regulations and unions, labour costs to large enterprises are high despite an abundant availability of low-wage labourers in the informal sectors. Therefore, strong incentives are at work among entrepreneurs in the formal sector to increase capital intensity by adopting labour-saving technologies. As a result, employment increases much less than increases in output and labour productivity in this sector. The income gap tends to widen cumulatively between employees in the formal sector, who can achieve handsome wage hikes through union bargaining under increases in labour productivity, and labourers in the informal sector, who continue on a subsistence level of living.[3]

In order to prevent this gap from widening, the same policies needed for suppressing the rise in capital's share would be effective. Namely governments should stop interventions into markets such as import licensing and foreign exchange allocations that favour large-scale enterprises. They should also endeavour to assist small and medium enterprises through development and diffusion of appropriate technologies and provision of technical and managerial know-how, including market information. Laws and regulations for the protection of labourers may be applied relatively loosely but as widely as possible to reduce segmentation of the labour market between the formal and informal sectors.

7.2.3 Agriculture–non-agriculture income differential

One of the major factors underlying inequality in the early stage of development is the widening income differential between the agricultural and non-agricultural population. When modern industries are introduced to an economy consisting primarily of traditional subsistence-orientated farmers, a major intersectoral differential in production is bound to emerge. This productivity differential tends to widen as productivity in the modern industrial sector increases faster (due to relative ease in technology borrowing) than productivity in agriculture in the early stage of development (Section 4.1).

Widening of the income differential between farm and non-farm households due to the widened productivity gap between agriculture and industry was a major factor accounting for inequality in Japan before World War II (Otsuki and Takamatsu, 1978). As shown in Table 7.3, the ratio of real labour productivity in agriculture to that of industry in Japan declined sharply from 75 per cent in 1885 to 24 per cent in 1935. Meanwhile, the intersectoral terms of trade remained largely stable, so that precipitous drops in the real productivity ratio against agriculture were mostly reflected in decreases in the ratio of farm household income to non-farm household income per capita from 76 per cent in 1885 to 38 per cent in 1935. It should

TABLE 7.3 *Historical changes in agriculture-manufacturing relative labour productivity, agriculture-industry terms of trade, farm-non-farm household relative income in Japan, 1985–1990*

	(1)	(2)	(3)
	Agriculture/industry real labour productivity ratio (%)	Agriculture/industry terms of trade (1885=100)	Farm/non-farm household relative income (%)
1885	75	100	76
1890	67	115	87
1900	49	102	52
1910	37	98	47
1920	50	99	48
1930	31	104	32
1935	24	136	38
1955	55	163	77
1960	39	169	68
1970	25	304	91
1980	17	347	115
1990	14	357	115

Sources: (1) 1885–1970: Calculated as ratio in real GDP per gainful worker between agriculture (including forestry and fishery) and industry (including mining) from Ohkawa and Shinohara (1979, pp. 278–82 and 392–95); the numbers of gainful workers for 1885–90 are estimated for agriculture by adding 3 per cent to the numbers of gainful workers in agriculture and forestry as fishery workers, and estimated for industry by assuming to be 72 per cent (1906–10 ratio) of the total number of gainful workers minus workers in agriculture, commerce and services based on Ohkawa, *et al.*, *LTES* vol. 1 (1974: 129). 1980–90: extrapolated from the Ohkawa–Shinohara series by GDP from Japan Economic Planning Agency's *National Accounts* and gainful workers from Ministry of Labour's *Labour Force Survey*.
(2) 1885–1970: Calculated as the ratio of the agricultural product price index to the industrial product price index from Ohkawa *et al. LTES* vol. 8 (1967: 165 and 192–3). 1970–90: extrapolated from the *LTES* series by Japan Ministry of Agriculture's agricultural product price index and Bank of Japan's wholesale price index for industrial commodities.
(3) 1885–35: The ratio of per capita income in farm households to that of non-farm households from Otsuki and Takamatsu (1982). 1955–90: The ratio of per capita income of farm households from Ministry of Agriculture's *Farm Household Economy Survey* to that of employees' households from Management and Coordination Agency's *Household Survey*.

be noted that rapid improvements in the farm–non-farm relative income after World War II resulted partly from improvement in the terms of trade partially due to agricultural protection policies, but more importantly from major increases in the off-farm income of farm households (Hayami, 1988: 92–3).

It is possible that the farm–non-farm income differentials in developing economies today will widen more sharply than in the history of Japan. Part of the reason is the weaker labour-absorptive capacity in the modern sector due to the institutional factors that strengthen the dual economic structure by promoting introduction of labour-saving technologies. Another reason is much stronger population pressure on limited land resources for agricultural production. In prewar Japan, increments of population were almost fully absorbed in non-agriculture so that the agricultural population remained nearly constant and farmland area per agricultural worker increased very slightly. In contrast, today's low- to lower-middle-income developing economies are experiencing absolute increases in agricultural population, and farm land area per agricultural worker is decreasing.

Under such strong population pressure on land, an extremely rapid rate of progress in land-saving technology is required to prevent labour productivity in agriculture from declining relative to that of industry. Such technological progress is possible if the potential of science-based agriculture is adequately exploited (Section 4.1). However, the potential cannot be realized without major public investment in farmers' education, agricultural research, irrigation, roads, and other infrastructure. Whether developing economies eager to achieve rapid industrialization allocate their limited budget to agricultural development investment will have a decisive effect on the trends in income distribution.

7.2.4 On the redistribution of incomes and assets[4]

It is well known that redistribution of incomes and assets (by such means as progressive tax, inheritance tax, and social security systems) underlies equalization in income distribution in advanced economies, especially since World War II.

However, these taxes and transfers can hardly be an effective means of equalizing income distribution in developing economies where the majority of the population engage in self-employment and casual hired work in agricultural and urban informal sectors. It is too costly to assess incomes and assets as the basis for taxation on a large number of self-employed producers. It is equally difficult to collect contributions to the social security fund from workers in the informal sector and make appropriate payments to them.

A redistributive policy which has hitherto been attempted to correct inequality in developing economies is land reform (or 'agrarian reform') aimed at redistributing farm lands from landlords to tenants and agricultural labourers. Implementation of redistributive land reform in Japan, Korea, and Taiwan immediately after World War II effectively transferred nearly all the farm lands owned by non-cultivating landlords to tenants, resulting in highly egalitarian agrarian structures. It is not very clear how much this reform contributed to increases in agricultural productivity. However, it cannot be denied that the establishment of egalitarian agrarian societies consisting of homogeneous small landholders increased social and political stability as the basis of rapid development of those economies (Hayami and Yamada, 1991: 83–5).

However, are there social and political conditions for effective implementation of redistributive land reform in developing economies today, where landlords constitute a very strong (often the strongest) political bloc? Past history shows that attempts at land reform patterned after the success in Japan, Korea, and Taiwan have not only failed to achieve the intended goals, but have often led to negative consequences (Warriner, 1969; Dorner, 1972; Ladejinsky, 1977). Plans and deliberations for land reform legislation have prompted landlords' evasive reactions to the reform, such as evicting tenants and hiring labourers to cultivate under landlords' direct management, and planting trees in arable lands to change the latter's classification. Such practices have reduced the opportunities for tenants to use their labour and managerial abilities. Indeed, the following statement about India is typical of developing economies in general:

Tenants have been evicted, sometimes beaten, their lives have been disrupted, sometimes ended, and they have watched the opportunities for sharecropping dry up and security guarantees from landlords disappear in the train of tenancy reform.(Herring, 1983: 48)

What had been overlooked were major differences in the social and political conditions in North-East Asian countries (Japan, Korea, and Taiwan) and in other developing countries. These conditions severely limited the likelihood of reproducing the land reform experience of the former. Japan's reform, for example, was directed by US occupation forces when the power and confidence of the ruling élite was at its lowest as a result of the Japanese defeat in World War II. The reform in South Korea was carried out under crisis conditions created by alleged aggression from the North. In Taiwan, the reform was enforced by the Nationalist Government which had just been exiled from mainland China and which was, therefore, alienated from the island's indigenous landed interests. Equally important was the existence of a relatively well-disciplined bureaucracy, together with a body of accurate data on land ownership and tenurial relations accumulated in those areas since before World War II. In addition, Japanese tenants had learned organization and unity from their long history of co-operativism and unionization.

The success of land reform in Japan, Korea, and Taiwan was thus based on very favourable conditions of demand for, and supply of, that particular institutional innovation in the political market. It was a situation that had rarely existed in the world's historical experience. It is therefore futile to blame 'lack of political will' for the failure of land reform in other countries without first considering the differences operating in these countries' political markets (for the economics of political markets, see Figure 1.3).

It is also usual to identify loopholes in laws and regulations as a source of failure of other land reform programmes. However, the fact is that an overabundance of rules and regulations, complicated further by numerous special clauses (some of them intended to close the loopholes), have not only reduced the chances of effective programme implementation, but have also induced the political élite and the bureaucracy to seek 'institutional rent' arising from those regulations, usually at the expense of the poor who have little legal knowledge. The regulatory programmes, which were barely successful under exceptionally favourable political market conditions in East Asia, were bound to fail in the absence of a relatively honest bureaucracy with a high level of administrative ability, accurate land-tenure records, and tenant political organizations (Hayami *et al.*, 1990: 2–4). Considering these conditions, the prospect is not bright for developing economies to use land reform as a practical means to counteract growing inequality.

Probably, a more effective policy instrument, which is administratively easier and subject to fewer negative side-effects than land reform, is taxation of land assets in proportion to the asset value, called 'land tax' or 'land property tax'. In developing economies today, cultivation frontiers have been pushed to less productive lands by population pressure resulting in increases in Ricardian differential rents (Section 3.3.2). Consequently, the income gap between land-owning and landless people has been widening. The equalizing effects of land tax would be especially large if increased rent incomes could be taxed and used as a source for public investment in irrigation and agricultural technology development to counteract population pressure. The tax revenue would achieve a very high pay-off in promoting both growth and equality if allocated to the propagation and strengthening of general education, as attested by recent developments in East Asia (Birdsall *et al.*, 1995).

Moreover, if the rate of tax as a proportion of land asset value is fixed for an extended period, land tax does not have the disincentive and distortive effects on production and resource allocation as created by excise tax and export duty, which are often levied to exploit agriculture (Section 4.3). Administratively, land taxation is easier to implement than land reform, because the information needed for the former is to identify who owns what parcels of land, while the latter must identify who are actual tillers of the lands in addition to the information on ownership.

However, effective land taxation requires establishment of a land registry system. Cadastral survey and land-mapping as the basis of a land registry are extremely time-consuming and expensive. For example, the cadastral survey for the reform of agricultural taxation—from the feudal tax-in-kind levied proportional to the harvest to the modern land tax (so-called the 'Land Tax Revision')—in Meiji Japan took eight years (1873–81) to complete and cost the government almost a full year's revenue (Niwa, 1962; Fukushima, 1970). However, its merit was great. Once land registry was completed, the government was able to continue raising a stable tax revenue at moderate administrative cost without distorting agricultural production incentives. On this tax basis Japan was able to promote modernization measures including education, research, and physical infrastructure such as roads and ports (as well as military build-up). Moreover, the land registry system reduced the cost of land transactions, and greatly facilitated mobilization of credit for long-term investment using land as collateral (Hayami and Yamada, 1991: 64–6). It must also be pointed out that the well-established land registration prepared an indispensable data base for effective implementation of land reform after World War II.

Considering these benefits, establishment of the land taxation system should represent a high pay-off investment opportunity for developing economies to promote both efficiency and equity. Yet, few developing economies have made serious efforts to institute land tax, partly because of the huge initial investment required, and partly because of strong opposition from landlords and owner-farmers, even though land tax could be less harmful to them than distortive taxes such as excise tax and export duty (Bird, 1974; Skinner, 1993).

7.3 Economic Stagnation and Poverty[5]

If low-income economies have to climb up the rising phase of inequality along Kuznets's inverted-U-shape curve when they begin modern development, do they have an option to maintain equality by avoiding the introduction of modern technology and development of market systems? It is a popular scenario that poor but egalitarian rural communities (characterized by mutual help and income-sharing) are destroyed by modernization forces (such as commercialization and modern technology), resulting in polarization between a small number of wealthy capitalist farmers and a large number of impoverished landless labourers (Lenin, [1899] 1960).

However, it is not possible today to maintain rural people's income level and equality by preserving the traditional mode of production. Population growth in developing economies today is more exogenous, brought about by importation of public health and medical technology, rather than induced by increases in income level (Chapter 3, Section 1). Explosive growths in population and the labour force under limited natural resource endowments will pull down the marginal productivity of labour and, hence, the wage rate as long as traditional technology continues. Correspondingly, the rent of natural resources, including land, is bound to rise. As a result, the income of landlords and large estate owners will increase at the expense of landless tenants and labourers.

7.3.1 Income distribution effects of the Green Revolution

To counteract population pressure which increases poverty and inequality, it is necessary to increase employment and output per unit of land area through the development of land-saving and labour-using technology. A significant achievement in this endeavor was the 'Green Revolution' (Section 4.2). Yet, strong criticism of the Green Revolution has prevailed on the grounds that new agricultural technology, based on modern high-yielding varieties and application of chemical fertilizers, aggravates inequality in the rural sector, causing social and political instability.

The critics of the Green Revolution have argued that the new technology tends to be monopolized by large farmers and landlords who have greater financial capacity and better access to new information. Small farmers are unable to use modern varieties efficiently since financial constraints make it difficult for them to purchase cash inputs such as fertilizers and chemicals. Monopoly of the new technology by large farmers enables them to use their profits to enlarge their operational holdings by consolidating small farmers' holdings. As farm sizes increase, it becomes profitable for large farmers to purchase large-scale machinery and reduce the cost of labour management. The effect is to reduce employment opportunities and to lower wage rates for the growing number of landless workers.[6]

How valid is the suggested sequence? Have large holders dominated the adoption of the modern-varieties technology? Does technology make large-scale operations relatively more efficient and profitable? Does modern-varieties technology induce mechanization and reduce employment earnings? The available evidence indicates that neither farm size nor tenure has been a serious constraint on the adoption of modern varieties. The data on adoption of modern wheat varieties in Pakistan, presented in Table 7.4, are fairly typical of those available for other areas where modern varieties are technically well adapted.

In the case of rice, the diffusion paths of modern varieties in three size classes of farmers (drawn in the upper diagram of Figure 7.3) indicate that small and medium farmers adopted modern varieties even faster than the large farmers did. It is true that adoption of tractors (small hand tractors) was led by large farmers. However, the popular perception that modern-variety technology stimulates the introduction of labour-displacing machinery has not been borne out by careful observation. A comparison between the upper and the lower diagram indicates that large farmers began to adopt tractors before the introduction of modern varieties. Nor was there any

TABLE 7.4 *Mexican wheat acreage as percentage of all wheat acreage by size and tenure of holdings: 1969–70 post-monsoon season in Lyallpur, Sahiwal, and Sheikhupura districts, Pakistan*

No. of acres per holding	Owner-holdings	Owner-cum-tenants	Tenant holdings	All holdings
Less than 12.5	71	80	67	73
12.5 to 25	63	72	69	68
25 to 50	72	93	82	82
Larger than 50	73	87	57	79
All sizes	69	81	70	73

Source: Azam (1973: 408).

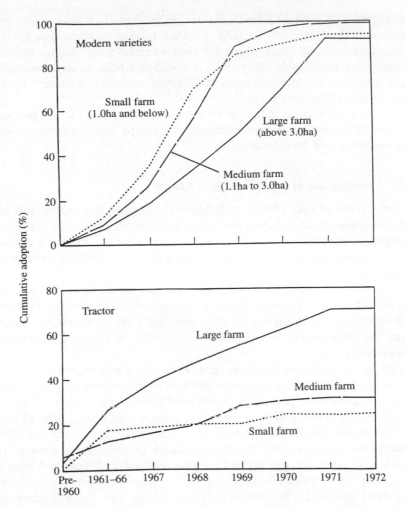

FIG. 7.3 *Cumulative percentage of farms in three size classes adopting modern varieties and tractors in thirty villages in Asia*
Source: Hayami and Kikuchi (1981: 54) based on data from the International Rice Research Institute (1978: 91).

indication that adoption of tractors was accelerated by the dramatic diffusion of modern varieties from the late 1960s to the early 1970s.

Probably the most important contribution of the Green Revolution was that it pinpointed the direction for solving the 'food problem' in the Ricardo–Schultz sense, or for escaping from the 'Ricardian trap'. If food production lags behind expansion in food demand, major damage from increased food prices will fall on agricultural labourers and marginal farmers who cannot produce sufficient food for their family consumption, while major gain will accrue to landlords and large farmers whose marketable surpluses of food products are large. Further, food price hikes raise the cost of living for urban workers, which will reduce employment through pressure on their wage increase. In this process it would be landlords alone who gain, since they can capture increased differential rents as predicted by the Ricardo model (Section 3.3.2).

Thus, if the direction indicated by the Green Revolution is not pursued, the possibility for low-income economies to escape from growing poverty and inequality will be reduced.

7.3.2 A comparison of two villages in Indonesia[7]

A comparison of two villages in Indonesia, based on field surveys at two different points in time during the Green Revolution, illustrates that developing economies under incessant population pressure fall into the Ricardian trap of stagnation and inequality in the absence of modern agricultural technology.

These two villages, located in the same regency (prefecture) in West Java, rely on wet-rice cultivation as the major source of employment and income. One village, in which modern varieties were diffused, is located in a coastal plain. The other, in which modern varieties failed to be adopted, is located in a mountain valley.

First, we will observe the latter case. This village was settled a long time ago beyond the villagers' memory, and was characterized by a high man-land ratio (seventeen persons per hectare of paddy-field area in 1978). The village records show that the population growth rate was as high as 3 per cent per year in the 1960s, but declined to less than 1 per cent in the 1970s. This decline represented a Malthusian check in population growth: the frontiers of new land opening had long been closed and there had been no significant improvement in the communal irrigation system, though it was well developed and efficiently maintained. In the late 1960s modern rice varieties were introduced in this village but failed since these varieties were attacked by brown planthoppers, presumably because of the relatively cool temperatures in the elevated location.

Economic changes in this village over a decade, from the 1968–71 survey and the 1978 survey, are summarized in Table 7.5. Farmers adopting modern varieties continued to be less than 20 per cent, and the absence of improvement in irrigation systems was reflected by the percentage of the double-cropped area (for wet and dry seasons) remaining unchanged at 90 per cent. Correspondingly, average rice yield per hectare did not show a statistically significant increase. A minor yield increase, if not due to weather fluctuations or statistical error, may have resulted from a modest increase in the input of chemical fertilizers induced by the almost 20 per cent decline in the real price of fertilizers (relative to the price of paddy) caused by the

TABLE 7.5 *Economic changes in a survey village^a in Indonesia in which modern rice varieties failed to be adopted, 1968–71 to 1978*

	1968 71 average	1978	Rate of change (%)
	(1)	(2)	[(2)–(1)]/(1)
Percentage of farmers adopting modern varieties	11	14	27
Percentage of double-cropped area	90	90	0
Paddy yield per hectare harvested (ton)	2.6	2.9	12
Inputs per hectare:			
Chemical fertilizer (kg)	191	229	20
Labour (work hours)	736	928	26
Carabao (work hours)	16	9	–44
Real input prices (in kg. of paddy):			
Chemical fertilizer (per kg)	1.5	1.1	–27
Labour^b (per work hour)	9.5	8.5	–11
Carabao (per work hour)	6.2	9.5	53
Factor shares of income^c (%):			
Labour	55.8	49.1	–12
Capital	6.0	4.7	–22
Land	38.2	46.2	21

^a Village S in Table 9.1
^b Sum of family and hired labour
^c Factor shares in value added after subtracting fertilizer cost from output value. Land's share is estimated as residual.
Source: Hayami and Kikuchi (1981: 180–1 and 191).

government's fertilizer subsidies. The real wage rate declined under population pressure, which was associated with increased input of labour, whereas the rental of water-buffalo increased and the use of water-buffalo decreased—reflecting substitution of buffalo ploughing by hand hoeing.

With the desperate efforts of villagers to work harder and longer to compensate for decreased wage rates, labour's share in the income from rice production decreased only about 10 per cent, while the share of capital (water-buffalo) decreased as much as 20 per cent. Meanwhile, land's share increased about 20 per cent. Accordingly, landless tenants and agricultural labourers were pauperized and their income position worsened *vis-à-vis* landlords and large owner-farmers under stagnant agricultural technology.

A sharp contrast to this case can be observed in the other survey village where the adoption modern rice technology was successful. This village was settled rather recently and was characterized by relatively low population density (twelve people per hectare of paddy-field area in 1978). However, the rate of population growth (including natural growth and immigration) was as high as 4 per cent per year within the inter-survey period. This rapid population growth was supported by developments in technology

TABLE 7.6 *Economic changes in a survey village[a] in Indonesia in which modern varieties were successfully adopted, 1968–71 to 1978*

	1968–71 average	1978	Rate of change (%)
	(1)	(2)	[(2)–(1)]/(1)
Percentage of farmers adopting modern varieties	7	100	1,329
Percentage of double-cropped area	50	100	200
Paddy yield per hectare harvested (ton)	2.4	3.4	42
Inputs per hectare:			
Chemical fertilizer (kg)	75	209	179
Labour (work hours)	638	701	11
Carabao (work hours)	7	13	38
Real input prices (in kg. of paddy):			
Chemical fertilizer (per kg)	1.5	1.0	–33
Labour[b] (per work hour)	7.9	11.5	46
Carabao (per work hour)	8.8	14.1	60
Factor shares of income[c] (%):			
Labour	43.2	45.6	6
Capital	2.2	5.2	14
Land	54.6	49.2	–10

[a] Village N in Table 9.1
[b] Sum of family and hired labour
[c] Factor shares in value added after subtracting fertilizer cost from output value. Land's share is estimated as residual.

Source: Hayami and Kikuchi (1981: 201–3).

and infrastructure, as summarized in Table 7.6. Originally the communal irrigation system in this village was poorly developed with only half of the paddy-field area double-cropped in the first survey period (1968–71). However, since a national irrigation system was extended to this village, all the paddy-fields were turned into double-cropped area. Meanwhile, farmers adopting modern varieties jumped from 7 to 100 per cent. Correspondingly, average rice yield per hectare increased more than 40 per cent. Adding to this yield increase, the effect of cropping-area expansion due to the irrigation improvement amounted to an increase in total rice output by 85 per cent in this village.

These developments in technology are reflected in changes in inputs. Although the rate of decline in the real price of fertilizers was about the same as in the other village analysed, the increase in fertilizer application was nearly three times faster. Most importantly, both the real wage rate and the input of labour increased. The use of water-buffalo also sharply increased, despite a large increase in the rental price for buffalo. These changes clearly indicate a major upward shift in the rice production function in this village. As the result of such technological progress, the income shares of labour and capital increased at the expense of land's share. Thus, the income position of landless people, who relied on subsistence earnings from their labour alone, improved both absolutely and relatively.

The comparison of experiences in these two villages clearly illustrates that it is not possible to escape from the Ricardian trap of poverty and inequality without adoption of modern technology and production systems. It is true that not all technological innovations promote equality. Innovations must have land-saving and labour-using characteristics. Mechanical technologies, such as tractors, tend to be monopolized by the large farmers (Figure 7.3), thereby widening the income gap against small farmers. Moreover, advances in mechanization are likely to facilitate substitution of capital for labour, resulting in a decline in the income share of labour.

The most effective way to prevent inequality in income distribution from increasing under strong population pressure is to expand demand for labour at a speed faster than growth in population and the labour force. In this regard, modernization of agriculture and the development of labour-intensive, small- and medium-scale manufacturers, especially in rural areas, are critically important (Stewart, 1977; Hayami and Kawagoe, 1993; Ranis and Stewart, 1993; Parikh and Thorbecke, 1996). Major efforts must be designated to promote innovations in the labour-using direction in both agriculture and non-agriculture. Otherwise, the inequalizing phase of the inverted-U-shape curve may become too steep for developing economies to climb over.

In this regard, the observation by Harry Oshima (1992) that inequality began to decline at a relatively low income level in the Asian economies—which did not neglect agriculture in the promotion of industrialization and achieved the success of the Green Revolution—seems to have very important policy implications.[8]

7.4 Environmental Problems in Economic Development

Growing inequality in the early stage of development was created through interactions between the traditional sector (pauperized under strong population pressure on limited land resources) and the modern sector (with increased capital intensity through technology borrowing). The same forces underlay degradation in natural environments.[9]

7.4.1 The environmental problems in developing economies

The environmental problem may be defined as the problem of natural resource exhaustion resulting from exploitation at speeds beyond their natural recovery rates, which endangers sustenance of life. This problem has existed almost from the beginning of human history. Primitive economies, based on hunting and gathering, could not have been sustained if people had killed wild animals and collected plants beyond their reproductive capacities to feed the multiplying mouths. This resource exhaustion crisis was over-come by development of agricultural technology and social institutions such as property rights (Section 1.1.2).

If property rights on certain resources are given to particular individuals or groups, they will utilize their resources efficiently with due consideration for future living, thereby avoiding resource exhaustion—such as one would not kill the goose yielding the golden eggs. However, the stipulation and protection of property rights entails large costs. Compared with arable land near villages, which is fairly easy for villagers to monitor, protection of property rights on remote forests and grazing lands is far more difficult and costly. Further, it is nearly impossible to establish property rights on air and running water. With no property-right assignment, people can use resources without paying costs. Then they will be likely to abuse these resources to the point of zero marginal private utility, even if this endangers everyone's living because of eventual resource exhaustion. This human propensity to be 'free-riders' underlies pervasive deforestation and air and water pollution.

Difficulty in fixing property rights on resources like forests and air implies that they have the attribute of 'non-excludability' (difficulty of preventing users who do not pay for the costs) in the theory of public good (Section 1.2.3). Because of this, private costs diverge from social costs on the use of these resources. This gap is called 'externality' or the 'external effect'. Environmental problems stem from negative externality in the use of natural resources.

However, the environmental problems do not emerge if these natural resources have another attribute of public good—'non-rivalness', or the nature of being utilized jointly by many people at the same time. For example, if forest resources are so abundant relative to population that someone's tree-cutting does not affect others' forest utilization, forests are non-rival resources. However, if forests become scarce owing to population growth and economic activities, non-rivalness is lost when someone's tree-cutting significantly reduces others' opportunities of forest use. Resources that are characterized by non-excludability but have lost the attribute of non-rivalness are called 'common-property resources' or 'common-pool resources'.

The reason that environmental problems are especially acute in developing economies is because changes in technology and institutions lag behind changes in resource endowments. Until the relatively recent past, many developing economies were characterized by sparse population and abundant natural resources. With the population explosion beginning during the 1920s and 1930s, scarcity of resources rose rapidly. Relative to this development, institutions for conserving scarce natural resources have been slow to develop. In terms of the theory of public good, compared with the increase in rivalry for natural resources, the development of institutions geared to increase excludability or decrease externality has lagged. Serious depletion of common-property resources has become inevitable in this situation.

This lag in institutional adjustment tends to become large in developing economies because of poverty and the high rates of discount for future consumption and income among people. Even if scarcity of natural resources increases, natural resources and environments can be adequately preserved by investment in conservation and anti-pollution activities such as reforestation, soil erosion prevention (such as terracing), and purification of gas emission. In order to promote these activities, institutional innovations are required, such as setting property rights where applicable, regulating and taxing natural resource utilization, and organizing governmental and non-governmental bodies for environmental monitoring.

These institutions raise the private cost of natural resource utilization, thereby lowering the current income of present users. This decrease in present-users' income is considered a part of investment in the conservation of the natural environment, which will contribute to increases in future income. However, attempts to build these conservation systems are bound to be strongly resisted by the current users who fear that their income will decline, especially amongst the poor who already live at a near-subsistence level and have very high discount rates on consumption.

Also, because the sacrifice of present income is borne by people currently using environmental resources without cost, these people are easily organized for political lobbying. Their collective action can be especially strong when the free-riders are politically powerful entities in small numbers, such as large enterprises which freely pollute air and water with industrial waste or receive logging concessions at prices lower than socially desirable. In contrast, the benefits of environmental conservation diffuse widely among many people over generations, who are unlikely to be organized for political action. Therefore, the institutions and policies to promote environmental conservation, to establish an equilibrium in the political market, are likely to be much less effective than is socially desirable (Section 1.2.3).

7.4.2 Rural poverty and environmental destruction

As in the case of income distribution, a major factor underlying environmental degradation in developing economies is pauperization of the rural population due to population pressure. As the supply of land suitable for cultivation becomes short relative to increased population under traditional agricultural technology, poor people are forced to cultivate fragile land for subsistence in hills and mountains, resulting in a high incidence of soil erosion. Also, they are forced to cut forests for timber and fuel as well as graze animals on pasture lands, exceeding the reproductive capacity of these natural resources. It is in such an environment that dire poverty or destitution typically becomes a vicious circle. Poverty results in malnutrition and reduces poor people's capacity for work, precluding them from wage employment opportunities. They are thereby forced to rely more heavily on the exploitation of fragile natural resources in marginal areas, to which property rights are not assigned (Dasgupta, 1993).

To prevent such environmental destruction due to rural poverty, government regulations on the use of environmentally fragile areas may be necessary. However, the administrative capacity of government in developing economies is usually too weak to prevent a large number of desperate squatters from encroaching on large remote areas of forests and grasslands. Moreover, if regulations were effectively strengthened, a means of subsistence for the poor would be closed. Short-run relief measures such as public distribution of food, water, and medical services might be necessary to rescue poor people from the trap of destitution. However, the fundamental solution to the problem should be directed to increasing employment and income by improving the productivity of the limited land already in use. This solution will not be possible without shifting from traditional resource-based to modern science-based agriculture, as symbolized by the Green Revolution (Sections 4.1 and 4.2).

There have been many criticisms of the Green Revolution for environmental reasons, e.g. directed against fertilizers and chemicals that poison soil and water causing ecological and human health damage. Also, it has been pointed out that irrigation without adequate drainage facilities tends to result in soil degradation through salinity and waterlogging. These effects are often serious. There is no question that major efforts must be allocated to overcome these defects through development of less poisonous chemicals, pest and insect control with reduced chemical application, and improved drainage facilities. However, if the efforts to develop modern technology were abandoned because of these defects, employment and income-earning opportunities for marginal farmers and agricultural labourers would continue to be reduced under population pressure. As a result, many would be forced to push cultivation frontiers into ecologically fragile lands, resulting in increased incidence of flood and soil erosion.

Indeed, according to a global survey commissioned by the UN Environmental Programme, soil degradation during the five decades after 1945 amounted to about two billion hectares or about 17 per cent of the total vegetative area in the world. As much as 80 per cent of the degraded area was located in Africa, Asia, and Latin America. About 30 per cent of this degradation was caused by deforestation, 7 per cent by overexploitation such as collection of fuels and fodder, 35 per cent by overgrazing, 28 per cent from agricultural activities, and 1 per cent from industrialization (Oldeman *et al.*, 1990). A significant portion of deforestation was caused by commercial logging. Degradation due to modern agricultural practices, such as an excess of irrigation water and chemical materials, cannot be overlooked. Yet, by far the largest cause is identified as the exploitation of natural resources by the poverty-driven population (Pinstrup-Anderson and Pandya-Lorch, 1994).

Therefore, the way to stop environmental destruction in the rural sector is not to curb development of modern agricultural technology for fear of its defects, but to strengthen scientific research to overcome the defects. Also, the development of agricultural technology should not be limited to favourable production environments with good irrigation conditions, but should extend to both productivity increases and environmental conservation in fragile areas through such means as agroforestry and complementary use of arable lands and grasslands (Garrity, 1993).

How can one mobilize the necessary resources for such research, development, and extension activities? How should these activities be organized? What kinds of institution should be developed to motivate private investment activities towards environmental conservation? These questions comprise an important policy agenda for developing countries. At the same time, considering the global externality of environmental conservation in developing economies (such as preservation of tropical rain forests), activities for this purpose should be very appropriate outlets for official development assistance (ODA) and volunteer activities by non-governmental organizations (NGOs) from developed countries.

7.4.3 Industrialization and environmental pollution

Parallel to pauperization in the rural sector, air and water pollution from urban economic activities is a cause of environmental degradation in developing economies. The problems of pollution due to such factors as emission of noxious gas and water from factories, and piles of waste from urban households are universal, but often more serious in developing economies. It is important to recognize that environmental pollution from these sources tends to progress faster in developing than in developed economies.

Advanced economies have reached a stage at which the weight of economic activities shifts from the industrial to the service sectors in response to economic growth, so that consumption of energy as the basic source of pollution grows slower than growth in national income. Moreover, people in the high-income economies have high preference for environmental amenity relative to present consumption. Therefore, they are more prone to accept environmental regulations and taxation at the expense of their present income.

In contrast, in the early phase of industrialization, the share of industry in domestic income expands, resulting in increases in energy consumption faster than growth in national product. This tendency is often exacerbated by the policy bias to promote heavy and chemical industries from the early stage of development (Section 8.2.4). Since anti-pollution regulations are usually weak in developing economies, increased energy consumption in the industrial sector tends to swell emission of noxious gas and water. Moreover, as many developing economies entered the era of motorization before railway networks were established, the density of automobiles has been high relative to their income levels, resulting in extreme city transportation congestion and serious air pollution.

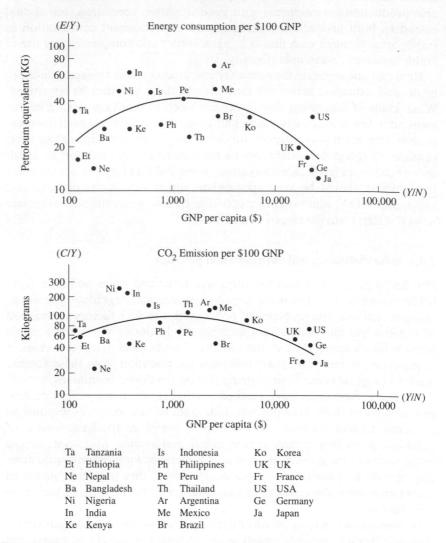

F IG . 7.4 *International comparison in commercial energy consumption and carbon dioxide emission from industrial processes, double-log scale*
Note: Commercial energy excludes traditional energy from such sources as fuel woods.
Source: Table 7.6.

Thus, it is hypothesized that energy consumption relative to national income, and the degree of pollution both rise initially in response to growth in income per capita, and decline after a certain threshold income level—an inverted-U-shape curve similar to the pattern of change in income distribution (Selden and Song, 1992; Grossman and Krueger, 1994, Dasgupta and Mäler, 1995: 2384–8). This pattern is illustrated by an international comparison in Figure 7.4. This figure compares the positions of twenty countries in commercial energy consumption per 100 dollars of GNP (upper diagram) and emission of carbon dioxide per 100 dollars of GNP (lower diagram) relative to GNP per capita, based on data presented in Table 7.7.

The curves in Figure 7.4 represent estimates of quadratic functions with respect to GNP per capita, as reported in Table 7.8—with regression (1) used for the upper diagram and regression (3) for the lower diagram. Even though the fits of quadratic equations to data are not very good, the coefficient of the linear term is positive and that of the quadratic term is negative, both

TABLE 7.7 *Commercial energy consumption and carbon dioxide emission from industrial processes for different levels of GNP per capita, selected countries*

	GNP per capita (1990 $US)	Kg per $100 GNP		Self-sufficiency rate of commercial energy (%)
		Commercial energy consumption (petroleum equivalent)	CO_2 emission	
	Y/N^a	E/Y^a	C/Y^b	X^c
Tanzania	110	35	64	7
Ethiopia	120	17	58	13
Nepal	170	15	24	20
Bangladesh	210	27	71	73
Nigeria	290	48	279	600
India	350	66	231	91
China	370	162	595	109
Kenya	370	27	49	27
Indonesia	570	48	161	276
Philippines	730	29	96	34
Peru	1,160	44	76	111
Thailand	1,420	25	129	41
Poland	1,690	202	477	109
Argentina	2,370	76	150	113
Mexico	2,490	52	157	167
Brazil	2,680	34	53	69
Hungary	2,780	116	218	54
Korea, Rep.	5,400	35	112	24
UK	16,100	23	62	97
France	19,490	20	34	48
USA	21,790	36	90	84
Germany	22,320	16	54	54
Japan	25,430	14	35	18

[a] 1990 value
[b] 1991 value
[c] 1971–91 average

Sources: World Bank, *World Development Report 1992*, World Development Indicators Tables 1 and 5; World Resources Institute, *World Resources 1994–95*, Tables 21.1, 21.2, 22.3 and 23.1.

TABLE 7.8 *Estimates of regression equations to explain commercial energy consumption and carbon dioxide emission from industrial processes per $100 GNP based on intercountry cross-section data*

Explanatory variable	Exclude ex-central planned economies (n=20)				Include ex-central planned economies (n=23)			
	Energy/GDP ln(E/Y)		CO_2/GNP ln(C/Y)		Energy/GDP ln(E/Y)		CO_2/GNP ln(C/Y)	
	(1)	(2)	(3)	(4)	(5)	(6)	(7)	(8)
GNP per capita ln(E/Y)	1.563** (3.19)	0.999* (1.96)	1.782* (2.51)	0.796 (1.16)	1.523** (3.24)	0.966* (2.05)	1.640* (2.35)	0.638 (0.99)
$ln(E/Y)^2$	-0.107** (3.32)	-0.071* (2.11)	-0.123** (2.62)	-0.159 (1.31)	-0.105** (3.38)	-0.069* (2.20)	-0.114* (2.47)	-0.049 (1.15)
Energy Self-sufficiency ln X		0.196* (2.22)		0.343** (2.89)		0.206* (2.49)		0.370** (3.28)
Central planning dummy D					1.353** (5.41)	1.352** (6.10)	1.282** (3.44)	1.281** (4.23)
Intercept	-1.910 (1.08)	-0.653 (0.39)	-1.662 (0.65)	0.537 (0.24)	-1.746 (1.04)	-0.564 (0.36)	-1.099 (0.44)	1.028 (0.48)
Coeff. of det.(R^2)	0.351	0.472	0.234	0.465	0.720	0.780	0.527	0.687
S.E. of estimates	0.394	0.355	0.570	0.477	0.384	0.340	0.571	0.465
Threshold value of Y/N (1990$)	1,486	1,136	1,400	850	1,411	1,097	1,330	672

Note: Equations linear in logarithms are estimates by the ordinary least-square method based on data in Table 7.7.

T-statistics are shown in parentheses.
** Significant at the 1 % level
* Significant at the 5 % level

statistically significant at conventional levels, supporting the inverted-U-shape hypothesis with respect to energy consumption and CO_2 emission.

Regressions (2) and (4) are the cases of assessing the energy self-sufficiency rate as an explanatory variable. Coefficients of this variable turned out positive and significant, which correspond to upward divergence of energy-exporting countries (such as Indonesia, Mexico, and Nigeria) from the quadratic curves in Figure 7.4. Such results appear to reflect the tendency that, in countries endowed with rich energy resources, energy prices are low, inducing high energy consumption in countries endowed with rich energy resources. If this conjecture holds true, elevation of energy prices by such means as carbon tax could promote savings in energy consumption, reducing emission of polluting gas.

Though not indicated on Figure 7.4, data in Table 7.7 reveal that former socialist economies (China, Poland, and Hungary) are characterized by abnormally high levels of energy consumption and CO_2 emission, relative to market economies at the same levels of income per capita. For example, energy consumption and CO_2 emission in China were about 2.5 times higher than in India despite almost the same level of GDP per capita in 1990. In regressions (5) through (8) in Table 7.8 the dummy variable representing former socialist economies was highly significant statistically.

Low energy efficiency in ex-socialist economies indicated by such statistical analysis seems to reflect the development strategy commonly adopted by the socialist states in accordance with the Soviet model. In this model, to assist industrial development, the cost of living for industrial workers and the prices of raw materials for industrial production were held low. Towards this end, the prices of foods and energy were set at very low levels. It is easy to imagine that these low prices induced abuse in energy consumption in both households and enterprises. Abnormally low efficiency in energy use was an unavoidable consequence when low energy prices were combined with low incentives to save cost by managers of state enterprises, whose achievements were assessed in terms of output quantities relative to assigned targets (Section 8.3.3).

Another factor underlying abuse in energy consumption with little regard for environmental externality may be the nature of the socialist political system, which was not responsive to anti-pollution movements among citizens but rather inclined to suppress such movements. Under Western democracy, government is at least officially supposed to mediate as a neutral third party between polluting firms and inflicted citizens. Under the one-party autocracy of communism, polluting firms are a part of government, against which citizens have difficulty in organizing opposition. They are also not equipped with such means as mass media and free voting rights to press the government. Under such a political regime, where industrialization was promoted with the compelling goal of achieving quantitative production targets, it was natural that state enterprises paid little attention to externality among surrounding dwellers. The experience in centrally planned economies clearly shows that state ownership (or 'people's ownership') of natural resources and capital does not at all guarantee environmental conservation.

The bottom row in Table 7.8 estimates the threshold levels of GNP per capita, which correspond to the peaks of the quadratic curves. The estimated thresholds range mostly from $1,000 to $1,500. As low-income economies begin industrialization and raise their per capita income to this range, they are likely to experience sharp increases in energy consumption and environmental pollution at rates much faster than growth in per capita income. Once they ride over this threshold, growth in energy consumption will become slower than per capita income growth. This does not mean that environmental conditions will improve after this threshold point is reached, because energy consumption will continue to increase although at a decelerating pace.

However, as income per capita continues to grow, technology and institutions will improve so that environmental pollution will eventually begin to decline absolutely. According to a study based on the data from the Global Monitoring System (a joint project of the World Health Organization and the UN Environmental Programme), conspicuous pollution (such as sulphur dioxide density in the air) begins to decrease from the income threshold of about $4,000 per person, and most other pollution decrease from about $8,000 (Grossman and Krueger, 1994).

7.4.4 Lowering the peak of the inverted-U-shape curve

Can developing economies allow environmental degradation to continue worsening until such high income levels are reached? In both rural and urban areas the poor are the first to be endangered by environmental degradation. If this damage to poor people coincides with unequal income distribution, social and political stability—the basis of economic growth—will be seriously undermined. It is, therefore, critically important for developing economies to lower the peaks of the inverted-U-shape curves for both income distribution and environmental quality in order to sustain their economic growth.

Technically it is not so difficult to counteract environmental degradation. Ways and means to prevent environmental destruction in the rural sector have already been discussed. Pollution arising from industrialization and urbanization can be suppressed in developing economies to a much lower level than experienced by advanced economies in the past if technologies and know-how accumulated in the latter are effectively applied to the former.

It is also theoretically easy to design the institutions and policies to promote adoption of such anti-pollution technologies. As explained at the beginning of this section, the core of the environmental problem is the divergence between private and social costs in the use of the environment, which induces exploitation of environmental resources above socially optimum levels. Therefore, the environmental problem can be solved by raising the private cost of utilizing the environment (such as discharging noxious gas into the air) to the social cost.

Policy means to achieve this equality are well known theoretically (Tietenberg, 1990; Cairncross, 1991, ch. 5). Assignments of property rights are effective where the rights can be assigned and protected at modest costs (Coase, 1960). Property rights on environmental resources such as air and water can be set by allocating 'marketable pollution rights' or 'tradable permits' among firms and households on emission of polluting material. For example, permits may be allocated among chemical manufacturers to emit sulphur up to a certain quantity. If a manufacturer wants to emit more than his quota, he may do so by purchasing the necessary quota amount from another manufacturer. Through such transactions, equality in the marginal costs of sulphur emission will be established across firms, resulting in an increase in social utility from the initial quota allocation. If the total quota volume is determined at a level to equate the market price of the quota with the social marginal cost of sulphur emission, socially optimum pollution control can be established.

The same optimum control can be achieved with tax and subsidy according to the well-known theorem by Arthur Pigou (1920). For example, when a firm is producing negative externality from the production of a certain commodity, a tax on this commodity, equivalent to the externality, will raise the private marginal cost to the social marginal cost. Then, social optimum will be obtained at the intersection between market demand and market supply—the latter corresponding to the private marginal cost schedule raised by the taxation. The same optimum can be achieved by giving the polluting firm, for unit reduction in output, a subsidy equivalent to the difference between the private and the social marginal cost.[10]

For the effective implementation of tradable permits as well as Pigovian tax and subsidy, the sources and quantities of pollution need to be identified and measured. Moreover, estimates of social and private costs are needed. Where such information is difficult to obtain, quantitative regulations, such as controls on the density of the pollutant in emission gas, are often applied. In the case of highly toxic materials, such as DDT and PCB, outright prohibition may be necessary.

However, in many cases market-based solutions such as marketable quotas and pollution tax are more effective in bringing resource allocations closer to social optimum than are direct quantitative regulations, even when available information is imperfect and indirect. It is often difficult to measure the quantity of noxious material that a particular enterprise is emitting. It is easier to measure the raw materials, such as coal and oil, that they are using as the sources of noxious materials. For this reason a feasible low-cost method of anti-pollution taxation is the imposition of a levy on the consumption or sale of coal and oil in proportion to carbon contained—the so called 'carbon tax'. Such taxation on energy materials raises the price of energy, thereby inducing its saving. It has been statistically confirmed that efficiency in the use of energy is low in economies where energy prices are lowered by government subsidy below international prices, while efficiency is high where energy prices are raised by taxation (Cairncross, 1991: 77–80).

Nevertheless, efficient and feasible anti-pollution measures such as carbon tax are not easily instituted even in high-income economies, for the very reason that they effectively raise energy prices and lower present incomes of energy consumers, who are apt to organize strong political opposition. This political barrier is even more insurmountable in low-income economies which are characterized by high preference of present to future consumption.

To overcome this barrier, the first requirement must be collection and dissemination of accurate information. Environmental degradation due to pollution tends to progress cumulatively and will reach devastating consequences in the long run. It is not easy in the early stage to accurately predict how dreadful the final consequence will be, as illustrated by wide variations in predictions of the greenhouse effect of carbon dioxide. The more uncertain the future prospect is, the weaker public opinion, and the less determined the government is to undertake countermeasures.

However, it should be easier for developing economies to predict the course and consequences of pollution than it was for advanced economies. The reason is that, if developing economies promote industrialization without appropriate countermeasures, they are likely to repeat the past tragedies of advanced economies (e.g. mercury poisoning of humans through fish from chemical factory waste in Minamata, Japan). If such failures in advanced economies are accurately portrayed to leaders and the public in developing economies, political feasibility will be greatly enhanced to institute appropriate anti-pollution measures.

In this connection, it is critically important to organize the people in a community who are directly subjected to the effects of pollution. The people who can best monitor pollution are those living in the polluted area (e.g. residents who suffer from asthma due to a nearby factory spewing sulphurdioxide gas, or fishermen whose catches decline because of polluted water). Traditionally, it has been the local communities, such as tribes and villages that have managed conservation of common property resources, such as forests, grazing-land, and fishing-grounds (Section 9.2.2). In modern societies also, if local communities are properly organized, they should be the most effective mechanism, not only for monitoring environmental conditions, but also for negotiating with polluters and lobbying the government.

7.4.5 Towards global co-ordination

Finally, the need for international co-operation on the environmental problems in developing economies must be emphasized. The influence of environmental pollution is not limited to a local area, but tends to spread widely on a national and global scale. Exhaustion of tropical rain forest in a mountain area damages not only mountain tribes in the area, but also increases the incidence of flood and drought for farmers in downstream plains, and further contributes to reduction in the global supply of oxygen. Likewise, industrialization in many developing economies, if promoted without appropriate measures, might aggravate air and water pollution to the level of global catastrophe. In the world today, when the limit of the earth has increasingly been felt under the pressure of growing population and economic activities, no country is free from the pollution caused by other countries.

This recognition has produced a series of attempts to establish international co-operation systems for conservation and the improvement of environments, from the UN Conference on Human Environment held in 1972 in Stockholm to the 1992 UN Conference on Environment and Development (the so-called 'Earth Summit') held in Rio de Janiero (Hashimoto, 1994). In these international forums, a major confrontation prevailed between developing and developed countries. Developed countries insisted that internationally uniform standards should be applied to environmental regulations on all nations, and that certain sanctions should be imposed, such as restrictions on import of commodities produced by violators of these regulations. On the other hand, developing countries argued that it is unfair for developed economies which achieved development in the past by freely polluting the environment, to impose severe environmental regulations on developing economies as a yoke on their development. Therefore, they demanded that, if advanced economies requested them to adopt severe environmental regulations, their consequent economic losses must be compensated by developed countries.[11]

In terms of the Pigou theorem, developed countries are demanding taxation of polluters based on the polluter-pay principle whereas developing countries are arguing for subsidies to polluters based on the polluter-be-paid principle or the victim-pay principle. Because both can achieve optimality, as the Pigou theorem predicts, the issue is equity. If this controversy is raised as a domestic issue, the polluter-pay principle seems to match the sense of equity and justice, since polluters are mainly large enterprises and wealthy people whose energy consumption is high. However, it does not appear unjust for low-income economies to be subsidized from high-income economies for reduction in pollution. Therefore, environmental conservation on a global scale should significantly progress if developed countries adopt the polluter-be-paid principle internationally *vis-à-vis* developing countries by advancing financial assistance and technical co-operation on condition that developing countries establish relevant anti-pollution measures based on the polluter-pay principle domestically, such as the carbon tax. Considering the global externality of environmental destruction in developing economies, compensation payments to developing countries as a part of ODA for adoption of anti-pollution policies should prove to be a high pay-off investment opportunity for high-income economies in the long run.

NOTES

1. Mathematically, the Gini coefficient can be expressed as

$$G = \sum_i \sum_j |y_i - y_j|/2n^2 u,$$

where y_i (or y_j) represents the income of i-th member in the group consisting of n persons (or households) and u is average income. Thus, the Gini coefficient is one-half of the ratio of average difference in income between all possible pairs among group members to the group's average income. For this and other measures of inequality, see Atkinson (1975, ch. 2), Fields (1980, ch. 2 and Lambert (1993, ch. 2).

2. Least-square estimation of the quadratic function produces the following results:

$$\ln G = -7.00 + 1.58 \ln(Y/N) - 0.10[\ln(Y/N)]^2, \quad \bar{R}^2 = 0.824$$
$$\quad\quad\quad\quad (9.24) \quad\quad\quad\quad (9.29)$$

where G is the Gini coefficient and (Y/N) is GNP per capita. Judging from t-values in parentheses, both the linear and the quadratic terms of Y/N are highly significant. As the coefficient of determination adjusted for the degree of freedom ($\bar{R}^2$) indicates, more than 80% of variations in G is explained by this regression equation. According to this equation, the income per capita that maximizes G is $2,700 —about the same as Brazil's income.

3. This tendency is said to be especially conspicuous in Africa and Latin America where the wage rates in the formal sector are often two to three times higher than in the informal sector for an identical task, whereas this wage gap is relatively modest in East Asia (about 20%). Relative flexibility and integrity of the labour market in East Asia, as indicated by each comparison, is considered a factor underlying good economic performances in this region (Field and Wan, 1989; World Bank, 1993: 266–73). The high wage rate in the urban formal sector raises rural people's expected benefits when they migrate to urban areas (Harris and Todaro, 1970). However, because most migrants find no employment in the formal sector they are forced to subsist on informal activities in urban slums. Thus, the segmentation of the labour market due to government labour regulations is a factor underlying the pathological growth of a metropolis in developing economies.

4. This section draws heavily on Hayami *et al.* (1990, ch. 1).
5. This section draws heavily on Hayami (1981), Hayami and Kikuchi (1981: 52–9), and Hayami and Ruttan (1985: 336–45).
6. This argument, commonly found in criticisms of the Green Revolution in its early stage, is typically advanced by Griffin (1974). For other variations, see Hayami and Kikuchi (1981, ch. 3). This type of naïve criticism has waned as the nature and effects of the Green Revolution have become clearer. However, criticisms have continued from a broader social and economic context, as presented by Lipton and Longhurst (1989). For comments on Lipton and Longhurst, see Hayami (1992). A recent comprehensive empirical study (David and Otsuka, 1994) leads to a conclusion opposite that of the Lipton and Longhurst argument.
7. This section draws heavily on Hayami and Kikuchi (1981, chs. 8 and 9).
8. Oshima argued that, while Kuznets's inverted-U-shape curve reached its peak at income per capita of about $2,000 (in 1972 prices) in Western Europe and North America, the threshold income in Asia was only about $600. Complementary, rather than trade-off, relationship between growth and equality in East Asia is also emphasized by Birdsall *et al.*,(1995).
9. Two especially useful references for general readers on environmental problems in economic development are Cairncross (1991) and the World Bank's *World Development Report 1992*.
10. The Pigou theorem establishes equivalence in efficiency in terms of social welfare maximization between taxation and subsidization on polluters. Of course, income distribution effects are different, with income transfer from polluters to taxpayers (who are usually victims of pollution) by taxation, and transfer from taxpayers to polluters by subsidies. A similar equivalence in efficiency and opposite income distribution effects are established by Ronald Coase (1960) on the assignment of property rights over environmental resources—i.e. equivalence in property-rights assignments over the environment between the polluters and victims.
11. For summary and assessment of those opposing views, see United Nations (1993), Whalley (1994), and *World Development Report 1992* (ch. 2). The opinion is especially strong among developed countries that imports should be restricted or prohibited of commodities produced by environmental-polluting methods. This issue is likely to be a major agenda in the next round of multilateral trade negotiations of the World Trade Organization.

8

Market and State

In this chapter and the next we will analyse economic systems to determine which is most appropriate to promote economic development. An economic system is defined as an institutional framework by which competition among people for the use of resources is co-ordinated.

In reality, an economic system is expressed as a combination of various economic organizations. In this chapter, we will focus on the relationship between market and state as two major organizations that determine the characteristics of the economic system. Much of the discussion in this chapter has been touched upon previously. This chapter will integrate those issues into a comprehensive and cohesive perspective on which economic systems should be chosen for different cultural and social heritage at different stages of development.

Before proceeding to substantive discussions, it is useful to develop clear definitions of 'institution' and 'organization'. Douglass North (1994) defined institution as a 'rule in society' and organization as a 'functional body or group' organized to act for a specific purpose. While this distinction is theoretically meaningful, institution and organization are inseparable in practice. For example, the state is an institution as it consists of a set of rules for governance. At the same time, it is a functional body consisting of various agencies and bureaux organized according to those rules. Similarly, the market is an institution comprised of rules for controlling voluntary transactions under the parameter of prices. It is also the functional body organizing various marketing agents, such as retailers and wholesalers, to bridge between consumers and producers. Thus, organization can be defined as 'a functional body organized by a set of rules', and institution can be defined as 'a set of rules to organize people into the functional body'. In the following discussion, we call market and state 'organizations' because we deal here mainly with their roles as agents of actions. However, it is perfectly legitimate to call them 'institutions'.

8.1 The Economic Functions of the Market and the State

A market is the organization that co-ordinates the production and consumption of goods and services through voluntary transactions. The simplest example may be a morning bazaar of vegetables in a local town plaza, at which producers and consumers get together and make transactions directly amongst themselves. It can take much more complicated forms in which consumers' demand meets producers' supply after passing through various marketing stages, transportation, and storage processes, across space and over time. By definition, transactions in the market are voluntary, based upon the free will of buyers and sellers. Any transfer of goods and services against their will (such as stealing or plundering) is not a market transaction. Therefore, if information is perfect, all the participants in market transactions gain, since sellers would not sell and buyers would not buy unless they were to gain. The market is, therefore, the organization to co-ordinate people's activities in seeking self-interest towards increasing social economic welfare.

In contrast, the state is an organization for monopolizing legitimate coercive power. Using this coercive force, the state co-ordinates people's activities according to set rules and regulations it stipulates. As a part of these rules, the state enforces conscription of resources, such as taxation and military draft, irrespective of an individual's will, while taking responsibility for providing such public goods as national defence, courts, police, and roads, which cannot be supplied by the market.

Despite their diametrically opposite roles in resource allocations, the market and the state are inseparably interdependent. The first condition for a market to function is a clear assignment of property rights on goods and services. Efficiency in market transactions would be greatly improved if mechanisms were established to resolve conflicts on contracts between sellers and buyers. Major means to protect property rights and enforce contracts are laws stipulated by the state, which are administered by such state organizations as courts and police. On the other hand, activities of state organizations are heavily dependent on the market. The state is authorized to conscript resources for its activities. However, the cost of governance would be extremely high if the state forced people to work against their will and procured innumerable goods necessary for its activities by coercion. Normally, the state relies upon the market for procurement of goods and services from revenue conscripted through taxation.

The interdependence of state and market may not exist in small subsistence economies (see Chapter 9), but is necessary at the scale of the nation-state and the national market—the core organizations of the modern world. Thus, no economy of any contemporary significance operates without the state and the market. Difference in economic systems reflects a difference in the way in which the state and the market are combined, i.e. which aspects of economic activities the state is in charge of, which aspects are left to the market, and how strongly and widely market activities are controlled by the state's administrative organization—the government. It is a matter of degree.

The question here is what combination of these two organizations would optimize the growth of developing economies. To answer this question, it is necessary to understand merits and demerits of the market and the state.

8.1.1 Efficiency of the competitive market

The orthodoxy of economics from Adam Smith and the English Classical School to the neoclassical school indicates that competition in a free market results in a socially optimum allocation of resources. Adam Smith clearly recognized that the mechanisms of a free market would guide people towards the promotion of total economic welfare in society. His famous thesis of 'invisible land' expressed this mechanism succinctly:

[E]very individual necessarily labours to render the annual revenue to the society as great as he can. He generally, indeed, neither intends to promote the public interest, nor knows how much he is promoting it. By preferring the support of domestic to that of foreign industry he intends only his own security; and by directing that industry in such a manner as its produce may be of the greatest value, he intends only his own gain, and he is in this, as in many cases, led by an invisible hand to promote an end which is no part of his intention. (Smith [1776] 1937: 423)

On the basis of this theory, Adam Smith advocated removal of trade restrictions in the Mercantile System as a major means of maximizing the wealth (or income) of nations. According to him, removal of trade restrictions would not only improve static efficiency in resource allocation in a single production period but would contribute to economic growth through the dynamic effect of increased division of labour stemming from an enlarged market over time (Chapter 5, Section 1).

In contrast, free-trade advocates, from David Ricardo to the neoclassical school, were mainly concerned about the proof of static efficiency in the free market, that is, efficiency in the allocation of existing resources in a given period while disregarding accumulation of the resources over time. Here, the neoclassical position will be summarized, leaving explanations of Ricardo's comparative advantage theory to the next section.

The first building block of the neoclassical theory is the mechanism of the market to equate demand and supply of a commodity (or service) through adjustments in its price. Obviously, a free market has the power to establish a single price. If a commodity is sold at different prices, all the buyers would be attracted to the low-priced supplier, bidding up his price, while no one would buy from a high-priced supplier, forcing his price down. The same mechanism continues to operate in adjusting the price to equate demand and supply of the commodity. If the price is too high, demand falls short of supply, piling up unsold surplus, which will force sellers to lower the price. On the other hand, if the price is too low and attracts too many buyers relative to supply, the price will be bid up through competition. If demand and supply are thus equated, waste from unsold surpluses and unproductive efforts of looking for the commodities in short supply (e.g. long queus at state stores, as commonly observed in the former Soviet Union) can be avoided.

According to neoclassical economics, this equilibrium between demand and supply in the free competitive market represents an efficient resource allocation for the production of a commodity to maximize economic welfare in society. In terms of Alfred Marshall's ([1890] 1953) concepts, the demand curve for a commodity in the competitive market is the schedule of decreasing marginal utility for increased consumption, while the supply curve is the schedule of marginal cost for increased production. Therefore, marginal utility and cost are equated at the demand–supply equilibrium, resulting in the maximum utility to society.

In terms of the general equilibrium theory of Leon Walras (1874) and Vilfredo Pareto (1906), the equilibrium reached through transactions in a free competitive market represents an efficient resource allocation in the sense that no participant in market transactions cannot increase his economic welfare without decreasing others' welfare—the so-called 'Pareto optimality'.

8.1.2 Market failure

If the market can achieve a socially desirable allocation of resources, there should be no need for government to coercively intervene in economic activities. However, the market is not able to achieve optimality in all economic activities. Divergence of market equilibrium from the point of Marshallian net utility maximization or Pareto optimality is called market failure. Government activities are needed to correct this failure.

First, market failure emerges in the supply of public goods. The market can achieve efficient resource allocations only to 'private goods' for which private property rights are established, so that only those who are assigned rights are entitled to use the goods—others are obliged to pay for the use of them. However, as for services provided by police and court to maintain peace and order, and basic scientific knowledge produced from academic research, for example, an unidentifiable number of people can use them jointly (non-rivalness), and it is difficult to impose appropriate payments on users (non-excludability). Everybody tries to utilize such 'public goods' without sharing the cost (free-riders). Since anyone seeking profit would not care to produce these goods, supply of them must rely on government (Section 1.2.3).

In the real world, both pure public goods endowed with perfect non-rivalness and non-excludability and pure private goods completely lacking these attributes are rare. For example, automobiles are private goods since only those who pay for transport costs can utilize them. However, since they pollute air and can be dangerous to humans when in accidents, automobiles are negative public goods ('public bads'). Therefore, the market equilibrium of automobile production tends to be larger than the social optimum level. For the correction of this market failure, government must take measures to curb production of automobiles, such as anti-pollution tax and quantitative restraint (Section 7.4.4).

Market failure can occur in the case of pure private goods also. For the market mechanism to achieve social optimality, the condition of 'perfect competition' must be satisfied—all the participants in market transactions must have perfect information on the prices and the qualities of commodities and no one can have monopolistic power to influence market prices.

In the real world, however, information is imperfect. Especially large gaps in information prevail between buyers and sellers on the qualities of products. Typically, it is difficult for ordinary citizens (customers) to judge the quality of professional services, such as those of medical doctors and lawyers. Likewise, financial services from banks and insurance companies, especially with respect to safety of deposit and insurance payment, are difficult for ordinary citizens to judge. If buyers are liable to incur loss from fraudulent sellers utilizing this 'asymmetry of information', then transactions in the market will be smaller than the socially optimum level or may even totally disappear (Arrow, 1963; Akerlof, 1970; Stiglitz and Weiss, 1981; Stiglitz, 1989*a*). In order to correct this type of market failure, the government may have to intervene in the market by limiting business permits and licences to qualified sellers as a means of increasing quality information to buyers.

Where market equilibrium diverges significantly from social optimality due to private monopoly by sellers and/or by monopsony buyers, corrective measures such as anti-trust laws may be required. Also, in some industries characterized by increasing returns to scale, such as electricity and water supplies, regional monopoly might be more efficient than competition. In this case, the government may have to regulate prices or undertake production by public corporations to avoid sellers' monopolistic pricing.

These government activities to correct market failures are a part of public goods. An even more important role that the government may have to play is redistribution of incomes. Equity in income distribution is a social objective that is as important as efficiency in economic production. At the same time, maintenance of decent equity is needed to enhance economic efficiency, because worsening of income distribution will endanger social stability, making normal economic transactions more difficult and costly due to increased crime and disruption.

The market is the mechanism used to promote economic efficiency but not to improve income distribution. If the income distribution realized through the free market is not socially desirable, it becomes necessary for government to attempt redistribution by use of its coercive power. Redistribution systems, such as progressive income tax and social security, are a type of public good to the extent that they increase economic welfare in society.

8.1.3 Government failure

However, since the supply of public goods is determined through a political process, there is no guarantee at all that their supply will be socially optimum (Section 1.2.3). In previous chapters it has repeatedly been emphasized that a short supply of public good represents a major bottleneck to the growth of developing economies. However, the danger of oversupply of public good should not be overlooked. The supply of public good entails costs which are ultimately financed through taxation. If a government activity to correct a market failure entails higher budgetary cost than social gain from the corrective measure, it represents an oversupply of public goods. The problem is that government is an organization inherently prone to oversupply those public goods of relatively low social demand at the expense of those public goods vitally needed for economic development.

What matters to political leaders or politicians is to maximize their likelihood of staying in office. Towards this goal, budget allocations among various public goods are based not so much on considerations of their contribution to social economic welfare, but on calculations on the strength of enhancing political support (Downs, 1957; Buchanan and Tullock, 1962; Breton, 1974). Accordingly, a public good, such as basic scientific research, which benefits society as a whole much greater than its cost, is likely to be undersupplied. Because its great benefit will be distributed widely among a large number of people in the future, it is unlikely that a strong pressure group will be organized for such public goods. In contrast, construction of local public infrastructure may be lobbied for very strongly, likely to result in an oversupply if it is expected to produce a large profit for a few contractors and/or a relatively small number of residents in a narrow local community.

Moreover, government is a monopolist of legitimate coercive power and has no danger of bankruptcy. In this organization, therefore, a strong incentive prevails to expand the organization for the sake of increasing the power and positions of bureaucrats. Since they command a large body of information, which ordinary citizens find difficult to access, they can easily manipulate the information to inflate the value of public goods they want to supply (such as exaggerating the danger of national security to increase the military). Also, government organizations are usually less efficient in the absence of profit incentive and bankruptcy incidence. These forces combine to produce oversupply of unnecessary public goods (Brittan, 1977; Buchanan and Wagner, 1977).

Because bureaucrats and pressure groups are strongly resistant to any reduction in vested interests, it is not easy to shift budget allocations from one category of public goods to another in response to changes in social needs. As the result, it is common to find that oversupply of unnecessary public goods coexists with sheer undersupply of public goods critically needed for economic development. Such inefficient budget allocation that results in reduction in net social welfare can be called 'government failure'.

The government failure is not limited to misuse of budget, but arises from undue regulations to bias resource allocations. There are many regulations that made positive contributions to such purposes as pollution control and safety when they were instituted, but later had socially negative effects. For example, the compulsory regular checking of automobiles by authorized garages in Japan (*Shaken*) made a high social contribution towards the safety of drivers and pedestrians as well as the control of noxious gas emission when automobiles made in Japan were low in quality and prone to trouble. However, since the quality of cars has greatly improved, this has become a system to protect the vested interests of the authorized garages at the expense of automobile users.

The danger is that the governments' regulations tend to become entrenched when those with vested interests seek 'institutional rents' or excess profits from regulations. Such rents are consumed for the sake of preserving the regulations (Tullock, 1967; Stigler, 1971; Tollison, 1982). Firms protected by a regulation raise funds and ballots to support politicians in exchange for their support on the preservation of this regulation. It is also common for firms to employ retired officials from regulating agencies. Through rent-seeking activities by bureaucrats and politicians as well as protected firms, socially negative regulations continue to be maintained and reinforced.

8.1.4 On the choice of economic system

According to the principle of democracy, the state is the possession of citizens, and government is an agent commissioned by citizens to exercise coercive power for the supply of public goods. More precisely, government may be conceptualized as an organization consisting of multi-layered agency contracts. In the case of parliamentary democracy, the citizens are the primary principal and the members of parliament are the primary agent. The parliamentary members act as the secondary principal to select chief executives of government as the secondary agent—such subagency contracts are linked in a chain from the top to the bottom layers to form the organization of government (Lin and Nugent, 1995). This structure is similar to other hierarchical organizations, such as joint stock companies, which consist of the nexus of principal–agency contracts across shareholders, board members, executives, and employees (Aoki, 1988).

Since politicians and bureaucrats are agents for the citizens, they must endeavour to do their best to serve the welfare of the nation. Yet, it is common that these agents yield to the temptation of placing higher priority on their own profit than on the people's or even their own nation's welfare. Such 'moral hazards' are not uncommon in the agency contracts in the private sector, such as financial agents managing entrusted funds for their own profit not for customers' profit (Arrow, 1985; Hart and Holmstrom, 1987).

Moral hazards are not a serious issue if a principal can recognize the agent's intent and action and discharge the agent before he causes moral hazards. In the real world, characterized by information asymmetry, however, moral hazards can be a major source of market failure, as explained before.

This problem is even more serious as a source of governmental failure. In principle, citizens should be able to discharge politicians and bureaucrats who commit moral hazards, (through political activities such as voting and rioting). However, the amount of information collected by government agencies for administrative purposes is usually incomparably greater than that available to individual citizens. It is not difficult for politicians and bureaucrats to cover up their moral hazards, often in collusion with private firms under their patronage, by manipulating information under their monopoly (Tirole, 1986; Laffont and Tirole, 1991). In contrast, the cost is usually very high for an ordinary citizen to detect moral hazards in government agencies. Even higher is his cost of disseminating this information to the majority of citizens and organizing political campaigns against corruption and misconduct by government agencies. Gains to the nation as a whole from his activities may be much larger than the cost he would incur. But these gains will be widely diffused among many citizens so that his own gain would be too small to cover the large cost of information collection and political campaign (Olson, 1965; Stigler, 1975). In such a situation, activities to prevent moral hazards in government are significantly smaller than is socially desirable. In contrast, political activities by small groups seeking institutional rents from socially negative controls and regulations are intensive. It is no wonder that social loss arising from government failure exceeds that from market failure (Krueger, 1974).

Both the market and the state are indispensable for allocating resources. The major task in choosing an economic system is to find the proper combination of market and state by clearly recognizing possible failures of these two organizations. For developing countries it is especially important to recognize that the types and magnitudes of both market and government failures are different for different cultural heritages as well as for different stages of development. In general, the less developed the economies are, the more imperfect the information is, and the less organized the institutions are in support of the market (such as protection of property rights). In such economies, market failures are pervasive and serious, thereby apparently demanding strong government action to correct them. However, in these less developed economies, the citizens' educational level is low and mass media for public opinion formation is underdeveloped. Correspondingly, the civic tradition of political participation and sense of national integrity are not well established among people. Under such social conditions, the possibility is greater for government failure to become more serious than market failures. With the recognition of this possibility, the choice of an optimum combination between the market and the state under given historical conditions is most fundamental in the design for development.

8.2 Around the Infant Industry Protection Argument

Throughout the history of modern economic growth, a major confrontation has persisted on the choice of development strategy between emphasis on the efficiency of the free market and the control on market activities through government planning and command. This confrontation has often revolved around two opposing views on international trade—the argument for free trade along Adam Smith's tradition, and the argument for trade protection, commonly called 'infant industry protection'. Examination of the theoretical contexts of these two doctrines greatly facilitates the understanding of the opposing perspectives on the choice of development strategy.

8.2.1 Market failure in dynamic economy

In general, the less developed the economies, the more imperfect the information, and, hence, the more prone they are to market failure. This problem is especially serious in the dynamic process of economic development involving capital accumulation and technological progress. Unlike the static economy that is assumed by the neoclassical school to prove the efficiency of the competitive market for one production period the dynamic development process over time is characterized by future uncertainty. The more uncertain the future is, the higher the risk is, and hence, the higher the discount rate on future revenues is, so that the rate of investment in the market will be lowered. Uncertainty inherent in the development process may thus represent a major bottleneck for development itself.

For example, assume that development of a particular industry in a developing economy, with importation of advanced technology, will contribute much to the growth of this economy in the long run. However, if importation of foreign technology and construction of production facilities takes a long time and requires a large investment, private entrepreneurs may hesitate to undertake such a project because of the high risk involved, despite a high probability of success. Moreover, efficient operation of new plants and machineries may require training of workers, engineers, and management staff. A private firm may worry that other firms will recruit its workers, trained with its time and costs. This externality, together with the high risk involved, would make it difficult for private entrepreneurs to develop this new industry under a free market. From the side of investible fund supply, too, the possibility would be low for private financial institutions in developing economies to advance a sufficient amount of credit to such a risky long-term project.

Accordingly, the logic was that it is necessary and desirable for government to protect 'infant industries' which have no chance of being established under free-market competition at present, but are expected to be major contributors to national development if they are protected until they grow to 'adults', able to compete in the free market. This infant industry protection can be promoted by such means as tariffs and other forms of border protection on domestic producers, allocations of subsidies and directed credits to target industries from state-owned financial institutions, favourable tax treatment, and nationalization of private enterprises. In this section, however, the analysis will be focused on confrontation between free trade and protective trade systems, which has traditionally been a major topic in the economics of development.

8.2.2 Ricardo vs. List

The theory of infant industry protection was advanced by Friedrich List (1789–1846) in Germany when this country explored the strategy to catch up with Britain in industrial power. His *Das Nationale System der Politischen Ökonomie* [National System of Political Economy] ([1841] 1930) rivalled the doctrine of free trade advocated by the English Classical School. It was structured as an antithesis to Ricardo's ([1817] 1966) theory of comparative advantage in international trade.

The theoretical basis of the two opposing doctrines may be explained in terms of an example of trade between England and Germany under the simplified assumption that both countries produce and exchange two commodities, cotton yarn and wheat, using labour as the sole factor of production.[1] As numerical illustrations, two hours of labour are required to produce one pound of cotton yarn and four hours are required to produce one kilogram of wheat in England, whereas eight hours are required for each in Germany. In this example, absolute costs of both commodities are higher in Germany than in England. Yet, according to Ricardo's theory, Germany can export one of the commodities based on difference in 'comparative costs' (or cost ratio) *vis-à-vis* England.

In autarky before international trade begins, the domestic terms of trade or the rate of exchange between the two commodities is determined by the ratio of production costs per unit of output, i.e. since four hours of labour are required to produce one kilogram of wheat and two hours to produce one pound of cotton yarn in England, then one kilogram of wheat should be exchanged for two pounds of yarn. On the other hand, because eight hours are required for unit production of both commodities in

Germany, then one kilogram of wheat should be exchanged for one pound of yarn.

Once international trade opens, it becomes less advantageous in England to produce one kilogram of wheat at home using four hours of labour than to export two pounds of yarn produced from the same amount of labour in Germany in exchange for two kilograms of wheat. Likewise, it becomes more advantageous in Germany to buy two pounds of yarn from England in exchange for one kilogram of wheat than to produce one pound of yarn at home, since both use eight hours of labour. As England and Germany specialize in the production of yarn and wheat respectively, through international trade both countries will be able to consume more goods, implying increased economic welfare in both countries.

As the example illustrates, as long as production costs remain unchanged for both commodities in both countries, free trade will result in specialization to maximize the economic welfare of all trade participants. List did not deny this logic of comparative advantage by Ricardo. What List did argue is that the proof of welfare maximization from free trade of all the participating countries is only valid under short-run static conditions characterized by fixed production cost structures but does not apply to the dynamic development process.

In terms of the previous example, List's argument is as follows: At present, the unit cost of cotton yarn in Germany may be four times higher than in England, resulting in Germany's comparative disadvantage in yarn production. However, if Germany builds modern cotton-spinning factories and trains workers appropriately, Germany should be able to cut down the cost of yarn production to a level less than twice that of England's. Then Germany can be transformed from an agrarian economy, based on the export of wheat, to an industrial economy exporting manufactured commodities such as cotton yarn. When this industrialization is achieved, the production possibility frontier of Germany should significantly expand with a major improvement in national economic welfare.

According to List, however, under free trade the market of manufactured commodities in Germany will continue to be occupied by English products, and there will be no incentive for domestic entrepreneurs to develop industries such as cotton-spinning to reduce the cost of manufacturing production through scale economies and workers' learning-by-doing. Therefore, List argued that government should protect domestic industries against competition from overseas by border protection measures such as tariffs until these infant industries become viable under free trade. Development of viable industries will be further facilitated if the increased budget from tariff revenue is used for the supply of such public goods as roads, harbours, and scientific and technical education in support of industrialization.

Infant industry protection entails social cost. If protective tariffs are imposed, for instance, consumers are forced to buy the protected commodities at higher prices, resulting in a loss in real income by consumers. If expected gains to producers from protection are so large that the sum of their present values (obtained by discounting future gains) is larger than the sum of present costs, infant industry protection can be justified. Since there is much room for developing economies to achieve major gains in productivity from technology borrowing, there should be many cases in which application of the Listian protection policy would be justified.

8.2.3 The Listian trap

As a theory, List's infant industry protection argument does not contradict Ricardo's theory of comparative advantage. List expanded Ricardo's static theory to a dynamic theory applicable to the long-run development process characterized by major changes in the production cost structure. In other words, the theory of comparative advantage was incorporated into the economics of development by List who recognized the possibility of serious market failure in dynamic economies.

In the controversy over the choice of development strategy, the real opposition to List's infant industry protection is Adam Smith's doctrine of free trade. In contrast to List, who emphasized the danger of market failure in the development process, Smith based his doctrine on the danger of government failure. Through observations of the Mercantile System (which was a predecessor to the Listian system), Smith clearly recognized how market regulations and trade monopolies emerged from rent-seeking activities by rulers of absolute monarchies and prestige merchants, and how those regulations suppressed wide development of entrepreneurial activities in agriculture, industry, and commerce by the bourgeois class (Ekeland and Tollison, 1981). Therefore, even though he recognized the possibility that 'by means of such regulations, indeed, a particular manufacture may sometimes be acquired sooner than it could have been otherwise, and after a certain time may be made at home as cheap or cheaper than in foreign countries', he had no hesitation asserting that 'it will by no means follow that the sum total, either of its industry, or of its revenue can ever be augmented by any such regulation' (Smith, [1776] 1937: 425).

List correctly pointed out the possibility that long-term investment in new industries tends to be smaller than optimum in the dynamic process characterized by high uncertainty and externality. This market failure is especially serious in the early stage of development. However, it is doubtful that he recognized the possibility that government interventions into the market for the sake of infant industry protection might produce government failure which could be more serious than market failure. This danger may be called the 'Listian trap'.

8.2.4 The import-substitution industrialization policy

The protective tariffs on major industrial commodities such as iron and steel, that List advocated, began to be applied in 1879 (after his death) in the second Reich led by Otto von Bismarck. In terms of its economic performance there was no sign that Germany was caught in the Listian trap—industrialization progressed rapidly and by the end of the nineteenth century surpassed England in the areas of heavy and chemical industries.

However, there are many that illustrate the danger of Listian trap. A typical example may be the 'import-substitution industrialization policy' widely adopted among developing economies after World War II. This policy is nothing but List's infant industry protection. It promotes industrialization of developing economies that were hitherto dependent on production and export of primary commodities, by substituting domestic supply of manufacturing products for those hitherto imported from abroad, by using tariffs and other measures. Leaders in newly independent nations in the Third World were very attracted by this strategy, partly because of their repulsion against the colonial system which imposed the role of the material supply base as well as the manufactured product market on them. Also, the memory of the collapse of primary commodity markets during the World Depression was still fresh in their minds during the period immediately after World War II, so that it was considered difficult for developing economies to earn sufficient income and foreign exchange. This view was represented by Nurkse (1959) who denied the possibility in the mid-twentieth century of such rapid expansions in external demand for primary commodities as was experienced in the nineteenth century, because consumption of tropical food crops such as sugar and coffee reached near saturation in high-income economies, and the substitution of synthetics for primary industrial raw materials such as copper and natural rubber was in rapid progress.

Such 'export pessimism' for primary commodity producers led to the theory of secular decline in the terms of trade (the ratio of primary to manufactured commodity prices) against developing countries by Raul Prebisch, a leading policy economist in Latin America. He argued that, because elasticities of world demand for primary commodities with respect to both income and price are much lower than those of manufactured commodities, competitive efforts of developing economies to increase their output and productivity are bound to depress the price of primary commodities relative to the price of manufactured commodities so that foreign exchange earnings decrease, resulting in trade deficits for developing economies. Free trade thus works as a mechanism of income transfer from developing to developed economies. Therefore, there is no other option for developing economies to sustain growth than to use the import-substitution industrialization policy (Prebisch, 1959).

On this apparently plausible theory, the import-substitution industrialization policy was widely adopted among developing economies. For this strategy, not only were border protection measures such as tariffs and import quotas used, but the setting of overvalued exchange rates for domestic currency was commonly practised. The higher the rate of exchange of local currency for foreign currency, the more advantageous are the industries that rely on imports for the supply of capital goods and intermediate products. A common policy mix for protection of target industries was to raise the domestic prices of their products by means of import restriction, and, at the same time, allocate to those industries an import quota of capital and intermediate goods so they could enjoy profits from imports under the overvalued exchange rate.

Victims of this policy were not only the consumers who were forced to purchase commodities at increased prices, but also unprotected industries. Especially, the unprotected industries producing tradable goods suffered from prices lowered by overvalued exchange rates, while they had to buy high-priced inputs produced by the protected domestic industries because little import licence was allocated to the unprotected industries.

The import-substitution industrialization policy was usually targeted to protect large-scale modern industries, such as the assembling of consumer durables and capital equipment (e.g. automobiles and televisions) and the manufacture of modern materials (e.g. synthetic fibres and chemical fertilizers). Correspondingly, agriculture and small- and medium-scale industries based on labour-intensive technology were victimized. While automobile assemblers benefited from both restrictions on automobile imports and a generous quota on the imports of parts at prices lowered by overvalued exchange rates, small-part manufacturers had to face international competition handicapped by overvalued exchange. Similarly, as synthetic fibre industries were protected, elevated domestic yarn prices rendered negative protection (or exploitation) to the weaving and garment industries which were run by small and medium enterprises based on labour-intensive technology.[2]

Thus, the import-substitution industrialization policy blocked wide autonomous developments in agriculture and industry supported by innovative activities of small and medium farmers and manufacturers (Little *et al.*, 1970). In this effect the import-substitution industrialization in the twentieth century shared common characteristics with mercantilism as Adam Smith observed in the eighteenth century (De Soto, 1989).

Despite such sacrifice, the cases were few in which protected industries were successful in achieving international competitive strength in due course. Instead, protection reduced the domestic producers' incentive to keep up productivity at an international level for the sake of survival, resulting in preservation of inefficient enterprises. This tendency is illustrated by the example in Latin America where a total of 600,000 automobiles was produced by as many as 90 assemblers with a production of only 6,700 cars per firm—far smaller than the minimum efficient plant scale (50,000 for passenger cars and 20,000 for trucks)—in the late 1960s, after twenty years of the import-substitution industrialization policy (Cardoso and Helwege, 1992: 96).

Excess profits produced from protection policies were consumed largely by rent-seeking activities, such as political lobbying for preservation and strengthening of trade regulations and foreign exchange controls, rather than for long-term investment aimed at productivity increases. A part of the excess profit was captured by labourers in large enterprises, who were able to achieve significant wage hikes under the pressure of labour unions. As a result, firms in the formal sector tried to replace labour with capital goods imported at relatively low prices (under the overvalued exchange rate), despite a large number of low-wage labourers desperately seeking formal employment. In this way, the import-substitution industrialization policy failed to achieve both the goals of economic growth and equality in income distribution (Bhagwati, 1978; Krueger, 1978; Balassa *et al.*, 1982).

8.3 The Rise and Fall of Developmentalist Models[3]

Then, why did the trade-protection policy fail so badly in developing economies after World War II, when it appeared to be successful in Germany before World War I? More generally, what conditions are necessary for the success of policies based on developmentalism?

'Developmentalism' is defined as the ideology that, in developing economies aimed at catching-up with advanced economies, economic development produces a higher value than its material value, such as satisfaction of national prestige and security. It is an ideology opposite to 'market liberalism' which measures the value of economic development in terms of additional utility from increased consumption to be determined by people's free choice in the market. A common element in economic policy based on developmentalism is establishment of the mechanism of 'forced saving' in a sense broader than Schumpeter's definition (Chapter 6, Section 3). It includes all the forced income transfers from households to target industries and enterprises, e.g. tariff protection for a particular industry raises the profit of firms in that industry at the expense of real household income and consumption which are reduced by elevated domestic prices. If people would accept the ideology of developmentalism, the social discount rate for future consumption would be smaller and, hence, the probability would be higher for the acceptance of such policies as infant industry protection that sacrifice present consumption for future economic growth.

A major question is what factors underlie the failure of developmentalist policies to achieve the original goal aimed for, as exemplified by the import-substitution industrialization policy. In other words, under what conditions did the developmentalist policies used to correct market failure in the development process produce more serious government failure?

8.3.1 The limit of information and the role of ideology

As explained in Section 1 of this chapter, one of the major factors that produces market failure in a dynamic economy is future uncertainty. Yet, there is no guarantee that government will be able to predict the future more accurately than will the private sector. It might not be so difficult to determine which industries should be protected by learning from the historical experiences of advanced economies. It is extremely difficult, however, to assess the long-run effects of protection policies on total economy through various interactions and reactions among industries and enterprises. For example, policy-makers in Latin America who designed the import-substitution industrialization policy may have had a decent estimation of how much profit it could render to automobile assemblers, but it may have not occurred to them what damage this policy would produce on automobile parts suppliers and other related industries.

It is also not easy for government to detect the moral hazards of protected enterprises. It is difficult for governments to determine how much of their failure to achieve international competitive strength is due to inevitable external forces, and how much is due to mismanagement such as the use of excess profits gained from protection for high manager and unionized labour salaries (and/or fringe benefits) instead of for productive investment.

Such failures, stemming from the government's limited capacity to collect and analyse information, should multiply as the means of intervention into the market increase in number and become more complex. In this respect, one reason for the success or lack of serious failure of the trade protection policy in Germany under the Second Reich might have been its simplicity, since it relied almost solely on tariffs. The import-substitution industrialization policy in post-independent developing economies was more complex, combining not only tariffs, but also many other measures, such as foreign exchange control, directed credit, and state enterprise. The informational requirement to manoeuvre such a complex system could have exceeded the capacity of their governments.

It has been pointed out previously that asymmetry of information (which is, of course, a part of imperfect information) is the basic factor underlying moral hazards among politicians and bureaucrats that create government failures. Development of mass media, such as newspaper and TV, could work as a significant check on self-interest-seeking politicians and bureaucrats who operate at the expense of the national interest. However, a more basic check on their moral hazards is the morale in society. The power of morale to check moral hazards depends on cultural tradition, but is also determined by people's desire for national economic development. In societies where people's desire to catch up with the economic power of advanced countries is strongly augmented by nationalism, those who promote economic development are likely to receive higher social praise than worthy of their material contributions. On the other side of the coin, moral hazards that obstruct economic growth are likely to be impeached in such societies.

We may hereafter call the system of institutions and policies based on developmentalism the 'developmentalist model'. The model's success depends on how to combine effective developmental policies while minimizing the sum of social costs arising from market and government failures, under a given value system and the capacity of information in society.

An indispensable element of the developmentalist model, which is aimed at catching up, is a mechanism of forced saving to enable accumulation of tangible and intangible capital in the late starter of industrialization at a much faster speed than in the early-starter country. Whether this mechanism would achieve the desired goal depends on how efficiently the model is structured to mobilize savings and allocate them among alternative investment opportunities to maximize the long-term growth rate of national product. Another requirement for the model's success is its ability to avoid social instability and political disruption often resulting from rapid economic growth, not only domestically but also in the international dimension, as to be discussed below.

8.3.2 Defeat of the old developmental market economies

In the history of modern economic growth, developmentalist models have emerged through confrontation between early and late starters of industrialization The first major confrontation between the early and the late starters occurred when Germany tried to catch up with England from the middle of the nineteenth century. England, which had established itself as the 'workshop of the world' by the early nineteenth century, followed the model of 'liberal market economies' in the tradition of Adam Smith (Chapter 5, Section 1). In this model, ordinary economic activities are left to decentralized private decisions under market competition, while government is supposed to maintain law and order as a basic framework within which the market operates.[4] Investment in human capital, such as education and research, was also left largely to the private sector.

When Germany accomplished national unification under the leadership of Bismarck and set out to industrialize, government invested heavily in industrial infrastructure including technical education and applied research and development (Section 6.2.1). At the same time, it installed tariff walls against imports of manufactured commodities according to List's thesis of infant industry protection.

Major achievements from the institutionalization of scientific education and research in Germany were illustrated by the fact that the number of new scientific discoveries during the last quarter of the nineteenth century in the areas of thermo, photo, electricity, electron and magnetism were 2.5 times greater in Germany than in England, and that as much as 60 per cent of the original research in physiology in the world was undertaken in this country (Shioki, 1993, p. i). There is little doubt that the government's investment in scientific education and research was a decisive factor underlying the supremacy of Germany in heavy and chemical industries in the new regime of 'invisible technology' based on scientific knowledge instead of traditional artisans' skill (Chapter 6, Section 2).

This development strategy in Germany was geared to accelerating capital (both tangible and intangible) accumulation and economic growth by suppressing consumption through government finance and border protection, within the basic framework of market economies. As such, it was a developmentalist model for catching up, which may be called the model of 'developmental economies'.

Germany's success convinced other late-starter countries, Czarist Russia and Imperial Japan among others, to imitate the model of the developmental market economy. In the Meiji period (1868–1912), in the absence of tariff autonomy due to unequal treaties forced by the Western powers, the Japanese government tried to promote industrialization by establishing model factories for the demonstration of borrowed technology (such as silk-reeling and steel-milling) and by giving subsidies to key industries (such as shipping and shipbuilding), while following Germany's model in building institutions related to education and research. Later, as tariff autonomy was recovered (partial recovery from 1899 and full recovery from 1911), escalated protective tariffs for heavy and chemical industries began to be applied (Yamazawa, 1984, ch. 17; Shimbo, 1995, pt. II, chs. 1 and 2).

It is important to note that the USA preceded Germany in the use of this model. Following the advocacy of Alexander Hamilton, 'the American System' had been established by the first half of the nineteenth century to protect domestic industries by tariffs and to invest the tariff revenue in public infrastructure, such as canals and highways, for integrating frontiers into a single domestic market. In fact, List developed his idea of infant industry protection from his personal observation of this 'American System' in the Hamilton tradition during his exile to the USA (List, 1827). Thus, the model of developmental market economies was universal in its appeal and applicability to the late starters in the nineteenth century.

Why did this model prove successful, at least economically, in Germany and Japan? How could their infant industry protection escape from the failure of the import-substitution industrialization after World War II? One reason could be that the system of protection was simple and transparent, using tariffs only for distorting market prices and thus not exceeding the informational capacity of government. Also, the tariff rates adopted by Germany and Japan were modest, ranging around the order of 20 per cent or less, which were significantly lower than the rates ranging from 50 to 100 per cent in many developing countries adopting the import-substitution industrialization policy (Yamazawa, 1984: 154; World Bank, *World Development Report 1991*, p. 87).

Probably, the more important factors were strong nationalism and the disciplined bureaucracy built for achieving the nationalistic goal. Given political and military confrontations pervasive in nineteenth century Europe, industrialization was one of various means in the overall geopolitical strategy of Germany. The situation was similar in Japan when it tried to industrialize a half century later than Germany in the era of colonialization of Asia by the Western powers. As a result, economic development was valued equally or even more highly as a means to build a strong army for achieving national supremacy than to increase consumers' utility. Under this narrow but strong nationalism, it would have been difficult for government officials to exercise those moral hazards that were an obvious hindrance to national economic development.

Of course, rent-seeking activities did exist. For example, tariff protection set out by the German Government in 1879 were applied to grain as well as major industrial commodities such as iron and steel. This policy was intended to protect the farm estates of *junkers* in Prussia—the political and military backbone of the Second Reich—from grain imports from Russia and Eastern Europe (Gerschenkron, 1943).

It is not clear how much Listian tariff protection contributed to industrialization in Germany and Japan. Germany was on the verge of supremacy in heavy and chemical industries when tariff protection was introduced. German industries were likely to have continued to dominate the world even in the absence of protective tariffs.

Also, it is important to point out that initial industrialization in Japan progressed before the recovery of tariff autonomy. In fact, there is evidence to suggest that the absence of tariff autonomy was favourable for industrial development. In the 1870s and 1880s, the Japanese Government tried to develop cotton-spinning industries in cotton-farming areas in order to rescue cotton producers about to be ruined by increased imports of cotton yarn and cloth after Japan's opening to foreign trade. To this end, government imported relatively small-scale plants consisting of about 2,000 spindles for lease or sale at subsidized prices to entrepreneurs in inland cotton-farming areas. However, factories equipped with these small-sized machines went broke as they failed to produce yarn at competitive prices from high-priced domestic cotton.

A little later, however, cotton-spinning in Japan was able to develop into a major export industry as large-scale modern factories equipped with machines made up of 15,000 spindles or more using cotton imported from India and the USA, were established by private entrepreneurs (Abe, 1990: 165–71; Francks, 1992: 43–6). If Japan had tariff autonomy in this period, it is quite possible that the government would have tried to protect the small-scale inefficient spinning-factories as well as domestic cotton farmers, by imposing high tariffs on foreign cotton and yarn imports. If so, the opportunity for cotton-spinning and weaving industries to grow as prime export industries would have been closed in Japan. Indeed, the dramatic development of the Japanese cotton textile industry thereafter, soon outstripping those of India and Britain, was accomplished with virtually no protection and subsidy from the government. This experience is clearly inconsistent with the assertion that government subsidies are indispensable for late-industrializing economies to foster export manufactures including textiles (Amsden, 1989: 143–4).

Thus considered, it is questionable how much the Listian tariff protection contributed to the success of industrial development in Germany and Japan. A more important factor might have been public investment in infrastructure for the support of private industrial activities, including scientific education and research systems.

The problem for the Kaiser's Germany as well as for Imperial Japan was that their successful economic development was tied to narrow nationalism or racism to promote imperialistic expansion for supporting industrial exports abroad. This nationalism could have contributed economic growth as it reduced moral hazards by politicians and bureaucrats. However, since such ideology had no universal appeal, expansionist policies inevitably resulted in isolation of these nations in the world community. In the end, the Second and the Third German Reichs, as well as Imperial Japan, had to experience disastrous defeats in the world wars. The USA was able to escape this route, partly because of its stronger liberalist tradition, but also because of open frontiers available for continued expansion of the domestic market until the Spanish–American War.[5]

In retrospect, while this 'old' model of developmental market economies was able to achieve success in fast economic growth, it failed because its supporting ideology was incompatible with the world system.

8.3.3 Collapse of the centrally planned economies

Upon the defeat of the old developmental market economies, the centrally planned economies of the Soviet type became the forefront of developmentalist models for catching up. This model represents an economic system design that minimized the role of the market and maximized the role of government planning and command within a feasible range of human organizations.

Centrally planned economies do not necessarily represent a developmentalist model. It is theoretically possible to envision a centrally planned economy which is managed so as to increase consumption by placing a low priority on investment. However, the centrally planned economies that existed historically in the former Soviet Union and Eastern Europe as well as China and Vietnam tried to suppress consumption to a politically feasible minimum so that capital accumulation and economic growth could be maximized. Indeed, it is estimated that the share of fixed capital investment in GNP in the Soviet Union increased from 19 per cent in 1928 to 29 per cent in 1970, while the share of household consumption decreased from 68 to 49 per cent (Ofer, 1987: 1788). This system of enforcing increased capital formation and economic growth at the expense of present consumption through government planning and command was the developmentalist model by nature.

Central planning and command can be an effective development model where income levels are low and people's wants are homogeneous enough to estimate demand and supply of commodities. Another condition contributing to the effective working of centrally planned economies is strong ideological belief preventing people, especially leaders, from free-riding and rent-seeking. The communist ideal, coupled with nationalism, could have served this purpose for the periods during and immediately following the revolution as well as during the war against Nazi Germany. In fact, GNP in the Soviet Union, which was only one-fourth that of the USA in 1920, grew rapidly to reach one-half in 1960 (Ofer, 1987: 1781).

This model was not only adopted in the communist bloc, but also incorporated into many national development programmes in the Third World. The attraction of this model to developing countries was, in part, based on a relatively good growth performance of the Soviet economy until the 1960s. This model's attractiveness to the Third World was also based on the ideological appeal of socialism for the period immediately after World War II. For newly independent nations, capitalism and the market were perceived as a mechanism of colonial exploitation. Socialism and central planning were a much more attractive system. Unlike narrow nationalism and racism which led pre-war Germany and Japan to isolation, socialist ideology was able to secure wide sympathy and alliance from the world for the communist bloc.

However, the ideology that immediately governed the economic management of the Soviet Union was developmentalism driven by haste and impatience to catch up with Western capitalist economies. The burning haste of Soviet leaders, exacerbated by their fear of Western capitalism, was typically expressed by Joseph Stalin:

We are fifty or a hundred years behind the advanced countries. We must make good this distance in ten years. Either we do it, or they will crush us. (Stalin, 1947: 356)

Based on this haste, the goal of economic planning was the maximization of material output growth in the short run (Ofer, 1987: 1798–1809). In order to achieve this goal, not only consumption but also investment in infrastructure requiring long gestation periods, such as transportation and communication systems, was sacrificed. Further, investment for environmental conservation was almost utterly neglected.

Short-run maximization of material output was enforced by quantitative production targets set each year, which were determined by the central planning committee (GOSPLAN) and allocated to state enterprises through ministries in charge of the respective industries. While annual targets were determined according to the five-year plan, enforcement was made strictly with respect to the annual assignments. For the executives of state enterprises as well as the managers of production lines it was imperative to fulfil those quantitative targets each year, for which they were rewarded or penalized. What mattered to them was to produce target quantities. Product quality and time of delivery were loosely specified and monitored and seldom used as criteria of reward and punishment. Also, the management of production costs was loose, and budget constraints worked weakly on the purchase of capital and intermediate goods. The necessary funds for current production and investment were allocated by the state bank (GOSBANK) according to production plans and targets. However, even if costs were to exceed revenues, state enterprises were in no danger of going bankrupt, because other state enterprises supplying these firms were satisfied with achieving their own quantitative production targets. Unpaid prices were simply counted as sales in credit. The state bank was also not particularly eager to recover loans and was tolerant to continue rescheduling. Such weak budget constraints—so called 'soft budgets' (Kornai, 1980)—were said to be ubiquitous in centrally planned economies.

Under production management based on quantitative targets, coupled with soft budget constraints, it was inevitable that moral hazards became pervasive at all levels of production. Executives of state enterprises as well as production line managers were strongly motivated to underreport on their production capacities and overreport on the input requirements. They were inclined to use connections, bribery, and intimidation to obtain approval for their production plans from higher-ranking officials in the management hierarchy. Because officials in industrial ministries usually had less information on production capacity and cost than the executives of state enterprises, who themselves had less information than line managers, it was difficult to prevent moral hazards from spreading from the top to the bottom.

This moral hazard problem, common in agency contracts due to information asymmetry, became especially serious in the total absence of market information. Since all the enterprises paid little attention to product quality and delivery date, they were subject to the danger of not being able to fulfil their assigned production targets, due to defects and/or late delivery of inputs.

This danger induced the managers of state enterprises to keep larger inventories of materials and equipment than necessary.[6] This tendency was augmented by low rates of interest—zero in principle according to the doctrine of Marx. Stagnation in the Soviet economy from the 1970s—especially negative growth in total factor productivity observed in Table 5.3—probably reflected the process in which rapid capital accumulation in the absence of incentives to economize on the use of capital resulted in a rapid decline in capital's marginal productivity almost to zero (Weitzman, 1970; Easterly and Fisher, 1994).[7]

The collapse of the Soviet Union in the 1980s appears to be the consequence of its economic system in which the role of government was expanded beyond the limit of its information capacity.[8] Centrally planned economies have a critical defect as a catch-up model. While resource allocations can be decently efficient under central planning in the low-income stage, errors in planning increase progressively as the level of income rises and people's wants diversify. Also, altruism based on communist ideology, which may be an effective enforcer of leaders' morals as well as workers' morale under the crisis situation of revolution or war, cannot be sustained for long in peace. As the income level rises under peace, both planning errors and rent-seeking behaviours accumulate to such an extent as to bring about the collapse of the economy. Thus, centrally planned economies are bound to fail before attaining the catch-up goal. From this perspective, the communist bloc failed not because of its ideology but because of the critical defect in its development model.

8.3.4 Trap of populism

Latin America was the cradle and the typical experimental ground for the import-substitution industrialization policy. The experience of Latin America provides valuable information on the relationship between the developmentalist model and ideology.

The import-substitution industrialization policy in Latin America is said to have been supported by populism or *populismo* (Cardoso and Helwege, 1992, ch. 8). In Europe and North America populism was developed as an ideology to protect peasants and artisans whose employment and skill were threatened by modern industries. Those subscribing to this ideology were Luddites in England, *Narodnik* in Russia, and populists in the USA. In contrast, populism in Latin America was an ideology for improving the status of organized labourers in urban-based, large-scale modern industries. It was a mixture of nationalism and social reformism advocating the transformation of semi-colonial economies based on primary commodity exports under domination by owners of large farm estates (*haciendas*) and foreign traders to a more independent and egalitarian structure. In order to break down the oligarchy of *hacienderos* and foreign capitalists, it was considered necessary to organize urban industrial workers.

A typical populist system was established under Juan Péron's regime in Argentina (1946–55). Péron came to power on the basis of the Facist-orientated military circle in alliance with urban industries and labourers. In contrast with free-trade orientation under the rule of *hacienderos*, the Péron administration promoted 'nationalistic' policies such as border protection on manufactured imports, foreign exchange control, and nationalization of foreign enterprises. At the same time, Péron tried to strengthen labour laws and social security systems. A result was that the number of labour union members increased from about a half million to five million during the regime. In particular, civil service employment increased much faster than total employment, reflecting expansion in the government sector, especially in areas of industrial policy and welfare programmes (Hosono and Tsunekawa, 1986: 209–10). In effect, by convention the populist system government provided a last resort for the employment of college and high school graduates from the middle class.

The populist governments in Latin America of Péron as well as others who followed Péronism collapsed by the end of the 1950s. Thereafter, various administrations, such as military juntas and socialist revolutionaries, alternated in their assumption of power with occasional revivals of populist governments. Yet, irrespective of their motivations and doctrines, they were not able to upset the vested interests of powerful organized labourers and thereby maintained the populist system to some extent.

It has already been pointed out that the import-substitution industrialization policy set out by the populist governments was not only able to achieve the original target of fostering viable large-scale modern industries but, also, blocked the wider autonomous development of agriculture and small and medium-scale enterprises. Another major failure in the populist system was self-multiplication of government organizations including state enterprises. High administrative costs, large transfer payments for social welfare programmes, and losses from inefficient state enterprises often added up to create large budget deficits. Also, under overvalued exchange rates, current balance of payments continued to record deficits except for occasional commodity boom periods. To cover these deficits, governments relied on foreign credits. However, as external debts accumulated and gave rise to fears of insolvency, inflows of foreign capital were bound to stop. In this situation, if governments were still unable to reduce expenditures, they were forced to print money to cover budgetary deficits resulting in inflation (Cukierman *et al.*, 1992).

Domestic inflation under fixed exchange rates made real exchange rates more overvalued and thereby widened the deficits in the balance of trade. The worsened trade balance, together with the increased outstanding external debts, gave rise to the expectation of domestic currency devaluation that depressed capital inflows and encouraged capital flights. Because of increased difficulty in securing external finance, government had to rely more heavily on printing money, further spurring inflation.

Governments in Latin America often failed to stop this vicious circle because the pressure of populism made it difficult to execute budget cuts. Also, devaluation of local currency was politically difficult as it was liable to meet opposition by people whose cost of living rises with increased domestic prices of tradable consumption goods, such as food and fuel, as well as by entrepreneurs and labourers in the protected industries that had benefited from imported materials made cheap under overvalued exchange rates. Thus, the vicious circle remained uncurbed until it culminated in hyperinflation of the order of several hundred to several thousand per cent per year, as experienced in the 1980s (Table 2.2).

Significant progress in industrialization had been recorded in Latin America. Especially in countries endowed with large domestic markets, such as Brazil and Mexico, the import-substitution industrialization policy resulted in rapid rates of industrial output growth comparable with those of Asian NIEs during the 1960s and 1970s. However, relative to the speed of output growth, increases in the exports of manufactured commodities were slow in Latin American NIEs, and were coupled with the tendency of external debts to accumulate. Their external debts increased considerably during the oil boom period beginning in 1973 due to large capital imports for ambitious development projects under the expectation of continued high prices of primary commodities. Subsequently, as international commodity markets collapsed after 1981 and interest rates were escalated by the Reagan administration's money supply control, these economies were doomed to suffer the worst inflation and external debt accumulation throughout the 1980s (Chapter 2, Section 2).

8.4 Rise of the New Developmental Market Economies[9]

The receding tide of centrally planned economies has coincided with the rise of a new developmentalist model which may be called 'new developmental market economies'. This is the developmental strategy that has been adopted by post-war Japan, followed by Asian NIEs such as Korea and Taiwan and more recently by economies in the Association of South-East Asian Nations (ASEAN). This model is similar to the old developmental market economies of pre-war Germany and Japan where the government promotes high capital accumulation by suppressing consumption through strong regulations and administrative guidance within the basic framework of market economies.

8.4.1 The system of new developmental market economies

Because this model incorporates a mechanism to promote exports, it is often called 'export-oriented industrialization' by contrast with 'import-substitution industrialization' adopted in Latin America and elsewhere. However, as an economic system (in terms of combination between the market and the state), this model has no intrinsic difference from that of import-substitution industrialization.

It has only been since the 1960s in Japan, and the 1980s in Korea and Taiwan, that market opening has been promoted in a major way. In a catch-up stage preceding this period protection of target industries was vigorously pursued by means of tariffs, import quotas, foreign exchange controls, directed credits (especially in Korea), and state enterprises (especially in Taiwan). Foreign direct investment and foreign enterprise activities were strongly controlled in Japan and Korea until recently, though liberalized in Taiwan much earlier.

It is true that these three economies have had a strong orientation to promoting exports. Simultaneously with the protection of target industries, export-promotion measures were instituted, such as application of low interest rates to discount export bills, accelerated depreciation for corporate income tax assessment, and tariff drawbacks on imported materials used for the production of export commodities. Also, preferential allocation of import quotas and foreign exchange licences was given to export enterprises. These export promotion policies were necessary for the purpose of import-substitution industrialization in resource-scarce economies such as Japan and Korea (unlike Latin American economies), which had to export for the sake of importing raw materials (Ranis and Mahmood, 1992).

Government regulations in the new developmental market economies have not been limited to the areas of international trade and capital movements, but have encompassed a wide range of domestic economic activities, including banking, insurance, communication, and transportation by such means as entry control and cartelization. Execution of these regulations has to a large extent been left to the discretion of bureaucrats. The role of administrative guidance not based on stipulated rules has been especially important in Japan (Johnson, 1982; Yamamura, 1990). The mode of government intervention in Japan has been to induce private business towards a policy goal through dialogue, persuasion, and signalling. For example, government-directed credits based mainly on postal savings and allocated through government banks (such as the Japan Development Bank and the Export-Import Bank) have been less than 10 per cent of total industrial loans. Yet, the allocation of the directed credits worked as a signal of government support to recipient industries to which private banks allocated a greater share of their lending under reduced risk.

In contrast, government control in Korea has been more direct and stronger, at least under the military administration of Park Chung Hee (1961–79). All formal credits were channelled from nationalized banks (before partial privatization in the 1980s) to targeted industries under the discretion of the government. Major recipients of these directed credits were the large conglomerates (*chaebol*) that have been the major carrier of industrialization. Not only formal domestic savings but also foreign credits were distributed mainly by the nationalized banks, while direct foreign investment was tightly controlled. This strategy has underlain the very high concentration of industrial production in the small number of large enterprises in Korea (Cole and Park, 1983; Amsden, 1989).

In a sense, government intervention has been even more direct in Taiwan, where major upstream industries (such as fertilizers, electricity, petrochemicals, and steel) have been set up as state enterprises (including enterprises owned by the Nationalist Party or *Kuomintang*), in which top management positions are manned by Nationalist Party élites exiled from mainland China. Most banks have also been state-owned and their credits have been directed mainly to state enterprises (Wade, 1990). Such centralization of resources served as a device for minority mainlanders to control the island economy. However, the government intervened little in the activities of small- and medium-scale enterprises, which are managed by native Taiwanese and refugee *petite bourgeois* from the mainland, at least until the 1970s when several financial institutions were established to assist small/medium enterprises. Because foreign direct investment was liberalized from a relatively early stage (outside the state enterprise sector) unlike Japan and Korea, many small- and medium-sized enterprises have entered contract relations with foreign firms from which they have received trade credits and technical guidance. In this way, small and medium enterprises in Taiwan have grown as the major export sector, with as much as 65 per cent of manufactured exports accounted for by firms with less than 300 employees in the mid-1980s (Wade, 1990: 70). As a result, relative to Korea, Taiwan's industrialization has been characterized by decentralization in the size distribution of manufacturing activities as well as their regional distribution between urban and rural areas (Ho, 1979, 1982).

It has commonly been considered that government intervention has been smaller in Taiwan than in Korea (Kuznets, 1988; Park, 1990). However, it is not quite certain whether this is really the case, at least in terms of government policy intention if not its outcome. Despite the remarkable development of the unregulated sector, formal bank credits have remained concentrated in the large state enterprise sector.

8.4.2 The source of success

Overall, the new developmental economies in East Asia, as practised in Japan, Korea, and Taiwan, represent a system in which the area under government control is wider than in the populist model in Latin America. Why has this system not been afflicted by a high incidence of government failure? Why has it been able to achieve such a degree of success in economic growth as to be called the 'East Asian Miracle' (World Bank, 1993)?

Despite their different organizational styles, Japan, Korea, and Taiwan developed a co-operative relationship between government and big business To outsiders this relationship looks like a corporative state or 'quasi-internal organization' (Chowdhury and Islam, 1993: 45–52) in which an elite bureaucracy staffed by the best managerial talent guides business activities through formal and personal networks according to an agreed-upon strategic plan. While such a system should be effective in co-ordinating economic activities between government and business corporations as well as among corporations, it could easily turn out to be a system of government-business collusion against the public's interest.

Indeed, this system has not been free from government failures. In Japan, for example strongly regulated industries, such as petroleum refining, electric power, telecommunications, and airlines, are characterized by large differences between domestic and border prices of their products. These industries are usually characterized by frequent employment of retired government officials (*amakudari*). It is no wonder that all the ministries and bureaux make maximum efforts to preserve regulations under their own auspices. Corruptive collusion and rent-seeking are more evident in the political circle as illustrated by recurrent scandals such as the Lockheed aircraft bribery made to Prime Minister Kakuei Tanaka through two major trading companies in Japan (Yamamura and Yasuba, 1987; Yamamura, 1990). The Japanese experience in this regard is far from an exception in the new developmental market economies, as demonstrated by the recent prosecution of two former presidents in Korea, Chun Doo Hwan and Roh Tae-Woo, on charges that 'secret funds' pooled contributions from *chaebol* seeking the government's patronage.

Earlier, evidence was cited to suggest that deprivation of tariff autonomy from Meiji Japan provided a favourable condition for the development of the cotton-spinning industry (Section 8.3.2). The opposite development has been happening within the silk industry due to import regulations on silk adopted for the protection of sericulture farmers. Because the domestic price of raw silk has been raised by means of an import levy and quota, while the imports of silk garments have been liberalized, silk-weaving and garment-manufacturing sectors are now on the verge of ruin. Despite this sacrifice, the trade protection has not been at all effective in preventing domestic sericulture from virtually disappearing. Yet, the public corporation in charge of the silk (and sugar) protection operation has been maintained on the pretext of farmer protection.

While these examples are countless, in the new developmental market economies in East Asia, government failures have not loomed large enough to destroy the basis of economic development. Although the scope of bureaucrats' discretion has been wide, incentives to private producers have been less seriously distorted than in Latin America and elsewhere. Generally, export incentives have been applied uniformly instead of favouring particular firms or industries over others. Often, rather than adding to distortions, subsidies on exports have effectively compensated for negative incentives faced by the producers of export products arising from import-substitution policies (Balassa, 1988; Krueger, 1990).

Meanwhile, large public investment has been undertaken in education and research organizations as well as physical infrastructure such as building of highway networks and modernization of railways (e.g. 'bullet trains' in Japan). Government intervention in the private sectors have not been limited to such rent-generating regulations as entry control and cartelization, but have also included provision of external market information (such as by the Japan External Trade Organization under the Ministry of International Trade and Industry) and guidance and persuasion on private firms to form R & D co-operatives for high-technology products, such as integrated circuit tips (Komiya *et al.*, 1984; Kosai, 1989).

In Japan strong regulations on entry to banking business and control on deposit interest rates had until recently given rise to large excess profits by established banks. Even though the lending rates were also controlled, the actual credit costs for the borrower firms were not so much different from the market rates because these firms were usually requested to deposit with the bank a certain portion of the credit they received at the regulated rates. The excess profit from the interest rate control (which represents an income transfer from depositors)—a kind of forced saving in our definition—together with stringent supervision by the Ministry of Finance and the Bank of Japan, had reduced the risk of banks' insolvency virtually to zero, resulting in increased bank deposits from households and thereby strengthening banks' lending to industries.

In this way, government regulations contributed to increased credibility of the financial system and thereby contributed to mobilization of household savings for industrial investment. In other words, banks' credibility enhanced by those regulations was a public good in the early development stage when their low credibility represented a block against mobilization of household savings, though this public good was provided at the expense of depositors (Hayami, forthcoming). This benefit could well have more than compensated for efficiency loss due to the interest rate distortion. The state-owned banking systems could have played a similar role in Korea and Taiwan.

This mechanism would not have worked effectively, however, unless macroeconomic management had been successful in curbing inflation to a moderate rate and thus preventing deposit rates from becoming negative in real terms. Otherwise, heavy 'financial repression' would have seriously undermined banks' capacity of mobilizing household savings for industrial development (McKinnon, 1973).

In fact, as represented by the strict balanced budgets in Japan from 1945 to 1960, the management of public finance in East Asia in their development process was relatively well disciplined, so that pernicious inflation endangering economic growth did not occur. The new developmental market economies are a system in which the market mechanism works, despite a wide area of government intervention. Government's stable macroeconomic management, maintenance of orderly financial systems, and provision of public infrastructure raised profit opportunities for private entrepreneurs' productive activities in the market. Such conditions were instrumental in inducing entrepreneurs to allocate more of their efforts to seeking profits from production under market competition rather than seeking institutional rents from lobbying for protective regulations

It is rather questionable whether 'industrial policies' aimed at promoting certain target industries have made any significant contributions to economic growth in East Asia. In the full-employment economies like Japan and Korea, favourable treatment of one industry implied maltreatment of another, since any resource added to the one industry would have been extracted from the other (Komiya, 1975, ch. 10). Under such conditions, heavy *de facto* subsidization of matured industries (such as steel mills and shipbuilding) through such means as favourable tax treatment and directed credits until the 1960s, concurrent with no significant assistance to emerging new export industries (such as household electric appliances) in Japan, does not seem justified in terms of the criteria of infant industry protection.

In fact, the major effort of industrial policies in post-war Japan has been directed towards protecting low-productive sectors such as retailing and agriculture as well as declining industries such as textiles, rather than towards promoting rising industries. While such a policy orientation contributed much to social stability as the basis for economic development, it was detrimental to the modernization of industrial structure.

It appears reasonable to conclude, at least for Japan, that 'significant achievements, such as advancements in the industrial structure and strengthened competitiveness in exports, resulted mainly from private firms' autonomous judgment and adjustment capability rather than based on the industrial policies' (Tsuruta, 1984: 76). If the industrial policies in Japan contributed to economic growth, the contributions came less from implementation of specific targeting policies than from the sharing of information between government and the private sector, which was promoted through dialogues in various committees and councils in the process of making indicative plans (Komiya, 1975, ch. 10). This information-sharing and consensus-making would have been effective in mobilizing concerted efforts by entrepreneurs to develop industries characterized by technological and pecuniary externalities (or 'strategic complementarities'), including forward and backward linkages, to enable exploitation of economy-wide increasing returns—thus avoiding so-called 'co-ordination failure' (Murphy *et al.*, 1989; Osano, 1990; Krugman, 1991; Matsuyama, 1991).

In this regard, large conglomerates like the *chaebol* in Korea, which diversify their activities into many different industries, might be considered a device to internalize inter-industry externalities. *Zaibatsu*, the powerful conglomerates organized by family-based holding companies in Japan before World War II, such as Mitsui and Mitsubishi (which were dissolved after the war under the direction of Allied occupation forces), could have played a similar role. Thus considered, concentration of resources in the *chaebol*-type organization might be one possible approach to avoid co-ordination failure in the early stage of development despite its adverse distributional effect.

However, the interindustry co-ordination for effective forward and backward linkages needs not be designed within the boundary of a national economy, as commonly assumed in the theory of interindustry co-ordination and strategic complementarity since the classic work of Rosenstein-Rodan (1943). The remarkable development of small and medium enterprises in Taiwan has been based more critically on their linkages with foreign enterprises rather than with domestic state enterprises. This, of course, has been the only strategy feasible for small port economies like Hong Kong and Singapore. The development experience of Taiwan, Hong Kong, and Singapore indicates that interindustry co-ordination can be structured at a global or regional scale under free trade and direct foreign investment so that both growth and equity can be promoted in developing economies.

Indeed, recent developments in South-East Asian economies, such as Thailand and Indonesia, as well as in the coastal areas of mainland China, have been proving the effectiveness of this strategy using direct foreign investment as a major linkage point with the world economy. Adoption of this strategy in South-East Asia has created the so-called 'wild-geese-flying' pattern (Akamatsu, 1962) with the development of Japan's capacity in manufacturing production, exports, and imports to be followed by NIEs and later by the ASEAN economies. The surge of industrial productivity in Japan created a forward linkage for small and medium enterprises initially in NIEs through direct investment and trade. Many of those local enterprises (including joint ventures) engaged in processing industrial materials and intermediate goods supplied from Japanese firms into final products for export to the market of high-income economies, especially the USA and Japan. Later, not only Japan but also NIEs began to provide this linkage to ASEAN and China, often through the network of overseas Chinese. India is also likely to join the flying geese as it began adopting the foreign linkage strategy in recent years. In this pattern of development in East Asia, Japan and Korea's approach of trying to develop the full set of industries by domestic entrepreneurs in each of their economies—Korea based on *chaebol* and Japan based on *zaibatsu* before World War II and on *keiretsu* (corporate group) after the war—under the strong regulation of direct foreign investment has been rather an exception.

Again, we return to the fundamental question: Why have government failures not loomed so large as to destroy the basis of economic development in the new developmental market economies? It has recently been popular to identify the export-oriented industrialization policy as the underlying reason for the success of development in East Asia. From this perspective, competition in the international market compelled domestic producers to improve product quality and reduce costs. They were more strongly driven to introduce new technologies from abroad. Using export promotion instead of import substitution as a yardstick, the failures of industrial policies can be more clearly visible. Corrective measures are thus likely to be implemented before the failures become very serious, because export promotion policies necessarily entail government budget costs, whereas costs of import substitution can be passed on to consumers and unprotected industries. These merits of the export-oriented system are said to have underlain the high rates of economic growth in East Asia as compared with the autarky oriented import-substitution system practised in Latin America and elsewhere (Krueger, 1978; 1990; Balassa, 1982).

This kind of argument is an insufficient answer to our question. In the early development stage of Japan, Taiwan, and Korea, export-promotion policies were superimposed on import-substitution policies. It is perfectly conceivable that the export-promotion policies could have been so structured as to seriously amplify distortions, e.g. giving very high export subsidies to inefficient protected industries (as practised in the EU's Common Agricultural Policy). Would this not have been the likely case if export promotion were attempted under Latin America's populist regimes? The question is really why the wide scope of government intervention in the new developmental market economies did not lead to policies involving so much distortion.

Several hypotheses may be postulated, albeit at a rather conjectural level. The organization of bureaucracy in Japan and Korea, which is structured highly independently of politics, may be more resistant against rent-seeking pressures from vested interest groups. The long-term stable employment of bureaucrats with high social prestige must be raising the expected cost of losing a position upon possible discovery of moral hazard and, therefore, working as a brake on taking such a risk. The fear of execution or other punishment may have been especially strong in Korea and Taiwan under the regimentation of militarized states. Largely homogeneous societies in East Asia characterized by low degrees of inequality in income distribution (as indicated in Figure 7.2) might have reduced distrust of citizens against ruling élites, resulting in relatively small need for the élite to purchase people's support by means of populist policies aimed at increasing their short-run income and consumption at the expense of long-run costs (Alesina and Rodrik, 1994; Rodrik, 1994). The high levels of education and mass media development would have contributed to reductions in information asymmetry between government and citizens. Further, rulers' ethics preached by Confucianism might invoke a guilty conscience among politicians and bureaucrats on their moral hazards (Kim, 1987; Vandermeesch, 1986; Mizo-guchi and Nakajima, 1991).

In addition, the role of a hidden ideology in the new developmental market economies might be pointed out. The old developmental market economies of the Kaiser's Germany and Imperial Japan were tied up with narrow nationalism or racism. Instead, it appears that the new model is implicitly based on 'developmentalism' or 'production fetishism' by which people judge whether or not certain policies are good and just in terms of their contributions to the growth of material output. This hidden ideology in the new model seems to have stemmed in Japan from deep disillusionment with the use of military power and sheer need for escape from hunger and poverty immediately after World War II, in addition to a century-long desire to catch up with the West. If the performance of politicians and bureaucrats is assessed in society in terms of contributions to material output growth, could it not be to their advantage to make major efforts to provide growth-enhancing public goods rather than to pursue rent-seeking activities?

A similar force seems to have been operating in South Korea and Taiwan also. In the Republic of Korea economic growth has commanded a much higher value than simply its contribution to material welfare, because of the need to prove superiority of this country's economic system over the People's Republic in the North as well as the national zeal to catch up with Japan. For Taiwan, since the Nationalist Government was denied international recognition as the ruler of China, surpassing the mainland in economic power has been almost the only means left to prove the state's legitimacy. Also, the memory of having lost the mainland based, to a large extent, on government failures should have strongly cautioned the Kuomintang not to repeat the past failures. These geopolitical conditions could have been even more compelling than those underlying the initial success of old developmental market economies such as the Second German Reich.

8.4.3 Beyond achieving the catch-up goal

The new developmental economies typically practised in North-East Asia comprised a catch-up model. As such, their positive role ends when the catch-up goal is achieved. Further improvements in economic welfare cannot be expected from this model, as it will face increasingly severe external and internal constraints.

Even before the process of catching up was completed, this model created serious international economic friction. The speed with which exports of manufactured commodities from these economies have entered the world market has often exceeded the capacity for industrial adjustment on the part of advanced economies, creating strong political demand for protectionism. The protectionist bloc tried to achieve its political goal by escalating economic conflicts to ideological confrontation. Their common strategy was to condemn advancement of developmental market economies to the world market as based on 'unfair' production and trade practices, and to characterize these 'unfair' practices as based on culture and ideology different from Western democracy and liberalism. They argued on these grounds that, since there is no common ground for settlement through rational dialogue, these economies must be 'contained' by force. This is typical of the arguments against 'the Japanese System' of so-called 'revisionists' (Johnson, 1982; Prestowitz, 1988; Fallows, 1989)

If such a political manoeuvre to escalate the economic problem to ideological confrontation were successful, it would result in popular criticism from the side of advanced economies on the social and cultural systems of developmental market economies. Resulting external pressures for reforms in these systems would evoke reactionary nationalism on the other side. If developmental market economies are thus pushed too hard, they may revert to the route followed by pre-war Germany and Japan. On the other hand, if developmental market economies are allowed to grow smoothly, their political systems which are now somewhat despotic and totalitarian are likely to move toward democracy and liberalism; this tendency is evident from the moves in Korea and Taiwan from autocracy to parliamentary democracy since the 1980s.

How can the confrontation between liberal and developmental market economies be structured so as to be constructive rather than destructive? In order to prevent the confrontation from turning into a negative-sum game, both sides must be freed from mutual fear and distrust. For that purpose, clear understanding must be established that liberal and developmental market economies are not really discontinuous. It must be recognized that, while the present system of Japan and Asian NIEs might be unique, it may not be quite so unique relative to 'the American System' or 'the German System' in the nineteenth century.

If a country wished to further promote the economic welfare of its people in a stage beyond the successful catch-up, the country would have to transform itself from developmental to a liberal market economy, because the system which can best serve consumers' (citizens') welfare at a high-income stage characterized by increased variations in people's wants is nothing but the free-market mechanism based on competition under transparent rules. This shift is also critically important for sustaining economic growth beyond the point of successful catch-up.

During the catching-up stage, it was not very difficult for governments to identify which kind of industries have high growth potential and which mechanisms should be designed to promote them, with reference to the experience of advanced economies. This reference was lost after the catching-up process was completed. At this point, failures in planning and coordination tend to multiply, especially in the affluent economies where people's wants are diversified and their demands are difficult to estimate. Adherence to government's guidance and command, which used to be a source of growth, has now turned into a block against further development.

In Japan, the strong community relationships both within and between corporations may also have to be restructured. The post-war success of Japanese manufacturing has rested on its ability to improve both the production process and product quality, while the basic ideas and concepts of technology were borrowed from abroad. For this approach, strong co-operative relationships among employees in a company as well as among companies within a corporate groups (such as between an automobile assembler and parts suppliers) have been highly instrumental in increasing efficiency in the mass production of high-quality products, accompanying such innovations as company-wide quality control movements and just-in-time parts supply systems (to be discussed in Chapters 9 and 10).

As such, Japan's success has thus far reflected success in technology borrowing, although the borrowing process involves a great deal of adjustment and improvements. No wonder that Japan's growth in its high economic growth period did not follow the Kuznets pattern typical of advanced economies, but remained in the Kuznets–Marx mongrel pattern characteristic of the economies based on borrowed technology (Tables 5.2 and 5.4). However, Japan's supremacy in the mass manufacture of high-quality products has been undermined as this approach has been effectively learned by Korea, Taiwan, and other East Asian economies having the advantage of lower wage rates. In order to sustain growth, it is vital for Japan to shift from being a borrower to being an originator of innovative ideas and concepts, so that its growth pattern will be transformed to the Kuznets pattern, in which economic growth is more dependent on improvement in efficiency than accumulation of tangible capital. Such a shift will also be necessary for Korea and Taiwan in the near future.

To accomplish this shift, major increases in government's investment in scientific research, education, and other public infrastructure are necessary but not sufficient. Vitally needed is the establishment of a free, competitive market in which entrepreneurs who achieve major innovations of high social demand can survive and prosper. In this process, restructuring of corporate management may be necessary to reward individually those employees who produce innovative ideas, rather than dispense rewards on a group basis and thereby bind innovative individuals to the mediocrity of pseudo-communities. Institutional infrastructure must be prepared for innovative talents to be able to spin out from the established large internal organizations to undertake new venture business.

This shift does not mean abandonment of Japan's cultural identity. The prevailing government controls and regulations were not necessarily rooted in the unique culture of Japan but were mostly created in the relatively recent past as a catching-up device. Somewhat unique business organizations and trade practices do exist that may appear to be strongly group-oriented and non-individualistic in the eyes of Westerners. However, real monopoly and inefficiency tend to arise where these group-oriented organizations are reinforced by government controls. Once those controls are removed, some of the apparently unique organizations and practices in Japan are likely to disappear as they lose to competition in the free market when inconsistent with the interests of consumers. Those institutions that survive through market competition, even if they originated in Japan's unique culture, will have universal applicability and contribute to revitalization of the world welfare, as attested by application of some Japanese management practices by US automobile makers.

However, the recognition that the highly effective system for catching up has been turning into a negative asset upon achievement of the catch-up goal has been slow to prevail among people, whose minds tend to be trapped by the past success. Meanwhile, resistance of vested interest groups to deregulation and liberalization has been intense. Whether or not Japan and East Asian NIEs will be able to slough off their hitherto successful systems will have a critical bearing on economic development in East Asia itself as well as in the world.

However, one issue low-income developing economies should be more concerned with at the moment is whether the catch-up model that proved effective in Japan, Korea, and Taiwan in the past may work under their own human capital accumulation and cultural heritage, or what adjustments may be required for the effective borrowing of this model for their development. They should also deliberate on the feasibility and effectiveness of replicating the strong developmental state model of the Korean type in an increasingly integrated world under uniform trade rules (as epitomized by the establishment of the World Trade Organization) with massive international capital movements and information flows. This issue should be considered in the light of a recent shift in the development paradigm as discussed in the next section.

8.5 An Emerging New Paradigm

The models of economic development that became dominant for nearly three decades following World War II emphasized the need to correct market failure in the development process by means of government's planning and command for the promotion of target industries. The defect of this developmentalist strategy has increasingly been felt since around the 1970s, from visible failures of the import-substitution industrialization policy as well as malfunctioning of centrally planned economies. These historical tests have led to the restoration of the market mechanism in the design of development policy, as traditionally emphasized in modern economics (neoclassical school). A newly emerging paradigm in development economics dictates that government should limit its activities to sound macroeconomic management and supply of public goods, while other economic activities should be left to the private sector under free market competition.

8.5.1 The structural adjustment policy by IMF and the World Bank

It was the World Bank and the International Monetary Fund (IMF) that led this change. Since the early and mid-1980s, the World Bank and IMF respectively have attempted to request basic policy reforms by the governments of developing economies as a condition for granting credits to overcome their economic crises arising from sharply decreasing world market prices for primary commodities and increasing interest rates after the collapse of the second oil boom in 1981. This new approach is commonly called the 'structural adjustment policy'.

This policy is based on the perception that the crisis of developing economies in the 1980s was not a temporary phenomenon resulting from the slump in primary commodity markets but was also the result of the accumulation of government failures inevitably produced by their economic systems. To correct these failures, government regulations, including import-restriction measures, which had constrained the market mechanism and biased its resource allocation, must be removed. Government must shoulder the cost of public goods, but it should be within the limit of available revenue so that decent stability can be maintained in the purchasing power of domestic currency.

The World Bank and IMF tried to guide developing economies towards such policy reform by setting conditionality for their lending. In 1980, the World Bank launched structural adjustment lending (SAL) as programme lending (or non-project lending) for general policy assistance rather than their traditional lending for specific projects (Ishikawa, 1994).

IMF's structural adjustment policy began with the establishment of the structural adjustment facility (SAF). The assistance by IMF to developing economies was to advance stand-by credits in the event of critical shortage of foreign exchange. In 1974, when non-oil-producing developing economies suffered from major deficits in the balance of payments, IMF established the extended fund facility (EFF) to advance medium-term loans (for three to ten years) to these non-oil-producers. SAF was a step forward from EFF, which aimed to advance medium-term loans on condition of policy reforms required for stable macroeconomic management.

SAL represents a sanction by the World Bank and IMF on the policy reform programmes of borrowers. As such, it has the effect of increasing the credibility of recipient governments, thereby reducing capital flight. Especially, IMF's consent is indispensable for rescheduling of external debts. Thus, SAL by the World Bank and IMF worked as a significant leverage to promote policy reform geared towards stability in macroeconomic management and efficient working of the market mechanism

The structural adjustment policy has been adopted by many developing economies not by the pressure of the international lending organizations alone. Some countries such as Chile and Thailand began the structural reform before SAL was formally launched. There are cases, such as India and Indonesia, in which the reform in the 1980s to the 1990s was promoted mainly by the domestic initiatives of enlightened technocrats, even though their reform was harmonized with assistance from the World Bank and the IMF (Kohama and Yanagihara, 1985). The fundamental force inducing structural reform was learning from the past failures. The World Bank and IMF gave a push to a boat on this running stream.

8.5.2 Renaissance of Latin America?

The history of structural adjustment policy in developing economies geared towards macroeconomic stability and microeconomic liberalization is yet too short to make correct assessment of its achievement. Recent recoveries of Latin American economies from the crisis in the 1980s, however, might represent an achievement of this policy reorientation. It was Chile that took the lead in the structural reform.

In Chile, in order to recover from the economic and political crisis created by socialist policies under Salvador Allende's administration (1970–3), the military government led by Augusto Pinochet (1973–89) attempted to cut the budget, liberalize trade, and reduce domestic regulations. As a result, the rate of inflation that had exceeded 500 per cent per year was reduced to two digits by 1977. Economic activities dropped initially due to the deflationary policy at the beginning but recovered soon with the inflow of foreign capital and achieved a GNP growth rate as high as 8 per cent per year for 1977–81 (Balassa, 1985; Kohama, 1995).

However, the Chilean economy was hit again by the crisis in 1982 corresponding to the collapse of the second oil boom. The crisis stemmed partly from the slump in the international copper market but more importantly from incomplete deregulation. Because the fixed rate of exchange was maintained under the higher than 30 per cent rate of inflation per year, overvaluation of local currency progressed, resulting in depressed exports and expanded imports. The two-digit inflation continued despite the government's deflationary policy because the wage indexation to determine wage hikes, corresponding to past inflation rates, was maintained as a remnant of the populist system (Cardoso and Helwege,1992: 162–6). Despite the worsened balance of trade, the Chilean economy was able to grow so long as foreign capital flowed in. It was inevitable, however, that economic activities precipitously shrank as capital flight began under the expectation of currency devaluation corresponding to accumulated outstanding external debts (Balassa, 1985).

To cope with the crisis, Chile accepted conditions on loans from the World Bank and IMF, and pushed forward structural adjustments, such as currency devaluation, deregulation, and privatization of state enterprises. Subsequently, the Chilean economy began to recover from 1984 and has been on the track of sustained growth (Corbo and Fischer, 1995: 2894–903). The policy orientation towards balanced budgets and market liberalization has also been maintained under the civilian government since 1989. While expenditures for education and social welfare programmes have increased, the tax basis has also been strengthened by such means as value added tax. As a result, not only has stable growth of the macroeconomy been achieved, but growth in agriculture and small- and medium-scale industries (such as farm-product-processing), which had hitherto been suppressed under the import-substitution industrialization policy, has now been activated (Imai, 1991; Yanagihara, 1991).

Following Chile, a number of Latin American economies such as Argentina, Bolivia, and Peru, have been undertaking structural adjustment reforms upon the conditions required by the World Bank and IMF. Especially noteworthy is the case of Argentina that began to undertake reform aimed at economic stabilization and liberalization in 1991 after prolonged stagnation for nearly five decades since the end of World War II. At least, for the first three years (1992–4), the inflation rate was reduced to the one-digit level and the GNP growth rate rose above 5 per cent per year, though not a small probability seems to exist for Argentina to face a similar crisis as experienced by Chile in its early reform phase.

8.5.3 On the effectiveness of structural adjustment policy

It is difficult to assess how sustainable the renaissance of Latin American economies will be. Crises similar to those experienced in Chile in 1982 and Mexico at the end of 1994 may be repeated in the future. However, such crises are likely to occur not so much from the defects of the structural adjustment policy (SAP) but rather from its incomplete implementation due to reactionary populism. In any case, the fact cannot be denied that SAP contributed to the rescue of Latin American economies from the major crisis of hyperinflation and external debt accumulation in the 1980s. Drawing from this and other success cases in Asia, like Thailand, Indonesia, and India, it appears that economic reforms of the SAP type geared towards macroeconomic stability and microeconomic liberalization are effective in supporting growth of wide-ranging developing economies.

Yet, strong criticism has prevailed on the IMF–World Bank approach. One major limitation of SAP may be little success in low-income economies such as in Sub-Saharan Africa, relative to the achievements in middle-income economies, as pointed out by the World Bank itself (World Bank Country Economics Department, 1988, 1990, 1992). In this connection, there has been an argument that the economic management dependent on the free market may be effective in middle-income economies endowed with relatively well-developed market organizations, but resource allocations must rely more heavily on the governments' directive for the 'customary economies' characterized by an underdeveloped market (Ishikawa, 1994). This argument correctly points out the greater incidence of market failure in underdeveloped market economies with highly incomplete information. In such economies, however, the incidence of government failure would be equally large or even larger. This danger is likely to be more serious in economies such as Africa where national boundaries were determined through the politics of colonialism and, therefore, where national integrity has been only weakly established (Sections 1.3 and 4.3). Is it not likely that the mounting crisis in Africa is rooted more deeply in government failure than in market failure?

Naturally, the effects of deregulation and liberalization are bound to be limited in a less developed market with severe information imperfection and high transaction costs. The best strategy to cope with such a situation, however, is to support the functioning of the market through appropriate investment in the basic public infrastructure that provides roads, electricity, telephone lines, commercial codes, and contract laws as well as law enforcement mechanisms such as courts, police, rather than to substitute bureaucracy for the market. For financing the provision of these public goods, it is necessary to prepare appropriate taxation systems, such as value added tax and real estate tax, which have a broad base of taxation and produce relatively small distortions in resource allocations (Ahmad and Stern, 1989). To emphasize the role of the free market for developing economies in the early development stage does not mean to advocate 'small governments' but to point out the need of concentrating governments' resources in the areas of their comparative advantage. If SAP is taken as a strategy of market liberalization with little regard to the need of major public investment in market development, it will have little chance of success in low-income economies.

Another criticism on SAP is the argument that a greater role should be assigned to government planning and guidance, considering the success in the new developmental market economies, such as Japan, Korea, and Taiwan. This view is especially strong among Japanese delegates to international development consortia, who, as formerly leading bureaucrats, are proud of their past role as the principal architect of 'government-led development' in Japan (Overseas Economic Cooperation Fund, 1991). Their position has also been supported by several Western scholars, whose perspective is based on the development experiences of Korea and Taiwan (Amsden, 1989; Wade, 1990). In this argument, even middle-income economies that have been successful with SAP, such as Thailand and Indonesia, must promote modern industries under government's protection and guidance in order to advance to the advanced stage of industrialization (Wade, 1994). In short, this view is nothing but a variation of the infant industry protection argument.

However, if this old doctrine were to be rearmed by the endogenous growth theory in current vogue, it could constitute a strong counter-doctrine to SAP based on the neoclassical orthodoxy. Since the seminal work by Romer (1986) and Lucas (1988), the endogenous growth theory has assumed that modern industries are characterized by increasing returns to scale, because returns from investment in research and development as well as education and training of workers (including the effects of learning-by-doing) are not fully captured by investing firms but spill over widely to other firms. Because of this externality effect, the rates of return to private investment are prevented from decreasing. Therefore, investment incentives can be maintained for private firms, guaranteeing continued capital accumulation and economic growth.

As this theory is applied to international trade, the same policy implication as List's proposal for infant industry protection can be obtained. If an economy succeeds in establishing an industry characterized by externality and increasing returns ahead of other economies, its advantage in this industry would increase cumulatively, while the chance would be closed for the other economies to build this industry under free competition. The theory, therefore, proposes that, if developing economies want to develop modern high-technology industries with intensive use of frontier knowledge and high human capital, they should promote domestic production by means of border protection, subsidies to private R & D, and public investment in basic research and scientific education (Krugman, 1987; Grossman and Helpman, 1991; Young, 1991). In fact, this was the strategy adopted by both the 'old developmental market economies' (such as pre-war Germany and Japan) and the 'new developmental market economies' (such as post-war Japan, Korea, and Taiwan).

The theoretical justification for this strategy was well grounded in List's theory, even without resort to the endogenous growth theory. The problem is whether this strategy might not produce the greater calamity of government rather than market failure within the cultural and social fabric of developing economies.

As discussed earlier, in Section 8.2.3, whether the infant industry protection policy is actually effective depends on the importance of the market failure to be removed by this policy, relative to the government failure to be created. In the past half-century, history witnessed the miserable failures of the import-substitution industrialization policy. In contrast, the developmentalist system that assigned greater mandate and discretion to government than the import-substitution industrialization strategy appears to have succeeded in East Asia. Does this difference depend on the difference in policy structures (e.g. absence versus presence of export-promotion measures)? Or is it based on the difference in the accumulation of human capital which government can mobilize for the policy implementation? Or is it based on differences in cultural and social traditions? The answers to these questions from the angle of culture and ideology have been sought in this chapter in a conjectural manner. Further exploration shall be attempted in the next chapter from the perspective of social organizations.

NOTES

1. In the original text of Ricardo ([1817] 1966), the exchange of cloth and wine between England and Portugal is used as an illustrative example. For introductory expositions, see Caves *et al.* (1993, ch. 3), and Krugman and Obstfed (1994, ch. 2).
2. Negative protection means the effective rate of protection (ERP) is negative. ERP measures the rate of change in value added due to border protection from the free trade situation, namely

$$\text{ERP} = \frac{(\text{Value added at domestic prices}) - (\text{Value added at border prices})}{(\text{Value added at border prices})}$$

which is calculated by

$$\text{ERP}_j = (t_j - \Sigma a_{ij} t_i)/(1 - \Sigma a_{ij}),$$

where ERP_j and t_j are ERP and the rate of difference between the border and the domestic prices (nominal rate of protection: *NRP*) for the *j-th* industry, t_i is *NRP* for the *i-th* intermediate good, and a_{ij} is the requirement of the *i-th* input for the unit output in the *j-th* industry (input–output coefficient).
3. This section draws heavily on Hayami (1995).
4. In the course of history, this model has undergone major modifications in North America and Western Europe including England itself under the tides of social democracy and Keynesianism. Yet, the model of liberal market economies based on the principles of equal opportunities, free competition, and consumer sovereignty has survived as an ideal to bind economic policies together in the Western economies.
5. Moreover, it would not be unfair to state that the model of liberal market economies in early-starter countries such as England and France was supported by the vast market in their overseas territories.
6. The unreliable supply of raw materials and parts also induced state enterprises to vertically integrate production of needed intermediate goods within their organizations, resulting in much larger than optimum size of enterprises.
7. Among the sectors of the Soviet economy, agriculture recorded the slowest growth in total productivity (Easterly and Fisher, 1994). As discussed in detail in the next chapter (Section 2), agriculture is characterized by the difficulty of monitoring labourers' work efforts because its biological production process is dispersed over a wide space and subject to environmental variations, for which small family farms are a more efficient production unit than large hierarchical organizations under central management. Nevertheless, Stalin collectivized family farms into

kolkhoz partly based on the Marxian doctrine (Mitrany, 1951) but more importantly with the intention of utilizing the collective farms for compulsory procurement of foodstuffs at low prices for urban industrial workers (Tang, 1967). The consequence was a shift of status for Russia from a major exporter of food grains to a major importer after World War II.

8. This consequence was anticipated by Friedrich von Hayek (1935) and Ludwig von Mises (1935) from the establishment of the Soviet communist regime. They argued that the nationalization of production factors by abolishing factor markets eliminates information on relative resource scarcities, hence making it difficult for the central planning authority to allocate resources efficiently under its limited information capacity. Their argument was rebutted by Oscar Lange (1938) on the grounds that the central planning authority can achieve efficient resource allocations through trial and error by utilizing market information on consumption goods. In fact, however, the Soviet system expanded government's planning and command over consumption goods, so that even Lange's solution was precluded.

9. This section draws heavily on Hayami (1996b).

9

The Role of Community in Economic Development

In the previous chapter the choice of economic system was discussed as the problem of how to combine the market and the state in organizing activities for economic development. To recapitulate, the market is the organization (and, at the same time, the institution) co-ordinating the activities of profit-seeking individuals through free transactions, under the guidance of prices, towards socially optimum production and consumption of private goods. The state is the organization supplying public goods by means of legitimate coercive power under its monopoly. If information is perfect so that transactions through the market are costless and agency contracts between citizens (principle) and government (agent) are faithfully enforced, the appropriate mix of these two organizations provides an adequate basis for developing economies to catch up with advanced economies.

In the real world, however, information is imperfect, and the degree of imperfection is especially large in developing economies, resulting in pervasive market and government failures. For example, when a producer delivers his product to the buyer and the buyer fails to honour the contracts of paying agreed-upon prices, the producer's supply will be short of the social optimum to the extent that his expected revenue decreases by the probability of the buyer's contract violation. It may appear that this market failure can be corrected by contract enforcement through legal procedures. However, judicial costs involved in formal court procedures are large, often exceeding the expected gains from dispute settlement on small transactions typical of less developed economies. Moreover, where judges and police are not necessarily the faithful agents of citizens, it can happen that the market failures are not only not corrected but even enlarged by government failures.

It has been pointed out that ideologies such as religious codes can play an important role in suppressing moral hazards under imperfect information. At the same time, the incidence of moral hazard should be smaller among people whose personal interactions are intense so that each can predict accurately the others' behaviour. Also, mutual trust nurtured through close personal relations should work as an effective brake on committing moral hazards.

A group of people tied by mutual trust based on intense personal interactions is a 'community' by our definition. Theoretically, communities range from the family to the 'national community' and further to the 'global (or international) community'. However, the communities discussed in this chapter are those in between this range, characterized by personal relationship closer than the arm's-length relation. In developing economies they are observed typically as tribes and villages tied by blood and locational affinities. However, in developed economies also, community relationships, which are formed through various channels such as the workplace, *alma mater*, church, sport and other hobby clubs, have significant influence on business transactions and political activities.

In the past, traditional communities such as tribes and villages have been regarded as a yoke or fetter on modernization. It must be recognized, however, that these communities provide a principle of organization critically needed to correct the failures of the market and the state, and, thereby, to support modern economic development. This chapter tries to make it clear that the economic system for the development of developing economies must be designed not as a combination of market and state alone but as a combination of the three organizations including community.

9.1 The Economic Functions of Community

What kind of role would the community play in economic development? As aptly pointed out by Adam Smith, advancement in the productive power of human society is brought about by progress in the division of labour. As people specialize in various activities, a system is required to co-ordinate them. The 'economic system' in our definition is a combination of the economic organizations that co-ordinate various economic activities so as to achieve a socially optimum division of labour. The market is the organization that co-ordinates profit-seeking individuals through competition under the signal of parametric price change. The state is the organization that forces people to adjust their resource allocations by the command of government. On the other hand, the community is the organization that guides community members to voluntary co-operation based upon close personal ties and mutual trust. In other words, the market by means of competition based on egoism, the state by means of command based on coercive power, and the community by means of co-operation based on consent, co-ordinate division of labour among people towards a socially desirable direction.

In practice, the community and the state often overlap. For example, a village is a community defined by the fact that villagers co-operate voluntarily. However, if villagers authorize a particular individual or individuals to exercise coercive power in the administration of village affairs, this village can be regarded as a small state.[1] In the real world, the community and the state are often inseparably combined in the economic system. However, they are functionally separable. The same applies to the relationship between community and market as well as between market and state.

9.1.1 Prisoner's dilemma

The importance of co-operation for efficient resource allocation can be understood by conceptualizing the 'prisoner's dilemma' situation in game theory (Luce and Raiffa, 1957: 94–7; Gibbons, 1992: 2–4).

The prisoner's dilemma can be explained by the example of two suspects charged with jointly committing a crime and taken into custody in separate cells. There they are interrogated by a prosecutor, who alternately threatens each suspect with a heavy penalty should he continue to deny the charges while the other suspect confesses, and tempts each with a reduced penalty should he confess while the other party continues denying.

A pay-off matrix for the two suspects (A and B) for their two strategies—co-operation with the partner meaning the continuation of the denial, and defection against the partner meaning the confession of the crime—is illustrated in Figure 9.1. In each cell of the matrix, A's profit is indicated above and B's profit below. If both continue co-operation (continued denial) the major crime (such as murder) will not be proven, so that both will receive only minor punishment for trumped-up charges such as illegal possession of a weapon. This mutual co-operation strategy is assumed to give a profit of three units for both A and B. If both defect from the partnership and confess the crime, both are supposed to incur loss of two units (or −2 of profit) from the sentence on the crime. If A continues to deny while B confesses, A's penalty will be elevated to a loss of five units (−5 of profit), but B's penalty is

A's Strategy \ B's Strategy	Co-operation	Defection
Co-operation	3 (A's Profit) 3 (B's Profit)	−5 5
Defection	5 −5	−2 −2

FIG. 9.1 *The pay-off matrix of the prisoner's dilemma game*

lightened equivalent to a profit of five units. Their profit positions will reverse when B denies and A confesses.

When B co-operates, A will be better off by defecting because A can elevate his profit to five units, as compared with a profit of three units should he continue co-operation. When B defects, A will be better off by also defecting in order to reduce his loss to only two units as compared with a loss of five units from continuing co-operation. The same applies to B's choice of strategy. Under this situation, both A and B will choose defection, each incurring the loss of two units, despite the possibility for both to earn a profit of three units through mutual co-operation.

This example of the prisoner's dilemma illustrates how much loss the inability among people to establish co-operative relationships, due to the absence of communication and trust, will produce for society. This loss can happen in all the economic transactions. For example, in the transaction of a commodity, a buyer may try to reduce payment to a seller on the false charge of quality deficiency in delivered commodities. Then, the seller will deliver low-quality commodities thereafter. As their mutual distrust is heightened, they will stop transactions and thereby close off a mutually profitable business opportunity.

As another example, consider the case of employment in a private firm or a governmental agency. If employment is insecure so that employees may be discharged any moment, employees would make little effort to acquire specific knowledge and skill for efficient work in this organization. Their employer would then be inclined to discharge these employees for their lack of effort. In this way, a co-operative relationship will not be established with the little accumulation of skill and knowledge needed for efficient functioning of this organization.

9.1.2 Trust as a social capital

Is it not possible to solve such a prisoner's dilemma situation in economic transactions with by the use of the legal apparatus provided by the state? In theory, in either commodity transaction or labour employment, the dilemma can be prevented from occurring if contractual terms and penalty clauses against their possible violation are stipulated in detail in a written agreement, and appeal to mediation by the third party, such as a court, is possible should a conflict arise. In practice, however, it is difficult to set a contract detailing all the possible conflicts about product quality and delivery time with due consideration for future contingencies. This difficulty is especially large for new products that are technologically complicated and for which it is difficult to predict beforehand what problems may arise in the development and production stages. As for employment, it is difficult to express by words clearly and in detail what specific skill and knowledge employees should be required to obtain. In general, possible contingencies that may influence a transaction are nearly infinite, so that it is not possible to stipulate in advance the appropriate counter-measures to all those contingencies under the 'bounded rationality' of human beings (Simon, 1957; Williamson, 1975).

Moreover, third party mediation, especially formal court procedure, entails significant costs and thus it does not pay to apply to conflicts involving small sums of money. Since scales of both production and transaction are typically small in developing economies, legal means have but very limited power to solve the prisoner's dilemma problem. Of course, this difficulty is augmented by insufficient development of laws and the judicial system.

Since the basic cause of the prisoner's dilemma situation is lack of communication and mutual trust between transacting parties, it should be prevented by the formation of trust through the development of a community relationship. One way to achieve this relationship is to shift from spot transactions between anonymous agents solely based on the price parameter to long-term continuous transactions or 'clientelization' in Clifford Geertz's term (1978). For example, a jeweller may be strongly tempted to cheat an unknown new customer to his shop by selling low-quality jewels at high prices. However, for a regular customer coming to his shop he would be inclined to feel guilty and less willing to risk losing a long-lasting business opportunity for a one-shot moral hazard. Thus, repeated transactions that are expected to continue over a long time have the power to protect transacting parties from the pitfall of the prisoner's dilemma, unless either party is myopic and discounts heavily the future penalty on exercising opportunism relative to the present gain, as the theory of repeated games predicts (Kreps and Wilson, 1982; Fudenberg and Maskin, 1986; Abreu, 1988; Gibbons, 1992: 82–115).

Mutual trust created by long-term continuous transactions can be further reinforced by multiple interlinked transactions (Bardhan, 1980; Bell, 1988; Hayami and Otsuka, 1993, ch. 5; Besley, 1995). For example, a trader not only purchases a commodity from a particular producer continuously year after year, but also supplies him with materials and credits. Mutual trust enhanced by intensified interaction and communication as well as fear of losing a multifaceted co-operative relationship is a strong force curbing moral hazards for both parties. The psychological basis of mutual trust could further be strengthened by incorporating personal elements in business transactions, such as exchange of gifts and attendance at weddings and funerals.

Relationships of mutual trust created through long-term and multiple transactions would not only be effective in suppressing moral hazards between the contracting parties but would also promote collaborative relationships within the wider community. Those who were benefiting from transactions based on trust would not want to trade with one who was known to have betrayed his business partner before, in terms of both moral sentiment and risk calculation. The cost of such social opprobrium and ostracism would be especially large in a small, closed community characterized by a high degree of information-sharing through close personal inter-actions. The stronger the fear of social sanction by the community, the more firmly would the convention of honouring contracts with the members of the same community be established.

If mutual trust between particular individuals were thus elevated to a moral code in society, large savings would be realized in transactions costs. The transaction costs include the costs of contract negotiation and enforce-ment concerning transactions. If one can trust the other party in a contract, there is little reason to worry about possible default. Contract partners would thus not need to specify *ex ante* detailed clauses on costs caused by possible contingencies outside the agreement but would renegotiate faith-fully to find the best solution for both in the event of an unexpected business outcome. If such co-operative *ex post* renegotiation could be guaranteed, business plans could be promoted much more flexibly and efficiently than by rigid *ex ante* specifications of contingencies, especially in long-term transac-tions subject to high risk and uncertainty.

Thus, trust accumulated through personal interactions in the community increases efficiency and reduces costs associated with the division of labour. In this regard, trust is a kind of 'social capital' similar to social overhead capital such as roads and harbours (Arrow, 1974; Dasgupta, 1988; Putnam, 1993; Seabright, 1993).

If the trust relationship is not sufficiently strong to suppress moral hazards in certain transactions, the co-operative relation may have to be structured by integrating participants in the transactions into a hierarchical organiza-tion (such as the 'firm'), allowing them work under the command and supervision of central management. Indeed, according to Ronald Coase (1937) and Oliver Williamson (1975, 1985) the origin of modern large-scale firms lay in their power of saving transaction costs. However, if mutual trust does not exist between workers and management, the cost of monitoring and enforcing the workers' efforts would become very large. Hierarchical organ-izations, including not only firms but also government agencies and non-governmental organizations, are likely to fall into functional disorder with a high incidence of moral hazards, unless the community mechanism of co-operation is incorporated in some form or the other.

9.1.3 Supply of local public goods

Mutual trust created through personal interactions in a community com-prises a social capital useful for community members alone. In that sense, such trust is a kind of 'local public good' whose benefit is limited to a particular group.

Generally speaking, the comparative advantage of community over the market and the state lies in the supply of local public goods (compared with the market's supply of private goods and the state's supply of 'global public goods'), because the community relationship is effective in preventing free-riders. When residents in one village have agreed to undertake collective work on construction of a country road, a villager's private benefit can be maximized if he becomes a free-rider, i.e. if he utilizes the road built by other villagers' work, while not contributing his own labour to the project in violation of the village community's agreement. How close to a social optimum level the supply of local public goods would increase depends, to a large extent, on how strong the trust has been forged among people in the community and, hence, how severe the social sanction would be against a violator of the community's agreement.

Local public goods can be supplied by the command of government also. However, in the process of raising necessary tax revenue and allocating it among alternative uses and areas, significant administrative as well as political lobbying costs are inevitably entailed. Also, governments are usually short of the capacity to accurately grasp the structure of demands for public goods at the grass roots. Therefore, if local communities (including local governments supported by community relationships) have the capacity to obtain consensus and prevent free-riders among community members, government should concentrate on the supply of global public goods, while leaving the supply of local public goods to beneficiary communities.

However, communities with scant accumulation of trust capital have no comparative advantage in the supply of local public goods and, hence, must rely on government for its supply even if its absolute cost is high. Gross undersupply of local public goods would be inevitable in such a society (Putnam, 1993).

9.2 Rural Organization in Developing Economies

It is in the rural sector of developing economies that a prototype of community can be observed. A concrete image of community organization can, therefore, be obtained from understanding the structure of rural villages in developing economies. This understanding is also necessary for the appropriate design of development strategy in developing economies characterized by high dependence on agriculture.

9.2.1 Dominance of peasants

The most common form of organization in the rural sector is the small-scale farm mainly based on family labour—popularly called 'peasants'. According to the 1970 World Census of Agriculture by the Food and Agriculture Organization (FAO), the average farm size in the world was 10 hectares. In Asia it was only 2.3 hectares, and in Africa 0.5 hectares. Cases are not scanty in which in the process of colonization in the Third World large farm estates under the administration of conquistadors were created by consolidating lands plundered from the natives. However, by far the largest share of agricultural production is shouldered by small family farms in developing economies as well as in the world

This dominance of family farms is based on trust and co-operation among members of a family as the smallest unit of community, which is diametrically opposed to the prisoner's dilemma situation. The labour of family members who exert proper work efforts without supervision is the source of the remarkable resilience and viability of family farms. This advantage of the family enterprise is especially evident in agricultural production, which is characterized by inherent difficulties in the enforcement of hired labour. In urban industries, work is standardized and relatively easy to monitor. The biological process of agricultural production, however, is subject to infinite ecological variations. Different ways of handling crops or animals are often necessary because of slight differences in temperature and soil moisture. The dispersal of agricultural operations over wide areas adds to the difficulty of monitoring. This difficulty multiplies as the farming system becomes more complex, involving more intensive crop care, crop rotations, and crop–livestock combinations: 'In areas more suitable for multiple enterprise farms, family operations have had the advantage. Increasing the enterprises so multiplies the number of on-the-spot supervisory management decisions per acre that the total acreage which a unit of management can oversee quickly approaches the acreage which an ordinary family can operate' (Brewster, 1950: 71). In fact, large plantations are limited largely to monoculture.

This constraint of managerial ability and family labour on operational farm size is exacerbated by the danger of reckless use of draft animals and machines by non-family operators that results in capital loss. Therefore, 'a landless person with a family who owns animals and/or machines and possesses some managerial skill will find it more profitable to rent in land than to hire out his endowments separately. Similarly, a large landowner will find it more profitable to rent out land than to manage a large operation because of scale diseconomies arising from the use of hired workers' (Binswanger and Rosenzweig, 1986: 254). In other words, technological scale economies arising from the use of indivisible inputs such as managerial ability and animals/machines are counterbalanced by scale diseconomies from the use of hired labour so that the nuclear family farm is the most effective except for some plantation crops that need close co-ordination with large-scale processing and marketing.

Another advantage of peasant operations is the ability to utilize the low-opportunity cost labour of women, children, and aged family members who have little employment opportunity outside their own farm. Although the wage cost is thus lower for peasants, their capital cost may be higher than for plantations because of more difficult access to the credit market. On this ground, the argument has been developed that plantations have an advantage in regard to tree crops that are characterized by long gestation periods from planting to maturity (Binswanger and Rosenzweig, 1986). However, the opportunity costs of labour and capital applied to formation of the tree capital are not necessarily high for peasants. Typically they plant the trees in hitherto unused lands. If such lands are located near their residence, they open new lands for planting by means of family labour at low opportunity cost during the idle season for the production of food crops on farm lands already in use. When they migrate to frontier areas, a typical process is to slash and burn jungles and plant subsistence crops such as maize, potatoes, and upland rice together with tree seedlings. Such complex intercropping is difficult to manage with hired labour in the plantation system.

Therefore, even in the export boom of tropical cash crops under colonialism from the nineteenth century to the early twentieth century, the plantation system failed to make inroads in regions where indigenous populations have established family farms (W. A. Lewis, 1970: 13–45). Western traders found it more profitable to purchase tropical agricultural commodities from peasant producers in exchange for imported manufactured commodities than to produce these commodities themselves in the plantation system. This was particularly convenient during the nineteenth century when the industrial revolutions in the Western nations made it possible for these countries to produce and supply manufactured products at much lower cost than if they had been produced by the manufacturing sector in the tropical economies (Resnick, 1970).

The establishment of plantations in less developed economies became a necessity when the demand for tropical products by the industrialized nations continued to rise, although the regions in the less developed economies physically suited for the production of these products had no significant peasant population that could produce and trade them. Opening frontier lands for the production of new crops entailed high capital outlays. Virgin lands had to be cleared and developed, and physical infrastructure such as roads, irrigation systems, bridges, and docking facilities had to be constructed. Capital, in the form of machinery and other equipment, had to be imported and redesigned to adapt to local situations. Labourers were not only imported from the more populous regions but also had to be trained in the production of these crops.

The establishment of plantations thus requires huge initial capital investment. For the investors to internalize gains from investment in infrastructure, the farm size must inevitably be large. Viewed from this perspective, it follows that the plantation system evolved not because it was generally a more efficient mode of productive organization than the peasant mode but because it was the most effective type of agricultural organization for extracting the economic benefit accruing from the exploitation of sparsely populated virgin areas (Hayami, 1994).

In this perspective it is easy to understand why the same crop is grown mainly by peasants in one place and by plantations in another. For example, for sugar-cane production the peasant mode is more common in old settled areas of Luzon while the plantation system predominates in the newly opened Negros, both in the Philippines (Hayami *et al.*, 1990, Chapter 5). The crops subject to scale economies sufficiently strong to make large-scale plantation operations necessary are rather few, namely tea and bananas among major tropical export crops (Pim, 1946; Wickizer, 1951; Binswanger and Rosenzweig, 1986). Even for these crops, scale economies are not decisive at the farm-level production, although the private profitability of some operations that have externalities, such as pest management, tends to be greater for larger operations.

Significant increasing returns emerge only at the level of the processing and marketing activities. The vertical integration of a large farm unit with a large-scale central-processing and/or marketing system is called for because of the need to supply farm-produced raw materials in a timely schedule. A typical example is fermented black tea. Black tea manufacturing for export requires a modern machine plant into which fresh leaves must be fed within a few hours after plucking (Wickizer, 1951). The need for close co-ordination between farm production and processing underlies the pervasive use of the plantation system for black tea manufacture. Unfermented green tea, in contrast, remains predominantly the product of peasants in China and Japan.

In the case of bananas for export, harvested fruits must be packed, sent to the wharf, and loaded to a refrigerated boat within a day. A boat full of bananas that can meet the quality standards of foreign buyers must be collected within a few days. Therefore, the whole production process from planting to harvesting must be precisely controlled so as to meet the shipment schedule (Hayami *et al.*, 1990, ch. 6). Although the plantation system has a decisive advantage for export banana production, bananas for domestic consumption are usually produced by peasants. For the crops which do not require centralized processing and marketing, plantations have no significant advantage over peasants. Typical examples are cocoa and coconuts. The fermentation of cocoa and the drying and smoking of coconuts to make copra can be handled in small lots with no large capital requirement beyond small indigenous tools and facilities.

Even in the production of plantation crops that require large-scale processing and marketing facilities, peasant households can be efficient production units if they are organized in the contract-farming system. In contract farming an agribusiness firm (or co-operative) manages processing and marketing but contracts for farm products from peasant farmers. The firm provides technical guidance, credit, and other services to peasants in return for their pledged production to the firm. In this way this system can take advantage of peasants in farm-level production without sacrificing scale economies in processing and marketing. The high efficiency of this system has been demonstrated by the fact that Thailand, which began canned pineapple production relatively recently based on this system, has surpassed the Philippines, formerly the world's leading exporter, whose production is based on the plantation system (Hayami, 1994)[2].

Cases are thus abundant to show that small peasants in developing economies, who may appear to be premodern and inefficient, are in fact superior to large farm estates based on hired wage labour at farm-level production, by taking advantage of the smallest unit of community organization. This does not mean that they are well-to-do. On the contrary, many of them are very poor, with a standard of living even lower than urban slum-dwellers. They are poor because they have little land and few capital assets as well as poor education. Moreover, they tend to be exploited by the élites through various taxations and regulations because of their weak capacity to organize politically (Lipton, 1976; Binswanger *et al.*, 1995).

They are poor not because their production organization—small family farms—is inefficient. If they are integrated into a large farm unit, both the productivity and the standard of living in the rural sector are bound to decline. This has been demonstrated by repeated failures of projects to develop large-scale modern commercial farm estates in developing economies (Johnson and Ruttan, 1994). A more dramatic example was the failure of collective farming in former socialist economies. Collectivization of family farms into *kolkhoz* resulted in a drop of status for Russia from a major exporter of food grains down to a major importer (see Chaper 8 n. 7). Equally illuminating were sharp increases in agricultural output and productivity in China, corresponding to a shift from collective farms ('people's communes') back to private family farms ('household responsibility system') in the 1980s (Lin, 1988, 1992). This experience shows unambiguously that agricultural development in developing economies cannot be achieved without taking advantage of the organizational merit of small-scale family farms.

9.2.2 Management of common-property resources

Family farms cannot fully realize their productive capacity unless a community mechanism operates to organize co-operation among them. The need for co-operation stems to a large extent from pervasive production externalities. By nature, agricultural production activities are strongly interdependent due to ecological interdependence of biological processes. Overgrazing in a mountain pasture may increase the incidence of flooding in nearby crop fields. Diversion of irrigation water in the upstream of a river may result in a water shortage for downstream farms. Inadequate rodent management in one warehouse may trigger a village-wide outburst of rodent calamity.

These external effects of individual farm activities are each small, though large in number, so that it is difficult to estimate their economic value.

Accordingly, formal measures to internalize externalities, such as assignments of property rights and imposition of pollution tax (Section 7.4.4) are often too costly to implement. A feasible alternative is to suppress negative externalities and promote positive externalities through co-operation among families within a local community. Typical forms of local community in developing economies may be classified as 'tribe' based on blood ties and 'village' based on locational ties, though these are more or less intertwined. The former is commonly observable among nomads and shifting cultivators, whereas the latter is common in the area of settled agriculture. In either case, the co-operative relationship created through intense personal interactions works as a mechanism to enforce mutual observance of traditional norms and conventions. As such, the community mechanism has been considered to be an effective control on 'common-property' or 'common-pool' resources, such as forests and grazing lands, that are subject to exhaustion by overexploitation while users who do not pay for the cost are difficult to exclude (Ostrom, 1990).

In many cases, however, the community mechanism has not been sufficiently effective for conservation of the common-property resources, as evident from denuded forests and desertified grazing lands. The community mechanism for enforcing rules is everyone's fear of the eyes and mouths of their fellow community members. In a small community everyone is watching everyone. Gossip about one's misconduct is circulated by word of mouth faster than modern communication means, sometimes culminating in social ostracism. For this mechanism to work, rules must be clearly established (if not written) by people's consensus. Externality of one's use of common-property resources, such as adding a goat to the flock in mountain grazing land, is typically too small to be visible. Unless a limit is clearly stipulated by a community rule on the number of animals per household on the common pasture for example, the community mechanism would be impotent in resource conservation. Such a rule is not easily achieved by community consensus, because some (or many) are worse off with it, at least, in the short run. Even if it is adopted as a community rule, it will take a long time to be established as a social norm.

The process by which norms and conventions to manage common-property resources are developed may be seen from the experience of Japan. Rural villages in Japan are characterized by detailed rules and their effective enforcement at the community level on the rights and the obligations regarding the use of common-property resources, such as forests, grazing lands, and water for irrigation. However, it was mainly during the eighteenth century that this strong control system was established. Throughout the seventeenth century from the formation of the Tokugawa Shogunate (1603), Japan had enjoyed rapid expansion in cultivation frontiers under secured peace, with an increase in area under cultivation from about two to three million hectares (Tamaki and Hatate, 1974: 247). As the frontiers closed but population continued to increase in the eighteenth century, competition for irrigation water and leaves and grasses in hills and mountains (as the source of compost) was intensified among rural people through their desperate efforts to compensate for decreases in per capita availability of farm lands by increased yields per unit of land area. As a result, conflicts occurred frequently, often involving bloodshed, among villagers as well as among villages on the use of rivers, forests, and grasslands. In order to escape from this negative-sum situation, conventional rules on the use of common-property resources at the village community level were gradually developed (Tamaki and Hatate, 1974; Tamaki, 1983).[3] This experience indicates the village communities had an ability to learn through repeated games how to escape from the prisoner's dilemma and to arrive at a co-operative game solution.

There is no reason to doubt that rural communities in developing economies today have the same ability. The problem is that the speed with which their institutions should be adjusted is incomparably higher than in eighteenth-century Japan corresponding to difference in the population growth rates. In many developing economies, such as South-East Asia and East Africa, population density had traditionally been low and natural resources were relatively abundant until only a half century ago. With explosive population growth of the order of 2–3 per cent per year, these economies have rapidly turned to a negative-sum situation with respect to the use of common-property resources. It is not surprising that many rural communities in developing economies have failed to strengthen controls on the resource use in keeping up with such rapid increases in population. This adjustment lag in community institutions has underlain pervasive incidence of deplorable resource depletion such as deforestation due to slash-and-burn cultivation and desertification due to overgrazing.

Despite the obvious failure of communities, it is dangerous to shift the role of common-property resource management to government. For example, in many developing economies, forests are formally owned by the state. This state ownership has often been a source of forest destruction. Usually, government's budget and manpower are grossly insufficient for adequately managing vast forest areas. For local inhabitants, on the other hand, government agencies are the 'outsider' to their community. In terms of the logic of community, exploitation of the outsider's properties for the benefit of community members is not something to be condemned. In these conditions, it is difficult to stop illegal timber-cutting and burning trees for shifting cultivation. Thus, exhaustion of community-property resources due to over-exploitation by free-riders—the so-called 'tragedy of commons' (Hardin, 1968)—tends to become more pervasive in state-owned than communally owned lands.

Moreover, under the asymmetry of information, it becomes a rather common practice for government officials to grant commercial logging concessions on large tracts of forest, at a price with little consideration for environmental externality. It is also not uncommon that, under the pressure of politically powerful estate owners and cattle ranchers, government provides subsidies and tax concessions for conversion of forests to arable land and ranches. As a result, the basis of livelihood for small indigenous tribes utilizing the forests in an eco-friendly manner tends to be destroyed (Binswanger, 1991; Dasgupta and Mäler, 1995: 2424–34).

Again, it must be emphasized that there is no reason to deny the potential of rural communities to develop the capacity of managing common-property resources adequately. There are cases in which they have demonstrated their capacity, such as the highly efficient communal irrigation management in Ilocos, the Philippines, and Bali, Indonesia. These cases tend to be found in areas with higher population density and environmental characteristics making community-level co-operation highly rewarding. (H. T. Lewis, 1971; Barker, 1978; Hayami and Kikuchi, 1981: 22–3).[4] The problem is how to realize this potential while keeping up with rapidly mounting population pressure. The appropriate attempt is not to substitute governmental organizations for communities but to improve the capacity of community organization by such means as education and technical assistance. The first requirement for this strategy is a correct understanding of the community mechanism. If government tries to reform community institutions without understanding what rational functions the apparently irrational conventions and customs are playing, such reform will but prove to be counterproductive for the development of communities' capacity.

9.2.3 Landlord–tenant relations

The community relationship is not only effective in managing common-property resources but also in reducing transaction costs of private goods and services. It has been pointed out in the previous section that trust accumulated through intensive personal interactions in a community has the effect of overcoming market failures stemming from information asymmetry. We will try to observe here how this community mechanism operates in the transactions of land and labour for agricultural production in developing economies.

As explained previously, efficiency of family-based farming is high, except with special commodities requiring centralized processing and marketing, so that operational farm sizes in developing economies are usually small and relatively homogeneous, within a range cultivable mainly by family labour. This does not mean that distribution of land ownership is homogeneous. Cases are not rare that large tracts of land in a village or over several villages have become private possessions through land accumulation by an indigenous ruling élite or plunder by colonizers. Also, there are cases in which originally homogeneous communities have been gradually stratified into landowners and the landless through rises in land rent under continued population pressure (Hayami and Kikuchi, 1981; Hayami *et al.*, 1990).

It is common to observe that rural villages in developing economies are stratified into classes based on ownership, such as landlords, owner-farmers, landless tenants, and agricultural wage-labourers. However, it is rather rare that landlords cultivate their holdings by hired wage-labour under their direct administration. It is much more common for large landowners to rent out areas in excess of their family cultivation in small parcels to tenants. Thus, land tenancy contracts work as a mechanism to create and maintain the agrarian structure consisting of small-scale family-based farms as the basic unit of agricultural production, despite unequal distribution of land-ownership. It must be noted, however, that due to seasonality in agricultural production family-based farms also have to employ outside labour in peak seasons, through wage hire contracts or through labour exchange among neighbours.

In contrast with urban industries in which labourers are alienated from the output of their labour as well as the means of production, in the peasant community even the landless have some claim to the use of land and to a share of output—typically through an arrangement such as sharecropping. As is typical in a sharecropping tenancy (though it often applies to fixed-rent tenancy also), a strong tendency exists in the village community for various transactions to be interlinked in a highly personalized relationship. A land-lord does not simply receive a share rent for his contribution of land to the production process, but also bears a part of the production cost (such as seeds and fertilizers) and advances credits for production and consumption purposes. Moreover, he often patronizes his tenant through gestures such as giving gifts at the birth of a child or the death of a father and using his connection and influence to solve the tenant's problems with other villagers or outsiders. The tenant reciprocates with the loyal service of himself and his family, including voluntary domestic help at the festive occasions of his landlord.

Such a relationship is commonly called by anthropologists and socio-logists a patron–client relationship—'a special case of dyadic (two-person) ties involving a largely instrumental friendship in which an individual of higher socio-economic status (patron) uses his own influence and resources to provide protection and/or benefits for a person of lower status (client) who, for his part, reciprocates by offering patronage' (Scott, 1972. 8). In the patron–client relationship, exchanges are multi-stranded and the balance is cleared in the long run. The patron–client relationship is a substitute for a set of specialized markets for labour, land, credit, and insurance (Bardhan, 1980; Hayami and Kikuchi, 1981; Hayami and Otsuka, 1993). As empha-sized previously, unlike urban industries characterized by the machine pro-cess, work is not standardized and is difficult to monitor. The scattering of agricultural operations over a wide area adds to the difficulty of monitoring. Under such conditions quality of labour (in terms of conscientious attention and adjustment) commands a high value. A market is bound to be inefficient or vanish altogether in the presence of asymmetry in such quality information between employers and employees—that is, when employees have full information on the quality of their own work while employers have difficulty in judging it. So far as an employment relationship is limited to a spot exchange among anonymous agents in the market-place, it is difficult to avoid hiring workers who are dishonest or shirkers, not so much in the duration and intensity of physical work but in its quality.

The multifaceted and enduring relationship of the patron–client type is clearly superior in the collection of quality information because performances in past transactions comprise a reliable data set for prediction of future performances. The chance of being cheated will be reduced, because the expected cost of committing one immoral or dishonest act is very great since its discovery by another party will endanger the whole set of transactions.

In this way, the patron–client relationship incorporated into the sharecropping contract is instrumental in shifting from the prisoners' dilemma to the co-operative game solution. Theoretically, the same outcome can be achieved by using the fixed-rent tenancy contract in which tenants capture all the benefits from their efforts (Cheung, 1969). Yet, because tenants have to shoulder all the risks of production fluctuations due to weather and other natural calamities, they often prefer a sharecropping contract, even if they have to pay a higher sharecropping rent than a fixed rent. The sharecropping tenancy was once believed to be exploitative and inefficient because a part of the gain from tenants' work effort is expropriated by landlords. However, recent theoretical and empirical studies indicate that inefficiency can be avoided by co-operative relationships between tenants and landlords to the advantage of both parties (Hayami and Otsuka, 1993).

The co-operative relationship between tenants and landlords is solidified within the total community relationship. A rumour about a tenant's shirking and cheating in his contract with a landlord will not only endanger the relationship with his present patron but also stop the possibility of his entering into contracts with other landlords in the same village. Likewise, if a landlord does not extend due assistance to a tenant at a time of misfortune, he will lose not only this tenant's loyal service but other villagers' co-operation. For example, if a cow belonging to a landlord known to be benevolent drops in a hole, it may be rescued by villagers passing by, whereas livestock belonging to a landlord with a reputation for maltreating his tenants may not be.

Of course, the relations between tenants and landlords are not always harmonious and co-operative. The larger the landlord's holding, the more difficult it is for him to establish a close personal relationship with many tenants. Therefore, he tends to rely more heavily on formal written contracts and legal enforcement—a tendency especially pronounced in the case of absentee landlords living outside the village. In the case of resident landlords, their behaviour may also change with exposure of rural communities to market economies. While their villages were largely isolated, goodwill and respect from their poor neighbours can be of important psychological as well as a practical value of protecting their properties. However, as the villages are integrated into a wider economic and political system, they may find it more effective to rely on court and police for the protection of properties, while the purchase of modern consumption goods from the market may become more attractive than the purchase of poor neighbours' goodwill. Accordingly, they may stop behaving as a generous patron to secure clients' minimum subsistence (Scott, 1976). Moreover, the possibility cannot be ruled out of a small number of landlords in an isolated village conspiring to impose unfavourable terms of contract on tenants (Popkin, 1979). These tendencies are exacerbated by increased scarcity of land relative to population.

Indeed, there is no denying that confrontation between tenants and landlords has been a major source of social instability in many areas in developing economies, especially in Asia. To resolve this conflict, land reform programmes geared for redistribution of landlords' holdings among tenants who are actual tillers of the land (land-to-tillers programmes) have been undertaken. However, these programmes have not been very successful in achieving the intended goal, except in Japan, Korea, and Taiwan. Instead, landlords' reform-evasion practices have often made the position of tenants worse than their pre-reform position (Section 7.2.4).

Especially noteworthy in the present context is the threat that landlords' evasion tactics destroy co-operative relationships between tenants and landlords. For example, because land-to-tillers programmes were targeted at tenanted lands alone, landlords tried to evict tenants from their lands which were consolidated into large estates under landlords' direct administration employing the evicted tenants as wage-labourers. Alternatively, to disguise tenants as wage-labourers, landlords stopped renewal of long-term tenancy contracts and tried to replace tenants by crop season. As a result tenants lost the opportunity of stable land utilization or declined in status from self-employed producers to wage-labourers (Cain, 1981; Herring, 1983).

These incidents demonstrate the danger of attempting reform of community relations without due understanding of their functions and mechanisms.

9.3 Economic Rationality in Community: A Perspective from Philippine Villages[5]

A traditional view on 'community' in sociology, from Karl Marx ([1939–41] 1953) to Ferdinand Tönnies ([1887] 1926) and Max Weber ([1909] 1924), has been to assume a small group of people (or families) bounded by blood and locational ties, in which different economic principles operate from those of the capitalist market economy. In this view, while the prime motivation in the capitalist economy is private profit-seeking by individuals, the principle of community is mutual help for guaranteeing subsistence to all its members. Therefore, economic rationality in terms of individual profit and utility maximization does not operate in a community of this definition.

If this traditional view is valid, contractual forms concerning labour employment and land utilization in traditional communities should be different from those of modern market economies, resulting in different patterns of resource allocation. This hypothesis is incorporated in the dual economy model by W. A. Lewis, and Ranis and Fei. In their model, in contrast to the modern sector (industry) in which the wage rate is determined by the neoclassical marginal principle, the wage rate in the traditional sector (agriculture) in developing economies is given exogenously as a social institution (Section 3.3.3). This 'institutional wage rate' was determined by equal sharing of agricultural output among villagers before the beginning of modern industrialization.

If the community principle is, in fact, mutual help and income-sharing instead of profit or utility maximization by individuals, community organizations should fail to achieve efficient resource allocations according to neoclassical criteria. However, many empirical studies following the lead of T. W. Schultz indicate that the wage rates in the rural sectors of developing economies are not significantly different from the marginal value products of labour, implying efficient resource allocations resulting from individuals' profit maximization (Schultz, 1964; Hopper, 1965, Yotopoulos, 1968). Moreover, recently accumulating micro-household studies in the rural areas of developing economies reveal the tendency that the healthier and stronger workers are (as measured by such indicators as body height and weight), the higher the remuneration they receive (Berhman and Deolalikar, 1989; Haddad and Bouis, 1991; Foster and Rosenzweig, 1993; Strauss and Thomas, 1995: 1908–18). Such results imply that farmer employers reward workers to correspond with their contributions to farm production rather than employ them with the altruistic motive of guaranteeing fellow-villagers' subsistence needs. Do these empirical findings imply that a community principle of mutual help is an illusion or a mere spoken moral code having no tangible power to control economic activities? Or have traditional communities already been destroyed by the introduction of the market economy into villages in developing economies?

An answer to this question will be sought in this section in terms of a concrete example of Philippine villages based on the field survey by Hayami and Kikuchi (1981, chs. 4, 5, and 6).

9.3.1 Labour hiring by peasants

When people familiar with agriculture in North-East Asia, including China, Korea, and Japan, visited rural villages in South-East Asia, such as the Philippines and Indonesia, they were intrigued by the observation that peasants and family members worked relatively little time on their own farms, leaving many of the tasks to hired labour. In recent years in Japan, reliance on hired labour for farm operations has increased as a result of increased off-farm employment opportunities. Before then, farm tasks were predominantly shouldered by family members with hired and exchange labour used as a minor supplement at peak seasons. According to a nationwide survey by the Japan Ministry of Agriculture for 1934–6, when the traditional pattern prevailed, the ratio of hired labour (including exchange labour) in the total number of workdays used for rice production was only 9.5 per cent for owner farms and 7.6 per cent for tenant farms (top two rows in Table 9.1).

In contrast, according to a survey of two rice villages in the Laguna Province, Philippines, the ratio of hired labour amounted to as high as 70 per cent, despite the fact that the average operational size of Philippine farms wasn't significantly different from the Japanese farms (middle two rows in Table 9.1). Farms dependent on hired labour for more than two-thirds of total labour input are not consistent with the traditional image of the 'peasant'—small, subsistence-orientated farms mainly dependent on family labour—since Alexander Chayanov ([1925] 1966). This high dependency on hired labour is not unique to these two surveyed villages but rather universal in the rice-farming areas of the Philippines (Takahashi, 1969).

How are such large amounts of external labour employed in small farms? Almost all the external labour is hired for casual work on a daily contract

TABLE 9.1 *Labour inputs per hectare of rice crop area in Japan, Philippines, and Indonesia*

	Workdays per hectare			Percentage of hired labour (%)	Operational holding per farm (hectare)
	Total	Family	Hired		
Japan (1934–6 average)					
Tenant	198	183	15	7.6	1.4
owner	200	181	19	9.5	1.6
Philippines					
Village E	105	31	74	70.5	2.0
Village W	105	37	68	64.8	1.4
Indonesia					
Village S	208	70	138	66.3	0.30
Village N	159	35	124	78.0	0.87

Sources: Japan: Japan Ministry of Agriculture and Forestry (1974); Philippines: Hayami and Kikuchi (1981: 118 and 137); Indonesia: Calculated from Hayami and Kikuchi (1981: 183 and 202) by assuming 6-hour work per day.

basis. Hired labour is used mainly for peak-season activities such as rice transplanting and harvesting. Both activities demand large quantities of labour in short periods and are visible in terms of work effort outcome (i.e. transplanted areas and harvested quantities). In contrast, family labour is used mainly for the tasks that require care and judgement without immediately visible outcomes, for which physical labour requirements are not so large, such as water and pest control, fertilizer application, and seed-bed preparation. Land preparation with the use of water-buffalo (*carabao*) is traditionally the task of family labour. However, it has increasingly been contracted out to tractor custom services in recent years.

This division of labour is understandable in view of seasonal fluctuations in labour demand as well as the relative ease (or difficulty) of monitoring work. In fact, it is applicable to Japan and elsewhere. A unique aspect is that family members rarely work at transplanting and harvesting. In the rice transplanting, seedlings are prepared and brought to fields by family members but transplanting itself is performed by a labour crew organized by a contractor called *kabisilya*. More intriguing is the system of harvesting which requires nearly 40 per cent of total labour input in rice production. The traditional system is called *hunusan*, a form of contract by which, when a farmer specifies a day of harvesting in his field, anyone can participate in harvesting and threshing, and the harvesters receive a certain share (traditionally one-sixth) of the output. By custom, the farmer can reject no one from harvesting his crop. Neither he nor his family members go to the harvesting field even to monitor the work

9.3.2 Income and work-sharing

Why do poor peasants employ external labour without fully utilizing family labour on their own farms? This behaviour is inconsistent with the Chayanovian concept of peasants who try to maximize the utilization of family labour even up to zero marginal productivity (Chayanov, [1925] 1966).

There is a theory to explain this apparent anomaly by absentee landlordism prevailing in the Philippines since Spanish colonial rule. A common form of land-tenancy contract in rice areas was a sharecropping contract by which both output and input costs (including hired wage costs) were shared 50–50 between tenants and landlords. Under this contract the larger the payment to hired labour, the smaller was the landlords' share of output. The tenants' share also became smaller with the larger payment to hired labour. However, this reduction in tenants' income could be recovered by receipt of output shares from neighbours, i.e. mutual employment among tenants would maximize their output share at the expense of landlords.

This hypothesis of 'tenants' collusion' (Takahashi, 1969) appears plausible in terms of agrarian history and organization in the Philippines. However, as a similar survey was conducted in West Java, Indonesia, where most farmers were owner-operators instead of tenants, it was found that dependency on hired labour was equally high, despite an average farm size significantly smaller than in the Philippines (bottom two rows in Table 9.1).

An alternative hypothesis may be that a social norm of income- and work-sharing prevails in the rural sector of South-East Asia. This norm dictates that well-to-do members in a village community should provide income-earning opportunities to poor neighbors by retreating themselves from work. It is a kind of community principle of mutual help to guarantee minimum subsistence to the poor.

The rural community characterized by the principle of income and work-sharing may sound like a Utopia of altruism. However, this principle is not necessarily inconsistent with economic rationality based on egoism. A condition for establishment of the sharing principle could have been a low level of agricultural productivity with high risk. Until relatively recently, South-East Asia had been characterized by sparse population relative to available land for cultivation. Before the Green Revolution (Section 4.2.1), rice farming was typically extensive with little fertilizer application and weeding practice, so that yield differences between diligent and idle farmers were much less pronounced than in Japan. Therefore, whether a farmer himself worked hard on his field or left the work to hired labourers did not much affect the level of yield.

On the other hand, production risk remained high. In drought, crops in the fields of elevated locations may be destroyed, whereas bumper crops may be harvested in lower-lying marshy fields. The reverse is likely to be the case in the season of heavy rain and flooding. Similarly, an outbreak of pest may eliminate crops in a certain area, while other areas might be left largely intact. Thus, it is hazardous to rely for subsistence on the production in a particular plot. Therefore, it is common for a peasant to hold his land in small parcels scattered over a wide area. Similarly, it greatly reduces risk if he allows other villagers to share work and output in his farm, while he is allowed to share work and output in others' farms. This insurance mechanism of work- and income-sharing should be especially valuable in economies where the market is underdeveloped so that villagers have no other means of insuring against risk in farm production, such as off-farm employment opportunities or formal insurance and credit systems. This is one of many insurance mechanisms in traditional societies, which generally involve diversifying family members' economic activities widely across different locations (Rosenzweig, 1988a, 1988b; Stark and Lucas, 1988).

Thus, it is hypothesized that the sharing principle observable in South-East Asian villages did emerge from people's need to secure subsistence at the low level of land productivity. It was established because it was mutually beneficial to sharing parties. As such, egoists would have found it profitable to observe this principle in terms of their rational economic calculations. However, the sharing system would have not been elevated to a social norm, unless violations from this norm (e.g. receiving shares from neighbours without reciprocating to them) were precluded by close community relationship.

9.3.3 Changes in the sharing system

If the community principle of work and income-sharing originated in rational choice under certain economic and technological conditions, its practice would have changed corresponding to changes in these conditions.

In the traditional *hunusan* system, every villager could participate in harvesting and normally receive one-sixth of harvested paddy. In the past when rice farming was associated with low yields, one-sixth of output could well be close to harvesting labour's contribution (or labour's marginal productivity) to output. However, as the use of modern rice varieties and chemical fertilizers has been promoted, yields per hectare have risen sharply with parallel increases in harvesters' receipts. On the other hand, the market wage rates have remained largely stable under the pressure of labour force growth. As the result, the rate of return to labour under the traditional *hunusan* contract has risen cumulatively above the market wage rate.

Such a tendency can be observed from the records of a survey village (Village E in Table 9.1). From 1966 to 1976, population in this village increased from 393 to 644 persons, while cultivated area remained virtually constant. On the other hand, average rice yield per hectare of paddy-field area increased from 2.2 tonnes in 1956 to 5.5 tonnes in 1966, and further to 6.8 tonnes in 1976 owing to progress in modern rice technology and improvements in irrigation systems. These technological advances significantly increased demand for labour in rice production. However, under the pressure of both high natural population growth and labour immigration from surrounding mountain areas, the real wage rate for casual farm work remained largely constant at about 9 kilograms of paddy per day. Thus, the *hunusan* contract of output-sharing, under which the real wage rate of harvesting labour increased parallel with paddy yields, has become a highly disadvantageous system for employer farmers-relative to the market wage contract. Moreover, unlike the old days when *hunusan* harvesters were largely neighbouring farmers, a majority of them consisted of landless agricultural labourers. Therefore, it has become difficult for an employer farmer to recover his high payment to harvesting labourers above the market wage rates from reciprocal employment. Corresponding to these changes, a new system called *gama* (meaning 'weeding' in Tagalog) has emerged. *Gama* is an output-sharing contract similar to *hunusan*, except that employment for harvesting is limited to workers who worked on the weeding of the field without receiving wages. In other words, in the *gama* system, weeding labour is a free service provided by workers to establish a right to participate in harvesting and to receive one-sixth of output. To the extent that weeding labour is additionally required for receiving the same share of output, the implied wage rate is lower in *gama* than in *hunusan*.

The role of *gama* as an institutional innovation to close the gap between harvesters' share and labour's marginal productivity under the traditional sharing arrangement consistent with the norm of community is confirmed by calculations in Table 9.2. The same calculations are applied to two data sets collected from employer farmers and employed *gama* workers. First, labour inputs per hectare per crop season are measured in workdays for both harvesting and weeding (first two rows). These labour inputs are imputed by market wage rates for estimating the market values of *hunusan* labour (A—the value of harvesting labour alone) and *gama* labour (B—the value of harvesting labour plus weeding labour). By comparing these market values of labour with the market value of one-sixth of paddy output (R), the rates of divergence of labour's remuneration under the sharing arrangement from its market value can be estimated. The results show that if *hunusan* had been used in 1976 when modern rice technology was widely diffused, harvesting labour's remuneration would have been about 30 per cent higher than its market value. This gap was nearly eliminated with adoption of the *gama* system. These results are consistent with the hypothesis that the *gama* contract represents an institutional innovation designed to reduce disequilibrium between labour's remuneration and marginal productivity within the framework of work and income-sharing in the community. In fact, the emergence and diffusion of the *gama* contract paralleled the increases in rice yield due to irrigation improvements and diffusion of modern rice

TABLE 9.2 *Comparisons between the actual revenue of harvesters and the imputed cost of harvesting labour under the* hunusan *and the* gama *contracts in a survey village (Village E) in the Philippines, 1976 net season*

	Based on employers' data	Based on employees' data
No. of work days of *gama* labour (days/ha)		
Harvesting	33.6	33.6
Weeding	20.9	18.3
Imputed cost of *gama* labour[a] (peso/ha)		
(A) Harvesting	369.6	369.5
(B) Harvesting + Weeding	536.8	516.0
(R) Actual revenue of harvesters[b] (peso/ha)	504.0	549.0
Percentage difference from the market wage rate (%)		
Hunusan (R-A)/R	26.7	32.7
Gama (R-B)/R	-6.5	6.0

[a] Imputation using the market wage rates of 8 pesos per day for weeding and 11 pesos for harvesting
[b] One-sixth of paddy harvest valued at the market price of 1 peso per kg
Source: Hayami and Kikuchi (1981: 121).

technology. These observations seem to indicate that villagers in the Philippines are applying the community principle of sharing based on rational economic calculation.

Such institutional adjustments were not limited to specific villages in Laguna. Similar changes in harvesting systems were observed widely over rice-producing areas in the Philippines as well as Indonesia (Hayami and Kikuchi, 1981, chs. 4, 7, and 8).

9.3.4 The role of community norm

It does not follow, however, that the community principle of sharing is a mere illusion or a superficial moral code with much shouting but no substantive impact on economic activities. The fact should not be overlooked that, when disequilibrium emerged between the market wage rate and the share of harvesting labourers under the *hunusan* system the output-sharing contract with the traditional one-sixth share was maintained instead of being replaced by the fixed daily (or hourly) wage contract. The daily employment contract at the fixed wage rate is a typical form of market exchange between labour and money. By nature, it is an impersonal spot transaction. Under such a contract, little incentive operates for employees to work properly and conscientiously. Therefore, employers must rely on supervision to enforce employees' work, resulting in high labour transaction costs as well as social confrontation between employers and employees.

In contrast, the community-type contract like *gama* in the Philippines encompasses several tasks, such as weeding and harvesting, over a season, and it usually continues to be renewed seasonally. Wages are not paid at the time of weeding. In the minds of villagers, weeding with no direct payment is considered to be not a part of a contract based on economic calculation, but an expression of gratitude by labourers for the goodwill of a farmer patron who provides them the opportunities of participating in harvesting and receiving the output share. Such a long-term personal relationship is further strengthened through exchanges of gifts, credits, and personal services in a manner similar to the relationship between landlords and tenants as described before. Both the sense of moral obligation and the fear of losing the patron–client relationship would motivate labourers to exert conscientious work efforts. Relative to the replacement of the community-type sharing contract by the market-type fixed-wage contract, the adjustment of the sharing contract by adding extra-work obligation, such as *gama*, should have reduced labour transaction costs. To that extent adherence to the community principle is effective in raising both economic efficiency and social stability.

It seems reasonable to hypothesize that the general moral principle calling for mutual help through work and income-sharing in village communities was instrumental in guiding institutional innovation towards *gama* instead of the fixed-wage contract. Significant psychological and social resistance against violations of an established social norm was demonstrated by an episode in a survey village in which, when a large farmer announced his intention to cut down harvesters' share from the traditional one-sixth to one-seventh under the *hunusan* system, his standing crop was burned during the night. Thus, the shift from the *hunusan* to the *gama* represents a case in which the social norms and moral codes long nurtured in village communities in the premodern period guided institutional change towards economic efficiency and social stability, when modernization forces (such as population explosion, modern agricultural technology, and commercialization) demanded institutional change.

However, it does not follow that the community-type of sharing arrangement is always preserved. In Indonesia, the institutional adjustment in the rice-harvesting system took place in West Java as diffusion of the *ceblokan* system which is essentially the same as the *gama* system in the Philippines. In Central Java, however, a different system called *tebasan* did emerge. *Tebasan* is a market-type contract in which farmers sell their standing crops immediately before harvest to a middleman who harvests the crops by labourers employed at the market wage rates (Collier *et al.*, 1973; Hayami and Kikuchi, 1981: 155–70). Because farmers, as members of a village community, were bound by the community obligation of sharing, they passed on to middlemen outside the community the task of executing the market-type labour contract. This example adds to the evidence of efforts by rural people in developing economies to achieve efficient resource allocations under the constraint of traditional community norms.

9.3.5 Egoism and altruism

The foregoing examples in rural South-East Asia give an important insight into the relationship between egoism and altruism, which are considered to be the motivational forces of market and community respectively. As human beings, members of a community also seek self-interests. However, self-interest-seeking by an individual without due regard to the interests of other community members is counterproductive to his goal of his profit maximization.

The possibility that egoists behave like altruists through intensive social interactions is elucidated by Gary Becker (1974). He defined 'social interactions' in terms of consumption externality or the utility function of a person to include other persons' reactions to his action. For example, A's welfare depends not only on his own personal income and consumption but also on how B looks at A's income and consumption levels. If A enjoys B's goodwill or fears his envy, A may transfer a part of his income to B up to a point where A's marginal loss of utility from the income transfer to B equals the marginal gain in A's utility due to the improvement in B's evaluation of A; at this point of equality A's total utility is maximized.

How far egoists would behave as altruists depends on the intensity of social interactions. In a closed small community in which people interact continuously, a wise egoist is likely to behave as an altruist. According to Becker, however, a person is altruistic to the extent that the return to his altruism exceeds the cost of so behaving. Farmers' work-sharing behaviour observed in Philippine villages seems to represent the equilibrium of their utility maximization under strong social interactions.

It might sound cynical to explain altruistic behaviour by egoism. However, self-restraint in consideration of other people's utility and sentiment can be interpreted as behaviour based on 'sympathy' which Adam Smith regarded as an indispensable moral sentiment for the harmonious organization of the market economy (A. Smith, [1759] 1976). Indeed, it is also consistent with the virtue of 'Consideration: Never do to others what you would not like them to do', advocated by Confucius (1938, trans. by Waley: 198). A major problem in developing economies is how to evolve this moral sentiment existing at a small community level to be generally applicable in wider modern industrial society.

9.4 The Community Failure and Its Correction

The community principle born in rural villages in developing economies has the potential to be an important part of modern organization in support of industrial development. However, traditional norms and conventions in village communities are not by themselves effective in organizing modern development. To be useful, the merits and demerits of community organizations must be clearly recognized. Similar to the cases of market and state, both subject to their particular failures, community is not free from its failings (Hayami, 1989). The problem is how to correct these failings so that community will become an effective component in the modern economic system.

9.4.1 Localized trust and co-operation

The role of trust and co-operation based on the community relations in reducing transaction costs, especially in developing economies characterized by a high degree of information imperfection and underdevelopment of a judicial system, has been emphasized in the first section of this chapter. However, mutual trust and co-operation among community members are often supported by rivalry (or hostility) against outsiders. Therefore, market transactions supported by the community relationship tend to be limited to a small area, and long-distance trade across regions often remains inactive because of the pervasive incidence of defection, including fraud and plunder.

A means of correcting this failure is the deployment of an ethnic community across regions. Typical examples are Jewish traders in medieval Europe and Chinese traders in South-East Asia. They were able to establish dominant positions in commercial and financial activities, as they were successful in reducing transactions costs across distant trading-posts among the traders and bankers bound by the ethnic community ties (Greif, 1989, 1993; Hayami and Kawagoe, 1993).

Another traditional device is the formation of trade associations such as guilds. A guild aimed at correcting the market failure arising from moral hazards under the asymmetry of information by controlling the quality standards of commodities and regulating the procedures of transactions among its limited members. It was a kind of artificial community with a strong entry barrier, which was formed originally by an agreement among participants that was enforced by social ostracism, and further reinforced by charters of feudal rulers and religious orders.

In both the ethnic group and the trade association, co-operative relationship within a closed community meant the community's ability to exercise opportunism against outsiders. Their success in reducing transaction costs, therefore, was inevitably accompanied by the formation of monopoly. It is well known that the trade monopoly of guilds became a major fetter on market expansion and economic development in late medieval to early modern Europe (Greif *et al.*, 1994).

In advanced market economies, too, it is not uncommon to observe cases in which a firm has long-term continuous transactions with a limited number of trading partners. A typical example is the relationship between automobile assemblers and part suppliers in Japan. Japanese automobile assemblers are characterized by high shares of parts supplied from outside firms. However, most of the parts are not of general specifications procured from market or open bidding, but of unique specifications to each assembler procured through long-term subcontracting arrangements with particular part manufacturers. Transactions between the assembler and the subcontractors are not only long-term but also multistranded including technical guidance and credit guarantee. The subcontractors try to observe product quality and delivery date requirements so as not to lose the benefits of long-term contracts with the assembler. The assembler also tries to guarantee appropriate treatment of subcontractors so as to maintain the source of reliable parts supply. Because of the mutual trust and co-operative relationship thus created, the subcontractors do not hesitate to invest heavily in the formation of specific skills and equipment consistent with demands of their assemblers. The artificial creation of a community relationship among business partners is said to underlie the highly competitive strength of the Japanese automobile industry (Abegglen and Stalk, 1985; Asanuma, 1985, 1988; Wada, 1991).

Why could the relatively closed corporate groups in the Japanese automobile industry escape from the evil of monopoly as produced by guilds? It should be because strong competition among the corporate groups (e.g.

Toyota versus Nissan) precludes the possibility of monopoly price-setting. Also, the assembler refrains from monopsonistic exploitation of part suppliers, because of the fear of the long-run exit of good part suppliers to the other corporate groups. Thus, clearly the existence of a contestable market is necessary to prevent community failure from becoming serious.

Also, it must be recognized that wide and complex transactions among enterprises cannot be controlled by the co-operative relationship of the community type alone. Even between firms within the same corporate group, there is the possibility of major conflicts emerging from contracts, especially those involving highly complicated and uncertain new technology developments, which cannot be compromised by co-operative spirit. As a last resort to conflict resolution, establishment of formal judicial systems is indispensable for co-ordinating the highly complex division of labour in modern economies. In fact, clear specifications of terms of contract in formal documents backed up by laws and courts are useful to minimize the chance of such conflicts emerging and reduces the present gain relative to the future loss from exercising opportunism, thereby maximizing the likelihood of sustaining a co-operative relationship.

Community relationship can play an important role in modern industrial organizations, but it cannot be a substitute for the market and the state.

9.4.2 Mutual cover-up and logrolling

The possibility should not be overlooked that mutual help and co-operation based on the community relationship work in some circumstances to promote mutual shirking and back-scratching. In the 'Japanese system of management' characterized by lifetime employment, seniority-based promotion and wage rates, and labour unions by corporation, a firm simulates a closed community, within which employees co-operate to work and monitor the efforts of each other for the common good of the company's prosperity (Dore, 1973; Morishima, 1982; Abbeglen and Stalk, 1985; Imai and Komiya, 1989; Aoki and Dore, 1994). However, state enterprises in China are even stronger communities than Japanese private firms, which not only preclude the possibility of lay-off and discharge but guarantee the full range of subsistence to employees and their families, including housing, schools, hospitals, and nursing homes. Nevertheless, employees' work morale is low and their co-operative efforts are directed at maintaining the *status quo* of living and working conditions rather than improving productivity (Wong, 1986; Walder, 1989). This condition is said to underlie rapid growth in 'village and township enterprises' in post-commune rural China, which has the advantage of utilizing low-cost labour free from the vested interests within state enterprises (Wong, 1987).

The community relationship serves as a mutual work-enforcement mechanism in Japanese private firms because they face market competition. If a company in Japan loses in the competition, all the employees would be seriously worse off because of the closed nature of its organization with little chance of exit. Given this fear, the community mechanism of co-operation operates in the direction of mutual work enforcement. In contrast, in the state enterprises in China, market competition is absent, which results in no fear of lay-offs, wage cuts, and bankruptcy. It is not surprising to find that both management and workers are motivated to mutually cover up shirking and to allocate their efforts in seeking institutional rents. Indeed, this tendency applies not only to state enterprises in China, but also to state enterprises (such as the National Railway Corporation before privatization) and semi-public organizations (such as agricultural co-operative associations) in Japan.

These observations indicate that any economic system built with disproportionate reliance on state and community is bound to be both inefficient and inequitable. Its shortcomings can only be corrected by appropriate incorporation of the competitive market. Without the compelling force of market competition, the community relationship tends to work as a social mechanism for penalizing and ostracizing innovators who deviate from established norms and conventions, thereby preserving obsolete technology and inefficient (or even dysfunctional) institutions and organizations (Akerlof, 1976, 1980, 1984). Internal organizations, not only private firms but also governmental agencies and non-profit organizations such as schools and hospitals, can best be made effective by the voice of insiders advocating organizational reforms, when coupled with the exit of customers and employees (Hirschman, 1970).

Since Thomas More's *Utopia* ([1516] 1989), there has always been great popular desire to build a Utopian state based on the community principle of mutual help and co-operation, while denying the market principle of competition as the system of exploitation by the rich and powerful. Countless failures in the attempt to build Utopia, often involving great tragedies such as the massacre of Cambodians by Pol Pot, have stemmed from oversight on the failures of state and community that are bound to become serious in the absence of market competition.

9.4.3 Is community inflexible?

It has commonly been argued that community institutions and organizations are inflexible and fail to adjust to changing economic needs. Traditional norms and conventions in communities have been formed slowly over many, many years. When created, these community institutions would have been appropriate social rules co-ordinating people's resource allocations in an efficient manner. However, the possibility cannot be denied that these community institutions may fail to adjust to changed resource endowments and technology, thus becoming fetters on efficient use of resources. Such adjustment lags in institutions are universal in the process of economic development (Chapter 1). It has often been argued that traditional norms and conventions, deeply rooted in people's minds, are more difficult to change than formal laws so that they are likely to become major fetters on modern economic development (North, 1994). However, it is not quite so obvious how serious the inflexibility of community institutions may be as an impediment to development.

In the history of Japan, in response to increased relative scarcity of common-property resources such as irrigation water and forests, institutions for conservation of these resources were well established at the village community level around the eighteenth century. The community-type co-operation learned through this process has provided a prototype of modern corporate management systems and interfirm co-ordination mechanism, as represented by the subcontracting system in the automobile industry. These examples seem to show the possibility that community institutions are sufficiently flexible in adjusting to changing economic needs so as to serve as an institutional basis for modern economic development. Such flexibility in community institutions is not unique to Japan but latent among developing economies, as inferred from the changes in the rice-harvesting system in the Philippines (Section 3 of this chapter).

The real danger is that the underestimation of communities' adjustment capability may result in attempts to substitute the functions of community by governmental organizations. As the deplorable consequences of state ownership of common-property resources such as forests indicate (Section 2 of this chapter), attempts to replace communities' functions with governmental agencies are likely to produce more serious failures of government rather than community.

How to combine community, market, and state in the economic system is probably the most important agenda in development economics. In finding the right combination, it is vital to understand how these three organizations are working under unique cultural and social traditions in each economy. It is indispensable to correctly identify the present role and future potential of community institutions through in-depth investigation at the grass roots.

NOTES

1. A concrete example may be the structure of corporate villages in South India, as depicted by Wade (1988), in which village councils are authorized to appoint agents for allocating irrigation water among individual farmers' fields and pro-

tecting standing crops from grazing animals, and to collect levies from beneficiaries to cover the remuneration of these agents.

2. A historical trend can also be observed that the smallholders' share of estate crop output rose as population increased and the land frontier was closed (Booth, 1988).
3. A similar process of tightening communal regulation in reponse to increased resource scarcity was found in medieval Europe. When grazing land had been abundant so that the grazing animals rarely encroached on cropland, crop rotation had been left to the decision of individual farmers. Later, when grazing land became scarce, the crop rotation schedule came to be determined according to village-wide planning so that cropland could be clearly separated from fallow land on which animals were allowed to graze (Hoffman, 1975).
4. A fascinating field study on South Indian villages by Wade (1988) also found a tendency for the community institution to tightly co-ordinate irrigation in villages located in the tail end of gravity-irrigation distributary. These villages were thus characterized by a high incidence of water shortage, so that the pay-off of coordination at the community level was high.
5. This section draws heavily on Hayami (1996a).

10

Tradition and Modernization: A Concluding Remark

As specified in the Introduction, the primary task of this book is to explore the possibility of setting low-income economies on the track of sustained economic growth, for the immediate goal of reducing poverty and the long-run goal of acquiring wealth comparable to that of developed economies.

This is indeed a difficult goal for low-income economies, as represented by those of Sub-Saharan Africa, to achieve. Developing countries' explosive population growth has caused the depletion of natural resources which traditionally supported low-income economies, resulting in increased poverty and environmental degradation. Moreover, as modern mass media conveys to poor people images of affluent living in developed economies and its simulation by a few élite in developing economies, dissatisfaction is amplified, resulting in serious social instability. People in developing economies no longer accept poverty as their destiny.

Thus, developing economies today cannot allow traditional stagnation to persist. Economic stagnation under explosive population growth means further pauperization and increasing inequality, which produce a high likelihood of social disruptions, including revolution and civil war. To avoid this crisis, developing economies need economic growth that brings improved living at a 'visible' speed. Is it possible to achieve such development with dwindling natural resources and poor capital accumulation?

10.1 Institutional Innovation for Technology Borrowing

In this apparently desperate situation, the only possible escape from poverty and stagnation would be the exploitation of the potential offered by technology borrowing. Effective borrowing of technologies developed in advanced economies is the key for late starters of industrialization to catch up with early starters. This is evident from the historical experiences of advanced economies today, as well as the dramatic rise of Asian NIEs such as Korea and Taiwan, followed by developments in South-East Asia and the coastal areas of China. As documented by Gerschenkron (1962), the later an economy's start towards industrialization, the larger the accumulation of technology borrowable by that economy is, so that the speed of its industrialization and economic growth is faster than those of early starters.

However, as Gerschenkron himself pointed out, effective technology borrowing requires institutional innovations. This relationship may be conceptualized in terms of the theoretical framework advanced in Chapter 1. The great opportunity of borrowed technology for developing economies means that the distance between old and new innovation possibility curves, as presented by I_0 to I_1 shown in Figure 1.2, is very wide. Under strong population pressure on natural resources, if developing economies that have based their production on a traditional technology (i_0) are able to adopt a new technology (i_1) appropriate for their new resource endowments along the innovation possibility frontier expanded by scientific and engineering knowledge accumulated in developed economies, they should be able to capture a major gain in cost saving, as measured by the distance between lines P_1 to P_1'. This technological innovation, represented by a move from point b to c cannot be realized unless accompanied by a major accumulation of capital (both tangible and intangible) as represented by a move from point d to point e. Capital accumulation on such a scale requires institutional innovations in various areas including taxation, financial systems, education, and research organizations.

Among many institutional innovations necessary for effective technology borrowing, Gerschenkron focused on the development of banking systems corresponding to increased capital requirements for late starters in industrialization in modern history of Europe. In general, at the beginning of industrialization, capital accumulated in the hands of entrepreneurs is small, whereas capital requirement is large for late starters to introduce advanced technology of high capital intensity from abroad. This was not a serious problem for England at the time of its Industrial Revolution from the late eighteenth to the early nineteenth century, as machines and plants were relatively small-sized, so that long-term investment in fixed capital could be financed by equity capital from the entrepreneurs' own savings and a few wealthy people's contributions. Therefore, the 'merchant banks' prevailed in England, engaging mainly in short-term production loans through discounting of bills. In contrast, a major source of finance for fixed capital investment in the industrial development of France in the mid-nineteenth century was credits from savings banks known as *Crédit Mobilier*, which collected savings from a wide range of citizens. To finance the heavy capital requirement for the spurt of industrialization in Germany in the late nineteenth century, large universal banks played a central role in converting household savings into lump-sum capital investments in large-scale industries. These banks evolved in response to high demands for long-term credits by industrialists, who themselves had little accumulation of equity capital relative to the requirement of borrowed technology (Section 6.3.3). As a means of mobilizing household savings from ordinary citizens, fixed-interest bank deposits would have been more effective than risky stock markets. As such, development of savings banks in France and universal banks in Germany were institutional innovations induced by expected high profits from borrowed technology (Chapter 1, Section 2).

It is important to recognize that these institutional innovations for the purpose of financing fixed capital for borrowing technology emerged in Western Europe within the market framework. Financial transactions including stock and credit are characterized by asymmetry of information and therefore, prone to suffering moral hazards (Stiglitz and Weiss, 1981; Stiglitz, 1989a, 1989b). The stock market in England and the credit market in France and Germany were able to develop and function as institutions to finance capital investment for modern industrial development, because moral norms and conventions on financial transactions had been accumulated in Western Europe through the experience of commercial transactions since the formation of medieval cities. Ratified by this tradition, modern laws and rules could have strong legitimacy and enforcing power.

In the absence of this commercial tradition, merchants in Czarist Russia, with its prevalence of fraud and fakery, had a strong preference for cash over credit transactions (Owen, 1981). Inevitably, Russian entrepreneurs in the late nineteenth century faced the difficulty of mobilizing through the market sufficient private funds for utilizing borrowed technology. Therefore, industrialization in Russia before the communist revolution was characterized by heavy reliance on the government budget as well as government-directed credits for financing investment in modern industries (Gerschenkron, 1962, chs. 3 and 6; Cameron *et al.*, 1967). In this regard, the Soviet system of central planning and command can be considered an extension of the Czarist system aimed at catching up with Western Europe in industrial development.

Sweeping generalization like Gerschenkron's is always hazardous in detail (Cameron *et al.*, 1967, 1972). Yet, looking at broad historical contrasts, as identified by Gerschenkron, from the model of interrelated developments in the social system (Figure 1.1), it is clear that appropriate institutional innovations are necessary for effective exploitation of borrowed technology and that forms of institutional innovation are fundamentally constrained by cultural tradition. In terms of the induced innovation model (Figure 1.2), expected profits would work as forces to induce technological and institutional innovations. However strong the inducing forces may operate, socially profitable innovations might not be realized if they are inconsistent with traditional norms deeply ingrained in people's minds.

10.2 The Experience of Japan[1]

What, then, was the system of financing fixed capital investment adopted in Japan for modern industrial development after the Meiji Restoration (1868)?

Initially, Japan borrowed an Anglo-Saxon system to rely on long-term capital finance by the stock market, as it looked attractive according to Britain's supremacy in international trade and finance in the nineteenth century. Private banks operated mainly in short-term production and trade loans, though advancement of long-term credits using companies' shares as collateral began to be practised from the early stage (Yamamura, 1972; Teranishi, 1982, ch. 3). At that time, it was not uncommon to find moral hazards by corporate executives, such as the issuing of stocks for fake companies and dressing up financial statements for raising dividends and/ or salaries (Takahashi, 1930; Okazaki and Okuno, 1993, ch. 4). Nevertheless, the stock market somehow worked as the major source of capital finance in the early phase of industrialization, presumably because of the accumulated experience of commercial and financial transactions since the middle of the Tokugawa period. The market development in eighteenth-century Japan was accompanied by formation of moral codes in business transactions.

Since its establishment in the early seventeenth century, the Tokugawa Shogunate adopted the Chu Hsi School of Confucianism, which originated in the Sung Dynasty in China. This school is called 'Neo-Confucianism', as it built a metaphysical foundation for Confucianism under the influence of Buddhism (De Bary *et al.*, 1964: 479–501). Based on a metaphysical construct of the universe, Chu Hsi philosophy rationalized the social hierarchy in the reign of an emperor in the world of Chinese civilization, who was believed to be ordained by heaven. As this philosophy was imported to Japan, it was used as an ideology to establish the legitimacy of the Tokugawa tycoon in Edo (Tokyo), who was commissioned by the emperor in Kyoto, the nation's symbolic leader similar to the Pope in medieval Europe, to rule over feudal lords, with subordinate warriors (*samurai*) governing people (mostly peasants) in each fiefdom. It was a twisted use of foreign philosophy, since the Tokugawa system, in which the emperor was deprived of any real power, was not really consistent with the authentic version of Chu Hsi philosophy in China. Recognition of this inconsistency later became the ideological basis of Meiji Restoration with which feudal fiefs were integrated into a nation-state under the emperor, when the aggression of Western powers was feared. Learning of this philosophy had been virtually monopolized by the *samurai* class in the early Tokugawa period.

In the eighteenth century, as the market economy developed during a longstanding peace, a new school of moral philosophy emerged and received support from merchants in Osaka—the commercial centre in Tokugawa Japan. There were several sects of this school. The best known was the Ishida School (*Sekimon Shingaku*) led by Baigan Ishida (1685–1744). In its logic and perspective it was an admixture of Confucianism, Buddhism, and Shintoism, but in substance it taught the same morals that Adam Smith considered to be the basis of the wealth of nations—frugality, industry, honesty, and fidelity (Yamamoto, 1992, chs. 25 and 26). Clearly this ideology was an important support for commercial and industrial development in the late Tokugawa period, as it suppressed moral hazards and reduced the costs of market transactions (Yamamoto, 1978). This ideological development may be considered to represent a case of 'induced cultural innovation'.

The role of this cultural heritage would not have been insignificant in supporting commerce and finance in the modern era after the Meiji Restoration. An example may be seen in the biography of Eiichi Shibusawa, the foremost leader of modern business in Meiji Japan. He was born the son of a prosperous peasant engaging in both farm and agribusiness activities. After working in administrative positions in both the Tokugawa and the Meiji governments, he established the first commercial bank in Japan, through which he promoted countless new business enterprises. He was an ardent admirer of Confucius, and advocated the promotion of national rather than private interests as the higher priority of business (Kaji, 1962: 254–9; Cho, 1991). Shibusawa promoted several hundred joint-stock companies as a founding board member. His reputation of having high morality is likely to have reduced the shareholders' expected loss from moral hazards in the management of the companies under his directorship and, therefore, reduced the cost of mobilizing equity capital for modern business from the stock market.

Thus, with the heritage of the cultural tradition and commercial practices from the Tokugawa era, Meiji Japan was able to simulate the Western economic system based on a free market and private entrepeneurship. For a decade after its establishment in 1869, the new Meiji government tried to establish several state enterprises for introducing modern industrial technologies. These state enterprises were largely experimental, however, as they were called 'model factories', set up for the purpose of industrial extension and demonstration. Most were quickly sold off to private concerns in the 1880s and 1890s (Minami, 1994: 24–6). Purchase of these state enterprises provided a momentum for the growth of large private conglomerates (*Zaibatsu*) such as Mitsui and Mitsubishi (Morishima, 1982: 90–4). Compared with Czarist Russia, the role of government in financing borrowed technology does not seem to have been very large in Meiji Japan.

The system of financing fixed-capital investment in Japan experienced a drastic change before and after World War II. During the war, the compelling need to concentrate large investment in military industries within a short period led to the allocation of investible funds through banks under the directive of the government. Though government control was gradually reduced after the war, the high dependency on bank credits and the low ratio of equity capital in companies' portfolios has continued to be one of the characteristics of the Japanese economy (Okazaki and Okuno, 1993; Komiya and Iwata, 1973). With much of the capital assets destroyed and the technology gap *vis-à-vis* the USA widening during the war, demands for investible funds from industries were explosive. Under such conditions banks which could mobilize savings from a wide range of households were more efficient and operational intermediaries than the stock market during the post-war recovery and the high economic growth period up to the first oil crisis in the early 1970s.

In the post-war system of capital finance, in each corporate group (*Keir-etsu*) in which enterprises are tied by long-term continuous transactions, a leading bank acts as a 'main bank' for members of the group (Aoki and Patrick, 1994). The main bank organizes the provision of syndicate loans with other banks outside the group to the in-group enterprises, while it takes full responsibility for both the pre-loan and the post-loan monitoring on borrowers. It is taken for granted that the main bank will shoulder a major portion of the default risk. If a bankrupt company is a member of the corporate group, the main bank is supposed to take responsibility for restructuring the company so that possible damage to the other banks in the syndicate as well as other firms in the corporate group having intensive transactions with this company can be minimized.

Long-term continuous transactions between the main bank and the in-group borrowers increase information and reduce the cost of monitoring credits, while the community relationship of trust and co-operation is effective in reducing moral hazards by the borrowers. The main bank also makes the maximum effort to accomplish its implicitly agreed-upon responsibility, because moral hazards in this regard (e.g. recovering its lending by utilizing insider information without paying due efforts to rescue the bankrupt company) give a bad reputation to the bank from both inside and outside the group, so that its business opportunities will diminish (Aoki, 1988, ch. 4; Okazaki and Okuno, 1993, ch. 3). Such a relationship between the main bank and member borrowers in the corporate group was effective in reducing risk and transactions costs associated with mobilization of large investible funds needed for rapid technology borrowing to close the technology gap between Japan and the USA that had widened during the war. In other words, the main bank system can be considered an institutional innovation induced by the need to reduce credit rationing due to the imperfect information characteristic of a highly dynamic economy (Stiglitz and Weiss, 1981; Aoki and Patrick, 1994, chs. 1 and 4).

Such a system was created through the shock of World War II. However, this institutional change can be viewed as a return from the market-based Anglo-Saxon system introduced at the beginning of modernization to a system more congruent with the traditional community principle in Japan. The organizational response of Japan to the war shock was rather unique. Japan's economic planning during the war was modelled on the Soviet Union in many respects. However, few attempts were made to organize small and medium enterprises into large state enterprises of the Soviet type, characterized by vertical integration from the production of raw materials up to the assembly of final products. Instead, to increase the precision of military equipment, subcontracting arrangements between small-scale part suppliers and large-scale assemblers involving technical guidance and co-operation were promoted. This organizational response to the war crisis was based probably on the common perception among economic planners and business people that, to achieve the goals of increased output and higher quality of military equipment in Japan, the subcontracting system structured according to the image of traditional community relationship would be more effective than the vertically integrated system under the command of central management.

This return to the proto-Japanese system is not limited to the corporate group formation. Although the so-called 'Japanese management system' characterized by lifetime employment, seniority wages, and company unions began to be structured during the interwar period, it was not until after World War II that this system was perfected, embracing not only white-collar but also blue-collar workers. The prototype of this system can be found in the organization of large merchants in the Tokugawa period, such as Mitsui and Sumitomo (Kitajima, 1963; Saito, 1987: 94–107). The internal organization of Japanese firms incorporating the community relationship has proved to be effective in guiding complex division of labour within modern enterprises to effective co-operation, and has contributed to improvements in both productivity and product quality, as represented by success in company-wide quality control (Abbeglen and Stalk, 1985; Imai and Komiya, 1989; Aoki and Dore, 1994).

The process by which the Japanese system of industrial organization and management has thus been created can be considered a case of the evolutionary dynamics of economic and social change. According to the theory of evolution, selection of the institutions and organizations suitable for new environments will proceed through random trial and error in response to external shocks, from a narrow feasible set determined by historical path and cultural heritage—analogous to genetic heritage in biological evolution (Alchian, 1950; Blume and Easley, 1993; Sobel, 1993; Nelson, 1995).

10.3 Multiple Paths to Economic Modernization

These institutional innovations in the modernization of Japan suggest that the organizational principles capable of supporting modern economic development are latent in the apparently premodern culture. The organization in support of industrialization in Japan is based heavily on personal relationships and relies less on explicitly stipulated laws and rules. The organization dominant in Western Europe and North America is structured on the premise that the specific rules agreed upon *ex ante* will continue to govern relations and activities uniformly within the organization. In contrast, the basic rule implicit in the organization in Japan is that the specific rules can be adjusted *ex post* according to convenience of human relationships. Relative to the Western system in which the enforcement of contracts is strongly based on formal rules (such as laws and court), there is greater reliance on personal relationships in Japan.

In her classic anthropological account, *The Chrysanthemum and the Sword* (1946), Ruth Benedict characterized Japanese culture as the 'culture of shame' in contrast to the 'culture of sin' in the West. While the sin that Westerners feel they should avoid is identified by a person as he contrasts his deeds with the commandments of an absolute being, shame is felt by a person when his behaviour is seen and gossiped about by other people.

Although the clear-cut dichotomy is somewhat artificial, there seems to be no denying that sin has a larger weight in the value system of Westerners relative to the weight of shame for the Japanese. Under the culture of shame, a personal relationship can work more effectively in enforcing contracts. It is yet to be explored how this difference in value system has been created. One tentative hypothesis may be that the strong aversion to shame or fear of social opprobrium is the sentiment long nurtured among Japanese through rice cultivation in mountainous topography, for which community-wide co-operation is indispensable especially in irrigation management.

Rooted in a different culture from the West, Japan was able to build an economic system effective for borrowing Western technology. The system's evolution has involved serious conflicts, compromises, and syntheses between the traditional value system and the imitated Western institutions and organizations. The Japanese system which thus evolved is a nexus of pseudo-community organizations. Not only does the internal organization of a firm simulate a community but, also, several firms form a corporate group under the community spirit. Further, another nexus of community is created among firms across different corporate groups by virtue of trade associations in different industries. Through the trade associations, private firms develop a nexus with governmental agencies, while the organizations of governmental agencies are also of the community type similar to private firms. The community mechanism of social opprobrium to reduce moral hazards and save transactions costs extends widely beyond a single firm through such a multi-stranded nexus.

The argument has been advanced that a condition for a modern market economy to develop is the existence of universal morality held in common by wider society beyond the small traditional community within which 'limited-group morality' based on personal relationship prevails. Because the emergence of a 'generalized morality' like that in Western Europe was a historical accident, market-based modern development is not open to many developing economies (Platteau, 1994). However, it is the limited-group morality rather than the generalized morality that controls market transactions in Japan. The multi-stranded nexus of communities enabled transmission of the community mechanism of contract enforcement (based on limited-group morality) from a single community to many other communities.

Supported by this community nexus mechanism, government's control over the market is strong in Japan, despite the relatively small size of government. Indeed, the share of government consumption in GDP in 1990 was only 9 per cent, while the other OECD members had shares higher than 10 per cent with an average of 17 per cent. In terms of central government's total expenditure including capital expenditure and transfers, Japan's 17 per cent was significantly lower than the other OECD members ranging from 20 to 40 per cent (World Bank, *World Development Report 1992*, World Development Indicators, tables 9 and 11).

The Japanese system is characterized by the ability of a relatively small government to strongly control private economic activities based on implicit agreements with firms through the community nexus such as trade associations. Because market transactions are largely controlled by the community mechanism, judicial organizations are small, representing a small burden on the government budget. In contrast, the role of the market in resource allocations is large in the West, especially in Anglo-Saxon countries. The administration of the market, such as stipulation and enforcement of laws controlling transactions, is mainly the responsibility of government. The redistribution of income for correcting the distributional consequence of market transactions is another prime responsibility of government. Relatively large budget shares of advanced market economies suggest that, in modern industrial societies characterized by highly complex division of labour, expansion in the role of the market does not necessarily result in a small government.

The problem is not which system—the Western or the Japanese—is superior. What is important is to recognize that both systems, created under different cultural traditions were successful in getting modern industrial technology to bring about high productivity and affluent living. Indeed, the traditional culture or value system is an important basis of economic modernization. However, it does not appear that the value system consistent with modernization is limited to a specific culture (such as the Protestant ethic). The success of industrialization in Japan, Korea, and Taiwan might reflect the possibility that religions and philosophies in East Asia, such as Confucianism, can also provide relevant morality for modern economic development. Further, rapid economic advance by Indonesia, Malaysia, and Thailand lends some support to the hypothesis that the principle of human organization with modernization is latent in Islam and Buddhism also.

The forms of organization of modernization are different for different cultural traditions and historical paths, as evident from the contrast between Japan and the West. Within North-East Asia, Korea and Taiwan are characterized by stronger command and more direct intervention by government than in Japan. This difference is represented by the fact that almost all formal credit is directed from state-owned banks to large conglomerates (in Korea) and to state enterprises (in Taiwan), in contrast to the Japanese approach of directing private bank credit mainly through administrative guidance and signalling along indicative plans (Section 8.4.2). The difference may to a large extent, be explained by lower capital accumulation and less developed financial intermediaries in the private sector, as well as much stronger autocracy of the militarized states in Korea and Taiwan which have been uniquely structured against possible communist aggression.

In part, however, the strong central command system in Korea might be based on the tradition of highly centralized governance structure established during the Yi dynasty supported by the authentic (or ultra-authentic) Chu Hsi philosophy (Pallais, 1975; Kim, 1987). Taiwan inherited a similar tradition, but its governance structure was influenced more directly by the perception of Sun Yat-sen (1866–1925), the founder of the Nationalist Party. Sun held that the Nationalist Party should be organized according to the Leninist model of a revolutionary vanguard in order to save the Chinese people, who had been rent into pieces (like 'sand' in his famous phrase) by recurrent foreign aggression and internal fighting among warlords since the Opium War (Huntington, 1970; Bedeski, 1981). The Japanese approach based on stable communities in which people are coagulated like clay under long domestic peace could hardly have been applicable to war-torn China suffering great social instability and uncertainty in the late nineteenth and early twentieth centuries. In fact, the Nationalist Government's inclination to organize major industries by state enterprises was consistent with Sun's advocacy of socialism in addition to nationalism and democracy in his 'Three Principles'.

Even greater differences exist between North and South-East Asia. For example, compared with Japan, Korea, and Taiwan, Thailand is characterized by relatively little control over resource allocations by government. In Thailand, 'protection of domestic manufacturing has been relatively moderate; the economy has been relatively open and trade-oriented. Foreign investment has been promoted, and the climate for foreigners has been receptive. Government has attempted relatively little dirigism in industrial investment, through either direct administration or credit allocation' (Muscat, 1994: 265). Moreover, 'for the most part, Thai governments have responded to pressures rather than attempting to shape the pattern of private-sector activity according to a technocratically predetermined set of objectives. In the Japanese and NIC models, government has played an initiating, leading, and directive role towards private investment and the evolution of the basic structural and comparative advantage characteristics of the economy' (Muscat, 1994: 5).

A part of the difference in the mode of governance between Thailand and the three North-East Asian economies might be explained by the difference between Buddhism and Confucianism. However, a more critical determinant could be the difference in traditional social structure. In premodern Japan, since at least the eighteenth century, what anthropologists call the 'tightly structured social system' had been created from the need for village communities to control the use of natural resources under strong population pressure. In contrast, in Thailand, which had been endowed with relatively abundant natural resources until very recently, a 'loosely structured social system' has been formed in which individuals' freedom is greater and people's behaviour is less strongly controlled by the community (Embree, 1950). As such, in Thailand, greater reliance on the free market mechanism could be more efficient in co-ordinating the division of labour in the industrial economy than strong government control of the Japanese type supported by tight community relationships.

Thus, similar to Japan, which was successful in developing a unique system for effective utilization of modern industrial technology, Thailand, now popularly called 'the fifth tiger', has been on the track of catching up with advanced economies by developing a unique system consistent with its cultural tradition. The same applies to several other Asian economies, such as Indonesia and Malaysia. Remember that a deep scepticism prevailed on the possibility of modernization of these Asian economies only a few decades ago.[2] Is there any strong reason to doubt that low-income economies suffering from poverty and stagnation today will be able to find their own unique systems consistent with modern economic development within their cultural and social traditions?

The task required for such a system design is not simply to adapt borrowed technology and institutions to traditionally given culture and value systems. Major efforts should also be made to change people's perception so that economically efficient technology and institution are acceptable to them. The design of an economic system endowed with economic efficiency and social legitimacy necessarily involves dialectic interactions among technology, institution, and culture, which can be realized only through trial and error by many people engaging in business and governmental activities as well as education, research, and information media. How to activate this process for effective working of the induced innovation mechanism to transform borrowed technology into economically and socially appropriate technology is the fundamental question in development economics.

This is an extremely difficult but not impossible task. The historical fact that Japan, Korea, Taiwan, and Thailand, among others, succeeded in getting on the track of sustained economic development, each based on their own unique system and tradition, strongly suggests the possibility that many low-income economies today will be able to achieve modern development in the future, not along a monolithic path, but along multiple paths according to their different traditions.

NOTES

1. This section and the next draw heavily on Hayami (1996*b*).
2. For example, Gunnar Myrdal (1968) characterized the political and social system in tropical Asia as a case in which a 'soft state' lacks the capacity to enforce rational modernization measures among people bound by traditional religion and beliefs, thus resulting in 'the resistance of that system to planned, induced changes along the lines of the modernization ideals' (p. 110).

Bibliography

Abe, T. (1990), 'Menkogyo' [Cotton Spinning Industries], in Nishikawa and Abe (1990), pp. 164–212.

Abegglen, J. C., and Stalk, G., Jr. (1985), *Kaisha: The Japanese Corporation* (New York: Basic Books).

Abramovitz, M. (1956), 'Resources and Output Trends in the United States since 1870', *American Economic Review*, 46 (Dec.) (Supplement): 5–23.

——(1986), 'Catching Up, Forging Ahead, and Falling Behind', *Journal of Economic History*, 46 (June): 385–406.

——(1993), 'The Search for the Sources of Growth: Area of Ignorance, Old and New', *Journal of Economic History*, 53 (June): 217–43.

Abreu, D. (1988), 'On the Theory of Infinitely Repeated Games with Discounting', *Econometrica*, 56 (Mar.): 383–96.

Ahluwalia, M. S. (1976), 'Income Distribution and Development: Some Stylized Facts', *American Economic Review*, 66 (May): 128–35.

Ahmad, E., and Stern, N. (1989), 'Taxation for Developing Countries', in H. Chenery and T. N. Srinivasan (eds.), *Handbook of Development Economics*, vol. 2 (Amsterdam: Elsevier), pp. 1005–92.

Ahmad, S. (1966), 'On the Theory of Induced Innovation', *Economic Journal*, 76 (June): 344–57.

Akamatsu, K. (1962), 'A Historical Pattern of Economic Growth in Developing Countries', *Developing Economies*, 1 (Mar.–Aug.): 3–25.

Akerlof, G. A. (1970), 'The Market for 'Lemons': Quality Uncertainty and the Market Mechanism', *Quarterly Journal of Economics*, 84 (Aug.): 488–500.

——(1976), 'The Economics of Caste and of the Rat Race and Other Woeful Tales', *Quarterly Journal of Economics*, 90 (Nov.): 599–617.

——(1980), 'A Theory of Social Custom, of Which Unemployment May Be One Consequence', *Quarterly Journal of Economics*, 94 (June): 749–75.

——(1984), *An Economic Theorist's Book of Tales* (Cambridge: Cambridge University Press).

Alchian, A. A. (1950), 'Uncertainty, Evolution, and Economic Theory', *Journal of Political Economy*, 58 (June): 211–21.

—— and Demsetz, H. (1973), 'The Property Rights Paradigm', *Journal of Economic History*, 33 (Mar.): 16–27.

Alesina, A., and Rodrik, D. (1994), 'Distributive Policies and Economic Growth', *Quarterly Journal of Economics*, 109 (May): 465–90.

Allen, R. C. (1992), *Enclosure and the Yeoman* (Oxford: Clarendon Press).

Amsden, A. (1989), *Asia's Next Giant: South Korea and Late Industrialization* (New York: Oxford University Press).

Anand, S., and Kanbur, S. M. R. (1993), 'Inequality and Development: A Critique', *Journal of Development Economics*, 41 (June): 19–43.

Anderson, K., and Hayami, Y., with Aurelia, G. (1986), *The Political Economy of Agricultural Protection* (Sydney: Allen & Unwin).

Aoki, M. (1988), *Information, Incentives, and Bargaining in the Japanese Economy* (Cambridge: Cambridge University Press).

—— and Dore, R. (eds.) (1994), *The Japanese Firm: Sources of Comparative Strength* (Oxford: Oxford University Press).

—— and Patrick, H. (eds.) (1994), *The Japanese Main Bank System: Its Relevance for Developing and Transforming Economies* (Oxford: Oxford University Press).

Arrow, K. J. (1963a), 'Uncertainty and the Welfare Economics of Medicare', *American Economic Review*, 53 (Dec.): 941–73.

—— (1963b), *Social Choice and Individual Values*, 2nd edn. (New York: Wiley).

—— (1974), *The Limits of Organization* (New York: Norton).

—— (1985), 'The Economics of Agency', in J. W. Pratt and R. J. Zeckhauser (eds.), *Principals and Agents: The Structure of Business* (Cambridge, Mass.: Harvard University Press), pp. 37–51.

Arthur, W. B. (1988), 'Self-reinforcing Mechanisms in Economics', in P. W. Anderson, K. Arrow, and D. Pines (eds.), *The Economy as an Evolving Complex System* (Redwood City, Calif.: Addison-Wesley), pp. 9–31.

Asanuma, B. (1985), 'Organization of Parts Purchases in Japanese Automobile Industry', *Japanese Economic Studies* 13 (Summer): 32–53.

—— (1988), 'Manufacturer-Supplier Relationships in Japan and the Concept of Relation-Specific Skill', *Journal of the Japanese and International Economy*, 3 (Mar.): 1–30.

Atkinson, A. B. (1975), *The Economics of Inequality* (Oxford: Clarendon Press).

Azam, K. M. (1973), 'The Future of the Green Revolution in West Pakistan: A Choice of Strategy', *International Journal of Agrarian Affairs*, 5 (Mar.): 404–29.

Bairoch, P. (1975), *The Economic Development of the Third World since 1900*, trans. by C. Postan (London: Methuen).

Balassa, B. (1985), 'Policy Experiments in Chile, 1973–83', in G. M. Walton (ed.), *National Economic Policies of Chile, Greenwich*, Conn.: Jai Press), pp. 203–38.

—— (1988), 'The Lessons of East Asian Development: An Overview', *Economic Development and Cultural Change*, 36 (Apr.) (Supplement): S273–90.

—— with Berlinksi, J., *et al.* (1982), *Development Strategies in Semi-Industrial Economies* (Baltimore: Johns Hopkins University Press).

Bank of Japan (1966), *Honpo Shuyo Keizai Tokei* [Hundred-Year Statistics of the Japanese Economy] (Tokyo: Bank of Japan).

Baran, P. A. (1957), *The Political Economy of Growth* (New York: Monthly Review Press).

Bardhan, P. K. (1980), 'Interlocking Factor Market and Agrarian Development: A Review of Issues', *Oxford Economic Papers*, 32 (Mar.): 82–98.

—— (1995), 'The Contributions of Endogenous Growth Theory to the Analysis of Development Problems: An Assessment', in J. Behrman and T. N. Srinivasan (eds.), *Handbook of Development Economics*, vol. 3B (Amsterdam: Elsevier), pp. 2983–98.

Barker, R. (1978), 'Barriers to Efficient Capital Investment in Agriculture', in T.W. Schultz (ed.), *Distortions of Agricultural Incentives* (Bloomington, Ind.: Indiana University Press), pp. 113–60.

Barker, R., and Herdt, R. W., with Rose, B. (1985), *The Rice Economy of Asia* (Washington, DC: Resources for the Future).

Barnum, H. N., and Squire, L. (1979), 'An Econometric Application of the Theory of the Farm-Household', *Journal of Development Economics*, 6 (Mar.): 79–102.

Barro, R. J. (1991), 'Economic Growth in a Cross-Section of Countries', *Quarterly Journal of Economics*, 106 (May): 407–43.

Basu, K., Jones, E., and Schlicht, E. (1987), 'The Growth and Decay of Custom: The Role of the New Institutional Economics in Economic History', *Explorations in Economic History*, 24 (Jan.): 1–21.

Bates, R. H. (1981), *Markets and States in Tropical Africa* (Berkeley and Los Angeles: University of California Press).

—— (1983), *Essays on the Political Economy of Rural Africa* (Cambridge: Cambridge University Press).

Baumol, W. J. (1986), 'Productivity Growth, Convergence and Welfare: What the Long-run Data Show', *American Economic Review*, 76 (Dec.): 1072–85.

Becker, G. S. (1974), 'A Theory of Social Interactions', *Journal of Political Economy*, 82 (Nov.–Dec.): 1063–93.

—— (1976), *The Economic Approach to Human Behavior* (Chicago: University of Chicago Press).

Bedeski, R. E. (1981), *State Building in Modern China: The Kuomintang in the Prewar Period* (Berkeley and Los Angeles: Institute of East Asian Studies, University of California).

Behrman, J. R., and A. B. Deolalikar (1989), 'Agricultural Wages in India: The Role of Health, Nutrition and Seasonality', in D. E. Sahn (ed.), *Seasonal Variability in Third World Agriculture* (Baltimore: Johns Hopkins University Press), pp. 107–17.

Bell, C. (1988), 'Credit Markets and Interlinked Transactions', in H. Chenery and T. N. Srinivasan (eds.), *Handbook of Development Economics*, vol. 1 (Amsterdam: North-Holland), pp. 763–830.

Bell, D. (1973), *The Coming of Post-Industrial Society* (New York: Basic Books).

Benedict, R. (1946), *The Crysanthemum and the Sword: Patterns of Japanese Culture* (Boston: Houghton Mifflin).

Berelson, B. (1974), *World Population: Status Report 1974* (New York: Population Council).

Bernsten, R. H., Siwi, B. H., and Beachell, H. M. (1981), 'Development and Diffusion of Rice Varieties in Indonesia', Paper presented at the International Rice Research Conference, IRRI, Los Baños, Philippines, photocopy.

Besley, T. (1995), 'Savings, Credit and Insurance', in J. Behrman and T. N. Srinivasan (eds.), *Handbook of Development Economics*, vol. 3A (Amsterdam: North-Holland), pp. 2123–207.

Bhagwati, J. (1978), *Anatomy and Consequences of Exchange Control Regimes* (Cambridge, Mass.: Ballinger).

Bicanic, R. (1962), 'The Threshold of Economic Growth', *Kyklos*, 15 (l): 7–27.

Binswanger, H. P. (1991), 'Brazilian Policies That Encourage Deforestation in the Amazon', *World Development*, 19 (July): 821–9.

—— and Rosenzweig, M. R. (1986), 'Behavioral and Material Determinants of Production Relations in Agriculture', *Journal of Development Studies*, 22 (Apr.): 503–39.

—— Delinger, K., and Feder, G. (1995), 'Power, Distortions, Revolt and Reform in Agricultural Land Relations', in J. Behrman and T. N. Srinivasan (eds.), *Handbook of Development Economics, vol.* 3B, (Amsterdam: North-Holland), pp. 2658–772.

Bird, R. M. (1974), *Taxing Agricultural Land in Developing Countries* (Cambridge, Mass.: Harvard University Press).

Birdsall, N. (1988), 'Economic Approaches to Population Growth', in H. Chenery and T. N. Srinivasan (eds.), *Handbook of Development Economics, vol.* 1 (Amsterdam: North-Holland), pp. 477–542.

—— Ross, D., and Sabot, R. (1995), 'Inequality and Growth Reconsidered: Lessons from East Asia', *World Bank Economic Review*, 9 (Sept.): 477–508.

Blume, L. E., and Easley, D. (1993), 'Economic Natural Selection', *Economics Letters*, 42 (2–3): 281–9.

Boeke, J. H. (1953), *Economics and Economic Policy of Dual Societies as Exemplified by Indonesia* (New York: Institute of Pacific Relations).

Booth, A. (1988), *Agricultural Development in Indonesia* (Sydney: Allen & Unwin).

Boserup, E. (1965), *The Conditions of Agricultural Growth* (Chicago: Aldine).

Breton, A. (1974), *The Economic Theory of Representative Government* (Chicago: Aldine).

Brewster, J. M. (1950), 'The Machine Process in Agriculture and Industry', *Journal of Farm Economics*, 32 (Feb.): 69–81.

Brittan, S. (1977), *The Economic Consequences of Democracy* (London: Temple Smith).

Brown, L. R., and Kane, H. (1994), *Full House: Reassessing the Earth's Population Carrying Capacity* (New York: Norton).

Buchanan, J. M., and Tullock, G. (1962), *The Calculus of Consent: Logical Foundations of Constitutional Democracy* (Ann Arbor: University of Michigan Press).

—— and Wagner, R. E. (1977), *Democracy in Deficit: The Political Legacy of Lord Keynes* (New York: Academic Press).

Cain, M. (1981), 'Risk and Insurance: Perspectives on Fertility and Agrarian Change in India and Bangladesh', *Population and Development Review*, 7 (Sept.): 435–74.

Cairncross, F. (1991), *Costing the Earth* (London: Business Books).

Cameron, R. (ed.) (1972), *Banking and Economic Development: Some Lessons of History* (New York: Oxford University Press).

—— with Crisp, O., Patrick, H., and Tilly, R. (1967), *Banking in the Early Stages of Industrialization* (New York: Oxford University Press).

Cardoso, E. A., and Helwege, A. (1992), *Latin America's Economy* (Cambridge, Mass.: MIT Press).

Cassen, R. H. (1978), *India: Population, Economy, Society* (London: Macmillan).

Caves, R. E., Frankel, J. A., and Jones, R. W. (1993), *World Trade and Payments: An Introduction*, 6th edn. (New York: HarperCollins).

Chambers, J. D., and Mingay, G. E. (1966), *The Agricultural Revolution, 1750–1880* (New York: Schocken Books).

Chayanov, A. V. (1966; original publication 1925), *Theory of Peasant Economy*, ed. D. Thorner *et al.* (Homewood, Ill.: Richard D. Irwin).

Cheung, Steven N. S. (1969), *The Theory of Share Tenancy* (Chicago: University of Chicago Press).

Childe, V. G. (1928), *The Most Ancient East* (London: Kegan Paul, Trench, Trubner).

Cho, Y. (1991), 'Jukyo to Shihonshugi no Kakawari' [Relationship between Confucianism and Capitalism], in Mizoguchi and Nakajima (1991), pp. 121–35.

Chowdhury, A., and Islam, I. (1993), *The Newly Industrializing Economies of East Asia* (London: Routledge).

Christensen, L. R., and Jorgenson, D. W. (1970), 'U. S. Real Product and Real Factor Input, 1929–1967', *Review of Income and Wealth*, 16 (Mar.): 19–50.

Clark, C. (1940), *The Conditions of Economic Progress* London: Macmillan.

Coase, R. H. (1937), 'The Nature of Firm', *Economica*, NS 4 (Nov.): 386–405.

——— (1960), 'The Problem of Social Cost', *Journal of Law and Economics*, 3 (October): 1–44.

Cole, D. C., and Park, Y. C. (1983), *Financial Development in Korea, 1945–1978* (Cambridge, Mass.: Harvard University Press).

Collier, W., Wiradi, G., and Soentoro (1973), 'Recent Changes in Rice Harvesting Methods', *Bulletin of Indonesian Economic Studies* 19 (July): 36–45.

Corbo, V., and Fischer, S. (1995), 'Structural Adjustment, Stabilization and Policy Reform: Domestic and International Finance', in J. Behrman and T. N. Srinivasan (eds.), *Handbook of Development Economics*, vol. 3B (Amsterdam: Elsevier), pp. 2845–924.

Corden, W. M., and Neary, P. J. (1982), 'Booming Sector and De-industrialization in a Small Open Economy', *Economic Journal*, 92 (Dec.): 825–48.

Council on Environmental Quality and U. S. Department of State (1980), *Global 2000 Report to the President* (Washington, DC: US Government Printing Office).

Crookes, W. (1899), *The Wheat Problem* (London: J. Murray).

Cukierman, A., Edwards, S., and Tabellini, G. (1992), 'Seigniorage and Political Instability', *American Economic Review*, 82 (June): 537–55.

Dalrymple, D. G. (1986), *Development and Spread of High-Yielding Rice Varieties in Developing Countries* (Washington, DC: US Agency for International Development).

Dasgupta, P. (1988), 'Trust as a Commodity', in D. Gambetta (ed.), *Trust: Making and Breaking Cooperative Relations* (Oxford: Blackwell), pp. 49–72.

——— (1993), *An Inquiry into Well-Being and Destitution* (Oxford: Clarendon Press).

——— and K. G. Mäler (1995), 'Poverty, Institutions, and the Environmental Resource Base', in J. Behrman and T. N. Srinivasan (eds.), *Handbook of Development Economics*, vol. 3A (Amsterdam: Elsevier), pp. 2371–463.

David, C. C., and Otsuka, K. (eds.) (1994), *Modern Rice Technology and Income Distribution in Asia* (Boulder, Colo.: Lynne Rienner).

David, P. A. (1985), 'Clio and the Economics of QWERTY', *American Economic Review*, 75 (May): 332–7.

Davis, L., and North, D. C. (1970), 'Institutional Change and American Economic Growth: A First Step towards a Theory of Institutional Innovation', *Journal of Economic History*, 30 (Mar.): 131–49.

De Bary, Wm. T., Wing-Tsit Chang, and Watson, B. (comp.) (1964), *Sources of Chinese Tradition* (New York: Columbia University Press).

Demsetz, H. (1967), 'Toward a Theory of Property Rights', *American Economic Review*, 57 (May) (Supplement): 347–59.

Denison, E. F. (1962), *The Sources of Economic Growth in the United States and the Alternatives before Us* (New York: Committee for Economic Development).

—— (1967), *Why Growth Rates Differ*: Post-War Experience in Nine Western Countries (Washington, DC: Brookings Institution).

—— and Chung, W. K. (1976), 'Economic Growth and its Sources', in H. Patrick and H. Rosovsky (eds.), *Asia's New Giant* (Washington, DC: Brookings Institution), pp. 63–151.

De Soto, H. (1989), *The Other Path*, trans. J. Abott (New York: Harper & Row).

Desai, P. (1976), 'The Production Function and Technical Change in Post-war Soviet Industry: A Reexamination', *American Economic Review*, 66 (June): 372–81.

Domar, E. (1946), 'Capital Expansion, Rate of Growth, and Employment', *Econometrica*, 14 (Apr.): 137–47.

Dore, R. (1973), *British Factory-Japanese Factory: The Origins of National Diversity in Industrial Relations* (Berkeley and Los Angeles: University of California Press).

Dorner, P. (1972), *Land Reform and Economic Development* (Harmondsworth: Penguin).

Downs, A. (1957), *An Economic Theory of Democracy* (New York: Harper).

Easterlin, R. A. (1975), 'An Economic Framework for Fertility Analysis', *Studies of Economic Planning*, 6: 54–63.

Easterly, W., and Fischer, S. (1994), *The Soviet Economic Decline: Historical and Republican Data*, Policy Research Working Paper 1284 (Washington, DC: World Bank).

Economic Intelligence Service (1990), *Basic Statistics Relating to the Indian Economy*, vol.1: *All India*, Aug. (Bombay).

Ekelund, R. B. and Tollison, R. D. (1981), *Mercantilism as a Rent-Seeking Society: Economic Regulation in Historical Perspective* (College Station, Tex.: Texas A & M University Press).

Embree, J. F. (1950), 'Thailand—A Loosely Structured Social System', *American Anthropologist* 52 (Apr.–June): 181–93.

Engels, F. (1953; original publication 1884), *Der Ursprung der Familie, des Privateigentums und des Staats* [Origins of the Family, Private Property, and the State] (Berlin: Dietz).

Evenson, R., and Westphal, L. E. (1995), 'Technological Change and Technology Strategy', in J. Behrman and T. N. Srinivasan (eds.), *Handbook of Development Economics*, vol. 3A (Amsterdam: Elsevier), pp. 2209–99.

Fallows, J. (1989), 'Containing Japan', *The Atlantic*, 263: 40–54.

Fei, J. C. H., and Ranis, G. (1964), *Development of the Labor Surplus Economy* (Homewood, Ill.: Irwin).

Fellner, W. (1961), 'Two Propositions in the Theory of Induced Innovations', *Economic Journal*, 71 (June): 305–8.

Fernandez, R., and Rodrik, D. (1991), 'Resistance to Reform: Status Quo Bias in the Presence of Individual-Specific Uncertainty', *American Economic Review*, 81 (Dec.): 1146–55.

Fields, G. S. (1980), *Poverty, Inequality, and Development*, (Cambridge: Cambridge University Press).

—— (1995), 'The Kuznets Curve: A Good Idea but...', Paper presented at the American Economic Association Annual Meeting, Washington, DC, Jan. 6–8, photocopy.

—— and Wan, Jr. H. (1989), 'Wage Setting Institutions and Economic Growth', *World Development*, 17 (Sept.): 1471–1483.

Food and Agriculture Organization of the United Nations (FAO) (1993), *Agriculture Towards 2010* (Rome).
—— (FAO), *Production Yearbook*, annual issues (Rome).
Food and Agriculture Organization and World Health Organization (FAO/WHO) (1992), *Nutrition and Development: A Global Assessement* (Rome).
Foster, A. D., and Rosenzweig, M. R. (1993), 'A Test for Moral Hazard in the Labor Market: Contractual Arrangements, Effort, and Health', *Review of Economics and Statistics*, 76 (May): 213–27.
Francks, P. (1992), *Japanese Economic Development: Theory and Practice* (London: Routledge).
Frank, A. G. (1967), *Capitalism and Underdevelopment in Latin America: Historical Studies of Chile and Brazil* (New York: Monthly Review Press).
Friedman, M. (1957), *A Theory of the Consumption Function* (Princeton: Princeton University Press).
Fudenberg, D., and Maskin, E. (1986), 'The Folk Theorem in Repeated Games with Discounting or with Incomplete Information', *Econometrica*, 54 (May): 533–54.
Fukushima, M. (1970), *Chiso Kaisei no Kenkyu* [Study of the Land Tax Revision] (Tokyo: Yuhikaku).
Furtado, C. (1963), *The Economic Growth of Brazil* (Berkeley and Los Angeles: University of California Press).
Garrity, D. (1993), 'Sustainable Land-Use Systems for Sloping Uplands in Southeast Asia', in *Technologies for Sustainable Agriculture in the Tropics*, ASA Special Publication no. 56 (Madison: Crops Science Society of America and Soil Science Society of America), pp. 41–65.
Geertz, C. (1978), 'The Bazaar Economy: Information and Search in Peasant Marketing', *American Economic Review*, 68 (May): 28–32.
Gelb, A., and associates (1988), *Oil Windfalls: Blessing or Curse?* (New York: Oxford University Press).
Gerschenkron, A. (1943), *Bread and Democracy in Germany* (Berkeley and Los Angeles: University of California Press).
—— (1962), *Economic Backwardness in Historical Perspective* (Cambridge, Mass.: Harvard University Press).
Gibbons, R. (1992), *Game Theory for Applied Economists* (Princeton: Princeton University Press).
Gillis, M., Perkins, D. H., Roemer, M., and Snodgrass, D. R. (1992), *Economics of Development*, 3rd edn. (New York: W. W. Norton)
Government of India. Ministry of Information and Broadcasting, Research and Reference Division (1994), *India 1993: A Reference Annual* (Delhi: Publications Division, Ministry of Information and Broadcasting).
Greif, A. (1989), 'Reputation and Coalitions in Medieval Trade: Evidence on the Maghribi Traders', *Journal of Economic History*, 49 (Dec.): 857–82.
—— (1993), 'Contract Enforceability and Economic Institutions in Early Trade: The Maghribi Traders' Coalition', *American Economic Review*, 83 (June): 525–48.
—— Milgrom, P., and Weingast, B. R. (1994), 'Coordination, Commitment, and Enforcement: The Case of the Merchant Guild', *Journal of Political Economy*, 102 (Aug.): 745–76.
Griffin, K. B. (1974), *The Political Economy of Agrarian Change: An Essay on the Green Revolution* (Cambridge, Mass.: Harvard University Press).

Griffith, G. T. (1926), *Population Problems of the Age of Malthus* (Cambridge: Cambridge University Press).

Grossman, G. M., and Helpman, E. (1991), *Innovation and Growth in the Global Economy*, trans. by R. W. de Aguilar and E. C. Drysdale (Cambridge, Mass.: M.I.T. Press).

—— and Krueger, A. B. (1994), 'Economic Growth and the Environment', NBER Working Paper, no. 4634 (Cambridge, Mass.: National Bureau of Economic Research).

Haddad, L. J., and Bouis, H. E. (1991), 'The Impact of Nutritional Status on Agricultural Productivity: Wage Evidence from the Philippines', *Oxford Bulletin of Economics and Statistics*, 53 (Feb.): 45–68.

Hannesson, R. (1991), 'From Common Fish to Rights Based Fishing: Fisheries Management and the Evolution of Exclusive Rights to Fish', *European Economic Review*, 35 (Apr.): 397–407.

Hardin, G. (1968), 'The Tragedy of the Commons', *Science*, 164: 1243–48.

Harrod, R. F. (1948), *Towards a Dynamic Economics: Some Recent Developments of Economic Theory and Their Application to Policy* (London: Macmillan).

Harris, J. R., and Todaro, M. P. (1970), 'Migration, Employment and Development: A Two-Sector Analysis', *American Economic Review*, 60 (Mar.): 126–42.

Hart, O. and Holmstrom, B. (1987), 'The Theory of Contracts', in T. Bewley (ed.), *Advances in Economic Theory* (Cambridge: Cambridge University Press), pp. 71–155.

Hashimoto, M. (1994), 'Development and Environment Problem', *Asian Economic Journal*, 8 (Mar.): 115–45.

Hayami, A. (1992), *Kinsei Nobichiho no Jinko Keizai Shakai* [Population, Economy and Society in the Nobi District in the Late Tokugawa Era] (Tokyo: Sobunsha).

Hayami, Y. (1981), 'Induced Innovation, Green Revolution, and Income Distribution: Comment', *Economic Development and Cultural Change*, 30 (Oct.): 169–76.

—— (1988), *Japanese Agriculture under Siege* (New York: St Martin's Press).

—— (1989), 'Community, Market, and State', The Elmhirst Memorial Lecture at the 20th International Agricultural Conference of Agricultural Economists, in A. Maunder and A. Valdes (eds.), *Agriculture and Governments in an Interdependent World* (Aldershot: Gower), pp. 3–14.

—— (1992), 'Agricultural Innovation, Economic Growth and Equity: A Critique of Michael Lipton, *Southeast Asian Journal of Agricultural Economics*, 1 (June): 1–9.

—— (1994), 'Peasant and Plantation in Asia', in G. M. Meier (ed.), *From Classical Economics to Development Economics* (New York: St Martin's Press), pp.121–34.

—— (1995), 'Japan in the New World Confrontation: A Historical Perspective', *Japanese Economic Review*, 46 (Dec.): 351–7.

—— (1996a), 'Community Mechanism of Employment and Wage Determination: Classical or Neoclassical?', Paper prepared for the Gustav Ranis Festschrift Conference (New Haven), 10–11 May.

—— (1996b), 'Toward an East Asian Model of Economic Development', Paper prepared for the IEA Round Table Conference on the Institutional Foundation of Economic Development in East Asia (Tokyo), 16–19 Dec.

—— (forthcoming), 'A Commentary on the Asian Miracle: Are There Lessons to be Learned?' *Journal of Japanese and International Economics*.

Hayami, Y., and Kawagoe, T. (1993), *The Agrarian Origins of Commerce and Industry: A Study of Peasant Marketing in Indonesia* (New York: St Martin's Press).

—— and Kikuchi, M. (1981), *Asian Village Economy at the Crossroads: An Economic Approach to Institutional Change* (Baltimore: Johns Hopkins University Press).

—— and Ogasahara, J. (1995), 'The Kuznets versus the Marx Pattern in Modern Economic Growth: A Perspective from the Japanese Experience', Department of Agricultural, Resource and Management Economics Working Paper, no. WP 95–13 (Ithaca, NY: ARME, Cornell University).

—— and Otsuka, K. (1993) *The Economics of Contract Choice: An Agrarian Perspective* (Oxford: Clarendon Press).

—— Quisumbing, Ma. A. R., and Adriano, L. S. (1990), *Toward an Alternative Land Reform Paradigm: A Philippine Perspective* (Quezon City: Ateneo de Manila University Press).

—— and Ruttan, V. W. (1985), *Agricultural Development: An International Perspective*, rev. edn. (Baltimore: Johns Hopkins University Press).

—— and Yamada, S., with Akino, M., *et al.* (1991), *The Agricultural Development of Japan* (Tokyo: University of Tokyo Press).

Hayek, F. A. von. (ed.), (1935) *Collectivist Economic Planning: Critical Studies on the Possibilities of Socialism* (London: Routledge & Sons).

Heer, D. M. (1972), 'Economic Development and the Fertility Transition', in D. V. Glass and R. Revelle (eds.), *Population and Social Change* (London: Edward Arnold), pp. 99–114.

Herdt, R. W., and Capule, C. (1983), *Adoption, Spread, and Production Impact of Modern Rice Varieties in Asia* (Los Baños, Laguna, Philippines: International Rice Research Institute).

Herring, R. J. (1983), *Land to the Tiller: The Political Economy of Agrarian Reforms in South Asia* (New Haven Yale University Press).

Hicks, J. R. (1932), *The Theory of Wages* (London: Macmillan).

—— (1960), *The Social Framework: An Introduction to Economics*, 3rd edn. (Oxford : Clarendon Press).

Hirschman, A. O. (1958), *The Strategy of Economic Development* (New Haven: Yale University Press).

—— (1970), *Exit, Voice and Loyalty: Responses to Decline in Firms, Organizations, and States* (Cambridge Mass.: Harvard University Press).

Hla Myint, U. (1965), *The Economics of the Developing Countries* (New York: Praeger).

—— (1971), *Economic Theory and the Underdeveloped Countries* (New York: Oxford University Press).

Ho, Ping-ti (1956), 'Early Maturing Rice in Chinese History', *Economic History Review*, ser. 9 (Dec.): 214–15.

Ho, S. P. S. (1979), 'Decentralized Industrialization and Rural Development: Evidence from Taiwan', *Economic Development and Cultural Change*, 28 (Oct.): 77–96.

—— (1982), 'Economic Development and Rural Industry in South Korea and Taiwan', *World Development*, 10 (Nov.): 973–90.

Hoffman, R. (1975), 'Medieval Origins of the Common Fields', in W. N. Parker and E. L. Jones (eds.), *European Peasants and their Markets: Essays in Agrarian Economic History* (Princeton, N.J.: Princeton University Press), pp. 23–71.

Hopper, D. (1965), 'Allocation Efficiency in a Traditional Indian Agriculture', *Journal of Farm Economics*, 47 (Aug.): 611–24.

Hosono, A., and Tsunekawa, K. (1986), *Latin America Kiki no Kozu* [Structure of Crisis in Latin America] (Tokyo: Yuhikaku).

Huntington, S. P. (1970), 'Social and Institutional Dynamics of One-Party System' in S. P. Huntington and C. H. Moore (eds.), *Authoritarian Politics in Modern Society* (New York: Basic Books), pp. 3–47.

Imai, J. (1991), 'Chile Keizai no Genjo to Kadai' [Present Situation and Future Problems of Chilean Economy], *Kikin Chosakiho* [Overseas Economic Cooperation Fund], 72 (Nov.): 22–33.

Imai, K., and Komiya, R. (1989), *Nihon no Kigyo* [Firms in Japan] (Tokyo: University of Tokyo Press).

Innis, H. A. (1933), *Problems of Staple Production in Canada* (Toronto: Ryerson Press).

International Labour Office (ILO), *Yearbook of Labour Statistics*. Annual issues (Geneva).

International Rice Research Institute (IRRI) (1978), *Interpretative Analysis of Selected Papers from Changes in Rice Farming in Selected Areas of Asia* (Los Baños, Laguna, Philippines).

Ishikawa, S. (1994), 'Kozo Chosei–Segin Hoshiki no Saikento' [Structural Adjustment: A Reassessment of the World Bank Approach], *Ajia Keizai* [Institute of Developing Economies], 35 (Nov.): 2–32.

Japan Ministry of Agriculture and Forestry (1974), *Nogyo Ruinen Tokei Hyo* [Historical Statistics of Agricultural Economy], vol. 4 (Tokyo: Norin Tokei Kyokai).

Japan Ministry of Education (1962), *Nihon no Seicho to Kyoiku* [Economic Growth and Education in Japan] (Tokyo).

Japan Science and Technology Agency, *White Paper on Science and Technology*. Annual issues (Tokyo).

Jimenez, E. (1995), 'Human and Physical Infrastructure: Public Investment and Pricing Policies in Developing Countries', in J. Behrman and T. N. Srinivasan (eds.), *Handbook of Development Economics*, vol. 3B (Amsterdam: Elsevier), pp. 2773–843.

Johnson, C. A. (1982), *MITI and the Japanese Miracle: The Growth of Industrial Policy, 1925–1975* (Stanford, Calif.: Stanford University Press).

Johnson, N. L., and Ruttan, V. W. (1994), 'Why are Farms So Small?' *World Development*, 22 (May): 691–706.

Johnston, B. F., and Kilby, P. (1975), *Agriculture and Structural Transformation: Economic Strategies in Late-Developing Countries* (New York: Oxford University Press).

Jorgenson, D. W. (1961), 'The Development of a Dual Economy', *Economic Journal*, 71 (June): 309–34.

——and Griliches, Z. (1969), 'The Explanation of Productivity Change', *Review of Economic Studies*, 34 (July): 249–83.

————and Dennison, E. F. (1972), *The Measurement of Productivity: An Exchange of Views between Dale W. Jorgenson and Zvi Griliches and Edward F. Dennison*, repr. no. 244 (Washington, DC: Brookings Institution).

Kaji, N. (ed.) (1962), *Rongo no Sekai* [The World of Confucius' Analects] (Tokyo: Iwanami Shoten).

Kaldor, N. (1961), 'Capital Accumulation and Economic Growth', in F. A. Lutz and D. C. Hague (eds.), *The Theory of Capital* (News York: St Martin's Press), pp. 177–222.

Kao, C. H. C., Anschel, K. R. and Eicher, C. K. (1964), 'Disguised Unemployment in Agriculture: A Survey', in C. K. Eicher and L. W. Witt (eds.), *Agriculture in Economic Development* (New York: McGraw Hill), pp. 129–44. .

Kikuchi, M., and Hayami, Y. (1985), 'Agricultural Growth against a Land Resource Constraint: Japan, Taiwan, Korea, and the Philippines', in K. Ohkawa and G. Ranis (eds.), *Japan and the Developing Countries: Comparative Analysis* (Oxford: Blackwell), pp. 67–90.

Kim, Il-Gon (1987), *Jukyo Bunkaken no Chitsujo to Keizai* [Order and Economy in the Confucian Culture Zone] (Nagoya: University of Nagoya, Department of Economics).

Kim, Jong-Il, and Lau, L. J. (1994), 'The Sources of Economic Growth of the East Asian Newly Industrialized Countries', *Journal of the Japanese and International Economy*, 8 (Sept.): 235–71.

Kirk, D. (1968), 'The Field of Demography', in *International Encyclopedia of the Social Sciences*, vol. 11 (New York: Macmillan), pp. 342–49.

Koguro, K., and Kohama, H. (1995), *Indonesia Keizai Nyumon* [Introduction to Indonesian Economy] (Tokyo: Nihon Keizai Hyoronsha).

Kitajima, M. (ed.) (1963), *Edo Shogyo to Iseten* [Commerce in Edo and a Merchant House in Ise] (Tokyo: Yoshikawa Kobunkan).

Kohama, H. (1995), 'Latin America Shokoku no Keizai Kaikaku' [Economic Reform in Latin American Countries], in S. Urata (ed.), *Boeki Jiyuka to Keizai Hatten* [Trade Liberalization and Economic Development] (Tokyo: Institute of Developing Economies), pp. 263–89.

——and Yanagihara, T. (eds.) (1995), *Higashi Ajia no Kozo Chosei* [Structural Adjustments in East Asia] (Tokyo: Nihon Boeki Shinkokai).

Komiya, R. (1975), *Gendai Nihon Keizai Kenkyu* [Study of the Modern Japanese Economy] (Tokyo: University of Tokyo Press).

——and Iwata, K. (1973), *Kinyu no Riron* [Theory of Finance] (Tokyo: Nihon Keizai Shinbunsha).

——Okuno, M., and Suzumura, K. (eds.) (1984), *Nihon no Sangyo Seisaku* [Industrial Policy in Japan] (Tokyo: University of Tokyo Press).

Kornai, J. (1980), *Economics of Shortage*, 2 vols. (Amsterdam: North-Holland).

Kosai, Y. (1989), 'Kodoseichoki no Keizai Seisaku' [Economic Policies in the Era of High Economic Growth], in Y. Yasuba and T. Inoki (eds.), *Nihon Keizaishi* [Economic History of Japan], vol. 8: *Kodoseicho* [High Economic Growth] (Tokyo: Iwanami Shoten).

Kreps, D. D., and Wilson, R. (1982), 'Reputation and Imperfect Information', *Journal of Economic Theory*, 27 (Aug.): 253–79.

Krueger, A. O. (1974), 'The Political Economy of the Rent-Seeking Society', *American Economic Review*, 64 (June): 291–303.

——(1978), *Liberalization Attempts and Consequences*, in *Foreign Trade Regimes and Economic Development*, vol. 10 (Cambridge, Mass.: Ballinger).

——(1990), 'Asian Trade and Growth Lessons', *American Economic Review*, 80 (May): 108–12.

——(1991) *A Synthesis of the Economics in Developing Countries*, vol. 4 of A. O. Krueger, M. Schiff, and A. Valdes (eds.), *The Political Economy of Agricultural Pricing Policy* (Baltimore: Johns Hopkins University Press).

—— (1995), 'Policy Lessons from Development Experience Since the Second World War', in J. Behrman and T. N. Srinivasan (eds.), *Handbook of Development Economics*, vol. 3B (Amsterdam: Elsevier), pp. 2497–550.

—— Schiff, M., and Valdes, A. (eds.) (1991), *Political Economy of Agricultural Pricing Policies*, 5 vols. (Baltimore: Johns Hopkins University Press).

Krugman, P. R. (1987), 'The Narrow Moving Band, the Dutch Disease and the Competitive Consequences of Mrs Thatcher', *Journal of Development Economics*, 27 (Oct.): 41–55.

—— (1991), 'History versus Expectations', *Quarterly Journal of Economics*, 106 (May): 651–67.

—— (1994), 'The Myth of Asia's Miracle', *Foreign Affairs* 73 (Nov./Dec.): 62–78.

—— and Obstfed, M. (1994), *International Economics: Theory and Policy*, 3rd. edn. (New York: HarperCollins).

Kush, G. S. (1995), 'Breaking the Yield Frontier of Rice', *Geojournal*, vol. 35 (3): 329–32.

Kuznets, P. W. (1988), 'An East Asian Model of Economic Development: Japan, Taiwan, and South Korea', *Economic Development and Cultural Change*, 36 (Apr.) (Supplement): S11–44.

Kuznets, S. (1955), 'Economic Growth and Income Inequality', *American Economic Review*, 45 (Mar.): 1–28.

—— (1966), *Modern Economic Growth: Rate, Structure and Spread* (New Haven: Yale University Press).

—— (1971), *Economic Growth of Nations: Total Output and Production Structure* (Cambridge, Mass.: Harvard University Press).

Ladejinsky, W. (1977), *Agrarian Reform as Unfinished Business: The Selected Essays of Wolf Ladejinsky*, ed. L. J. Walinsky (New York: Oxford University Press).

Laffont, J. J., and Tirole, J. (1991), 'The Politics of Government Decision Making: A Theory of Regulatory Capture', *Quarterly Journal of Economics*, 106 (Nov.): 1089–127.

Lambert, P. J. (1993), *The Distribution and Redistribution of Income: A Mathematical Analysis*. 2nd edn. (Manchester: Manchester University Press).

Landes, D. S. (1965), 'Technological Change and Development in Western Europe, 1750–1914', in J. K. Habakkuk and M. Postan (eds.), *The Cambridge History of Europe*, vol. 6, p. I, *The Industrial Revolutions and After* (Cambridge: Cambridge University Press), pp. 274–601.

—— (1969), *The Unbound Prometheus: Technological Change and Industrial Development in Western Europe from 1750 to the Present* (Cambridge: Cambridge University Press).

Lange, O. (1938), 'On the Economic Theory of Socialism', in B. E. Lippincott (ed.), *On the Economic Theory of Socialism* (Minneapolis: University of Minnesota Press), pp. 57–143.

Leibenstein, H. (1954), *A Theory of Economic-Demographic Development* (Princeton: Princeton University Press).

—— (1957), *Economic Backwardness and Economic Growth, Studies in the Theory of Economic Development* (New York: Wiley).

Lenin, V. I. (1960; original publication 1899), *The Development of Capitalism in Russia: The Process of Formation of a Home Market for Large-Scale Industry*, in Lenin, *Collected Works*, vol. 3, 4th edn. (Moscow: Foreign Language Publishing House), pp. 23–607.

Levine, D. (1978), 'Some Competing Models of Population Growth during the First Industrial Revolution', *Journal of European Economic History*, vol. 7 (2–3), pp. 499–516.

Lewis, H. T. (1971), *Ilocano Rice Farmers: A Comparative Study of Two Philippine Barrios* (Honolulu: University Press of Hawaii).

Lewis, Jr., S. (1989), 'Primary Exporting Countries', in H. Chenery and T. N. Srinivasan (eds.), *Handbook of Development Economics*, vol. 2 (Amsterdam: Elsevier), pp.1541–99.

Lewis, W. A. (1954), 'Economic Development with Unlimited Supplies of Labor', *Manchester School of Economic and Social Studies*, 22 (May): 139–91.

—— (ed.) (1970), *Tropical Development, 1880–1913: Studies in Economic Progress* (London: Allen & Unwin).

Lin, J. Y. (1988), 'The Household Responsibility System in China's Agricultural Reform: A Theoretical and Empirical Study', *Economic Development and Cultural Change*, 36 (Apr.) 199–224

—— (1992), 'Rural Reforms and Agricultural Growth in China', *American Economic Review*, 82 (Mar.): 34–51.

—— and Nugent, J. B. (1995), 'Institutions and Economic Development', in J. Behrman and T. N. Srinivasan (eds.), *Handbook of Development Economics*, vol. 3A (Amsterdam: Elsevier), pp. 2301–370.

Lipton, M. (1976), *Why Poor People Stay Poor: Urban Bias in World Development* (London: Temple Smith).

—— and Longhurst, R. (1989), *New Seeds and Poor People* (London: Unwin Hyman).

List, F. (1930; original publication 1841), *Das Nationale System der Politischen Ökonomie* [The National System of Political Economy], vol. 6 of List, *Schriften, Reden, Briefe*, ed. Artur Sommer (Berlin: Reimar Hobbing).

—— (1827), *Outlines of American Political Economy* (Philadelphia: S. Parker).

Little, I. M. D., *et al.* (1993), *Boom, Crisis, and Adjustment: The Macroeconomic Experience of Developing Countries* (Oxford: Oxford University Press).

—— Scitovsky, T., and Scott, M. (1970), *Industry and Trade in Some Developing Countries* (Oxford: Oxford University Press).

Luce, R. D., and Raiffa, H. (1957), *Games and Decisions* (New York: Wiley).

Lucas, R. E., Jr. (1988), 'On the Mechanics of Economic Development', *Journal of Monetary Economics*, 22 (July): 3–42.

Luttrell, C. B., and Alton, G. R. (1976), 'Crop Yields: Random, Cyclical, or Bunchy', *American Journal of Agricultural Economics*, 58 (Aug.): 521–31.

Maddison, A. (1987), 'Growth and Slowdown in Advanced Capitalist Economies: Techniques of Quantitative Assessment', *Journal of Economic Literature*, 25 (June): 649–98.

—— (1991), *Dynamic Forces in Capitalist Development* (Oxford: Oxford University Press).

—— (1995), *Monitoring the World Economy, 1820–1992* (Paris: OECD Development Center).

Mahalanobis, P. C. (1955), 'The Approach of Operational Research to Planning in India', *Sankhya: Indian Journal of Statistics*, 16 (1-2): 3–80.

Malthus, T. R. (1926; original publication 1798), *An Essay on the Principle of Population, As It* Affects the Future Improvement of Society, with Remarks on the Speculation of Mr. Godwin, Mr. Condorcet and Other Writers, reproduced for the Royal Economic Society (London: Macmillan).

Marshall, A. (1953; original publication 1890), *Principles of Economics*, 8th edn. (London: Macmillan.)

Martin, M. V., and Brokken, R. F. (1983), 'The Scarcity Syndrome: Comment', *American Journal of Agricultural Economics*, 65 (Feb.): 158–59.

Marx, K. (1904; original publication 1859), *Contribution to the Critique of Political Economy*, trans. and ed. N. I. Stone (Chicago: Charles Kerr) [Original publ. in German with title: *Zur Kritik der politischen Ökonomie*].

——(1909–12; original publication 1867–94), *Capital: A Critique of Political Economy*, ed. F. Engels; trans. S. Moore and E. Aveling; rev. Ernest Untermann, 3 vols. (Chicago: Charles H. Kerr) [Original publ. in German with title: *Das Kapital: Kritik der Politischen Ökonomie*].

——(1953; original publication 1939–41), *Grundrisse der Kritik der politischen Ökonomie: (Rohentwurf), 1857–1858* [Foundations of the Critique of Political Economy (Rough Draft)] (Berlin: Dietz).

Matsuyama, K. (1991), 'Increasing Returns, Industrialization, and Indeterminancy of Equilibrium', *Quarterly Journal of Economics*, 106 (May): 617–50.

McKeown, T., and Brown, R. G. (1955), 'Medical Evidence Related to English Population Changes in the Eighteenth Century', *Population Studies*, 9 (Nov.): 119–41.

McKinnon, R. I. (1973), *Money and Capital in Economic Development* (Washington, DC: Brookings Institution).

Meadows, D. H., Meadows, D. L., Randers, J., and Behrens, W. W. (1972), *The Limits to Growth* (New York: Universe Books).

Mellor, J. W. (1966), *The Economics of Agricultural Development* (Ithaca, NY: Cornell University Press).

Minami, R. (1994), *The Economic Development of Japan*, trans. by Ralph Thompson et al., 2nd edn. (New York: St Martin's Press). [Original publ. in Japanese with title: *Nihon no Keizai Hatten*]

——and Ono, A. (1977), 'Yososhotoku to Bunpairitu no Suikei' [Estimation of Factor Income and Factor Shares: Non-Primary Industry], *Keizai Kenkyu*, 29–1 (Apr.): 143–69.

——Kim, K. S., and Tanizawa, H. (1993), 'Shotoku Bunpu no Choki Hendo' [Long-term Changes in Income Distribution: Estimation and Analysis], *Keizai Kenkyu*, 44 (Oct.): 351–73.

Mises, L. von (1935), 'Economic Calculation in the Socialist Common Wealth', in Hayek (1935), pp. 87–130.

Mitchell, B. R. (1980), *European Historical Statistics 1750–1975*, 2nd edn. (London: Macmillan).

Mitrany, D. (1951), *Marx against the Peasant: A Study in Social Dogmatism* (Chapel Hill, NC: University of North Carolina Press).

Mizoguchi, T. (1986), 'Nihon no Shotoku Bunpu no Choki Hendo' [Long-term Changes of Size Distribution of Income in Japan], *Keizai Kenkyu*, 37 (Apr.): 152–8.

Mizoguchi, T., Takayama, T., and Terasaki, Y. (1978), 'Sengo Nihon no Shotoku Bunpu' [Size Distribution of Household Income, 1953–75], *Keizai Kenkyu*, 29 (Jan.): 44–60.

Mizoguchi, Y., and Nakajima, M. (eds.) (1991), *Jukyo Renaissance o Kangaeru* [Thinking about the Renaissance of Confucianism] (Tokyo: Daishukan Shoten).

More, T. (1989; original publication 1516), *Utopia*, ed. G. M. Logan and R. M. Adams (Cambridge: Cambridge University Press). [Original publ. in Latin with title: *Libellus vere avreus nec minus salutaris quam festivus de optimo reip, statu deque nova insula utopia*].

Morishima, M. (1982), *Why Has Japan Succeeded?: Western Technology and the Japanese Ethos* (Cambridge: Cambridge University Press).

Murphy, K. M., Shleifer, A., and Vishny, R. W. (1989), 'Industrialization and the Big Push', *Journal of Political Economy*, 97 (Oct.): 1003–26.

Muscat, R. J. (1994), *The Fifth Tiger: A Study of Thai Development Policy* (Armonk, NY: M. E. Sharpe).

Musgrave, R. A. (1959), *The Theory of Public Finance* (New York: McGraw-Hill).

Myrdal, G. (1968), *Asian Drama; An Inquiry into the Poverty of Nations* (New York: Twentieth Century Fund).

Nakamura, T., and Odaka, K. (1989), *Nihon Keizaishi* [Economic History of Japan], vol. 6, *Niju Kozo* [Dual Structure] (Tokyo: Iwanami-Shoten).

Negishi, T. (1989), *History of Economic Theory* (Amsterdam: North-Holland).

Nelson, R. R. (1956), 'A Theory of the Low-Level Equilibrium Trap', *American Economic Review*, 46 (Dec.): 894–908.

——(1991), 'Diffusion of Development, Post-World War II Convergence among Advanced Industrialized Nations', *American Economic Review*, 81 (May): 271–5.

——(1995), 'Recent Evolutionary Theorizing about Economic Change', *Journal of Economic Literature*, 33 (Mar.): 48–90.

——and Winter, S. G. (1982), *An Evolutionary Theory of Economic Change* (Cambridge, Mass.: Harvard University Press).

Nishikawa, S., and Abe, T. (eds.) (1990) *Nihon Keizaishi* [Economic History of Japan], vol. 4, *Sangyoka no Jidai* [The Era of Industrialization] (Tokyo: Iwanami-Shoten).

Niwa, K. (1962), *Meiji Ishin no Tochi Kaikaku* [Land Reform at the Meiji Restoration] (Tokyo: Ochanomizu Shobo).

North, D. C. (1955), 'Location Theory and Regional Economic Growth', *Journal of Political Economy*, 63 (June): 243–58.

——(1981), *Structure and Change in Economic History* (New York: Norton).

——(1990), *Institutions, Institutional Change and Economic Performance* (Cambridge: Cambridge University Press).

——(1994), 'Economic Performance Through Time', *American Economic Review* 84 (June): 359–68.

——and Thomas, R. P. (1973), *The Rise of the Western World: A New Economic History* (Cambridge: Cambridge University Press).

Nugent, J. B., and Sanchez, N. (1989), 'The Efficiency of the Mesta: A Parable', *Explorations in Economic History*, 26 (July): 261–84.

Nurkse, R. (1952), 'Some International Aspects of the Problem of Economic Development', *American Economic Review*, 42 (May) (Supplement): 571–83.

Nurkse, R. (1953), *Problems of Capital Formation in Underdeveloped Countries* (Oxford: Blackwell).

—— (1959), *Patterns of Trade and Development* (Stockholm: Almquist & Wiskell).

Odaka, K. (1984), *Rodo Shijo Bunseki* [Analysis of Labor Market] (Tokyo: Iwanami Shoten).

Ofer, G. (1987), 'Soviet Economic Growth: 1928–85', *Journal of Economic Literature*, 25 (Dec.): 1767–833.

Ohkawa, K., and Rosovsky, H. (1973), *Japanese Economic Growth* (Stanford, Calif: Stanford University Press).

—— and Shinohara, M. (1979), *Patterns of Japanese Economic Development: Trend Acceleration in the Twentieth Century* (New Haven: Yale University Press).

—— and Umemura, M. (eds.), (1964–1988), *Estimates of Long-term Economic Statistics of Japan Since 1868*, 14 vols. (Tokyo: Tokyokeizai Shimposha).

Okazaki, T., and Okuno, M. (eds.) (1993), *Gendai Nihon Keizai System no Genryu* [The Origin of Modern Japanese Economic System] (Tokyo: Nihon Keizai Shimbunsha).

Oldeman, L. R., van Engelen, V. W. P., and Pulles, J. H. M. (1990), 'The Extent of Human-Induced Soil Degradation', in L. R. Oldeman, R. T. A. Hakkeling and W. G. Sombroek (eds.), *World Map of the Status of Human-Induced Soil Degradation: An Explanatory Note* (Nairobi: UNEP, and Wageningen: International Soil Reference and Information Center).

Olson, M. (1965), *The Logic of Collective Action* (Cambridge: Havard University Press).

Ono, A., and Watanabe, T. (1976), 'Changes in Income Inequality in the Japanese Economy', in H. Patrick (ed.), *Japanese Industrialization and its Social Consequences* (Berkeley and Los Angeles: University of California Press), pp. 363–89.

Osano, H. (1990), 'Coordination Failure and Long Run Growth', *Osaka Economic Papers*, 40 (Sept.): 102–25.

Oshima, H. T. (1992), 'Kuznets' Curve and Asian Income Distribution Trends', *Hitotsubashi Journal of Economics*, 33 (June): 95–111.

Ostrom, E. (1990), *Governing the Commons* (New York: Cambridge University Press).

Otsuki, T., and Takamatsu, N. (1978), 'An Aspect of the Size Distribution of Income in Prewar Japan', Tokyo: International Development Center of Japan, mimeo.

—— (1982), 'On the Measurement of Income Inequality in Prewar Japan', IDCJ Working Paper, no. 09 (Tokyo: International Development Center of Japan).

Overseas Economic Cooperation Fund (1991), 'Issues Related to the World Bank's Approach to Structural Adjustment: A Proposal from a Major Partner', OECF Occasional Paper No.1 (Tokyo).

Owen, T. C. (1981), *Capitalism and Politics in Russia: A Social History of Moscow Merchants, 1855–1905* (Cambridge: Cambridge University Press).

Pack, H., and Westphal, L. E. (1986), 'Industrial Strategy and Technological Change: Theory Versus Reality', *Journal of Development Economics*, 22 (June): 87–128.

Pallais, J. B. (1975), *Politics and Policy in Traditional Korea* (Cambridge, Mass.: Harvard University Press).

Pareto, V. (1906), *Manuale di economia politica con una introduzione alla scienza sociale* [Manual of Political Economy with an Introduction to Social Science] (Milano: Societa Edetrice Libraria).

Parikh, A., and Thorbecke, E. (1996), 'Impact of Rural Industrialization on Village Life and Economy: A Social Accounting Matrix Approach', *Economic Development and Cultural Change*, 44 (Jan.): 351–77.

Park, Y. C. (1990), 'Development Lessons from Asia: The Role of Government in South Korea and Taiwan', *American Economic Review*, 80 (May) 108–12.

Paukert, F. (1973), 'Income Distribution at Different Levels of Development: A Survey of Evidence', *International Labor Review*, 108 (Aug.-Sept): 97–125.

Perkins, D. H., with Yeh-Chien Wang, Kuo-Ying Wang Hsiao, and Yung-Ming Su (1969), *Agricultural Development in China, 1368–1968* (Chicago: Aldine).

Phelps, E. S. (1966), 'Models of Technical Progress and the Golden Rule of Research', *American Economic Review*, 33 (Apr.): 133–45.

Pigou, A. C. (1920), *The Economics of Welfare* (London: Macmillan).

Pim, A. (1946), *Colonial Agricultural Production* (London: Royal Institute of International Affairs).

Pinstrup-Andersen, P., and Pandya-Lorch, R. (1994), *Alleviating Poverty, Intensifying Agriculture, and Effectively Managing Natural Resources* (Washington, DC: International Food Policy Research Institute).

Pinto, B. (1987), 'Nigeria during and after the Oil Boom: A Policy Comparison with Indonesia', *World Bank Economic Review*, 1 (May): 419–45.

Platteau, J-P. (1992), 'Formalization and Privatization of Land Rights in Sub-Saharan Africa: A Critique of Current Orthodoxies and Structural Adjustment Programmes', London School of Economics Research Programme, DEP no. 34, Suntory-Toyota International Centre for Economics and Related Disciplines, (London: London School of Economics).

——(1994), 'Behind the Market Stage where Real Societies Exist, Parts I (The Role of Public and Private Order Institutions) and II (The Role of Moral Norms), *Journal of Development Studies*, 30 (Apr.): 533–77 and 30 (July): 753–817.

Popkin, S. L. (1979), *The Rational Peasant: The Political Economy of Rural Society in Vietnam* (Berkeley and Los Angeles: University of California Press).

Prebisch, R. (1959), 'Commercial Policy in the Underdeveloped Countries', *American Economic Review*, 49 (May): (Supplement): 251–73.

Prestowitz, C. V., Jr. (1988), *Trading Places: How We Allowed Japan to Take the Lead* (New York: Basic Books).

Putnam, R. D. (1993), *Making Democracy Work: Civic Traditions in Modern Italy* (Princeton: Princeton University Press).

Ranis, G., and Fei, J. C. H. (1961), 'A Theory of Economic Development', *American Economic Review*, 51 (Sept.): 533–65.

——and Mahmood, S. A. (1992), *The Political Economy of Development Policy Change* (Cambridge, Mass.: Blackwell).

——and Stewart, F. (1993), 'Rural Nonagricultural Activities in Development: Theory and Application', *Journal of Development Economics*, 40 (Feb.): 75–101.

Resnick, S. (1970), 'The Decline in Rural Industry under Export Expansion: A Comparison among Burma, Philippines and Thailand, 1870–1938', *Journal of Economic History*, 30 (Mar.): 51–73.

Ricardo, D. (1966; original publication 1817), *On the Principles of Political Economy and Taxation*, ed. P. Sraffa (Cambridge: Cambridge University Press).

Rodrik, D. (1993), 'King Kong Meets Godzilla: The World Bank and East Asian Miracle', in A. Fishlow *et al.*, *Miracle or Design* (Washington, DC: Overseas Development Council), pp. 15–53.

Romer, P. M. (1986), 'Increasing Returns and Long-run Growth', *Journal of Political Economy*, 94 (Oct.): 1002–37.

—— (1987), 'Growth Based on Increasing Returns due to Specialization', *American Economic Review*, 77 (May): 56–62.

Rosenberg, N., and Birdzell, Jr., L. E. (1986), *How the West Grew Rich: The Economic Transformation of the Industrial World* (New York: Basic Books).

Rosenstein-Rodan, P. N. (1943), 'Problems of Industrialization of Eastern and South-Eastern Europe', *Economic Journal*, 53 (June/Sept.): 202–11.

Rosenzweig, M. R. (1984), 'Determinants of Wage Rates and Labor Supply Behavior in the Rural Sector of a Developing Country', in H. P. Binswanger and M. R. Rosenzweig (eds.), *Contractual Arrangements, Employment, and Wages in Rural Labor Markets in Asia* (New Haven: Yale University Press), pp. 211–41.

—— (1988*a*), 'Risk, Private Information, and the Family', *American Economic Review*, 78 (May): 245–50.

—— (1988*b*), 'Risk, Implict Contracts and the Family in Rural Areas of Low Income Countries', *Economic Journal*, 98 (Dec.): 1148–70.

Rostow, W. W. (1960), *The Stages of Economic Growth: A Non-Communist Manifesto* (Cambridge: Cambridge University Press).

Saito, O. (1987), *Shoka no Sekai Uradana no Sekai* [The World of Merchants and the World of Petty Traders and Laborers] (Tokyo: Rebroport).

Samuelson, P. A. (1965), 'A Theory of Induced Innovation along Kennedy–Weisacker Lines', *Review of Economics and Statistics*, 47 (Nov.): 343–56.

—— and Nordhaus, W. D. (1985), *Economics*, 12th edn. (New York: McGraw-Hill).

Sauer, C. O. (1952), *Agricultural Origins and Dispersals* (New York: American Geographical Society).

Schultz, T. P. (1988), 'Education Investments and Returns' in H. Chenery and T. N. Srinivasan (eds.), *Handbook of Development Economics*, vol. 1 (Amsterdam: North-Holland), pp. 543–630.

Schultz, T. W. (1953), *The Economic Organization of Agriculture* (New York: McGraw-Hill).

—— (1964), *Transforming Traditional Agriculture* (New Haven: Yale University Press).

Schumpeter, J. A. (1942), *Capitalism, Socialism and Democracy* (New York: Harper).

—— (1961; original publication 1912), *The Theory of Economic Development: An Inquiry into Profits, Capital, Credit, and the Business Cycle*, trans. R. Opie (New York: Oxford University Press). [Original publ. in German with title: *Theorie der Wirtschaftlichen Entwicklung*].

Scott, J. C. (1972), 'The Erosion of Patron-Client Bonds and Social Change in Rural Southeast Asia', *Journal of Asian Studies*, 33 (Nov.): 5–37.

—— (1976), *The Moral Economy of the Peasant: Rebellion and Subsistence* (New Haven: Yale University Press).

Seabright, P. (1993), 'Managing Local Commons: Theoretical Issues in Incentive Design', *Journal of Economic Perspectives*, 7 (Fall): 113–34.

Selden, T.M., and Song, D. (1992), *Environmental Quality and Development: Is there a Kuznets Curve for Air Pollution?*, Syracuse University, photocopy.

Sen, A. (1992), *Inequality Reexamined* (New York: Russell Sage Foundation).

Shimbo, H. (1995), *Kindai Nihon Keizaishi* [Economic History of Modern Japan] (Tokyo: Sobunsha).

Shinohara, M. (1966), *Sangyo Kozoron* [Treatise on Industrial Organization] (Tokyo: Chikuma Shobo).

Shioki, M. (1993), *Doitsu Kindaika o Sasaeta Kanryo* [A Bureaucrat Who Supported Modernization of Germany] (Tokyo: Chuo Koronsha).

Simon, H. A. (1957), *Models of Man: Social and Rational* (New York; Wiley).

Simon, J. L. (1992), *Population and Development in Poor Countries* (Princeton: Princeton University Press).

——and Kahn, H., (eds.) (1984), *The Resourceful Earth: A Response to Global 2000* (Oxford: Blackwell).

Singer, H. W. (1950), 'The Distribution of Gains between Investing and Borrowing Countries', *American Economic Review*, 40 (May): 473–85.

Skinner, J. (1993), 'If Agricultural Taxation Is So Effective, Why Is It So Rarely Practiced?', in K. Hoff, A. Braverman, and J. E. Stiglitz (eds.), *Economics of Rural Organization* (New York: Oxford University Press), pp. 352–73.

Slicher van Bath, B. H. (1963), *The Agrarian History of Western Europe, A.D. 500–1850*, trans. Olive Ordish (London: Arnold). [Original publ. in Dutch with title: *De agrarische geschiedenis van West Europa (500–1850)*].

Smith, A. (1937; original publication 1776), *An Inquiry into the Nature and Causes of the Wealth of Nations*, ed. E. Cannan, 6th edn. (New York: Modern Library).

——(1976; original publication 1759), *The Theory of Moral Sentiment*, 6th edn. (Indianapolis, Ind.: Liberty Press).

Smith, V. L. (1975), 'The Primitive Hunter Culture, Pleistocene Extinction, and the Rise of Agriculture', *Journal of Political Economy*, 85 (Aug.): 729–56.

Sobel, J. (1993), 'Evolutionary Stability and Efficiency', *Economics Letters*, 42 (2–3): 301–12.

Solow, R. M. (1956), 'A Contribution to the Theory of Economic Growth', *Quarterly Journal of Economics*, 70 (Feb.): 65–94.

——(1957), 'Technical Change and Aggregate Production Function', *Review of Economics and Statistics*, 39 (Aug.): 312–20.

——(1970), *Growth Theory: An Exposition* (Oxford: Oxford University Press).

——(1994), 'Perspective on Growth Theory', *Journal of Economic Perspective*, 8 (Winter): 45–54.

Spencer, D. S. C. (1994), *Infrastructure and Technology Constraints to Agricultural Development in the Humid and Subhumid Tropics in Africa*, EPTD Discussion Paper No. 3 (Washington, DC: International Food Policy Research Institute).

Srinivasan, T. N. (1990), 'Development Thought, Strategy and Policy: Then and Now', Background paper prepared for World Bank Report, 1991 (Washington, DC), photocopy.

Stalin, J. (1947), *Problems of Leninism* (Moscow: Foreign Languages Publishing House).

Stark, O., and Lucas, R. E. B. (1988), 'Migration, Remittance, and the Family', *Economic Development and Cultural Change*, 36 (Apr.): 465–81.

Stewart, F. (1977), *Technology and Underdevelopment* (Boulder, Colo.: Westview Press).

Stigler, G. J. (1971), 'Theories of Economic Regulation', *Bell Journal of Economics*, 5 (Spring): 3–21.

—— (1975), *The Citizen and the State: Essays on Regulation* (Chicago: University of Chicago Press).

Stiglitz, J. E. (1989a), 'Markets, Market Failures, and Development', *American Economic Review*, 79 (May): 197–203.

—— (1989b), 'Financial Markets and Development', *Oxford Review of Economic Policy* 5, (Winter): 55–68.

—— and Weiss, A. (1981), 'Credit Rationing in Markets with Imperfect Information', *American Economic Review*, 71 (June): 393–410.

Strauss, J., and Thomas, D. (1995), 'Human Resources: Empirical Modelling of Household and Family Decisions', in J. Behrman and T. N. Srinivasan (eds.), *Handbook of Development Economics*, vol. 3A (Amsterdam: North-Holland), pp. 1883–2023.

Summers, R., and Heston, A. (1988), 'A New Set of International Comparisons of Real Product and Price Level Estimates for 130 Countries', *Review of Income and Wealth*, 34 (Mar.): 1–25.

—— (1991), 'The Penn World Table (Mark 5): An Expanded Set of International Comparisons 1950–1988', *Quarterly Journal of Economics*, 106 (May): 327–68.

Swan, T. W. (1956), 'Economic Growth and Capital Accumulation', *Economic Record*, 32 (Nov.): 334–61.

Syrquin, M., and Chenery, H. B. (1988), *Patterns of Development, 1950 to 1983* (Washington, DC: World Bank).

Takahashi, A. (1969), *Land and Peasants in Central Luzon* (Tokyo: Institute of Developing Economies).

Takahashi, K. (1930), *Kabushiki Kaisha Bokokuron* [Joint Stock Company Ruins the Nation] (Tokyo: Banrikaku Shobo).

Tamaki, T. (1983), *Mizushakai no Kozo* [Structure of Hydraulic Society] (Tokyo: Ronsosha).

—— and Hatate, I. (1974), *Hudo: Daichi to Ningen no Rekishi* [Environment: History of Land and Man] (Tokyo: Heibonsha).

Tang, A. M. (1967), 'Agriculture in the Industrialization of Communist China and the Soviet Union', *Journal of Farm Economics*, 49 (Dec.): 1118–34.

Tanizawa, H., and Minami, R. (1993), 'Dainiji Taisen Chokugo ni okeru Bunpu no Byodoka Yoin' [Factors Underlying Equalization of Income Distribution Immediately after World War II], *Keizai Kenkyu*, 44 (Oct.): 365–73.

Teranishi, J. (1982), *Nihon no Keizai Hatten to Kinyu* [Economic Development and Finance in Japan] (Tokyo: Iwanami Shoten).

Thorbecke, E. (1995a), 'Causes of African Development Stagnation: Policy Diagnosis and Policy Recommendations for a Long-term Development Strategy', in J. C. Berthelemy (ed.), *Whither African Economies* (Paris: OECD), pp. 117–43.

—— (1995b), 'Health, Nutritional and Demographic Trends with Particular Emphasis on Sub-Saharan Africa', in Advisory Committee on Health Research, *The Impact of Scientific Advances on Future Health* (Geneva: World Health Organization), pp. 75–87.

Tietenberg, T. H. (1990), 'Economic Instruments for Environmental Regulation', *Oxford Review of Economic Policy*, 6 (Spring): 17–33.

Tiffen, M., and Mortimore, M. (1994), 'Malthus Controverted: The Role of Capital and Technology in Growth and Environment Recovery in Kenya', *World Development*, 22 (July): 997–1010.

Timmer, C. P. (1969), 'The Turnip, the New Husbandry, and the English Agricultural Revolution', *Quarterly Journal of Economics*, 83 (Aug.): 375–95.

Tirole, J. (1986), 'Hierarchies and Bureaucracies: On the Role of Collusion in Organizations', *Journal of Law, Economics and Organization*, 2 (Fall): 181–214.

Tollison, R. (1982), 'Rent-seeking: A Survey', *Kyklos*, 35 (4): pp. 575–602.

Tönnies, F. (1926; original publication 1887), *Gemeinschaft und Gesellschaft: Grundbegriffe der reinen Soziologie* [Community and Society: Basic Concepts in Pure Sociology] (Berlin: K. Curtius).

Tobata, S., and Ohkawa, K. (1937), *Chosen Beikoku Keizairon* [Treatise on Rice Economy in Korea] (Tokyo: Nihon Gakujutsu Shinkokai).

Tsuruta, T. (1984), 'Kodo Seichoki' [The Era of High Economic Growth], in Komiya, Okuno, and Suzumura (1984), pp. 45–76.

Tullock, G. (1967), 'The Welfare Costs of Tariffs, Monopolies and Theft', *Western Economic Journal*, 5 (June): 224–32.

United Nations (1993), *Agenda 21: Program of Action for Sustainable Development* (New York).

United Nations. Department of International Economic and Social Affairs, Statistical Office. *Industrial Statistics Yearbook*. Annual issues (New York).

Vandermeersch, L. (1986), *Le Nouveau Monde Sinise* [The New Sinitic World] (Paris: Presses Universitaires de France).

Vernon, R. (1966), 'International Investment and International Trade in the Product Cycle', *Quarterly Journal of Economics*, 80 (May): 190–207.

Von Braun, J., et al. (1993), *Aid to Agriculture: Reversing the Decline* (Washington, DC: International Food Policy Research Institute).

Wada, K. (1991), 'The Development of Tiered Inter-firm Relationships in the Automobile Industry: A Case Study of Toyota Motor Corporation', *Japanese Yearbook on Business History*, 8: 23–47.

Wada, R. O. (1975), *Impact of Economic Growth on the Size Distribution of Income: The Postwar Experience of Japan* (Geneva: ILO).

Wade, R. (1988), *Village Republics: Economic Conditions for Collective Action in South India* (Cambridge: Cambridge University Press).

—— (1990), *Governing the Market: Economic Theory and the Role of Government in East Asian Industrialization*, (Princeton: Princeton University Press).

—— (1994), 'Selected Industrial Policies in East Asia: Is the East Asian Miracle Right?' in A. Fishlow et al., *Miracle or Design?* (Washington, DC: Overseas Development Council), pp. 55–84.

Walder, A. G. (1989), 'Factory and Manger in an Era of Reform', *China Quarterly*, 118 (June): 242–64.

Waley, A., trans. and annot. (1938), *The Analects of Confucius* (London: Allen & Unwin).

Walras, Leon (1874), *Élements d'économie politique pure, ou, Theorie de la richesse sociale* [Elements of Pure Economics, or, The Theory of Social Wealth] (Lausanne: L. Corbaz).

Wan, H. Y., Jr. (1971), *Economic Growth* (New York: Harcourt, Brace, Jovanovich).

Warriner, D. (1969), *Land Reform in Principle and Practice* (Oxford: Clarendon Press).

Watkins M. (1963), 'A Staple Theory of Economic Growth', *Canadian Journal of Economics and Political Science*, 29 (May): 141–58.

Weber, M. (1920), 'Die Protestantische Ethik und der Geist des Kapitalismus' [The Protestant Ethic and the Spirit of Capitalism], in Weber, *Gesammelte Aufsätze zur Religionssoziologie* (Tübingen: J. C. B. Mohr), pp. 17–206

——(1924; original publication 1909), 'Agrarverhältnisse im Altertum' [Agrarian Relations of Ancient Civilizations], in Weber, *Gesammelte Aufsätze zur Sozial- und Wirtschaftgeschichte* (Tübingen: J. C. B. Mohr), pp. 1–288.

Weitzman, M. L. (1970), 'Soviet Postwar Economic Growth and Capital-Labor Substitution', *American Economic Review*, 60 (Sept.): 676–92.

Whalley, J. W. (1994), 'Compensation or Retaliation: Developed and Developing Countries and the Growing Conflict over Global Environmental Conservation', IPR Discussion Paper 93 (Washington, DC: Institute for Policy Reform).

Wickizer, V. D. (1951), *Coffee, Tea, and Cocoa: An Economic and Political Analysis* (Stanford, Calif.: Stanford University Press).

Williamson, J. G. (1990), *Coping with City Growth During the British Industrial Revolution* (Cambridge: Cambridge University Press).

Williamson, O. E. (1975), *Markets and Hierarchies, Analysis and Antitrust Implications: A Study in the Economics of Informal Organizations* (New York: Free Press).

——(1985), *The Economic Institutions of Capitalism* (New York: Free Press).

Wittfogel, K. A. (1957), *Oriental Despotism: A Comparative Study of Total Power* (New Haven: Yale University Press).

Wong, C. P. W. (1986), 'The Economics of Shortage and Problems of Reform in Chinese Industry', *Journal of Comparative Economics*, 10 (Dec.): 363–87.

——(1987), 'Between Plan and Market: The Role of the Local Sector in Post-Mao China', *Journal of Comparative Economics*, 11 (Sept.): 385–98.

World Bank, *World Development Report* (New York: Oxford University Press). Annual issues.

——(1993), *The East Asian Miracle: Economic Growth and Public Policy* (Oxford: Oxford University Press).

World Bank Country Economics Department (1988), *Adjustment Lending: An Evaluation of Ten Years of Experience* (Washington, DC).

——(1990), *Adjustment Lending Policies for Sustainable Growth* (Washington, DC).

——(1992), *Adjustment Lending and Mobilization of Private and Public Resources for Growth* (Washington, DC).

World Resources Institute, *World Resources* (New York: Oxford University Press). Annual issues.

Woytinsky, W. S., and Woytinsky, E. S. (1953), *World Population and Production* (New York: Twentieth Century Fund).

Wrigley, E. A. (1969), *Population History* (New York: McGraw-Hill).

——and Schofield, R. S. (1981), *The Population History of England 1541–1871* (Cambridge, Mass.: Harvard University Press).

Yamamoto, H. (1978), *Nippon Shonin* [Nippon Merchants] (Tokyo: Bengei Shunjusha).

——(1992), *Nihonjin Towa Nanika* [What Are the Japanese?], vol. 2 (Tokyo: PHP Shuppan).

Yamamura, K. (1972), 'Japan, 1868–1930: A Revised View', in Cameron (1972), pp. 168–98.

—— (ed.) (1990), *Japan's Economic Structure: Should It Change?* (Seattle: Society for Japanese Studies).

—— and Yasuba, Y. (1987), *The Political Economy of Japan, vol. 1, The Domestic Transformation* (Stanford, Calif.: Stanford University Press).

Yamazawa, I. (1984), *Nihon no Keizai Hatten to Kokusai Bungyo* [Economic Development and International Division of Labor in Japan] (Tokyo: Toyokeizai Shimposha).

Yanagihara, T. (1991), 'Chile no Keizai Chosei' [Structural Adjustment in Chile], *Kikin Chosakiho* [Overseas Economic Cooperation Fund], 72 (Nov.): 34–51.

Yasuba, Y. (1980), *Keizai Seichoron* [Treatise on Economic Growth] (Tokyo: Chikuma Shobo).

Yoshida, Y. (1990), *Soren, Toou Shokoku no Keizai Hatten to Seisansei no Susei* [Economic Development and Productivity Trends in the Soviet Union and Eastern European Countries] (Tokyo: Kazama Shobo).

Yotopolos, P. A. (1968), 'On the Efficiency of Resource Utilization in Subsistence Agriculture', *Food Research Institute Studies in Agricultural Economics, Trade, and Development*, 8 (2): 125–35.

Young, A., (1991), 'Learning by Doing and the Dynamic Effects of International Trade', *Quarterly Journal of Economics*, 106 (May): 369–405.

Index of Names

Index of Subjects